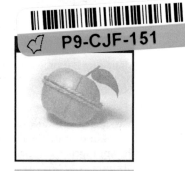

Converged Networks and Services

Internetworking IP and the PSTN

Igor Faynberg
Lawrence Gabuzda
Hui-Lan Lu

Wiley Computer Publishing

John Wiley & Sons, Inc.

NEW YORK · CHICHESTER · WEINHEIM · BRISBANE · SINGAPORE · TORONTO

Publisher: Robert Ipsen
Editor: Carol Long
Assistant Editor: Margaret Hendrey
Managing Editor: Micheline Frederick
Text Design & Composition: North Market Street Graphics

This book is printed on acid-free paper. ♾

Published by John Wiley & Sons, Inc.

Published simultaneously in Canada.

This publication is designed to provide accurate and authoritative information in regard to the subject matter covered. It is sold with the understanding that the publisher is not engaged in professional services. If professional advice or other expert assistance is required, the services of a competent professional person should be sought.

Library of Congress Cataloging-in-Publication Data:

Faynberg, Igor.
    Converged networks and services : Internetworking IP and the PSTN / Igor Faynberg, Hui-Lan Lu, Lawrence Gabuzda.
        p.   cm.—(Wiley networking council series)
    "Wiley Computer Publishing."
    Includes bibliographical references and index.
    ISBN 0-471-35644-1 (pbk. : alk. paper)
    1. Internet telephony. 2. TCP/IP (Computer network protocol) I. Lu, Hui-Lan.
II. Gabuzda, Lawrence. III. Title. IV. Series.

TK105.8865. F39 2000
004.6'2—dc21   00-039240

Printed in the United States of America.

10 9 8 7 6 5 4 3 2 1

Wiley Networking Council Series

Scott Bradner
Senior Technical Consultant, Harvard University

Vinton Cerf
Senior Vice President, MCI WorldCom

Lyman Chapin
Chief Scientist, BBN/GTE

Books in the Series

For more information, please visit the Networking Council Web site at www.wiley.com/networkingcouncil.

For
Anne Bishop Faynberg
Aida, Danielle, and Nicholas Gabuzda
盧三讓 *and Hai-Chen Tu*

Contents

networking council foreword

The Networking Council Series was created in 1998 within Wiley's Computer Publishing group to fill an important gap in networking literature. Many current technical books are long on details but short on understanding. They do not give the reader a sense of where, in the universe of practical and theoretical knowledge, the technology might be useful in a particular organization. The Networking Council Series is concerned more with how to think clearly about networking issues than with promoting the virtues of a particular technology—how to relate new information to the rest of what the reader knows and needs, so the reader can develop a customized strategy for vendor and product selection, outsourcing, and design.

In *Converged Networks and Services: Internetworking IP and the PSTN*, by Igor Faynberg, Lawrence Gabuzda, and Hui-Lan Lu, you'll see the hallmarks of Networking Council books—examination of the advantages and disadvantages and the strengths and weaknesses of market-ready technology, useful ways to think about options pragmatically, and direct links to business practices and needs. Disclosure of pertinent background issues needed to understand who supports a technology and how it was developed is another goal of all Networking Council books.

The Networking Council Series is aimed at satisfying the need for perspective in an evolving data and telecommunications world filled with hyperbole, speculation, and unearned optimism.

In *Converged Networks and Services: Internetworking IP and the PSTN*, you'll get clear information from experienced practitioners.

We hope you enjoy the read. Let us know what you think. Feel free to visit the Networking Council Web site at www.wiley.com/networkingcouncil.

Scott Bradner
Senior Technical Consultant, Harvard University

Vinton Cerf
Senior Vice President, *MCI WorldCom*

Lyman Chapin
Chief Scientist, *BBN/GTE*

Acknowledgments

We admit we could not possibly have completed a project of this scope without the help we received from others.

First, we wish to thank Scott Bradner for giving us the idea for this book, pointing us to many essential sources of material, and subsequently guiding the project from conception to delivery. Scott has read and reread this manuscript at least one more time than we did, and his tactful advice and many incisive suggestions were a constant source of improvement in both technical precision and readability.

We are indebted to Bell Labs experts who consulted us about (and also carefully reviewed and commented on) the relevant parts of the manuscript: Brian Allain, Herb Bertine, Bill Byrne, Nury Dagdeviren, Gary Fisman, Glen Freundlich, Eric Gray, Jack Kozik, Peter Kroon, Terry Lyons, Harry Mildonian, Dan Romascanu, Jonathan Rosenberg, Greg Vaudreuil, John Wachter, and Reza Zarafshar. (If Jack Kozik had not brought to our attention the developments in the area of unified messaging, this fascinating subject would have never made it into the book.) Many, many thanks to Suzanne Smith for her cheerful help with the figures and tables!

In the process of research and writing, we also received invaluable advice from our Bell Labs colleagues Scott Alexander, Grenville Armitage, Alec Brusilovsky, Walter Buga, Rex Coldren, Janusz Dobrowolsky, Marilyn Holda-Fleck, Murali Krishnaswamy, Chinmei Lee, Argy Milonas, Jackie Orr, Dan Raz, John Segers, Pida Srisuresh, Ben Tang, Zheng Wang, and Wayne Zeuch.

We have learned a great deal from professional interactions with our colleagues from across the industry and academe. We are particularly grateful to Steve Bellovin, Vint Cerf, Lawrence Conroy, France Haerens, Jean-Pierre Hubaux, Christian Huitema, Zhengkun Mi, Lyndon Ong, Dave Oran, Scott Petrack, Noah Prywes, Henning Schulzrinne, Chip Sharp, Henry Sinnreich, Lev Slutsman, Tom Taylor, Houlin Zhao, and Huiling Zhao.

We want to acknowledge our employer, Lucent Technologies—specifically our managers Herb Bertine and George Arnold. Although this book was not a Bell Labs project, we were warmly encouraged to work on it and given access to the world's best technical expertise and information resources.

We are indebted to our editors, Marjorie Spencer, Margaret Hendrey, Micheline Frederick, and Stephanie Landis, for their titanic professional effort, to which this book owes much in the way of sanity, consistency, and style.

Even with all the help we got, we expect that the very scope of this project will likely result in undetected errors and omissions, for which, of course, we are solely responsible.

Introduction

This introduction provides a brief overview of the book and the Internet-telecommunications convergence technology that is its subject. It also describes how the book is organized, our intended audience, and how we feel readers will benefit.

Overview of the Book and Technology

Today, one of the hottest topics in all of technology is the convergence between the worlds of the Internet and telecommunications, and in particular between the Internet and the existing telecommunications infrastructure known as the *public switched telecommunications network* (PSTN). The Internet, of course, is the worldwide public network based on *Internet Protocol* (IP), which provides the basis for popular consumer applications such as Web browsing, e-mail, and chat rooms, and is rapidly growing up to provide the underpinnings for the global electronic commerce market as well. The PSTN is the familiar phone network, also worldwide in scope, and famed for its ability to deliver its target application of person-to-person voice communications with extremely high quality and astonishing reliability.

These networks represent radically different application requirements, design philosophies, and institutional histories. At the same time, the Internet and the modern PSTN share a basis in digital technology and have already developed some important symbiotic relationships, such as the pervasive use of dial-up over the PSTN for consumer Internet access.

The rapid growth of the Internet naturally stimulates the question of what happens when it gets to be as big as the PSTN—an event that, depending on how you define it, may be imminent!

This is a very big story, and it can be approached in several ways. One way is as a sort of fascinating wrestling match in which the two network giants contest and we all watch, speculate, take bets on the outcome, and cheer for our favorite. Another is as a purely technological tale that, if we were to tell it, would focus exclusively on analyses comparing the domains of application for circuit switching and packet switching, the statistics of different types of traffic and their requirements for quality of service, and so on.

We have chosen in writing this book to treat Internet-telecommunications convergence neither as a spectator sport nor as grist for the academic mill, but rather as a practical business problem and opportunity. That is, given that network managers for both enterprises and carriers now have the opportunity to choose technologies, products, and services that have their basis in either the Internet or the traditional PSTN, or in some hybrid combination of the two, how can they go about making choices that optimize today's bottom line while maintaining service quality and providing a smooth path to the future?

How This Book Is Organized

In constructing the plan of the book, our guiding idea was to walk readers through the key steps needed in deciding what sorts of Internet- and PSTN-based technologies, products, and services to apply to their specific applications. Thus, Part One (Chapters 1 through 3) begins with some additional background and the essentials of emerging technologies, and Part Two (Chapters 4 through 7) continues with an overview of the relevant standards. Part Three (Chapters 8 through 11) is a methodical guide to understanding your own applications, considering potentially relevant products and services, and then making appropriate choices. Part Four is a little different: In the concluding Chapter 12 it delves in some depth into the tricky question of the economic feasibility of Internet-telecommunications integration, and then provides handy reference material, including a reference list, glossary, and index.

To complete this overview of how the book is organized, here is a chapter-by-chapter summary:

Chapter 1: A Context for Convergence. This introductory chapter of Part One provides historical context for the notion of overlapping and converging network infrastructures, as well as a high-level framework for understanding the different types of relationships that potentially exist between the Internet and the PSTN. Many readers will find it fascinating to learn a bit more about how things got to be the way they are, but if you tend to be impatient with history and philosophy and want to get right on to leading-edge technology, you may want to fast-forward to Chapter 2.

Chapter 2: Adjusting the PSTN to the Internet. This chapter gives some background on the structure and technology of the PSTN, and goes on to discuss how aspects of the PSTN are being modified and upgraded to provide appropriate support for the Internet, including access and signaling.

Chapter 3: Adjusting the Internet to the PSTN. This chapter captures some of the key technologies underlying IP telephony, including quality of service, gateways, and the coding of digitized speech. IP telephony, also called *voice over IP*, is an industry "hot topic" in its own right; but, with the background provided by the two preceding chapters, readers will already appreciate that carrying packetized voice over the Internet is only one of the many ways to usefully combine the technologies of the Internet and the PSTN.

Chapter 4: ISDN, SS No. 7, IN, and CTI. This first chapter of Part Two covers the basic standards for switching and signaling that underlie the modern digital telephone network and support its remarkable robustness and huge scale.

Chapter 5: IP Telephony-Related Standards. This chapter covers the standards in place and emerging for transporting and controlling packetized voice streams over IP networks.

Chapter 6: Messaging, Directory, and Network Management Standards. This chapter covers the current standards for voice and text messaging, directory, and network management and their integration.

Chapter 7: Remote-Access-Related Standards. This chapter covers the standards for achieving remote access to the Internet over dial-up connections, including the Point-to-Point Protocol and important standards for accounting and security in the remote access environment.

Chapter 8: Identifying Your Environments. This first chapter of Part Three walks readers through a survey of application environments as an important exercise in beginning to understand their own Internet/telecommunications requirements.

Chapter 9: Identifying Your Applications. This chapter lists and describes some of the most important categories of applications in which Internet-PSTN convergence can play a key role.

Chapter 10: PSTN-Internet Interworking Products. This chapter lists and describes the key characteristics of the product categories available today for Internet-PSTN interworking.

Chapter 11: Choosing the Right Products for Your Applications. Here we get to the "bottom line": Based on understanding the underlying technology and standards, knowing the kinds of products available, and reflecting on your key applications and requirements, how do you go about selecting the products that address your actual business situation?

Chapter 12: The Technology Is Relevant. For readers who want to go a little deeper, this chapter provides some of the latest thinking on the fundamental economic case for Internet-PSTN convergence, and also considers the effect of other factors such as government regulation.

Who Should Read This Book

This book is intended to be of particular value to networking professionals who need to solve practical business problems where the convergence of the Internet and the PSTN may provide innovative solutions. The target audience definitely includes network managers who operate the telecommunications, data, and multimedia networks of businesses large and small. It also includes many types of professionals who work for different kinds of carriers, such as telecommunications carriers and Internet service providers. These may be, for example, the managers, engineers, architects, and planners who propose, dimension, create, and evolve the networks, as well as marketing people and sales engineers whose jobs involve helping customers understand and use innovative new services. Equipment providers, system integrators, and anyone who needs to understand and use industry standards for Internet-PSTN convergence will also benefit from the book. Professors responsible for undergraduate or graduate courses in computer science, electrical engineering, or telecommunications management may want to consider using it as a textbook. Finally, because of its coverage of the technology and economics of convergence, as well as its historical context, the book should be of interest to anyone who is just trying to get a better understanding of this major technological trend and its long-term significance.

Summary

In conclusion, we would like to express the hope that you will find the subject of convergence between the Internet and the PSTN to be as fascinating as we do, and that in reading the chapters that follow you will glean much information that will allow you to apply this rapidly emerging technology in a way that satisfies your needs, whatever they may be.

Background and Emerging Technologies

Chapter 1 provides historical context for the subject of network infrastructure convergence and a high-level framework for understanding possible relationships between the Internet and the Public Switched Telecommunications Network. Chapters 2 and 3 delve into emerging technologies that are bringing the Internet and telecommunications networks closer together.

A Context for Convergence

Whether you are a network manager for a large or small business, or just a technically savvy user of telephone services and the Internet, you are probably well aware by now that the networking industry is frantically trying to create *convergence* between telecommunications and the Internet.

Much venture capital money has been invested to seed start-ups that are preparing to offer Internet telephony gateways, *Internet Protocol private branch exchanges* (IP PBXs), and other gadgets combining Internet and telephony technology. Oceans of high-yield bond offerings (they're not called junk bonds anymore) are financing *new carriers* who plan to package voice and all other forms of communication into *Internet Protocol* (IP) datagrams and send them zipping around the world on brand-new infrastructures of wavelength-division-multiplexed fiber optics. Not wanting to be left behind, the giant incumbents of the telecommunications world—equipment vendors and carriers alike—are very much a part of the game. They have their own early offerings and are gobbling up start-ups and midsize firms in mergers and acquisitions. Competing visions of the technical underpinnings for the converged world are the main subject of animated debate at meetings of standards organizations, such as the *Internet Engineering Task Force* (IETF).

All of this activity surrounding convergence may be diverting to watch and to read about in the trade press. There is no doubt, however, that the current state of affairs can be confusing as well—and if your job is to manage and plan the growth of a network (or even your home office), you have the right to ask questions like: "Is this stuff real?" "Is it ready for prime time?" "Are the standards stable?" and, ultimately, "What's in it for me?"

We believe that, amid the welter of offerings available and soon to come, there are products and services that can provide real value to network managers and users. In order to make well-informed decisions, you must have a basic understanding of the underlying technologies and standards and be able to match product capabilities with the demands of your environments and applications. We hope to provide the background information you need, in addition to a guided tour through emerging product categories.

This introductory chapter continues with some reflections about innovations and infrastructures, and it makes the reassuring point that we have been through this kind of evolution before.

Innovations and Infrastructures

On August 10, 1876, Alexander Graham Bell conducted the first successful transmission of telephone speech over outdoor wires. For the preceding five months, all of the world's telephone conversations had taken place over wires strung through enclosed spaces such as laboratories and electrical shops. When it came time to test the new wonder on a larger geographical scale, Bell followed the easiest and most obvious course of action: He took advantage of an existing highly developed network technology for long-distance electrical communication. Bell borrowed the telegraph line between Brantford and Paris in Ontario, stationed his father at one end with a transmitter and orders to shout and speak distinctly, and repaired to the other end with a receiver, where his sensitive 30-year-old ears were able to make out a few words.

Throughout 1877, public demonstrations of the telephone and long-distance experiments continued to rely on borrowed telegraph wires (Figure 1.1). It was not until the emergence of public subscription and the first exchanges in 1878 that a significant purpose-built telephone infrastructure came to exist. In the early years of public telephone service, Western Union, the giant nationwide telegraph monopoly, had an edge in competing with the struggling Bell companies because it could leverage its telegraph infrastructure to quickly start up telephone service in new areas.

The example of early telephony and its relationships with the existing technology of telegraphy suggests the following three principles, which are relevant to today's discussion of the convergence (or, possibly, integration) of telecommunications and the Internet.

1. *The power of network scale.* This first principle is well known to economists as *network externality* (Economides, 1996). Essentially, it means that the bigger a network is and the more places it interconnects, the more valuable it

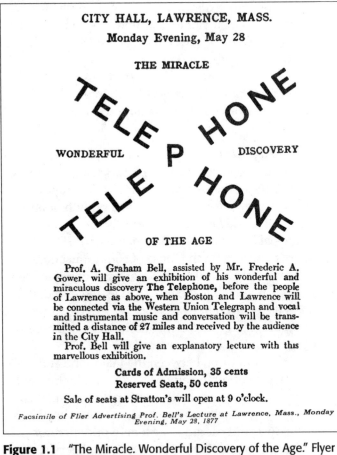

Figure 1.1 "The Miracle. Wonderful Discovery of the Age." Flyer advertising Professor Bell's lecture at Lawrence, Massachusetts, Monday evening, May 28, 1877, demonstrating transmission of music and speech over telegraph wires between Boston and Lawrence.

Source: Property of AT&T Archives. Reprinted with permission of AT&T.

is. This truth provides a strong incentive for new operators (like the Bell companies in the 1870s or so-called new carriers today) to build out their networks as quickly as possible, and for regionally based networks to seek interconnection.

The second principle derives in part from the first, but it also takes into account the fact that building networks that span physical space inevitably runs into money.

2. *The power of incumbency.* To build a network, you must construct enormous physical structures like continent-spanning cables buried in trenches or chains of tall towers. Whether the network operator builds the infrastructure or plans to lease it from a third party, someone must raise funds in the capital

markets to finance the construction. The expense and enormity of the task, along with network externality, raises a barrier to new entrants and provides a natural advantage to incumbents (like Western Union in the 1870s or the corporate descendants of the Bell companies today).

Much more can be said about the economics of the carrier business in relation to convergence, and we will return to this subject in Chapter 12.

You can deduce the last principle from our little parable about early telephony as follows:

3. *The ability of existing network infrastructures to boost new applications.* Because Bell was able to wire his crude telephones to existing telegraph lines, he could give public demonstrations of the technology and build support for his fledgling business. Closer to our own time, the explosive growth of fax technology in the 1980s owed a lot to the fact that Group 3 fax machines were completely compatible with the *public switched telephone network* (PSTN). And when the modern era of data networking (in the sense of communications between computers and between terminals and computers) got going in the 1960s, wide area communications relied almost entirely on leased and dial-up telephone circuits. Before there were such entities as *Internet service providers* (ISPs), the nodes of the early Internet in government and university laboratories were interconnected using telephone circuits as well (Figure 1.2).

We all know how the story of competition between the telephone and telegraph companies worked out: The telephone networks won big. By the mid-twentieth century, what telegraph traffic remained was largely multiplexed onto telephone carrier circuits, and just a little later Western Union itself suffered a multistage financial collapse and ceased to be a network operator.

The vanquishing of the telegraph by the telephone is quite a cheery story from the vantage point of a new carrier, because it suggests that, in spite of the aforementioned three principles—all of which emphasize the advantages of already having a large network—the big guys don't always win. So, what else is involved? Well, a lot of really nasty stuff like legal fights over patents and regulation and quite a bit of bare-knuckled business competition, no doubt. But let's stay on the high ground and suggest two more principles that seem to drive the outcome when different communication infrastructures compete head to head.

4. *The necessity of matching network characteristics to application needs.* It's all well and good to propose a universal network that can carry all applications, and with modern technology we may be able to come closer to that ideal. But back in the early telephony era, it quickly became clear that telegraph networks and technology were not well suited to the telephone application. One-wire circuits with their return path through the earth itself were the norm in telegraphy, but they induced a lot of noise in sensitive telephone receivers. Also, while some businesses had private telegraph networks, the public telegraph network actually connected a nationwide system of local

Figure 1.2   Data transmission over the telephone network.
Photograph taken in 1963 shows a woman in a computer center
dialing a telephone to transmit data between IBM facilities in
Greensboro, North Carolina, and New York City using an AT&T
201A Data Phone.
Source: Property of AT&T Archives. Reprinted with permission of AT&T.

telegraph offices (post offices, in the many parts of the world where the mail
and telegraph services were run by the same government department). To
send a message, you first walked, rode, or sent a messenger to the local telegraph office.

   The telephone application was clearly developing into something much
more personal and spontaneous than the telegraph. So, to support the needs
of the application for high-quality transmission and to provide the essential
ubiquitous reach into homes and offices, telephone companies began building extensive local loop networks of two-wire twisted pairs, which still exist
today. These networks grew with the astonishing popularity of the telephone,
and, in a few decades, overwhelmed the telegraph networks in size.

   This brings us to one last principle—the most important one, of course.

   5. *The primacy of the application and the power of the well-satisfied need.* There
was (and is) something almost mysterious about the telephony application. It
seems to satisfy a deep-seated human need for intimate communication, deliv-

ering the closest thing possible to a direct brain-to-brain link over distance and a quality of private communication otherwise difficult to experience outside the bedroom or the confessional. People get quite annoyed when essential qualities of telephony are compromised (as they sometimes are by things like bad speakerphones, cell phone dropouts, and voice prompt systems).

Telephony is mysterious enough that the very telephone companies that owed all their growth to high-quality satisfaction of the needs of the telephony application have sometimes misunderstood it as simply transmission of voice over distance and stumbled when they poured millions into building failed services aimed at transmission of images or data over distance.

People do tolerate things like cell phones and bad speakerphones, and the voice quality of Internet telephony can be very good under the right circumstances. So voice quality per se is secondary to our point: You can reap rewards when the characteristics of an application are completely understood and satisfied—tricky when the characteristics are somewhat mysterious.

There is some serendipity to the discovery of such applications—witness the much more recent emergence of the World Wide Web as a consumer application from its beginnings in the world of physics research. The Web, of course, relies on the infrastructure of the Internet and has driven much of the Internet's recent growth. The Web also presents an interesting case because the application seems to be so powerful that it grows in spite of the fact that the existing infrastructure of the Internet is less than ideal for it, inducing the delayed and interrupted transfers that everyone has experienced. When the Internet grows up enough to support a uniformly good Web experience, it will truly be unstoppable!

Living in Interesting Times

The preceding section explored some of the relationships that can exist between innovative communications applications and embedded communications infrastructures. In sequence, telephony was first carried over telegraph networks; then telegraphy and data communications were both carried over telephone networks; now, many applications, including voice and the Web, are carried over the Internet. This is perhaps interesting, but what does it mean to the harried network manager and to purchasers of Internet and telecommunications products and services?

A number of points stand out as potentially good news. These include the following:

- The world has gone through overlapped transitions of network infrastructure before and survived more or less intact.

- When, as is the case today, multiple large infrastructures coexist (that is, the telecommunications networks and the Internet), the options for the purchaser are multiplied.

■ The applications that users run and network managers must deploy and support are of prime importance and drive all other needs. Nobody is going to make any money in the convergence business unless customer needs are satisfied!

We will consider each of these three points in more detail before moving on to Chapter 2.

Precedents for Network Infrastructure Transition

Since the time when networks for communication at a distance were first deployed, there have been a number of technological discontinuities that have resulted in periods (some relatively short, others much longer) when multiple network infrastructures coexisted. Whether multiple networks continued to exist side by side or were subsumed into one entity depended on business dynamics and the role of government as much as on technology.

When historians of technology go looking for the origins of rapid long-distance communication, after pausing briefly to consider smoke signals and hilltop bonfires, they usually come upon the French optical telegraph system, which was deployed initially for military purposes in the 1790s. The system consisted of chains of towers, mostly laid out in radiating fashion from Paris to reach provincial cities. At the top of each tower was a set of arms that could be wagged to spell out words using a code. Within each tower was stationed an operator, who moved the arms via a mechanical linkage and who observed the next tower in the chain using a telescope to read its messages. This system was quite successful and ultimately was used for commercial as well as military purposes. By 1844, the French network connected 29 cities to Paris and consisted of 533 relay stations placed 8 to 10 km apart, for a total of approximately 5000 route-km. Optical telegraph networks deployed elsewhere in Europe and Britain brought the total number of stations to around 1000. (The British system wagged paddles instead of arms, but was otherwise similar to the French system.)

In the late 1830s, the electrical telegraph was developed, and it immediately offered obvious advantages of communication at night and in bad weather as well as in speed of transmission. While the optical telegraph persisted for a while in places (particularly France) where the system was highly developed and government supported, it was soon overwhelmed by the electrical telegraph, and the optical telegraph towers decayed into quaint landmarks (one can be seen, for example, on the label of a rather nice French wine that is marketed in the United States).

By the 1880s, electrical telegraph networks were in a state of advanced deployment in all the industrialized nations of the world. Table 1.1 gives some statistics regarding telegraph deployment in Europe and North America as of the year 1880.

Table 1.1   Telegraph Deployment in Europe and North America in 1880

COUNTRY	TOTAL LINES (KM)	OFFICES
Great Britain	42,347	5,433
France	69,030	5,426
Switzerland	6,556	1,108
United States	178,270	12,510

Source: *Journal Telegraphique*, 1881.

The telephone was invented in 1876, and by the next year, telephone networks were already being deployed. By 1880, the year of the aforementioned telegraph statistics, there were already 30,000 telephones in use throughout the world. Just as the electrical telegraph offered clear technological advantages over the optical system, the telephone represented another level of improvement, notably in ease of use: No special skill was required either to send or receive. However, while demand for the service was high and growth was rapid, there was significant resistance from operators of the telegraph networks, which were larger and more deeply embedded than the optical telegraph had been at the analogous moment of transition.

In the United States, where both telegraph and telephone networks were privately owned, resistance took the form of a protracted legal fight over patent claims between Western Union (the private telegraph monopoly) and the Bell companies. The Bell companies ultimately won in court, and rapid development of the U.S. telephone network proceeded.

In Europe, where the telegraph networks were government owned, the tools of the state were employed to deliberately limit the penetration of the telephone. For example, in 1892, the British government initiated actions to purchase all existing telephone trunk lines. To describe the government's motivations, the postmaster general released this startling statement:

> If the telephone companies were in communication with all the large towns and sent messages all over the country, undoubtedly the system would to a large extent supersede the telegraphs and consequently largely diminish the telegraph revenue. Therefore, it is an essential feature of the scheme, if carried out, that the Government should have possession of the trunk wires.

> *Robertson, 1947.*

A result of these somewhat different dynamics in Europe and the United States was that telephone density increased more slowly in Europe, and the period of overlap between the two technologies and two network infrastructures was longer in Europe than in the United States. Thus, in 1934, telephone density (phones per 100 people) was reported as 13.29 in the United States, but only 4.78 in Britain and 3.19 in France. By 1997, according to the ITU, the gap had closed significantly, with the United States at 64.37, Britain at 54.00, and France at 57.5. In 1988, France still had 150,000 telex subscribers and Britain 116,000, compared with 81,000 in all of the United States. By 1996, telex subscribers were down to 39,000 in France and 20,000 in Britain, and the United States had stopped reporting the figure to the ITU.

It should be stated, by the way, that the persistence of the telegraph was not entirely due to the machinations of evil government monopolists. While the telephone was superior in ease of use, some characteristics of the telegraph provided differential advantages for certain applications. For example, the fact that telegrams were printed on paper provided a permanent record and eased language barriers for those who could read or write but not necessarily converse in a foreign language. Telegrams could also be sent without concern about whether the intended recipient was awake and ready to receive. Also, while some business cultures, notably the American one, thrive on the informal interaction enabled by the telephone, others are more likely to require written records for most transactions. It was only the widespread availability of fax, voice mail, and e-mail, all developments of the last 20 years, that made it possible to do away just about entirely with the telegraph (and its last incarnation, the telex) in almost all business applications.

From the optical telegraph to the electrical telegraph to the telephone to—the Internet? By now, the Internet certainly qualifies as the next great technology for rapid communication at a distance. But it is only very recently that it has begun to acquire the status of a distinct communications infrastructure. Initially, the nodes of most data communications networks, and of the Internet itself, were usually connected with leased telephone circuits of one kind or another. This was partly an accommodation to reality and partly a matter of design. The reality was the overwhelming dominance of the telephone network infrastructure. For the Internet, this was also a reflection of the design principle, "IP over everything, and everything over IP." IP stands for *Internet Protocol*, the ubiquitous network layer protocol of the Internet, and the meaning of this phrase is that the design of IP is simple and flexible enough so that no dedicated, specially designed lower-layer infrastructure is required. Therefore the infrastructure of the Internet—to the extent there can be said to be one—has consisted of higher-layer routing, naming, and addressing structures operating over the same wires, optical fibers, and coaxes used by telephone calls, faxes, and TV signals.

In very recent times, the Internet infrastructure has begun to change a bit, due to two developments. First, a few companies have announced that they will build new optical networks dedicated to IP routing. (One prominent new carrier is Level 3.) Second, the bandwidth demands of Internet links have grown so rapidly that there is strong interest in interfacing IP routers directly to optical fibers. In this case, even if transmission capacity is leased from a carrier, it would be obtained as an entire wavelength on a wavelength division multiplexing system, or even as a whole dedicated fiber. This scenario begins to look very much like a whole top-to-bottom infrastructure dedicated to Internet, and raises the questions, "How long will the overlap with the older (in this case, telephone) infrastructure persist, if not indefinitely?" and, "What will be the driving technical, business, and regulatory factors?"

The Infrastructure Bazaar

Predicting a future paced by foreshortened Internet time is a risky exercise indeed, but there are a number of reasons to think that the near to medium term will see not a single infrastructure winner, but rather the availability of multiple infrastructures competing for the attention and business of end users. We might even call this the *infrastructure bazaar*. One important factor encouraging this direction is the continuing rapid privatization and deregulation of the telecommunications world. We've seen that the status of telegraph networks as government-owned monopolies helped them resist the advent of the telephone and then to co-opt it, leading to government-owned (or, in a few places like the United States, private, government-sanctioned) telephone monopolies. This either/or dynamic, in which the old infrastructure persists until the technical advantages of the new one become overwhelming, whereupon it becomes the basis for a new monopoly, is unlikely to be repeated in today's world, where carriers are private and set in competition against one another.

The possibility of multiple competing infrastructure options is further enhanced by the availability of multiple infrastructure technologies and combinations thereof. Despite the meteoric trajectory of IP, it is not the only game in town. Many big carriers are making major investments in *asynchronous transfer mode* (ATM), a technology whose obituary has been written too many times by followers of technology fashion. One highly publicized example is the *Sprint Integrated On-Demand Network* (ION) project in the United States. In many other cases, however, significant ATM infrastructure is being purchased and installed more quietly as a logical technical choice to underlie multiservice offerings. Wireless networks, many of them operated by highly competitive new carriers, have their own rapid growth curve and are evolving to *third-generation systems* intended to support multimedia applications in addition to voice. The existing circuit-switched telephone infrastructure, still unsurpassed for reliability and the quality of voice transmission, has been rendered more and more efficient by the rigors of competition in those parts of the world where deregulation and privatization have been in place for a decade or more.

Even within the world of IP, there are technical choices that can be the basis for differentiation among providers. Who is to say for sure, for example, that the idea of building an all-IP network from fiber-optic glass in the ground up through routers and switches will give a lower cost per bit and better service than can be delivered by an IP specialist who leases transmission capacity from a facilities-based carrier, or in comparison with another network that combines and interworks IP, ATM, and circuit switching?

At the moment, all of these are plausible business models that are capable of attracting investment. In the near to medium term, all will also be options available to the network manager who needs to obtain carrier services to support the voice, data, and multimedia needs of end users. In the infrastructure bazaar, no less than in any other market, having a wide set of vendors offering goods in a variety of packagings, quality levels, and price points is a favorable situation for the savvy shopper!

Applications: The Driving Factor

The ITU estimates that in 1998 there were over 800 million main telephone lines in operation in the world. The staggering fact is that this immense network is rigged for a single application (voice telephony) and represents over $1 trillion in capital investment and untold millions of person-years of engineering and operational experience. With the proliferation of network applications and the burgeoning of network technology, intuition may tell you that no such monolithic network will ever be built again.

On the other hand, the opposite of the traditional telephone network would appear to be a network that supports all applications on a single highly flexible technology platform. This is an idea that never seems to go away in spite of the fact that it has yet to be realized. The idea appeals strongly in various ways to carriers, technology vendors, and standards makers—and ISDN, ATM, and IP have all had their turn as the core technology concept. But does it merely represent a lazy wish by vendors to offer a single product so appealing that everyone will want to buy it, no matter what their spectrum of needs or applications? The hardest job for vendors, as always, is to understand user needs in detail and to construct products to support those needs, even if the result is that one size does not fit all.

If the telecommunications world continues to develop toward ever greater competition among universally privatized networks, the relationships among user applications and network technologies may assume a much greater variety of forms than we have seen in either the telephony model or the one-network-does-everything vision. We may see large, publicly available, multiservice networks; but if these fail to optimally meet the needs of particular user applications, the business and technology environment will readily support the development and deployment of more specialized networks, including ones based on new network technologies that do not exist today. There will also be a wide spectrum of options for enterprises to either own or outsource any or all elements of network operation.

We are the first to admit that we don't have an unclouded crystal ball, and that the preceding paragraphs represent speculation no more (or less) reliable than other speculation you may have read about the future of the network. If we retreat a bit to the near term, however, we can say with much more confidence that two of the most powerful technologies available to help you address your business networking needs will be the Internet and traditional telecommunications. The rest of this book is dedicated to helping you understand and choose the best technologies from these converging worlds of networking.

Convergence, Integration, and Interworking

Up to this point, we have been using words like *convergence, integration,* and *interworking* loosely and interchangeably. To prepare for the discussion of technology and standards in the following chapters, we need to be a little more precise. Following are some scenarios that show the possible relationships between the Internet and telecommunications that we consider in this book.

Given the existence of both the public Internet and the *public switched telephone network* (PSTN), as well as their private network equivalents [private IP-based networks and private telephone networks based on PBXs and circuit-switched *virtual private network* (VPN) services], the zero-order relationship is simple coexistence. From the user point of view, coexistence means an either/or choice: Either economics, quality, security, and other key requirements together mandate the choice of Internet, or you have a traditional telecommunications network for a given application.

However, especially because we are living in an era of infrastructure overlap, in which both technologies are highly developed and widely available, many other more intricate combinations are possible. As a framework for understanding the possible relationships at a high level, we will introduce the simple functional division shown in Figure 1.3 and assert that it can be applied to all networks, including the Internet and telecommunications networks.

Transport aspects of networks are those dedicated to successfully moving bits and signals from one place to another and include things like physical layer functions and encoding. *Control aspects* help ensure that the bits and signals go to the particular place intended, and include things like signaling protocols and routing tables. Large-scale circuit-switched telephone networks often

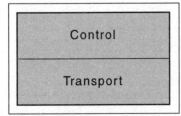

Figure 1.3   High-level functional layering of networks.

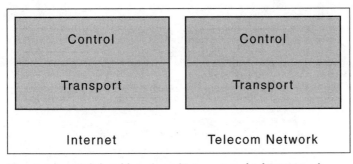

Figure 1.4 High-level layering of Internet and telecommunications networks.

have architectures that strongly separate these functional groupings, with control residing in SS No. 7 signaling networks and the control computers of switches, and transport being handled by digital transmission systems. On the Internet side, there is typically less gross physical separation of these functional groups in implementations, but they may be sorted out by examining the set of functions performed by each protocol layer. Routing, for example, clearly belongs in the control category, while physical and link layer functions would be grouped under the transport function. (Apologies to internauts for usurping the term normally used for the third layer from the bottom of the Internet stack.)

Now, if you accept this extremely simple network model as universal, or at least agree that it roughly applies to the Internet and telecommunications networks, imagine putting the two side by side, as in Figure 1.4.

Now we will consider some useful relationships between the control and transport structures of the Internet and telecommunications networks.

First, the straightforward approach is to directly connect the control and transport structures of the two networks via interposed *gateways,* as shown in Figure 1.5.

The gateway interconnection scenario applies to *Internet telephony* and, in particular, the interworking of IP telephony with circuit-switched telephony.

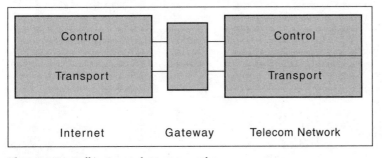

Figure 1.5 Full gateway interconnection.

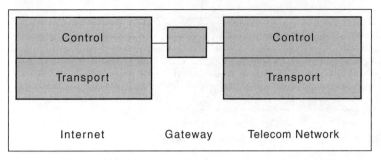

Figure 1.6   Control-only interconnection.

The gateway at the transport level transforms the encoding of speech from a form that is appropriate for transport on a circuit-switched network to one that is appropriate for transport on a variable-length packet network, and the gateway at the control level uses control information (for example, signaling and address information) from one network to determine the proper onward routing. This scenario is the focus of much (to put it mildly) current technology and standards development, and we will elaborate on it greatly in the chapters that follow.

Figure 1.6 shows a less obvious potential relationship, but one that is the subject of current work in the IETF PSTN/Internet Internetworking (*pint*) and Service in the PSTN/IN Requesting Internet Service (*spirits*) working groups, and is already the basis for a number of quite powerful products and services. As shown in Figure 1.6, the interconnection is purely in the control dimension. There is no gateway for encoded speech at the transport level, because the speech information remains entirely on the telecommunications network side. In effect, the routing and even initiation of calls within the telecommunications network are controlled via the Internet.

Finally, Figure 1.7 shows another relationship that has already proved to be of high practical importance. The transport facilities of the telecommunications network may be used to carry a portion of the Internet, with all its control and transport information, in a transparent fashion, with no direct

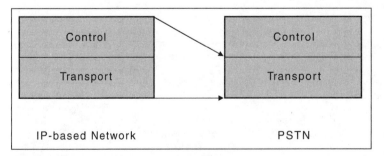

Figure 1.7   Carriage of an IP-based network on the PSTN.

interaction between Internet and telecommunications network control. This is an instance of *tunneling*—precisely what happens when remote access to the public Internet or to a private IP network is accomplished by dial-up over the PSTN.

With these potential relationships between the Internet and telecommunications networks in mind, we are ready to discuss the technologies that enable integration of the Internet and telecommunications.

Adjusting the PSTN to the Internet

One gray and rainy February morning, the authors landed in Frankfurt Airport on their way from Newark, New Jersey, to Geneva, Switzerland. Frankfurt Airport is a hub for Lufthansa Airlines; we were supposed to get on a plane to Geneva an hour and a half after we arrived.

That was not to be, however. Just as we entered the terminal, all flights were canceled, and furthermore, the whole airport was closed indefinitely because of the freezing rain. The temperature was falling. It was Sunday, and we absolutely had to be in Geneva by Monday morning for a meeting. A short conversation with a Lufthansa customer service representative made it clear that this would be impossible if we chose to stay in Frankfurt overnight. On the other hand, the representative said, our goal would be quite easy to achieve if we went by train: We would be in Geneva in six hours.

By train? What about the tickets? Where was this train?—we were in the airport, after all. What about our heavy bags with the suits and shoes, which we had not received back anyway?

Very simple: The train station was right below the luggage carousel— we would just take the elevator, which incidentally did accommodate luggage carts. The luggage was being offloaded at that very moment and would be there in 10 minutes. The station ticket office would exchange our boarding passes for the train tickets. Indeed, this is precisely what happened! Granted, we did need to change trains twice—in Frankfurt central station and in Bern—but we found it quite remarkable that it was so easy to change the mode of transportation from an airline (run by a private company) to a train system (which at the time was run by the German government). Not only did the more-than-a-century-old technology happen to be an excellent fallback for a much newer technology (which could not be used under the circumstances anyway), but the systems supported by these technologies *interworked* perfectly in all aspects, including accounting! We thought momentarily that we still had a problem—our rented car in Geneva was waiting for us at the Geneva airport—but even that proved to be no problem at all: The very train we took terminated at the Geneva airport. In fact, as we found out later, throughout the world, railroads strategically build their gateways at the international airports.

You probably already see what we are getting at. Our experience has provided us with a powerful allegory for the very subject of this book. That the transportation and communications industries have had many common tasks is well known. As a matter of fact, the same results of an area of applied mathematics called operations research have been applied with equal success to the problems in both industries. It is the degree of cooperation and interworking among old and new technological infrastructures of the transportation industry that should give us a clue as to the directions for the future in the ever developing world of communications.

And not only cooperation but competition between these infrastructures is there, too! Going back to the rail-versus-air theme, note that for decades it was commonplace knowledge that if you wished to get from the center of London to the center of Paris (or vice versa) as fast as possible, you would need to fly. Now, however, you are likely to do better by taking a train: The development of the Eurotunnel and fast trains is an example of the evolution of the old infrastructure that enables it to compete successfully with a new one. Thus, we cannot give a simple answer to the question, Should I take a plain or train from London to Paris? We can give you a more or less accurate answer only after we learn (1) where exactly you are in London, (2) what time of day it is, and (3) what the weather is going to be like over the next few hours. In fact, once you understand the present capabilities of the rail and air infrastructures (including the schedules), you will be able to make your own decisions easily.

In this chapter and the next, we specifically concentrate on infrastructure technologies that support the PSTN and Internet infrastructures. In this chapter, we show how the PSTN is evolving in response to the IP challenge, while in Chapter 3 we demonstrate how the Internet (and the IP infrastructure in general) is adjusting to interworking (and, in some cases, competing) with the PSTN. Naturally, Chapters 2 and 3 overlap—there would not have been convergence to speak of if it were possible to clearly delineate all subjects as belonging to one or another chapter!

The Public Switched Telephone Network (PSTN)

PSTN is an old-fashioned term; today, it is more politically correct to substitute "G" (which stands for *global*) for "P," and call the thing the *GSTN*. Sometimes the infrastructures such as the *integrated services digital network* (ISDN) are mentioned as though they are somehow not part of the PSTN (as in a combination PSTN and ISDN or PSTN/ISDN). In this book, we refer to the PSTN in its most general sense—that is, the telephone system in public use. The fact that it is used globally does not warrant—in our opinion—creation of another acronym. As we demonstrate further in this chapter, the ISDN is a technology and infrastructure supported within the PSTN, not a separate network type. Furthermore, inasmuch as private (specifically, enterprise) telephony networks interconnect with the PSTN, we include the relevant apparatus [such as *private branch exchange* (PBX) switches] in the description of the PSTN infrastructure for the same reason that we consider our own telephones a part of the same infrastructure. As the Internet is a conglomerate of different IP networks, so the PSTN is a conglomerate of different telephone networks.

The situation is somewhat different with the cable and wireless networks, which until very recently have existed independently from the PSTN. To this end, the wireless network technologies have been developing toward blending with the PSTN (the wireless part deals only with access to the nearest "wireline" switch), and the wireless services have much in common with those of the PSTN; the blending of cable networks with the PSTN has started very recently, however. In any event, in this book we make only passing references to these technologies—each of which has had many books written about it—and only so long as they are used to access the PSTN or Internet. To this end, we should note that the *Intelligent Network* (IN) technology has been systematically used as the means of integrating various infrastructures (for example, wireless access) into the PSTN. We will keep returning to the topic of IN throughout the book.

Our goal here is to provide the basics of the PSTN structure to help you understand what can be done and what is being done in order to make both networks work together. We don't take for granted that you know these basics of the PSTN. (On the other hand, we *do* take for granted that you know the basics of data communications technologies in general and IP technologies in particular. Our recent experience in giving seminars to graduate students and engineers and in teaching a postgraduate course on telephony has convinced us that these people's curricula had included very little or no material on telephony, while they had studied data communications in detail and had firsthand experience with the Internet.)[1]

---

[1]Lack of telephony in the curriculum can be easily explained: The Internet has been built by graduate students, and universities have played a major role in running it. PSTN expertise, on

For example, we found that many people were amused when they learned that the PSTN has had a packet network (for its own use in support of signaling) that was developed at the same time as the Internet, or that the telephone switches were actually fault-tolerant computers whose operating systems were specialized for real-time control of fast devices, or that variants of the Unix operating system (which has always been associated with the Internet) were used in the development of such switches from its early days (Pekarich, 1978). Many students were even surprised when they heard that voice was digitized in the PSTN from the moment it entered local switches.

To familiarize readers who are similarly unacquainted with the PSTN, we start the chapter by introducing several key PSTN technologies, specifically the ones dealing with switching, signaling, service support, and operations. Then we proceed with the evolution of the PSTN on its path of convergence with IP networks. To this end, we consider two of the three subjects of this book: PSTN-based access to IP networks and IP-based support of PSTN telephony services. (We address the third subject—interworking with IP telephony—in Chapter 3.)

The PSTN: Switching, Signaling, Services, and Operations

The goal of this section is to provide a brief overview of the development of the PSTN as the means of delivering services with an emphasis on the need for network programmability. The best way to address this topic is to follow the development historically—an approach that should eliminate many potential whys. To that end, we describe the basic structure of the PSTN, address the evolution of switching and signaling, and then move to the edge of the network by describing the PSTN offer of integrated voice and data services to the end user—the *integrated services digital network* (ISDN). After that, we move into the core of the network and introduce the subject of *Intelligent Network* (IN)—the means to achieve network-wide service programmability. Finally, we attend to the issues of operation, administration, and maintenance of the PSTN, where we particularly focus on network traffic management problems and solutions.

Structure of the PSTN

At the very beginning of the telephony age, telephones were sold in pairs; for a call to be made, the two telephones involved had to be connected directly.

---

the other hand, until very recently belonged to a handful of corporations, which were in most countries either run or regulated by governments. Following the breakup of the Bell Telephone System in the United States in 1984, the worldwide telecommunications industry development called *liberalization* is resulting in a surge of new, competing companies (which is what makes the structure of the PSTN look more and more like that of the Internet). In this situation, the demand for telephony engineering education has grown, but is still hardly met by academe.

So, in addition to the grounding wire, if there were 20 telephones you wanted to call (or that might call you), each would be connected to your telephone by a separate wire. At certain point, it was clear that a better long-term solution was needed, and such a solution came in the form of the first Bell Company *switching office* in New Haven, Connecticut. The office had a switching board, operated by human operators, to which the telephones were connected. An operator's job was to answer the call of a calling party, inquire as to the name of the called party, and then establish the call by connecting with a wire two sockets that belonged to the calling and called party, respectively. After the call was completed, the operator would disconnect the circuit by pulling the wire from the sockets. Note that no telephone numbers were involved (or needed). Telephone numbers became a necessity later, when the first automatic switch was built. The automaton was purely mechanical—it could find necessary sockets only by counting; thus, the telephones (and their respective sockets in the switch) were identified by these telephone numbers. Later, the switches had to be interconnected with other switches, and the first telephone network—the Bell System in the United States—came to life. Other telephone networks were built in pretty much the same way.

Many things have happened since the first network appeared—and we are going to address these things—but the structure of the PSTN in terms of its main components remained unchanged as far as the establishment of the end-to-end voice path is concerned. The components are:

- *Station equipment [or customer premises equipment (CPE)].* Located on the customer's premises, its primary functions are to transmit and receive signals between the customer and the network. These types of equipment range from residential telephones to sophisticated enterprise *private branch exchange* systems (PBXs).

- *Transmission facilities.* These provide the communications paths, which consist of transmission media (atmosphere, paired cable, coaxial cable, light guide cable, and so on) and various types of equipment to amplify or regenerate signals.

- *Switching systems.* These interconnect the transmission facilities at various key locations and route traffic through the network. (They have been called switching offices since the times of the first Connecticut office.)

- *Operations, administration, and management (OA&M) systems.* These provide administration, maintenance, and network management functions to the network.

Until relatively recent times, switching boards remained in use in relatively small organizations (such as hotels, hospitals, or companies of several dozen employees), but finally were replaced by customer premises switches called *private branch exchanges* (PBXs). (PBXs, as a primary IP telephony application for enterprise networks, are given extensive coverage in Chapter 10.) The

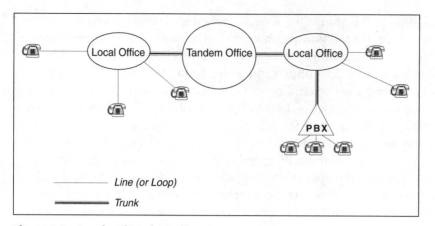

Figure 2.1   Local and tandem offices.

PBX, then, is a nontrivial, most sophisticated example of station equipment. On the other end of the spectrum is the ordinary single-line telephone set. In addition to transmitting and receiving the user information (such as conversation), the station equipment is responsible for *addressing* (that is, the task of specifying to the network the destination of the call) as well as carrying other forms of *signaling* [*idle* or *busy* status, *alerting* (that is, ringing), and so on].

As Figure 2.1 demonstrates, the station equipment is connected to switches. The telephones are connected to *local* switches (also interchangeably called *local offices, central offices, end offices,* or *Class 5 switches*)[2] by means of *local loop* circuits or *channels* carried over local loop transmission facilities. The circuits that interconnect switches are called *trunks.* Trunks are carried over *interoffice* transmission facilities. The local offices are, in turn, interconnected to *toll offices* (called *tandem* offices in this case). Finally, we should note that in all this terminology the word *office* is interchangeable with *exchange,* and, of course, *switch.* It is very difficult to say which word is more widely used.

The trunks are grouped; it is often convenient to refer to trunk groups, which are assigned specific identifiers, rather than individual trunks. Grouping is especially convenient for the purposes of network management or assignment to transmission facilities. (A trunk is a logical abstraction rather than a physical medium; a trunk leaving a switch can be mapped to a fiberoptic cable on the first part of its way to the next switch, microwave for the second part, and four copper wires for the third part.)

In the original Bell System, there were five levels in the switching hierarchy; this number has dropped to three due to technological development of *nonhierarchical routing* (NHR) in the long-distance network. NHR was not adopted by the local carriers, however, so they retained the two levels—local and tandem—of switching hierarchy.

---

[2]The pre-1984 Bell telephone system hierarchy of switches had five ranks or *classes,* with the fifth class—the lowest in the hierarchy—designating local switches.

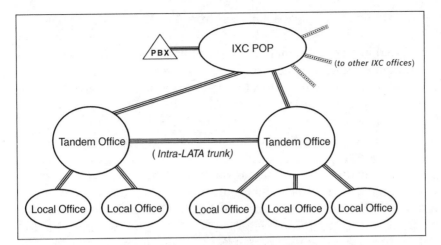

Figure 2.2   The interconnection of LATAs and IXCs.

Local switches in the United States are grouped into *local access and transport areas* (LATAs). You can find a current map of LATAs at www.611.net/NETWORKTELECOM/lata_map/index.htm. A LATA may have many offices (on the order of 100), including tandem offices. Service within LATAs is typically provided by *local exchange carriers* (LECs). Some LECs have existed for a considerable time (such as original Bell Operating Companies, created in 1984 as a result of breakup of the Bell system), and so are called *incumbent LECs* (ILECs); others appeared fairly recently, and are called *competitive LECs* (CLECs). Inter-LATA traffic is carried by *interexchange carriers* (IXCs). The IXCs are connected to central or tandem offices by means of *points of presence* (POPs).

Figure 2.2 depicts an interconnection of an IXC with one particular LATA. The IXC switches form the IXC network, in which routing is typically non-hierarchical. Presently, IXCs are providing local service, too; however, since their early days IXCs have had direct trunks to PBXs of large companies to whom they provided services like *virtual private networks* (VPNs).[3] We should mention that IXCs in the United States can (and do) interconnect with the overseas long-distance service providers by means of complex gateways that perform call signaling translations, but the IXCs in the United States are typically not directly interconnected with each other.

Evolution of Switching

As noted, the first switch was a switching matrix (board) operated by a human. The 1890s saw the introduction of the first automatic *step-by-step* sys-

---

[3]The most important feature of a VPN service is that a multilocation enterprise can have its own numbering plan. We will return to this service—and its namesake in the IP world, with which it must *not* be confused—several times in this book.

tems, which responded to rotary dial pulses from 1 to 10 (that is, digits 1 through 9 to 0). *Cross-bar* switches, which could set up a connection within a second, appeared in late 1930s. Step-by-step and cross-bar switches are examples of *space-division* switches; later, this technology evolved into that of *time-division*. A large step in switching development was made in the late 1960s as a consequence of the computer revolution. At that time computers were used for address translation and line selection. By 1980, *stored program control* as a real-time application running on a general-purpose computer coupled with a switch had become a norm.

At about the same time, a revolution in switching took place. Owing to the availability of digital transmission, it became possible to transmit voice in digital format. As the consequence, the switches went digital. For the detailed treatment of the subject, we recommend Bellamy (2000), but we are going to discuss it here because it is at the heart of the matter as far as the IP telephony is concerned. In a nutshell, the switching processes end-to-end voice in these four steps:

1. A device scans in a round-robin fashion all active incoming trunks and samples the analog signal at a rate of 8000 times a second. The sampled signal is passed to the *coder* part of the coder/decoder device called a *pulse-code modulation* (PCM) *codec*, which outputs an 8-bit string encoding the value of the electric amplitude at the moment of the sample (see Chapter 3 for more on codecs).

2. Output strings are fed into a frame whose length equals 8 times the number of active input lines. This frame is then passed to the *time slot interchanger*, which builds the output frame by reordering the original frame according to the connection table. For example, if input trunk number 3 is connected to output trunk number 5, then the contents of the 3rd byte of the input frame are inserted into the 5th byte of the output frame. (There is a limitation on the number of lines a time slot interchanger can support, which is determined solely by the speed at which it can perform, so the state of the art of computer architecture and microelectronics is constantly applied to building time slot interchangers. The line limitation is otherwise dealt with by cascading the devices into multistage units.)

3. On outgoing digital trunk groups, the 8-bit slots are multiplexed into a transmission carrier according to its respective standard. (We will address transmission carriers in a moment.) Conversely, a digital switch accepts the incoming transmission frames from a transmission carrier and switches them as described in the previous step.

4. At the destination switch, the decoder part of the codec translates the 8-bit strings coming on the input trunk back into electrical signals.

Note that we assumed that digital switches were toll offices (we called both incoming and outgoing circuits *trunks*). Indeed, initially only the toll switches on the top of the hierarchy went digital, but then digital telephony moved quickly down the hierarchy, and in the 1980s it migrated to the central offices and even PBXs. Furthermore, it has been moving to the local loop by means of the ISDN and *digital subscriber line* (DSL) technologies addressed further in this part.

The availability of digital transmission and switching has immediately resulted in much higher quality of voice, especially in cases where the parties to a call are separated by a long distance (information loss requires the presence of multiple regenerators, whose cumulative effect is significant distortion of analog signal, but the digital signals are fairly easy to restore—0s and 1s are typically represented by a continuum of analog values, so a relatively small change has no immediate, and therefore no cumulative, effect).

We conclude this section by listing the transmission carriers and formats, which are referenced systematically in Chapter 10. The *T1* carrier multiplexes 24-voice channels represented by 8-bit samples into a 193-bit frame. (The extra bit is used as a framing code by alternating between 0 and 1.) With data rates of 8000 bits per second, the T1 frames are issued every 125 µs. The T1 data rate in the United States is thus 1.544 Mbps. (Incidentally, another carrier, called *E1*, which is used predominantly outside of the United States, carries thirty-two 8-bit samples in its frame.)

T1 carriers can be further multiplexed bit by bit into higher-order carriers, with extra bits added each time for synchronization:

- Four T1 frames are multiplexed into a T2 frame (rate: 6.312 Mbps)
- Six T2 frames are multiplexed into a T3 frame (rate: 44.736 Mbps)
- Six T3 frames are multiplexed into a T4 frame (rate: 274.176 Mbps)

The ever increasing power of resulting pipes is depicted in Figure 2.3.[4]

Evolution of Signaling

Now that we know *what* the voice circuit between the switches is, we can talk about *how* it is established. In the so-called *plain old telephone service* (POTS), establishing a call *is* routing, for once the call (for example, an end-to-end virtual circuit) is established, no routing decisions are to be made by the switches. There are three aspects to call establishment: First, a switch must understand the telephone number it receives in order to terminate the call on a line or route the call to the next switch in the chain; second, a switch must choose the appropriate circuit and let the next switch in the chain know what it is; third, the switches must test the circuit, monitor it, and finally release it at the end of the call. We will address the (quite important) concept of *understanding* the tele-

---

[4]You may have noticed that 4×1.544 equals 6.176, not 6.312. The extra bits here and in the rest of T-streams are added for framing and error control and recovery.

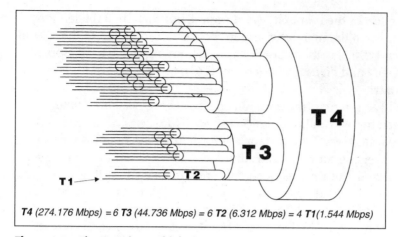

*T4 (274.176 Mbps) = 6 **T3** (44.736 Mbps) = 6 **T2** (6.312 Mbps) = 4 **T1** (1.544 Mbps)*

Figure 2.3   The T-carrier multiplexing nomenclature.

phone number later. The other two circuit-related steps require that the switches exchange information. In the PSTN, this exchange is called *signaling*.[5]

Initially, the signaling procedure was much closer to the original meaning of the word—the pieces of electric machinery involved were exchanging electrical signals. The human end user was (and still is) signaled with audio tones of different frequencies and durations.

As far as the switches are concerned, in the past, signaling was not unlike what our telephones do when we push the buttons to dial: switches exchanged audio signals using the very circuit (that is, trunk) over which the parties to the call were to speak. This type of signaling is called *in-band* signaling, and quite appropriately so, because it uses the voice band. There are quite a few problems with in-band signaling. Not only is it slow and quite annoying to the people who have to listen to meaningless tones, but also telephone users can produce the same tones the switches use and thereby deceive the network provider or disrupt the network.[6]

To prevent fraud and also to improve efficiency, another form of signaling that would not use the voice band was needed. This could be achieved by using for signaling the frequencies that were out of the voice band (thus called *out-of-band* frequencies). Nevertheless, a channel in the telephone network is limited to the voice band, so there is no physical way to send frequencies beyond the voice band on such a channel. This limitation necessitated *out-of-channel* rather than out-of-band signaling. It was also obvious that

---

[5]The international standard uses the British spelling of the word *signaling* (that is, *signalling*). We use the British spelling whenever we refer to standard terms.

[6]Before 1995, there was a mandatory "Introduction to Telephony" course that all Bell Laboratories employees were required to take soon after they joined the company. The course listed cases of fraud where people whistled the signaling information in order to make free long-distance calls (long distance was quite expensive at that time), or whistled wrong charging signals—an entertaining illustration of what was wrong with in-band signaling.

much more information (concerning the characteristics of the circuits to be established, calling and called parties' numbers, billing information, and so on) was required, and that this information could be stored and passed in the same form that was used for data processing. Hence (1) the information had to be encoded into a set of data structures and (2) these data structures had to be transformed over a separate data communications network. Thus, the concept of *common channel signaling* was born. Common channel signaling is signaling that is common to all voice channels but carried over none of them. Although it is clearly a misnomer, this type of signaling is often still called *out-of-band signaling.*

Let's get back to the question of the switch understanding the telephone number. First of all, there are two types of numbers: those that actually correspond to the telephones that can be called and those that must be translated to the numbers of the first type. An example of the first type is a U.S. number +1-732-555-0137, which translates to a particular line in a particular central office (in New Jersey). An example of the second type is any U.S. number that starts with 1-800. The 800 prefix signals to the switch that the number by itself does not identify a particular switch or line (there is no 800 area code in the United States). Such a number designates a service (called *toll-free* in the United States or *freephone* in Europe) that is free to the caller but paid by the organization or person who receives calls.

Handling numbers of the first type is relatively straightforward—they end up in a switch's routing table, where they are associated with the trunks or lines to be used in the act of establishing a call. The other (toll-free) numbers need translation. Naturally, a switch could translate the toll-free number, too, but such a solution would require tens of thousands of switches to be loaded with this information. The only feasible solution is to let a central database do the translation.[7] The switch then needs to communicate with the database. [Note: The solution was figured out as early as 1979—see Faynberg et al. (1997) for the history.]

Another example where a database lookup is needed is implementation of *local number portability* (LNP). In the United States, the Telecommunications Act passed by the U.S. Congress in 1996 mandates the right of telephony service subscribers to keep their telephone numbers even when they change service providers. With that, subscribers can keep not only the numbers but also the features (such as call waiting) originally associated with the numbers. In the United States, the solutions are based on switches' capabilities to query databases so as to locate the terminating switch when they encounter numbers marked as ported. (To be precise, this process requires two database dips—one to determine whether a dialed number is portable and the other to find the terminating switch.)

---

[7]The word *central* as used here means accessible to all switches in the network. As far as its actual structure is concerned, the database is distributed.

For both types of communications—out-of-band signaling among the switches and querying the database—the Bell Telephone System has designed a special data network called a *common channel interoffice signaling* (CCIS) network. When this network was introduced—in 1976—it was used only for out-of band signaling (hence *interoffice*). Thus the network served as a medium for communicating information about any trunk (channel) without being associated with that particular trunk. In other words, it was a medium common to all trunks, hence the term *common channel*. In the early 1980s, the network databases were connected to the network; thus signaling ceased to be strictly interoffice, and the I was taken away from the CCIS. Both the network and the concept became known as *common channel signaling* (CCS).

The architecture of the CCS network is depicted in Figure 2.4. The endpoints of the system are switches and network databases. The CCS routers are called *signaling transfer points* (STPs). Since all signaling has been outsourced to it, the CCS network must be as fast and as reliable as the network of the telephone switches. The reliability has been achieved through high redundancy: All STPs within the network are fully interconnected. Furthermore, each STP has a *mated* STP, with which it is connected through a high-speed link (*C*-link). Interconnection with other STPs is achieved through a backbone link (*B*-link). Finally, switches and databases are connected to STPs by *A*-links.

Historically, there are two distinct types of protocols within common channel signaling: (1) interactions between the switches and databases that started

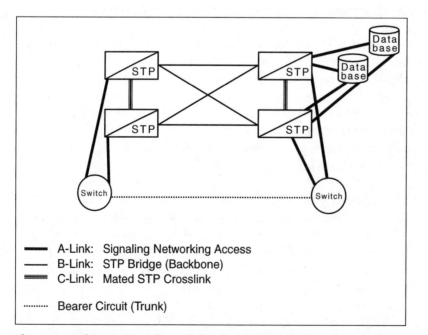

Figure 2.4 The common channel signaling (CCS) architecture.

as simple query/response messages for number translation and have evolved into service-independent protocols that support multiple services for IN technology, described later in this chapter; and (2) the protocols by means of which the switches exchange information necessary to establish, maintain, and tear down calls.

The CCS network has evolved through several releases and enhancements in the Bell System, and subsequently other telephone companies, which eventually resulted in multiple CCS networks. To ensure the interoperability of these networks as well as multivendor equipment interoperability in each of them, ITU-T has developed an international standard for common channel signaling. The latest release of this standard is called *Signalling System No. 7* (SS No. 7); it is described in Chapter 4. Note that the official ITU-T abbreviation of this term is *SS No. 7*; however, the unofficial (but much easier to write and pronounce) term *SS7* is used throughout the industry. In this book, we use the official term whenever we refer to the standard or its implementation in the network; we use SS7 when we refer to new classes of products (such as the SS7 gateway).

Integrated Services Digital Network (ISDN)

The need for data communications services grew throughout the 1970s. These services were provided (mostly to the companies rather than individuals) by the X.25-based *packet switched data networks* (PSDNs). By the early 1980s it was clear to the industry that there was a market and technological feasibility for integrating data communications and voice in a single digital pipe and opening such pipes for businesses (as the means of PBX access) and households. The envisioned applications included video telephony, online directories, synchronization of a customer's call with bringing the customer's data to the computer screen of the answering agent, telemetrics (that is, monitoring devices—such as plant controls or smoke alarms—and automatic reporting of associated events via telephone calls), and a number of purely voice services. In addition, since the access was supposed to be digital, the voice channels could be used for data connections that would provide a much higher rate than had ever been possible with the analog line and modems.

The ISDN telephone (often called the *ISDN terminal*) is effectively a computer that runs a specialized application. The ISDN telephone always has a display; in some cases it even looks like a computer terminal, with a screen and keyboard in addition to the receiver and speaker. Several such terminals could be connected to the *network terminator* (NT) device, which can be placed in the home or office and which has a direct connection to the ISDN switch. Non-ISDN terminals (telephones) can also be connected to the ISDN via a terminal adapter. As far as the enterprise goes, a digital PBX connects to the NT1, and all other enterprise devices (including ISDN and non-ISDN terminals and enterprise data network gateways) terminate in the PBX.

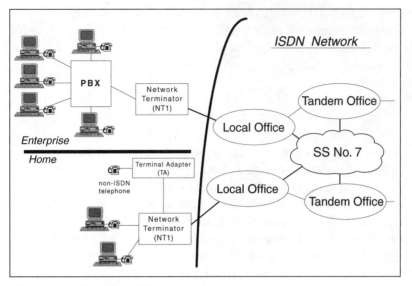

Figure 2.5   The ISDN architecture.

These arrangements are depicted on the left side of Figure 2.5. The right side of the figure shows the partial structure of the PSTN, which does not seem different at this level from the pre-ISDN PSTN structure. This similarity is no surprise, since the PSTN had already gone digital prior to the introduction of the ISDN. In addition, bringing the ISDN to either the residential or enterprise market did not require much rewiring because the original *twisted pair* of copper wires could be used in about 70 percent of subscriber lines (Werbach, 1997). What has changed is that codecs moved at the ultimate point of the end-to-end architecture—to the ISDN terminals—and the local offices did need to change somewhat to support the ISDN *access signaling* standardized by ITU-T. Again, common channel signaling predated the ISDN, and its SS No. 7 version could easily perform all the functions needed for the intra-ISDN network signaling.

As for the digital pipe between the network and the user, it consists of *channels* of different capacities. Some of these channels are defined for carrying voice or data; others (actually, there is only one in this category) are used for out-of-band signaling. (There is no in-band signaling even between the user and the network with the ISDN.) The following channels have been standardized for user access:

A. 4-kHz analog telephone channel.

B. 64-kbps digital channel (for voice or data).

C. 8- or 16-kbps digital channel (for data, to be used in combination with channel **A**).

D. 16- or 64-kbps digital channel (for out-of-band signaling).

H. 384-, 1536-, or 1920-kbps digital channel (which could be used for any-thing, except that it is not part of any standard combination of channels).

The major regional agreements support two combinations:

- *Basic rate interface.* Includes two **B** channels and one **D** channel of 16 kbps. (This combination is usually expressed as **2B+D**.)

- *Primary rate interface.* Includes 23 **B** channels and 1 **D** channel of 64 kbps. (This combination is accordingly expressed as **23B+D**, and it actu-ally represents the primary rate in the United States and Japan. In Europe, it is **30B+D**.)

The ISDN has been deployed throughout mostly for enterprise use. The residential market has never really picked up, although there has been a turn-around because of the demand for fast Internet access (it is possible to use the **2B+D** combination as a single 144-kbps digital pipe) and because ISDN con-nections are becoming less expensive.

Even before the ISDN standardization was finished, the ISDN was renamed *narrowband ISDN* (N-ISDN), and work began on *broadband ISDN* (B-ISDN). B-ISDN will offer an end-to-end data rate of 155 Mbps, and it is based on the *asynchronous transfer mode* (ATM) technology. B-ISDN is to sup-port services like video on demand—predicted to be a killer application; however, full deployment of B-ISDN means complete rewiring of houses and considerable change in the PSTN infrastructure.

Although the ISDN has recently enjoyed considerable growth owing to Internet access demand, its introduction has been slow. The United States until recently trailed Europe and Japan as far as deployment of the ISDN is concerned, particularly for consumers. This lag can in part be explained by the ever complex system of telephone tariffs, which seemed to benefit the development of the business use in the United States. Another explanation often brought up by industry analysts is *leapfrogging:* by the time Europe and Japan developed the infrastructure for total residential telephone service pro-vision, the ISDN technology was available, while in the United States almost every household already had at least one telephone line long before the ISDN concept (not to mention ISDN equipment) existed.[8]

Intelligent Network (IN)

The first service introduced in the PSTN with the help of network databases in 1980 was calling card service; soon after that, a series of value-added ser-

---

[8]Leapfrogging is a typical phenomenon in the developing world. The authors were surprised to find in 1995 that many of their Beijing colleagues whom they met at a telecommunications con-ference had wireless telephones, which were at the time not nearly as ubiquitous in the United States as they are now. The explanation was that the owners of wireless telephones had no resi-dential telephone lines, for which they would need to wait for years!

vices for businesses called *inward wide area telecommunications service* (INWATS) were introduced. When the U.S. Federal Communications Commission (FCC) approved a tariff for expanded 800 service in 1982, the Bell system was ready to support it with many new features due to the distributed nature of the implementation. For example, a customer dialing an 800 number of a corporation could be connected to a particular office depending on the time of day or day of week. As the development of such features progressed, it became clear that in many cases it would be more efficient to decide how to route a customer's call after prompting the customer with a message that provided several options, and instructions on how to select them by pushing dial buttons on the customer's telephone. For the purpose of customer interaction, new devices that could maintain both the circuit connections to customers (in order to play announcements and collect digits) and connections to the SS No. 7 network (to receive instructions and report results to the databases) were invented and deployed. The network database ceased to be just a database—its role was not simply to return responses to the switch queries but also to instruct the switches and other devices as to how to proceed with the call. Computers previously employed only for storing the databases were programmed with the so-called *service logic*, which consisted of scripts describing the service. This was the historical point at which the service logic started to migrate from the switches.

After the 1984 court decree broke up the Bell System, the newly created Regional Bell Operating Companies (RBOCs) ordered their R&D arm, Bell Communications Research, to develop a general architecture and specific requirements for central, network-based support of services. An urgent need for such an architecture was dictated by the necessity of buying the equipment from multiple vendors.[9] This development resulted in two business tasks that Bellcore was to tackle while developing the new architecture: (1) The result had to be equipment-independent and (2) as many service functional capabilities as possible were to move out of the switches (to make them cheaper). The tasks were to be accomplished by developing the requirements and getting the vendors to agree to them. As Bellcore researchers and engineers were developing the new architecture, they promoted it under the name of *Intelligent Network*. The main result of the Bellcore work was a set of specifications called *Advanced Intelligent Network* (AIN), which went through several releases.

AT&T, meanwhile, continued to develop its existing architecture, and its manufacturing arm, AT&T Network Systems, built products for the AT&T network and RBOCs. Only the latter market, however, required adherence to the AIN specifications. In the second half of the 1980s, similar developments took place around the world—in Europe, Japan, and Australia. In 1989, a

---

[9]In the pre-1984 Bell System, most of the equipment was manufactured in house; after the breakup, the manufacturing facilities stayed with AT&T, which also provided long-distance telephone service.

standards project was initiated in ITU to develop recommendations for the interfaces and protocols in support of *Intelligent Network* (IN). (You can find a description of IN standards in Chapter 4.)

To conclude the historical review of IN, we give you some numbers: Today, in the United States, at least half of all interexchange carrier voice calls are IN supported. This generates on the order of $20 billion in revenue for IXCs. LECs use IN to implement *local number portability* (LNP), calling name and message delivery, flexible call waiting, 800 service carrier selection, and a variety of other services (Kozik et al., 1998). The IN technology also blends wireless networks and the PSTN, and, as we demonstrate further in this chapter, is being used strategically in the PSTN-Internet convergence.

We are ready now to formulate a general definition of IN: IN is an architectural concept for the real-time execution of network services and customer applications. The architecture is based on two main principles: network independence and service independence. *Network independence* means that the IN function is separated from the basic switching functions as well as the means of interconnection of the switches and other network components. *Service independence* means that the IN is to support a wide variety of services by using common building blocks.

The IN execution environment includes the switches, computers, and specialized devices, which, at the minimum, can communicate with the telephone user by playing announcements and recognizing dial tones. (More sophisticated versions of such devices can also convert text to voice and even vice versa, send and receive faxes, and bridge teleconferences). All these components are interconnected by means of a data communications network. The network can be as small as the *local area network* (LAN), in which case the computers and devices serve one switch (typically a PBX), or it can span most switches in an IXC or LEC. In the latter case, the data network is SS No. 7, and usually the term *IN* means this particular network-wide arrangement. [In the case of a single switch, the technology is called *computer-telephony integration* (CTI).]

The overall IN architecture also includes the so-called *service creation* and *service management* systems used to program the services and distribute these programs and other data necessary for their execution among the involved entities.

Figure 2.6 depicts the network-wide IN execution environment. We will need to introduce more jargon now. The service logic is executed by a *service control point* (SCP), which is queried—using the SS No. 7 transaction mechanism—by the switches. The switches issue such queries when their internal logic detects *triggers* (such as a telephone number that cannot be translated locally, a need to authorize a call, an event on the line—such as called party being busy, etc.). The SCP typically responds to the queries, but it can also start services (such as wake-up call) on its own by issuing an instruction to a switch to start a call.

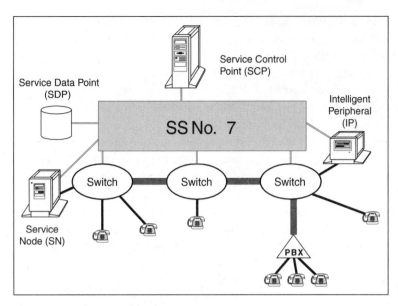

Figure 2.6 The IN architecture.

As we noted before, to support certain service features (such as 800 number translation), the SCP may need to employ special devices (in order to play announcements and collect digits or establish a conference bridge). This job is performed by the *intelligent peripheral* (IP). The IP is connected to the telephone network via a line or trunk, which enables it to communicate with a human via a voice circuit. The IP may be also connected to the SS No. 7 network, which allows it to receive instructions from the SCP and respond to them. (Alternatively, the SCP instructions can be relayed to the IP through the switch to which it is connected.) As SCPs have become executors of services (rather than just the databases they used to be), the function of the databases has been moved to devices called *service data points* (SDPs).

Finally, there is another device, called a *service node* (SN), which is a hybrid of the IP, the SCP, and a rather small switch. Similar to the SCP, the SN is a general-purpose computer, but unlike the SCP it is equipped with exotic devices such as switching fabric and other things typically associated with an IP. The SN connects to the network via the ISDN access mechanism, and it runs its own service logic, which is typically engaged when a switch routes a call to it. An example of its typical use is in voice-mail service. When a switch detects that the called party is busy, it forwards the call to the SN, which plays the announcement, interacts with the caller, stores voice messages and reads them back, and so on. The protocols used for the switch-to-SCP, SCP-to-SDP, and SCP-to-IP communications are known as *Intelligent Network Application Part* (INAP), which is the umbrella name. INAP, further discussed in Chapter 4, has evolved from the CCS switch-to-database transaction inter-

the day and day of the week in a given time zone, and the PSTN has consequently been engineered to handle just as much traffic as needed. (Actually, the PSTN has been slightly overengineered to make up for potential fluctuations in traffic.) If a particular local switch is overloaded (that is, if all its trunks or interconnection facilities are busy), it is designed to block (that is, reject) calls.

Initially, the switches were designed to block calls only when they could not handle them independently. By the end of the 1970s, however, the understanding of a peculiar phenomenon observed in the Bell Telephone System—called *the Mother's Day phenomenon*—resulted in a significant change in the way calls were blocked (as well as other aspects of the network operation).[11]

Figure 2.7 demonstrates what happens with the toll network in peak circumstances. The network, engineered at the time to handle a maximum load of 1800 erlangs (an *erlang* is a unit measuring the load of the network: 1 erlang = 3600 calls × sec), was supposed to behave in response to ever increasing load just as depicted in the top line in the graph—to approach the maximum load and more or less stay there. In reality, however, the network experienced inexplicably decreasing performance way below the engineered level as the load increased. What was especially puzzling was that only a small portion of switches were overloaded at any time. Similar problems occurred during natural disasters—earthquakes and floods. (Fortunately, disasters have not occurred with great frequency.) Detailed studies produced an explanation: As the network attempted to build circuits to the switches that were overloaded, these circuits could not be used by other callers—even those whose calls would pass through or terminate at the underutilized switches. Thus, the root of the problem was that ineffective call attempts had been made that tied up the usable resources.

The only solution was to block the ineffective call attempts. In order to determine such attempts, the network needed to collect in one place much information about the whole network. For this purpose, an NTM system was developed. The system polled the switches every now and then to determine their states; in addition, switches could themselves report certain extraordinary events (called *alarms*) asynchronously with polling. For example, every five minutes the NTM collects the values of *attempts per circuit per hour* (ACH) and *connections per circuit per hour* (CCH) from all switches in the network. If ACH is much higher than CCH, it is clear that ineffective attempts are being made. The NTM applications have been using artificial intelligence technology to develop the inference engines that would pinpoint network problems and suggest the necessary corrective actions, although they still rely on a human's ability to infer the cause of any problem.

---

[11]Mother's Day is often used as a charming example of the phenomenon, but it appears that the actual annual peak long-distance day is the Monday after Thanksgiving. Mother's Day and Christmas are typical peaks in residential calling.

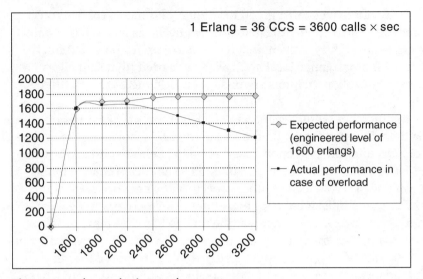

Figure 2.7   The Mother's Day phenomenon.

Overall, the problems may arise because of transmission facilities malfunction (as in cases when rats or moles chew up a fiber link—sharks have been known to do the same at the bottom of the ocean) or a breakdown of the common channel signaling system. In a physically healthy network, however, the problems are caused by use above the engineered level (for example, on holidays) or what is called *focused overload,* in which many calls are directed into the same geographical area. Not only natural disasters can cause overload. A PSTN service called *televoting* has been expected to do just that, and so is—for obvious reasons—the freephone service, such as 800 numbers in the United States. (Televoting has typically been used by TV and radio stations to gauge the number of viewers or listeners who are asked a question and invited to call either of the two given numbers free of charge. One of the numbers corresponds to a "yes" answer; the other to "no." Fortunately, IN has built-in mechanisms for blocking such calls to prevent overload.)

Once the cause of the congestion in the network is detected, the NTM OSS deals with the problem by applying *controls,* that is, sending to switches and IN SCPs the commands that affect their operation. Such controls can be *restrictive* (for example, *directionalization* of trunks, making them available only in the direction leading from the congested switch; cancellation of alternative routes through congested switches; or blocking calls that are directed to congested areas) or *expansive* (for example, overflowing traffic to unusual routes in order to bypass congested areas). Although the idea of an expansive control appears strange at first glance, this type of control has been used systematically in the United States to fix congestion in the Northeast Corridor between Washington, D.C., and Boston, which often takes place between 9 and 11 o'clock in the morning. Since during this period most offices are still closed in California (which is three hours behind), it is not unusual for a call from Philadelphia to Boston to be routed through a toll switch in Oakland.

Overall, the applications of global network management (as opposed to specific protocols) have been at the center of attention in the PSTN industry. This trend continues today. The initial agent/manager paradigm on which both the *Open Systems Interconnection* (OSI) and Internet models are based has evolved into an agent-based approach, as described by Bieszad et al. (1999). In that paper, an (intelligent) agent is defined as computational entity "which acts on behalf of others, is autonomous, . . . and exhibits a certain degree of capabilities to learn, cooperate and move." Most of the research on this subject comes in the form of application of artificial intelligence to network management problems. Agents communicate with each other using specially designed languages [such as *Agent Communication Language* (ACL)]; they also use specialized protocols [such as *Contract-Net Protocol* (CNP)]. As the result of the intensive research, two agent systems—*Foundation for Intelligent Physical Agents* (FIPA) and *Mobile Agent System Interoperability Facilities* (MASIF)— have been proposed. These specifications, however, are not applicable to the products and services described in this book, for which reason they are not addressed here. Consider them, though, as an important reference to a technology in the making.

The PSTN Access to IP Networks

Most of the technologies in the area of PSTN access to IP networks have been relatively well understood—that is, supported by the standards and widely implemented in products. For this reason, much material on this subject resides in the next two parts (which cover available standards and products, respectively). The technologies we describe here relate to physical access to the network. We have already described the ISDN; with the growing demand for the Internet access, residential subscription to the ISDN has grown (although not necessarily for the purposes for which the ISDN was invented). Typically, users bundle the B and D channels to get one big data pipe, and use this pipe for Internet access. Other types of access technologies are described in the following section.

An important problem facing the PSTN today is the data traffic that it carries to IP networks; the PSTN was not designed for data traffic and therefore needs to offload this traffic as soon as possible. We describe the problem and the way it is tackled by the industry in a separate section, which, to make the overall picture more complete, we tie in with the technique of *tunneling* as the paradigm for designing IP VPNs. Both technologies have been developed independently and for different purposes; both, however, work together to resolve the access issues.

Physical Access

In much of this book, we talk about approaches to integration of the Internet with telephony in which the action occurs at the network layer or higher—things like carrying voice over IP or using control signals originating within the Internet to cause connections to appear and disappear within the telephony network. However, integration at the lowest level—the physical level—is also of great practical importance, and nowhere more so than in the access portion of the network. Here, advances in digital signaling processing techniques and in high-speed electronics have resulted in remarkable progress in just the last few years, allowing access media originally deployed more than a century ago for telephony to also support access to the Internet at previously unimagined speeds. In our brief survey of these new access technologies, we will first provide an overview of the access environment, and then go on to describe both the 56-kbps PCM modem and the xDSL class of high-speed digital lines.

The Access Environment

Today it is quite possible, and not at all uncommon, for business users to obtain direct high-speed optical fiber access to telephony and data networks, including the Internet. For smaller locations, such as individual homes and small business sites, despite experiments in the 1980s with fiber to the home and in the early 1990s with hybrid fiber coax, physical access choices mostly come down to twisted pair telephone line and cable TV coax. We will not cover business fiber access or the cable modem story here, on the grounds that the former is a relatively well understood if impressively capable technology and that the latter is somewhat outside the scope of our Internet/telephony focus. Instead, we will look at recent developments in greatly speeding up access over ordinary telephone lines.

The twisted pair telephone line was developed in the 1880s as an improvement over earlier single-wire and parallel-wire designs. The single-wire lines, which used earth return, were noisy and subject to the variable quality of grounding connections, while the parallel-wire lines were subject to cross talk from one line to another. The twists in a twisted pair set up a self-canceling effect that reduces electromagnetic radiation from the line and thus mitigates cross talk. This simple design creates a very effective transmission medium that has found many uses in data communication (think of 10BaseT LANs and their even higher-speed successors) as well as in telephony. Two-wire telephone access lines are also called *loops,* as the metallic forward and return paths are viewed as constituting a loop for the current that passes through the telephone set.

In modern telephone networks, homes that are close enough to the central office are directly connected to it by an individual twisted pair (which may be spliced and cross-connected a number of times along the way). The twisted pair from a home farther away is connected instead to the remote terminal of a *digital loop carrier* (DLC) system. The DLC system then multiplexes together the signals from many telephone lines and sends them over a fiber-optic line (or perhaps over a copper line using an older digital technology like T1) to the central office. In the United States, close enough for a direct twisted pair line generally means less than 18,000 feet (18 kft). For a variety of reasons (including installation prior to the invention of DLCs), there are a fair number of twisted pair lines more than 18 kft in length. These use heavy-gauge wire, loading coils, or even amplifiers to achieve the necessary range. The statistics of loop length and the incidence of DLC use vary greatly among countries depending on demographic factors. In densely populated countries, loops tend to be short and DLCs may be rare. Another loop design practice that varies from country to country is the use of *bridged taps.* These unterminated twisted pair stubs are often found in the United States, but rarely in Europe and elsewhere.

From the point of view of data communication, the intriguing thing about this access environment is that in general it is less band-limited than an end-to-end telephone network connection, which of course is classically limited to a 4-kHz bandwidth. While there is indeed a steady falloff in the ease with which signals may be transmitted as their frequency increases, on most metallic loops (the exceptions are loops with loading coils and, more rarely, loops with active elements such as amplifiers) there is no sharp bandwidth cutoff. Thus, the bandwidth of a twisted pair loop is somewhat undefined and subject to being extended by ingenious signal processing techniques.

For decades, the standard way of pumping data signals over the telephone network was to use *voiceband modems.* Depending on their vintage, readers may remember when the data rate achievable by such devices was limited to 2400, 4800, or 9600 bps. This technology finally reached its limit a few years ago at around 33.6 kbps. By exploiting the extra bandwidth available in the loop plant, xDSL systems are able to reach much higher access speeds. We will describe these systems shortly, but first will take a small detour to talk about another intriguing recent advance in access that exploits a somewhat more subtle reservoir of extra bandwidth in the telephone network: the 56-kbps PCM modem.

The PCM Modem

Conventional voiceband modems are designed under the assumption that the end-to-end switched or private line connection through the telephone network is an analog connection with a bandwidth of just under 4 kHz, subject to the distortion of *additive white Gaussian noise* (AWGN). When the first practical voiceband modems were designed about 40 years ago, this was literally true. The path seen by a signal traveling from one telephone line to another over a long-distance switched network connection might be something like this: First over an analog twisted-pair loop to an electromechanical step-by-step switch, then over a metallic baseband or wireline analog carrier system to an electromechanical crossbar toll switch, then over a long-haul analog carrier system physically implemented as multiple microwave shots from hill to hill across a thousand miles, to another electromechanical crossbar toll switch, and back down through another analog carrier system to a local crossbar switch to the terminating analog loop. Private line connections were the same, except that permanently soldered jumper wires on cross-connect fields substituted for the electromechanical switches. Noise, of course, was added at every analog amplifier along the way for both the switched and private line cases.

A remarkable fact is that although when modeled as a black box the modern telephone network at the turn of the twenty-first century looks exactly the same as it did 40 years ago (a band-limited analog channel with some noise added to it), the interior of the network has been completely transformed to a concatenation of digital systems—mostly fiber-optic transmission systems and digital switches. Voice is carried through this network interior as sequences of 8-bit binary numbers produced by *pulse-code modulation* (PCM) encoders. Only the analog loops on both ends remain as a physical legacy of the old network.

By the way, what is it that makes these loops analog? After all, they are only long thin strands of copper metal—the most passive sort of electrical system imaginable. How does the loop know whether a signal impressed upon it is analog or digital? The answer is that it doesn't know! In fact, in addition to the smoothly alternating electrical currents of analog voice, loops can carry all sorts of digital signals produced by modems and by all the varieties of *digital subscriber line* (DSL) systems, which we will discuss in the next section. Ironically, the analog quality of the loop really derives from the properties of the analog telephone at the premises end of the loop and of the PCM encoder/decoder at the central office end—or, more precisely, from the assumption that the job of the PCM encoder is to sample a general band-limited analog waveform and produce a digital approximation of it, distorted by quantization noise—inevitable because the finite-length 8-bit word can only encode the signal level with finite precision.

It is this quantization noise, which averages about 33 to 39 dB, in combination with the bandwidth limitation of approximately 3 to 3.5 kHz, that limits conventionally designed modems to just over 33 kbps as calculated using the standard Shannon channel capacity formula (Ayanoglu et al., 1998).

Enter the PCM modem. Quoting Ayanoglu et al., who developed this technology at Bell Labs in the early 1990s: "The central idea behind the PCM modem is to avoid the effects of quantization distortion by utilizing the PCM quantization levels themselves as the channel symbol alphabet." In other words, rather than designing the modem output signals without reference to the operation of the PCM encoder and then letting them fall subject to the distortion of randomly introduced quantization noise, the idea is to design the modem output so that "the analog voltage sampled by the codec passes through the desired quantization levels precisely at its 8-kHz sampling instants." In theory, then, a pair of PCM modems attached to the two analog loops in an end-to-end telephone connection could commandeer the quantization levels of the PCM codecs at the central office ends of the loops and use them to signal across the network at something approaching the 64-kbps output rate of the voice coders. Actually, filters in the central office equipment limit the loop bandwidth to 3.5 kHz, and this in turn means that no more than 56 kbps can be achieved. Also, it turns out that there are serious engineering difficulties with attempting to manipulate the output of the codecs by impressing voltage levels on the analog side.

Fortunately, there is an easier case that is also of great practical importance to the business of access to data networks—including the Internet. Most ISPs and corporate remote access networks employ a system of strategically deployed points of presence at which dial-up modem calls from subscribers to their services are concentrated. At these points, the calls are typically delivered from the telephone company over a multiplexed digital transmission system, such as a T1 line. The ISP or corporate network can then be provided with a special form of PCM modem at the POP site that writes or reads 8-bit binary numbers directly to or from the T1 line (or other digital line), thus permitting the modem on the network side to directly drive the output of the codec on the analog line side as well as to directly observe the PCM samples it produces in the other direction. The result is that, in the direction from the network toward the consumer (the direction in which heavy downloads of things like Web pages occur), a rate approaching 56 kbps can be achieved. The upstream signal, originating in an analog domain where direct access to the PCM words is not possible, remains limited to somewhat lower speeds— an asymmetry we will see again in the next section when we discuss certain popular types of DSLs.

So hungry are residential and business users for bandwidth that 56-kbps modems became almost universally available on new PCs and laptops shortly after the technology was reduced to silicon—and even before the last wrinkles of standards compatibility were ironed out. The standards issues have since been worked through by ITU-T study group (SG) 16, and the 56-kbps modem is now the benchmark for dial-up access over the telephony network to the Internet.

Digital Subscriber Lines

Digital subscriber line (DSL) is the name given to a broad family of technologies that use clever signal design and signal processing to exploit the extra bandwidth of the loop plant and deliver speeds well in excess of those achievable by conventional voiceband modems. The term is often given as xDSL, where x stands for any of many adjectives used to describe different types of DSL. In fact, so many variations of DSL have been proposed and/or hyped, with so many corresponding values of x, that it can be downright confusing—too bad, really, since DSL technology has so much to offer. We will attempt to limit the confusion in this book by describing the types of DSL that appear to be of most practical importance in the near term, with a few words about promising new developments.

The term *DSL* first appeared in the context of ISDN—which struggled with low acceptance rates and slow deployment until it enjoyed a mini-Renaissance in the mid-1990s, buoyed by the unrelenting demand for higher-speed access to the Internet. The ISDN DSL sends 160 kbps in both directions at once over a single twisted pair. The total bit rate accommodates two 64-kbps B channels, one 16-kbps D channel, and 16 kbps for framing and line control. Bidirectional transmission is achieved using an echo-canceled hybrid technology in most of the world. In Japan, bidirectionality is achieved using Ping Pong, called *time compression multiplexing* by the more serious-minded, in which transmission is performed at twice the nominal rate in one direction for a while, and then, after a guard time, the line is turned around and the other direction gets to transmit. ISDN DSLs can extend up to 18 kft, so they can serve most loops that go directly to the central office or to a DLC remote terminal. Special techniques may be used to extend the range in some cases, at a cost in equipment and special engineering. ISDN DSL was a marvel of its day, but is relatively primitive in comparison to more recently developed varieties of DSL.

HDSL

The next major type of DSL to be developed was the *high-bit-rate digital subscriber line* (HDSL). The need for HDSL arose when demand accelerated for direct T1 line interconnection to business customer locations providing for 1.544-Mbps access. T1 was a technology for digital transmission over twisted pairs that was originally developed quite a long time ago (the early 1960s, in fact) with application to metropolitan area telephone trunking in mind. With its 1.544-Mbps rate, a T1 line could carry twenty-four 64-kbps digital voice signals over two twisted pairs (one for each transmission direction). In this application, T1 was wildly successful, and by the late 1970s it had largely displaced baseband metallic lines and older analog carrier systems for carrying trunks between telephone central offices within metropolitan regions—distances up to 50 miles or so. However, applying T1 transmission technology directly to twisted pairs going to customer premises presented several difficulties. A basic one was that T1 required a repeater every 3000 to 5000 feet. This represented a major departure from practice in the loop plant, which was engineered around the assumption that each subscriber line was connected to the central office by a simple wire pair with no electronics along the way—or at least for up to 18 kft or so when a DLC system might be encountered. Also, T1 systems employ high signal levels that present problems of cross talk and difficulties for loop plant technicians not used to dealing with signals more powerful than those produced by human speech impinging on carbon microphones.

A major requirement for the HDSL system was therefore to provide for direct access to customer sites over the loop plant without the use of repeaters. The version of HDSL standardized by the ITU-T as G.991.1 in 1998 achieves repeaterless transmission over loops up to 12 kft long at both the North American T1 rate of 1.544 Mbps and the E1 rate of 2.048 Mbps used in Europe and some other places. Repeaters can be used to serve longer loops if necessary. When employed, they can be spaced at intervals of 12 kft or so, rather than the 3 to 5 kft required in T1. The repeaterless (or few-repeater) feature greatly reduces line conditioning expenses for deployment in the loop plant compared to traditional T1. In addition, HDSL can tolerate (within limits) the presence of bridged taps, avoiding the expense of sending out technicians to remove these taps.

HDSL systems typically use two twisted pairs, just as does T1. However, rather than simply using one pair for transmitting from east to west and the other for west to east, HDSL reduces signal power at high frequencies by sending in both directions at once on each pair, but at only half the total information rate. The two transmission directions are separated electronically by using echo-canceled hybrids, just as in ISDN DSL.

Overall, HDSL provides a much more satisfactory solution for T1/E1 rate customer access than the traditional T1-type transmission system. Work is currently under way in the standards bodies on a second-generation system, called SDSL (for "symmetric" or "single-pair" DSL) or sometimes HDSL2, which will achieve the same bit rates over a single wire pair. To do this without recreating the cross talk problems inherent in T1 requires much more sophisticated signal designs borrowed from the most advanced modem technology, which in turn requires much more powerful processors at each end of the loop for implementation. By now the pattern should be familiar—to mine the extra bandwidth hidden in the humble loop plant, we apply high-speed computation capabilities that were quite undreamed of when Alexander Graham Bell began twisting pairs of insulated wire together and observing what a nice clean medium they produced for the transmission of telephone speech!

ADSL

The second major type of DSL of current practical significance is *asymmetric digital subscriber line* (ADSL). Compared to HDSL, ADSL achieves much higher transmission speeds (up to 10 Mbps) in the downstream direction (from the central office toward the customer) and does this over a single wire pair. The major trade-off is that speeds in the upstream direction (from the customer toward the central office) are reduced, being limited to 1 Mbps at most. ADSL is also capable of simultaneously supporting analog voice transmission.

Considering these basic characteristics, it is clear that ADSL is particularly suited to residential service in that it can support:

- High-speed downloading in applications like Web surfing
- Rather lower speeds from the consumer toward the ISP
- Ordinary voice service on the same line

On the other hand, these characteristics also meet the needs of certain small business (or remote business site) applications as well. The basic business proposition of ADSL is that these asymmetric characteristics, which are the key to achieving the high downstream rate, represent a significant market segment. Time will tell how ADSL fares against other access options such as cable modems and fixed wireless technologies, but the proposition seems to be a plausible one.

The way ADSL exploits asymmetry to achieve higher transmission rates has to do with the nature of cross talk and with the frequency-dependent transmission characteristics of telephone lines. Earlier we noted that there is not a sharp frequency cutoff on unloaded loops, but there is a steady decline in received signal power with increasing frequency. If a powerful high-frequency (high-bit-rate) transmitter is located near a receiver trying to pick up a weak incoming high-frequency signal, the receiver will be overwhelmed by near-end cross talk. The solution is to transmit the high-frequency (high-bit-rate) signal in only one direction. A basic ADSL system is thus an application of classic frequency division multiplexing, in which a wide, high-frequency band is used for the high-bit-rate downstream channel, a narrower and lower-frequency channel is used for the moderate-bit-rate upstream transmission, and the baseband region is left clear for ordinary analog voice (see Figure 2.8).

The basic concept of ADSL is thus rather simple. However, implementations utilize some very advanced coding, signal processing, and error control techniques in order to achieve the desired performance. Also, a wide variety of systems using differing techniques have been produced by various manu-

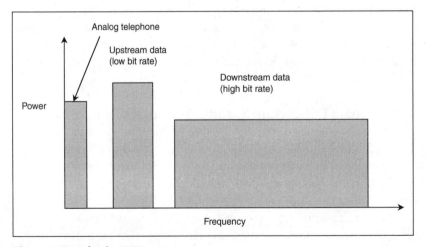

Figure 2.8 A basic ADSL system.

facturers, making standardization something of a challenge. Key ITU-T standards are G.992.1 and G.992.2. The latter provides for splitterless ADSL, which deserves some additional description.

ADSL Lite

In the original ADSL concept, a low-pass filter is installed at the customer end of the line to separate the baseband analog voice signal from the high-speed data signals (see Figure 2.9). In most cases, this filter requires the trouble and expense of an inside wiring job at the customer premises. To avoid this expense, splitterless ADSL, also known more memorably as *ADSL Lite*, eliminates the filter at the customer end. This lack of a filter can create some problems, such as error bursts in the data transmission when the phone rings or is taken off hook, or hissing sounds in some telephone receivers. However, the greatly simplified installation was viewed as well worth the possible small impairments by most telephone companies, and they pushed hard for the adoption of splitterless ADSL in standards.

Factors Affecting Achieved Bit Rate

Like ISDN DSL and HDSL, a basic objective of ADSL is to operate over a large fraction of the loops that are up to 18 kft long. However, the actual bit rate delivered to the customer may vary depending on the total loss and noise characteristics of the loop. The ANSI standard for ADSL (T1.413) provides for rate-adaptive operation much like that employed by high-speed modems. The downstream rate can be as high as 10 Mbps on shorter, less noisy loops, but may go down to 512 kbps on very long or noisy loops. Upstream rates may be as high as 900 kbps or as low as 128 kbps.

Future DSL Developments

We have already mentioned that work is under way on an improved version of HDSL, called HDSL2. Another name for this sometimes seen in the literature is *symmetric DSL* or *single-pair DSL* (SDSL).

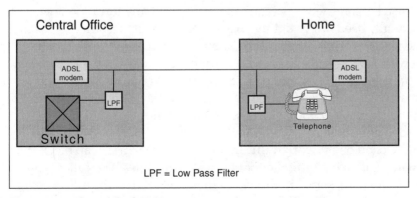

Figure 2.9 The original ADSL concept.

Another new system, called *very-high-rate DSL* (VDSL), is under discussion in standards bodies. It will provide for very high downstream rates of up to 52 Mbps. VDSL would work in combination with optical transmission into the neighborhood of the customer. High-speed transmission over the copper loop would only be used for the last kilometer or so.

Applicability

We've described a number of advanced access technologies that can support remarkably high-data-rate access to data networks (including the Internet) over the existing telephone plant. How do you decide which ones, if any, to use?

In the case of the 56-kbps PCM modem, the decision will likely be made for you by the manufacturer of your PC or laptop. It's simply the latest in modems and is often supplied as a standard feature.

For xDSL, the situation is a bit more complex. In most cases, you obtain a service from a telephone company or other network provider that uses HDSL or ADSL as an underlying transmission technology. The technology may or may not be highlighted in the service provider's description of the offering. Essentially, the decision comes down to weighing the price of the service against how well it satisfies the needs of the application, including speed but also such factors as guarantees of reliability, speed of installation, whether an analog voice channel is included or needed, and so on. If you are more adventurous, you may try obtaining raw copper pairs from a service provider and applying your own xDSL boxes. If you contemplate going this route, you really need to learn a lot more about the transmission characteristics of these systems than we've covered here, and you should perhaps start by consulting some of the references listed in our bibliography.

Internet Offload and Tunneling

Internet traffic has challenged the foundation of the PSTN—the way it has been engineered. Contrary to the widespread view (based on the perceived high quality that users of telephony have enjoyed for many years), which holds that the telephone networks can take any calls of any duration, the PSTN has actually been rather tightly engineered to use its resources so as to adapt to the patterns of voice calls. Typical Internet access calls last 20 minutes, while typical voice calls last between 3 and 5 minutes (Atai and Gordon, 1997). The probability of the duration of a voice call exceeding one hour is 1 percent, versus 10 percent for Internet access calls. As the result, the access calls tie up the resources of local switches and interoffice trunks, which in turn increases the number of uncompleted calls on the PSTN. (As we mentioned in the section on network traffic management, the PSTN can block calls to a switch with a high number of busy trunks or lines. The caller typically receives a *fast busy* signal in this case.) In today's PSTN, the *call blocking rate* is the principal indicator of the quality of service. The actual bandwidth of voice circuits is grossly wasted—Internet users consume only about

20 percent of the circuit bandwidth. The situation is only further complicated by flat-rate pricing of online services—believed to encourage Internet callers to stay on line twice as long as they would with a metered-rate plan.

The three problem areas identified in Atai and Gordon (1997) are (1) the local (*ingress*) switch from which the call has originated; (2) the tandem switch and interoffice trunks; and (3) the local (*egress*) switch that terminates calls at the ISP modem pool (Atai and Gordon, 1997). (The cited document does not take into account the IXC issues, but it is easy to see they are very similar to the second problem area.) The third problem area is the most serious because it can cause focused overload. Presently, such egress switches make up roughly a third of all local switches. The acuteness of the problem has been forcing the carriers to segregate the integrated traffic and offload it to a packet network as soon as possible.[12]

The two options for carrying out the offloading are (1) to allow the Internet traffic to pass through the ingress switch, where it would be identified, and (2) to intercept the Internet traffic on the line side of the ingress switch. In all cases, however, the Internet traffic must first be identified. Identifying Internet traffic is best done by IN means. One way (which is unlikely to be implemented) is to collect all the ISP and enterprise modem pool access numbers and trigger on them—not a small feat, even if a feasible one. This triggering would slow down all local switches to a great extent. The other solution is to use local number portability queries; to implement the solution, all modem pool numbers would have to be configured as ported numbers. The third, and much better, way to carry out the offloading is for ISPs and enterprise modem pools to use a single-number service (an example is an 800 number in the United States) and let the IN route the call. The external service logic would inform the switch about the nature of the call (this information would naturally be stored). Many large enterprises already use 800 numbers for their modem pools. The fourth solution is to assign a special prefix to the modem pool number; then the switch would know right away, even before all the digits had been dialed, that it was dealing with an Internet dial-up. (Presently, however, switches often identify an Internet call by detecting the modem signals on the line.)

Two post-switch offloading solutions are gaining momentum. The first is terminating all calls in a special multiservice module—effectively a part of the local switch—in the PSTN. The multiservice module would then send the data traffic (over an ATM, frame relay, or IP network) to the ISP or enterprise access server (which would no longer need to be involved with the modems). The other solution (also illustrated by products described in Chapter 10) is to terminate all calls at network access servers that would act as switches in that they would establish a trunk with the ingress switch. The access servers

---

[12]One short-term solution that has been considered is to identify Internet users (which is by itself a nontrivial problem that we will address) and terminate their lines on the modules with low line concentration ratios so as to eliminate blocking at the line concentration level of the switch. The engineering levels of both the switches and trunks must be modified to eliminate blocking. This approach can be costly, and, in any event, it would provide only a short-term solution.

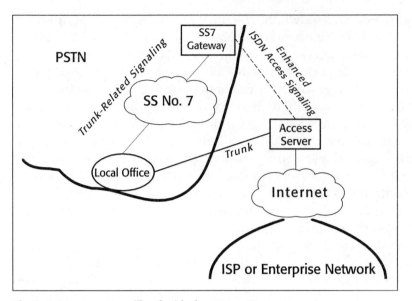

Figure 2.10   Internet offload with the SS7 gateway.

would then communicate with the ISP or enterprise over the Internet. One problem with this solution is that access servers would have to be connected to the SS No. 7 network, which is expensive and, so far, hardly justified. To correct this situation, a new SS No. 7 network element, the SS7 gateway, acts as a proxy on behalf of several access servers (thus significantly cutting the cost). The access servers communicate with the SS7 gateway via an enhanced (that is, modified) ISDN access protocol, as depicted in Figure 2.10.

At this point you may ask: How are the network access servers connected to the rest of the ISP or enterprise network? Until relatively recently, this was done by means of leased telephone lines (permanent circuits) or private lines, both of which were (and still are) quite expensive. Another way to connect the islands of a network is by using *tunneling,* that is, sending the packets whose addresses are significant only to a particular network. These packets are encapsulated (as a payload) into the packets whose addresses are significant to the whole of the Internet, and they travel between the two border points of the network through what is metaphorically called a *tunnel.* Again, the packets themselves are not looked at by the intermediate nodes, because to nodes the packets are nothing but the payload encapsulated in outer packets. Only the endpoints of a tunnel are aware of the payload, which is extracted by and acted on by the destination endpoint. As you will see in Parts Two and Three, tunnels are essential for an application called the *virtual private network* (VPN).[13] With tunneling, for example, the two

---

[13]The IP VPN is not to be confused with the PSTN VPN. We will always clarify the context in which this term is used when we use it.

nodes of a private network that have no direct link between them may use the Internet or another IP network as a link. In Parts Two and Three, we will address tunneling systematically as far as security and the use of the existing protocols is concerned. Another essential aspect of tunneling is quality of service (QoS), so we address that issue again when reviewing the *multiprotocol label switching* (MPLS) technology. As you have probably noticed, we have already ventured into a purely IP area. This is one example where it is virtually impossible to describe a PSTN solution without invoking its IP counterpart.

Going back to the employment of the SS7 gateway, we should note one important technological development: With the SS7 gateway, an ISP can be connected to a LEC as a CLEC (Kozik et al., 1998).

Internet-Supported PSTN Services

Last year a colleague of ours was called by a reporter from a well-known technical publication and asked to describe the effort of the PSTN/Internet Internetworking (*pint*) working group in the Internet Engineering Task Force (IETF). Our cautious colleague wisely decided that the best he could do under the circumstances was to read out to the reporter a few selected sentences from the working group charter published by the IETF on its Web page. Specifically, he stressed—prompted by the *pint* Web page—that the purpose of *pint* was to "address connection arrangements through which Internet applications can request and enrich PSTN . . . telephony services." The reporter wrote down what she heard. Later, in accordance with her agreement with our colleague, she sent to him the draft of the article. The article was accurate except for one word: *enrich* had turned into *unleash*—this is what the reporter heard over the telephone line (an atypically imperfect telephone line, we presume). When the amazed author called the reporter with the correction, she seemed to be disappointed. (And so are we. We wish the *pint* charter really did talk about unleashing the telephone services, because this is precisely what the Internet-supported PSTN services are all about!)

In his recent article on Intelligent Network, Scott Bradner correctly observes that the intelligence of IN is strictly in the network, not on its edges (Bradner, 1999).[14] This lack of edge intelligence is precisely what the interworking of the Internet and IN is to change—once and forever!

The basic goal of the IN technology is to allow the user of an Internet host to create, access, and control the PSTN services. A simple example of what the technology can do is the click-to-dial-back service, where you click on an icon

---

[14]Actually, there is a device called the *intelligent call processor* (ICP) that AT&T puts on the premises of large enterprises and then connects to its common channel signaling network. The ICP then routes the calls in cooperation with the AT&T *network control point* (NCP). To this end, the ICP has been an edge device; however, this is an exotic exception, and even then the one suitable only to a large businesses—hardly an example of *volks*-IN.

displayed on a Web page and the PSTN call is established as the result.[15] This service and its counterparts are described in more detail in Chapter 9. As simple as it sounds (and a crude implementation of this service is just as simple), the unleashing quality of this service alone should not be underestimated. The competition among the long-distance service providers is such that they would do almost anything to get a call flowing through their networks. With Web-based access, their customers are around the world! There are still countries that protect their networks by forbidding the call-back service; people may get angry about such backward and anticompetitive practices, but click-to-dial-back, which technically is not a call-back service, is a way to get even.

Once you start thinking about the possibilities of tweaking this basic concept, you will find that the possibilities for creating new services are virtually unlimited. We will demonstrate a straightforward extension of click-to-dial-back to drastically improve on a PSTN-only service.

The service in question, interestingly enough, came to life as an application of the Web business model (but not the Web technology) to the PSTN.[16] Telephony service providers in Europe started to market free telephone calls to those who would agree to listen to several minutes of audio advertising. The advertisers have so far found the approach ineffective—pure audio is hardly the best means of delivering advertising today. This already bad effect is further worsened by the "push" nature of audio advertising.

Now, with the technology just described, the prospective caller can access the service provider's page on the Web, where he or she can also subscribe to the service and register a profile stating the preference for the types of products he or she wishes to learn about. Every time a call is to be made, the caller can then be walked through a video presentation of the advertisement on his or her Internet appliance—possibly accompanied by the audio portion over the PSTN line. The caller can control the pace of the advertisement; when it is finished, the caller will be prompted for the number he or she wishes to call and then connected to that number.

There are several early developments in this area (Hubaux et al., 1998). In the relevant architecture (depicted in Figure 2.11), the SCPs and SNs are connected to the Internet (which is fairly easy to achieve because they are almost invariably implemented on the Unix system platform).[17] It is important to

---

[15]If you wonder how a voice call can take place when the telephone line has been occupied by the Internet connection, note that there are modems that allow the line to be split to maintain both the data and the voice connections. In addition, many households have two telephone lines or a wireless telephone that can receive a call. The ISDN is another answer.

[16]Access is free of charge to the user; the profit is made through advertising.

[17]Parts Two and Three, respectively, point to the developing standards and existing products in this area. We just briefly note that the IETF PSTN/Internet Internetworking (*pint*) working group has defined a general architecture and completed a protocol in support of the services initiated by an IP host. The protocol is based on the extended Session Initiation Protocol (SIP), also developed in the IETF. (SIP is described in Chapter 5.) For the services that originate in the PSTN, this task is presently tackled by the Service in the PSTN/IN Requesting Internet Service (*spirits*) working group.

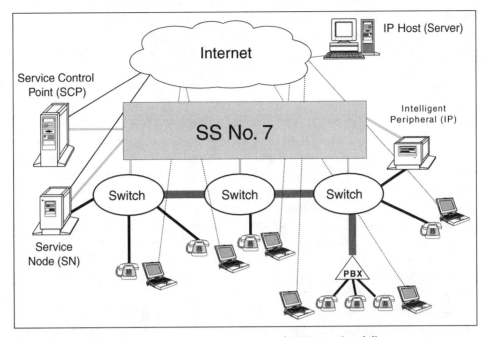

Figure 2.11   The architecture for Internet-supported PSTN service delivery.

repeat that with this arrangement *only* SCPs and SNs—but by no means the switches—are connected to the Internet and thus can communicate with other IP hosts.

The service control function can be distributed to Internet hosts as much as the PSTN service provider allows and the owner of a particular IP host (who may be the same PSTN service provider) wishes to handle. In the *WebIN*, the IP host is actually a Web server, and part of the service control function (called *WebSCP*) is moved into the Internet (Low, 1997; Low et al., 1996). This arrangement can be used to provide the main features of the PSTN VPN service—the private numbering plan and closed user group in particular (Hubaux et al., 1998). The translation map of the enterprise-significant numbers to the PSTN-significant ones, as well as the specification of the closed groups (including the calling privileges of each group member), are kept in the databases accessible through the Internet. Part of the SCP service logic is executed by the WebSCP. While there is very little interoperability among the legacy IN implementations, integrating them with the Internet immediately establishes a common language for interworking.[18] Even more significant is that the service creation and service management are also moved (via the Internet) to the edge of the network.

As exciting as the opening of PSTN call control to the Internet hosts may be, there is a serious and not completely solved problem associated with it. This problem is security, and it is ubiquitous in the Internet. While trusted

---

[18]See also the section on address translation in Chapter 3.

relations between the PSTN and IP entities can be established between the enterprise networks, opening IN control fully to anyone on the Internet remains problematic. There may be no need for IN control to be fully opened, except in the cases of some well-understood services.

Potential security issues also prevent (at least for the time being) direct connection of the switching offices to the Internet. If that were done, the SCP itself could be placed on the Internet, and subsequently anything that IN does presently could be done in the Internet.[19] Although there is a single ITU-T standard, it specifies different options. These options reflect implementations that differ not only between different continents (that is, Europe and North America) but also among the network operators in the United States. (Bell Operating Companies use the option corresponding to the Bellcore AIN; some IXCs use proprietary or European versions of IN.) Thus, direct interconnection of the PSTN switches and Internet SCPs, even if secure, would not provide global interoperability. Only interworking of the PSTN service control with the Internet hosts holds the promise (on which it has already started to deliver) of universal, global access to service control of the PSTN.

To conclude this section, we would like to repeat that so far we have taken an intentionally one-sided approach to the role of IN in the integration of PSTN and the Internet. Our only goal was to demonstrate how IN can be used to give more control in creating and executing services to the edge of the network. At this point, it is important to observe an interesting duality: While the PSTN benefits from Internet-based service creation and control, the IP networks greatly benefit from the existing PSTN-based service control for at least three different reasons: (1) efficiency of the access to IP networks; (2) provision of certain combined PSTN-Internet services;[20] and (3) support of the existing PSTN services in the IP telephony environment. The last item is the subject of Chapter 3.

---

[19]Communications between a switch and the SCP could now take place over an IP network as a result of the effort of the IETF Signaling Transport (*sigtran*) working group, which has developed a transport protocol for carrying SS No. 7 and enhanced Q.931 messages. Since INAP is based on SS No. 7, it can be transported over an IP network, too. The problem is, however, that there are at least two different versions of INAP. Actually, the same is true of other SS No. 7 protocols as well.

[20]An example of *combined services* is *unified messaging,* as described in detail in Chapter 9. The gist of the service is that its user can choose any medium for both sending and receiving his or her message. A user can, for instance, send an e-mail message that would be received as voice mail; conversely, the user can read an e-mail message that was originally spoken over telephone lines and stored as voice mail.

CHAPTER 3

Adjusting the Internet
to the PSTN

In this chapter we address the technologies that change the infrastructure of IP networks and the Internet so as to place them on the convergence path. Whenever an infrastructure is designed—no matter how general the design plan—it is invariably done with some particular application(s) in mind. The original Internet applications—file transfer, virtual terminal for remote host access, and later e-mail—had never concerned themselves with preserving bandwidth or giving more to a user who would pay more. In fact, the whole issue of accounting (not to mention the security) was not an issue at all. Researchers were building the network for themselves and whomever else would enjoy its wonderful connectivity services. The end users never paid for it; no one expected them to. Also, in the 1960s and even the 1970s, there was no technology for voice on the Internet available to anyone with a PC— in fact, there were no PCs. But the landscape has changed a lot since then. In particular, IP telephony has become an important application for the Internet as we move into the twenty-first century.

The basic and most widely used telephony application is a simple two-person call. The ability of one (*calling*) party to signal another (*called*) party by dialing its *address* (telephone number) and the ability of the called party to hear the signal and respond to the call have been so fundamental to modern society that the look and feel of the telephone terminal and the sequence of the calling process have hardly changed in decades. Whatever small changes have taken place have actually been mere enhancements compared with what has happened to the underlying technologies and networks. The very fact that telephone numbers have remained archaic strings of decimal digits (in the age of highly computerized digital switches, which long ago replaced mechanical step-by-step switches that actually counted digits) is the testimony to the fact that the basic telephony call has reached true perfection in the PSTN.[1]

If the PSTN is perfect, then why change to IP? There are at least three reasons:

1. In certain environments (such as enterprise networks), the prices of calls can still be lowered significantly without lowering the quality. Under the current telecommunications tariff regulations, the Internet can be effectively employed to bypass those parts of the PSTN used in long-distance calls (thus eliminating long-distance call charges).

2. As the World Wide Web phenomenon has demonstrated quite convincingly, the services that accompany basic calls can be improved. Limits are set only by the creativity of the people making telephone calls (because they will be able to customize these services by linking them with other computer applications). We will further explore the enhancement of services in Chapter 9.

3. Maintaining only one type of a network for both voice and data is much easier than maintaining two types of specialized networks.

One can successfully argue that the real technologies that made the Internet killer application—the World Wide Web—available were those that (1) made computing fast and cheap (that is, semiconductors and integrated circuits), (2) brought graphics-based user interfaces to life, and (3) vastly increased the performance of transmission media (due to advances in optical networking). The same factors (especially factors 1 and 3) are significant to IP telephony, in addition to the promise of more efficient use of the bandwidth of the IP networks. Nevertheless, in this book, we don't address these factors; instead, we concentrate on a bigger picture—that is, the architectures of the IP networks and their evolution toward interworking with the PSTN.

In what follows, we first address the most burning issue—*quality of service* (QoS). As you may recall, QoS is essential for the support of voice over IP as well as the IP-based VPNs, where the leased or private *physical* lines connecting routers that belong to the same IP network are replaced with the *logical*

---

[1]The word *archaic* is used here in connection with the semantics (rather than syntax—no one would dispute the use of decimal numbers) of the telephone numbers today. At the time of step-by-step switches, the telephone numbers were actually the numbers of telephones in the list of telephone exchanges maintained by a switch. Today, however, a telephone number is no more than a string of digits that may identify a particular telephone line (without reflecting its order in any switching system) or even a service (such as freephone or an 800 number in the United States). In the latter case, the final translation of the number to the line may never take place.

connections that traverse other IP networks. In order for the voice call application to work over the Internet, the packets that carry voice must arrive in the order in which they were sent and at about the same rate at which they were transmitted. Dissimilarity of the requirements of voice traffic with those of data traffic is visible in tolerating packet loss, too: Occasional loss of packets has little or no effect on the quality of a call, while the delay of a stream of packets caused by the retransmission of the lost one is simply unacceptable. So, support of voice calls requires significant reengineering of the IP networks with many paradigm changes.

We then address the IP endpoint architecture in support of voice over IP—the telephony gateways and their components. Strictly speaking, *IP telephony* refers to real-time voice communications over the Internet or enterprise IP networks. In contrast to the POTS or ISDN calls, IP telephony calls are not supposed to involve PSTN switches (or other circuit telephony equipment) at all. Nevertheless, such a pure form of IP telephony has not yet spread outside enterprise-only networks. What has happened instead is that the industry came up with the equipment and applications that deliver calls by interworking the IP networks and the PSTN (or private circuit-switched networks), and, as a result, created a hybrid network.

In addition to interworking of physical components, the IP and PSTN naming and addressing schemes must interwork; we dedicate a section to this subject. Finally, we move to one low-level technology that has become a real enabler of IP telephony—codecs. As we mentioned in Chapter 2, codecs have slowly traveled down in the PSTN hierarchy from toll switches to local switches and, finally, to the endpoints (that is, the ISDN terminals). The availability of inexpensive and efficient (in terms of using whatever bandwidth the Internet can provide) codecs that can be placed in a PC or Internet appliance has been a true enabler of IP telephony and its specialized network-enabled telephones (or *netphones*)—the true IP telephones.

Quality of Service (QoS)

The Glossary of the Telecommunications Terms of the U.S. Federal Standard 10377 (available at www.its.bldrdoc.gov/fs-1037/fs-1037c.htm) defines *quality of service* (QoS) as:

> *1. The performance specification of a communications channel or system. . . . 2. A subjective rating of telephone communications quality in which listeners judge transmissions by qualifiers, such as excellent, good, fair, poor, or unsatisfactory.*

This definition best expresses both the objective (that is, something based on a computable metrics) and subjective (that is, perception-based) aspects of the QoS concept. Three objectives that drive the need to integrate the Internet and the PSTN relate to QoS: (1) carrying voice across both the IP networks and the PSTN, (2) combining the PSTN transport and IP access to services, and (3) accessing the IP networks over the PSTN lines. The first item is associated with the most perceivable QoS requirements. Nevertheless, the IP network access aspect (and connected to it, issues of supporting VPNs) is equally important, as we will demonstrate. Ferguson and Huston (2000) address the subject in detail, although it is relatively high level. For a more theoretical treatment of QoS support in IP routing, we recommend Chapter 13 of Huitema (1995). In addition, Weiss (1998) and other articles in the same issue of *Bell Labs Technical Journal* deal with many technical details and provide the latest results of ongoing research on the subject.

To begin with, different applications (or, rather, their users) have different perceptions of what the QoS is. Using an application called *telemedicine* (further described in Chapter 9), a doctor may expect a copy of a brain tomogram taken in a remote laboratory. The transmission can be delayed for a few minutes; however, the doctor cannot afford to have any detail of the tomogram compromised (a missing detail could wrongly suggest a tumor or leave it undetected)—the chief QoS requirement here is that no data arrive in error. On the other hand, in an IP telephony application, an occasional error in the signal would cause no problem; however, a long delay (or a variable delay, called *jitter*) is likely to be unacceptable.

The model of routing for the PSTN is based on the concept of *circuits*, which are created end to end for the duration of the session. Circuits are mapped into fixed switched physical connections. Thus, any message between two end users in a session always traverses the same physical path for the duration of a session. [For conferencing, such circuits can be *bridged* (that is, joined) by switches or other devices that have switching fabric; thus, any multicast message will follow the same, predetermined set of physical circuits.] With this routing model, it is possible to determine whether a session that requires certain characteristics (such as bandwidth or loss tolerances) can be established. Once the session is established, it is relatively straightforward to guarantee that the requested characteristics will remain constant for the duration of the session.

One important factor in PSTN routing is the time that it takes to set up a circuit; the *call setup time* has traditionally been an essential QoS metric in the PSTN. Incidentally, this model, which naturally grew out of telephony, was applied by the ITU-T to the definition of *virtual circuit* for data communications standards. First, this concept was defined in X.25 and, subsequently, frame relay and asynchronous transfer mode (ATM) networks—technologies outside the scope of this book. For the use of ATM in public networks, we strongly recommend the excellent book by Davis (1999). ISDN access guarantees certain bandwidth (depending on a particular national standard) to the subscriber. Broadband ISDN (B-ISDN) access, in addition, specifies parameters that are needed by the ATM network. At this very moment, the mechanisms are being developed to back up B-ISDN by Intelligent Network, which could ensure policy-based networkwide QoS enforcement. Overall, in today's PSTN, the main QoS metric is, as mentioned before, the call blocking rate.

The Internet routing model, on the other hand, has traditionally avoided stressing any built-in mechanism for creation and maintenance of virtual circuits. In the Internet, QoS issues (which also define their respective metrics) include bandwidth availability, latency (that is, end-to-end delay) control, jitter (that is, delay variation) control, and packet loss. Historically, the IP networks have been supporting what is called the *best effort* (but no guarantees) of packet transmission. In this system, no differentiation among different types of traffic is made, and neither the sequence of packet arrivals nor the arrival itself is guaranteed.

Whatever the end-to-end QoS requirements may be, at the network layer the packets travel (similarly to those of us who take airplanes) from hub to hub (that is, from router to router). Each router queues newly arriving packets for retransmission over the link to the most suitable (according to the routing table) router or destination host. Until very recently, most routers used a first-come, first-served queuing discipline, which is fair to all packets and, for this very reason, cannot make some packets more equal than others.

Overall, for applications such as voice or video over IP, a new network layer model was clearly needed, and such models have been researched and implemented since the 1990s. Two new approaches proposed mechanisms that are now called *fair queuing* and *weighted fair queuing* (Nagle, 1987; Demers et al., 1990; Zhang, 1991). With fair queuing and weighted fair queuing, routers are no longer required to treat packets equally. The incoming traffic is separated into well-defined *flows*. (A TCP connection is an example of a flow, although it may be difficult to detect by a router—all TCP connections between the same pair of hosts is a more realistic example; a voice session is another one.)

Fair Queuing and Weighted Fair Queuing

Using the new queuing schemes, each flow now has its own queue. With the fair queuing policy, the packets are transmitted round-robin in order to guarantee each flow an equal share of the capacity (possibly penalizing flows that have large packets at times of network congestion). Weighted fair queuing—an algorithm that is widely used in today's advanced QoS-capable routers—assigns each different type of flow its (by no means necessarily identical) share of bandwidth. Figure 3.1 illustrates the concept: In Figure 3.1*a*, with the first-come, first-served queue, airplanes, cars, and elephants move in the same order in which they have arrived (a scheme that would cause plane crashes and annoy the drivers of the cars following elephants!). In Figure 3.1*b*, with fair queuing, the queues are formed per each flow (defined here as a formation of planes or cars or a caravan of elephants), but they are preempted so that bigger things have to wait until an equivalent number of

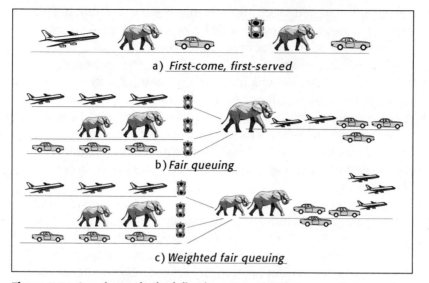

a) *First-come, first-served*

b) *Fair queuing*

c) *Weighted fair queuing*

Figure 3.1   Queuing and scheduling in routers. (*a*) First-come, first-served queuing. (*b*) Fair queuing. (*c*) Weighted fair queuing.

smaller things passes (still, a maddening experience for elephants!). In Figure 3.1*c*, with weighted fair queuing, the planes are given the right of way, so they move through the queue almost without slowing down and always keeping formation; the planes are followed by cars, and the cars by the caravan of elephants. This property of keeping the packet "formation" eliminates delay variance (called *jitter*).

In 1992, A. Parekh and R. Gallager of MIT demonstrated that a flow that experiences a service rate slightly higher than the flow's data rate has a bounded delay. In other words, by requesting that a flow not exceed a certain rate, the network can guarantee that the delay experienced by the flow does not exceed a certain value. (A good example of a similar result is *green streets* in cities, where stoplights are adjusted so that a car traveling at a certain speed—for example, 25 mph—is guaranteed a green light at about 9 out of 10 intersections.)

The scientists then augmented the weighted fair queuing with the specification of guaranteed delay for each flow. This work resulted in a new architecture for what its creators called *integrated services packet networks* [compare with the expansion of the *integrated services digital network* (ISDN)] in Clark et al. (1992). Two types of services—*guaranteed* (which supports real-time traffic with determined latency and jitter bounds) and *controlled-load* (which deals with relaxed traffic)—were defined. At that point, the groundwork was laid for the standardization work in the *Internet Engineering Task Force* (IETF). This work is further addressed in Chapter 5, as is the protocol that defines integrated services, called the *Resource Reservation Setup Protocol* (RSVP)—which is not a routing protocol. In a nutshell, RSVP, which was designed with multicasting (that is, sending a message to multiple receivers) in mind, makes bandwidth reservations—from destination to source—in the routers along the spanning tree covering multicast group members. The routers store the necessary state information, which is then maintained by sending specific RSVP messages in both directions.

The integrated services approach has been comprehensive, but apparently far too ambitious to implement widely. One recurring sentiment is that the overhead associated with reservations is far too large; the other is that it is overkill as far as the short-lived flows (of which most of the present Internet traffic consists) are concerned. (The counterargument to the latter is, of course, that the model was not created with the short-lived flows in mind; but then, something needs to be done about the short flows, too.) The third concern (Weiss, 1998) regarding the integrated services approach is that it would make charging those who request a higher QoS difficult. In any event, while the applicability of the RSVP to wide area networks and the Internet is questioned, it is being implemented for smaller enterprise networks. In essence, the integrated services approach has been a top-down one—guaranteeing absolute QoS in the network on a per-flow basis.

A bottom-up alternative technology, where QoS building blocks (which routers can recognize and act on) are defined, is called *differentiated services* (Kumar et al., 1998; Weiss, 1998). This technology has been actively addressed by the IETF and has resulted in a standard (also described in Chapter 5). The concept behind the technology is definition of various classes of services. The service provider establishes with each customer a *service level agreement* (SLA). Among other things, an SLA specifies how much traffic a user may send within any given class of service. A particular class of service of a packet is encoded in its IP header. The traffic is then policed at the border of the service provider's network. Once the traffic enters the network, specialized routers provide it with differentiated treatment, but—unlike the case with the integrated services approach—the treatment is based not on a per-flow basis, but solely on the indicated class of service. The overall network is set up so as to meet all SLAs.

Label or Tag Switching

We now move to *label switching* or, as called by some implementations, *tag switching*, which is standardized by the IETF [see the description of the output of the IETF multiprotocol label switching (*mpls*) working group in Chapter 5]. The technology was initially developed for the purpose of interworking between the IP-based and ATM and frame relay networks, and it was later developed to apply to any network layer protocol (hence the *multi-* designation). The ATM (B-ISDN) switches follow the PSTN model in establishing and maintaining virtual circuits and virtual paths. The B-ISDN access protocol specifies the QoS, which is then guaranteed by the network.

To get an idea of MPLS, try to answer the following question: If the ATM and IP networks are to interwork, what should the router on the border of the ATM and IP networks do? The most straightforward answer is *try to maintain the virtual circuits and virtual paths.* To do so, the first router in a chain would need to "understand" the "ATM language" and act (that is, route the packet) based on the connection identifier established by the ATM switch. The next router on the path to the destination does not necessarily have to "understand" the same "ATM language," but then it needs to understand whatever means the first router uses to identify a connection. The same applies for the rest of the routers on the path to the destination.

This is precisely how the MPLS routers work. They make forwarding decisions based on a fixed-length string called a *label* to decide how to forward the packet. The labels are meaningful only to the pair of routers sharing a link, and only in one direction—from a sender to the receiver. The receiver, however, chooses the label and negotiates its semantics with the sender by means of the *Label Distribution Protocol* (LDP). The label can indicate not only where to forward the packet (that is, which port to use), but also the QoS characteristics of the packet that specify its priority and suggest an appropriate treatment.

This approach is very different from the traditional (that is, non-MPLS routing) approach, where a router makes forwarding decisions based on the IP header. In the traditional approach, the routing table must be searched, which takes more time and processing power than a lookup in a label table, which the label-based forwarding requires. Furthermore, the routers that are not capable of analyzing the network layer packet can still perform the label lookup and replacement (a much simpler operation). Another advantage of MPLS is that using the labels (that is, in a sense, maintaining the history of the path) allows the forwarding decisions to be made based on the identity of the router at which the packet enters the network—packets entering the network via different routers are likely to be assigned different labels. Finally, when a packet is to be forced to follow a particular explicit route (rather than be left to the mercy of routing algorithms), the MPLS label can be used to represent the route. RSVP can be extended to complement MPLS by associating labeled paths with the flows. With that, resource reservations associated with an explicit route can be made to guarantee QoS.

We should mention one more important MPLS application: MPLS provides an excellent mechanism for tunneling by stacking the labels and thus supporting nested routing decision making. One important potential application of combining RSVP and MPLS is that the resulting tunnels can be routed away from the points of network failure or congestion. We highly recommend the work of Armitage (2000) as a comprehensive review of the subject.

Another means for ensuring QoS is network-wide enforcement policies, which are rules for control of the network resources and services. In describing these, we follow Kozik et al. (1998). Quality of service is only one aspect of policy-based networks; others are security, authorization, and accounting.

These aspects are often inseparable—the accounting function, for example, may determine whether the present level of use has been paid for (by keeping track of the use of the resource). If use has not been paid for, policies can restrict access to the resource or affect QoS by downgrading the level of use.

The architecture of policy-based networks—sometimes also called *directory-enabled networks*—is depicted in Figure 3.2. The architecture actually repeats the IN conceptual pattern in both the way that the policies are stored and the way that they are accessed by network elements (for example, routers, access servers, or telephony gateways). The policies are stored centrally in a *policy database* by a *policy management system.* When a network element detects an event that requires policy access (such as a request to provide bandwidth in order to establish an IP telephony call), the network element queries a policy server, which in turn consults the policy database and then either denies the request or carries it through by instructing all concerned entities to perform the actions that would enforce the policy.

The IETF is addressing the subject of policy-based networks in the Policy Framework (*policy*) working group.

Active Networks

Some implementations of *active networks* (AN) exist (for example, see www.cccc.com), but no standards projects are currently associated with them. The area of the application of AN is larger than ensuring QoS, but AN is viewed with much interest in the research and development communities as a possible means of ensuring and supporting QoS.

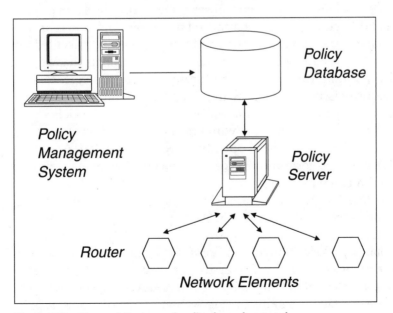

Figure 3.2   The architecture of policy-based networks.

As Calvert et al. (1998) observe, AN means different things to different people. In a sense, this is true, although everyone seems to agree that, in a nutshell, AN is about programmability of network elements (for example, routers) and—to an extent—bypassing, if not totally eliminating, standardized protocols, replacing them with dynamic, created-on-the-fly protocols. Marcus et al. (1998) lament that "existing protocols do not operate well for emerging applications or take advantage of novel network technologies," citing "IP's inability to capitalize on sub-networks which offer quality of service . . . guarantees." While one could argue with this particular example by using the facts presented in this very book, there is a point in the complaint. It is indisputable, however, as the authors further note, that "Forming a consensus within large groups is a slow process, and is likely to remain slow; therefore, protocol standards will continue to evolve at a slow pace." The question, of course, is whether this pace is sufficient for the market development, and only the future will bring the answer. The idea behind AN is quite similar to (if not influenced by) the idea that resulted in the creation of Java. The language [Hypertext Markup Language (HTML)] and the protocol [Hypertext Transfer Protocol (HTTP)] that made possible the Internet killer application—the World Wide Web—do not support rapid interaction of the user with the page. Such interaction has been made possible by the invention of the principle by which a program (*applet*) written in Java is sent to the user's personal computer (PC) or Internet appliance and then interpreted locally (by a Java interpreter). The user actually sees no difference (unless a silly message on a screen proudly announces that a Java program is being executed). The user simply clicks on an object, and HTTP carries the Java code to the user's machine. Now, AN proposes pretty much the same mechanism, except that the active code is to be carried not in the application protocol message but in a network layer packet, and this code is to be executed not (or, in general, not only) at the host, but by the network elements themselves. Although many questions can be asked (most cannot yet be answered) regarding the security issues involved with this approach and its exact applications, it is relatively straightforward to see how in principle the QoS-related state of a router can be changed with unprecedented efficiency, and how the network-wide services could potentially be implemented. A specific and somewhat less futuristic application of AN to network management is described in Raz and Shavitt (1999).

The overall architecture for AN is being developed in the Defense Advanced Research Projects Agency (DARPA), the same organization that sponsored the development of what has now become the Internet. Several universities (notably Berkeley University, Columbia University, Georgia Tech, MIT, the University of Arizona, the University of Kansas, the University of Pennsylvania, and Washington University—by no means an exhaustive list), as well as the research facilities of major corporations, have AN projects.

There are two things on which the AN community agrees: (1) Networks must be service independent and (2) end-to-end service programs must be network independent. Do these sound like early IN principles? Exactly! After all, the more things change, the more they stay the same. [For a tutorial on applications of AN to IN, see Prywes (2000).]

IP Telephony Gateway

If a call is to be made from a PC or specialized IP phone to a regular PSTN telephone or vice versa, both the PSTN and IP network are involved in making the call. As we noted earlier in this chapter, the PSTN may also use an IP network for so-called *trunk replacement*, or *IP trunking*, where the long-distance portion of the PSTN voice traffic between two PSTN telephones is carried over an IP network. (You will find a detailed description of all relevant service scenarios in Chapter 9.)

When it comes to delivering real-time voice, the PSTN and an IP network are different in a number of ways, as summarized in Table 3.1. For establishing a call, for example, SS No. 7 has been traditionally used within the PSTN, while H.323 is the most prevalent protocol suite [with Session Initiation Protocol (SIP) as a viable alternative] in the Internet to date. In general, the connection of two dissimilar networks is achieved through some sort of a device—called a *gateway*—that compensates for the differences in the networks. There is no exception when it comes to interconnecting the PSTN and IP networks for supporting IP telephony. In this case, the interconnecting device is called an *IP telephony gateway* and will link users of IP telephony with a billion or so PSTN users.

Table 3.1 Key Differences between Telephony over the PSTN and the Internet

DISTINGUISHING ASPECT	PSTN	INTERNET
Bandwidth allocation for voice transport	A dedicated circuit (e.g., 64 kbps) set up for each two-party communications session.	Best-effort delivery of IP packets.
Numbering and addressing scheme	14-bit point code for network nodes and E.164 for endpoints.	4-byte IP address, domain name system (DNS), e-mail address, uniform resource locator (URL), etc.
Voice representation	Typically analog in the loop and G.711 (either A- or μ-law) in the backbone.	G.711, G.723.1, G.729, etc.
Signaling protocols	Signalling System No. 7, Q.931, etc.	H.323, SIP, etc.
Availability	99.999% (5 min downtime per year).	99% (88 h downtime per year).

Figure 3.3 illustrates the integration of the PSTN and the Internet (or any IP network) through gateways in support of IP telephony. It distinguishes four types of IP telephony gateways based on the PSTN interfaces and certain specific functions that they support.

1. *Trunking gateway.* Connects a central office (CO) switch to an IP router. Such a gateway typically has an SS No. 7 signaling interface and manages a large number of 64-kbps digital circuits and Real-Time Transport Protocol (RTP) streams. It is used in the trunk replacement application where the long-distance portion of a call between two telephones is made over the IP network instead of the PSTN. (In IP telephony parlance, such calls are known as *phone-to-phone calls.*)

2. *Access gateway.* Connects telephones or PBXs to an IP router through an access interface [such as ISDN primary rate interface (PRI)]. It supports calls between two telephones with the IP network as an intermediary transport or between a telephone and a PC. (Again, in IP telephony parlance, calls between a telephone and a PC are also known as *PC-to-phone calls* or *phone-to-PC calls.*)

3. *Network access server.* Connects a central office switch to an IP router. (Though previously discussed, it is included for completeness, because this type of gateway can be controlled in exactly the same manner as others.) Such a gateway may have an ISDN interface similar to that of the access gateway.

4. *Residential gateway.* Connects analog phones to an IP router. Such a gateway typically supports a small number (two to four) of analog lines and is located on the customer premises. It brings the Internet interconnection point directly to the curb and maximizes the use of the IP network for calls between two telephones as well as between a telephone and a PC.

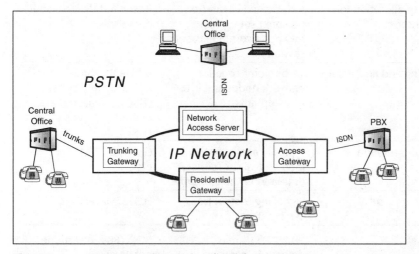

Figure 3.3 PSTN-Internet integration through gateways.

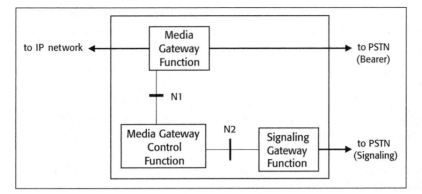

Figure 3.4   Components of a decomposed PSTN-Internet gateway.

Gateway Decomposition

The different types of gateways described in the previous section are specific instances of a generic gateway notion. It is useful to decompose the generic gateway into several functional components. Figure 3.4 depicts a common view of such a decomposed gateway. Three components are identified: (1) the *media gateway* (MG) function, (2) the *signaling gateway* (SG) function, and (3) the *media gateway control* (MGC) function. We describe these functions next.

Physically, the media gateway function terminates PSTN circuits and connections to IP routers (in relation to which it is a host). It also performs all the necessary transformation to convert bit streams received from the sending network into bit streams particular to the receiving network. The transformation occurs at two levels: transmission and application.

At the transmission level, the MG function converts the bit streams between two different framing schemes. This usually involves multiplexing of bit streams of distinct communication sessions and the reverse operation—demultiplexing. In the PSTN, fixed-size digital channels (each typically carrying a voice conversation) are multiplexed based on the *time division multiplexing* (TDM) scheme at various hierarchical levels (for example, T1 and E3) and packed into frames for transmission over high-capacity facilities. In the IP networks, bits representing a voice conversation are packetized according to the *Real-time Transport Protocol* (RTP) profile for audio and video payloads (RFC 1890).[2] (You can find a brief discussion of RTP in Part Two.)

At the application level, the transformation takes place between different media-encoding schemes (see the section on codecs for more information)

---

[2]It is important to note an issue that is unique in transporting voice packets over IP networks: the practical size of the payload encapsulated in the RTP packets. The payload size determines the minimum end-to-end delay. Larger packets introduce less header overhead but higher delay and make packet loss more noticeable. Presently, a payload of the recommended size holds 20 ms of voice data. With some technological advances, different RTP streams can also be multiplexed at certain network nodes. This should result in a reduction of header overhead and a more efficient transmission over IP networks.

and is commonly known as *transcoding*. In IP telephony, two prevalent speech encoding schemes are G.711 and G.729. Operating at a bit rate of 64 kbps, G.711 is used ubiquitously in the digital backbone of the PSTN and sets what is known as the *toll-quality voice standard*. G.729 operates at a much lower bit rate of 8 kbps but still supports near-toll-quality voice service. For this reason, it is widely used in IP networks where bandwidth is constrained. Note that transcoding is computationally intensive and thus causes delays. In addition, transcoding results in degradation of voice fidelity, in particular when a speech coder uses compression.

Another important task of the MG function is to support the use of the QoS facilities of the IP network. Other tasks include echo cancellation (if required), event detection, signaling generation, usage recording, and support of specialized resources such as conference bridges, fax machines, modem pools, and interactive voice response units.[3]

The SG function receives and sends PSTN signaling (such as SS No. 7 or ISDN access) messages. Depending on the arrangement, it may relay, translate, or terminate the PSTN signaling. It exchanges signaling information with the MGC function over IP, and with the PSTN using the SS No. 7.

The MGC function provides control of the media gateway function, including call and connection control and resource management. To this end, it terminates and originates all the relevant signaling. In addition, the MGC function keeps an inventory of the MG resources (for example, bearer circuits and RTP streams) and instructs the MG to reserve or release resources as required. (Naturally, some sort of local policy will govern the use of resources.) With its central role in call and connection control, the MG function logically also provides support for Internet offloading (as described in Chapter 2) or advanced services and features (such as freephone or call-forwarding). It has the ability to detect data calls from the PSTN and to direct the data traffic straight to a network access server as well as to launch queries to SCPs for instructions for further call processing.

Distributed Gateways

With the many complex tasks that the gateway has to perform, its scalability becomes an important issue. An effective approach to scalability is to allow for a distributed design of the gateway. This way the MG, SG, and MGC functions can be grouped in a number of ways, with functions implemented in separate devices or combined in single physical units, depending on the actual interconnection arrangement.

---

[3]The inclusion of fax machines as specialized resources lets the media gateway support real-time IP fax in addition to real-time voice communications. Being a data application in nature, real-time IP fax actually has requirements different from those of IP telephony and calls for specific MG solutions. For further information, consult Tebbs (1999) and ITU-T Recommendation T.38.

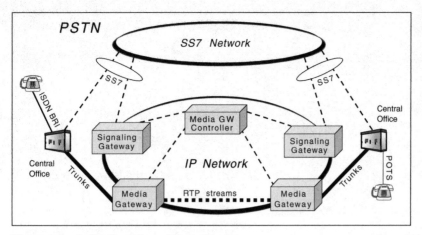

Figure 3.5   A distributed trunking gateway.

Figure 3.5 shows an example of trunking gateways with the MG, SG, and MGC functions implemented in separate boxes. In particular, the media gateways happen to be under the control of the same media gateway controller.

Another example is shown in Figure 3.6, where the access gateway is distributed over two boxes, one implementing the MGC function and the other the MG as well as SG functions. When the MG and SG functions are colocated, the signaling information is hauled back to the controller for handling.

Figure 3.7 shows yet another example. There, the SS No. 7 SG and MGC functions are combined in a physical box, called a *software switch* (or a *soft switch*), which controls the boxes implementing the rest of the function for access and trunking replacement applications. The soft switch is an increas-

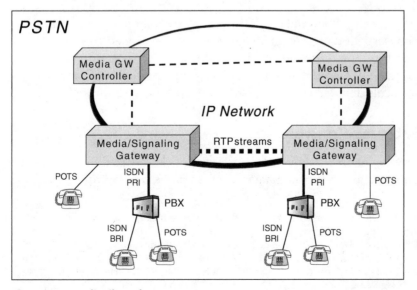

Figure 3.6   A distributed access gateway.

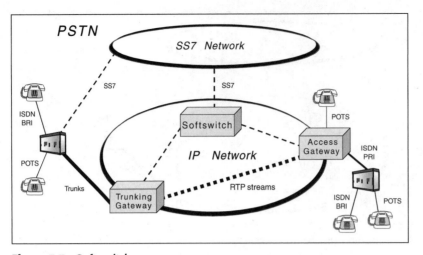

Figure 3.7 Soft switch.

ingly popular device for supporting full-featured IP telephony services across the PSTN and the IP network. In a nutshell, soft switches are distributed call control servers that emulate circuit switches in a packet network. A consortium devoted to the subject has been formed and is named, for obvious reasons, the *International Softswitch Consortium* (www.softswitch.org). Lakshmi-Ratan (1999) also describes a particular soft switch implementation.

Common to these examples is the physical separation of the MG and MGC functions. This allows for the deployment of fewer MGC devices than MG devices in the network such that one MGC device controls multiple MG devices. In addition, there tends to be a separate device that is dedicated to the SS No. 7–only SG function. Naturally, the number of dedicated SG devices is even smaller than that of MGC devices for their specific function and for the conservation of (scarce) SS No. 7 network entity addresses.

Gateway distribution results in new interfaces between the components, such as the N1 and N2 interfaces in Figure 3.4, or the multitude of proprietary signaling protocols denoted by the dashed lines in Figures 3.5 through 3.7.[4]

Media Gateway Control

An application-level protocol over the N1 interface can be used by the media gateway controller to run the media gateway (as far as call control, connec-

---

[4]Naturally, these interfaces are considered for standardization, which is essential for the interoperation of equipment from different vendors. ITU-T and the IETF are jointly defining the protocol for the N1 interface. The protocol will be published as Recommendation H.248 by ITU-T and as a request for comments (RFC) by the IETF. With respect to the N2 interface, there may be multiple protocol standards defined in the end. At least two protocols for reliable in-sequence carriage of PSTN signaling (for example, SS No. 7 and enhanced Q.931) over IP are under development in ITU-T and the IETF respectively.

tion control, and resource allocation are concerned). Industry approaches vary in the way that resources are represented and calls and connections are modeled. Huitema et al. (1999) describe an early approach. Supplanting it is the approach that has been pursued jointly by ITU-T and the IETF *media gateway control* (MEGACO) named after the IETF working group [see www.ietf .org/html.charters/megaco-charter.html]. While bearing resemblance to Huitema's approach, MEGACO differs in a considerable way as well.

At the heart of the MEGACO approach is its connection model, which consists of two types of objects: a termination and a context. A *termination* is a source or sink of one or more flows on a media gateway. It has properties (for example, media characteristics, a set of events that can be detected, and a set of signals that can be acted on) describing the nature of the termination. Bearer circuit channels and RTP streams are examples of terminations. In particular, bearer circuits, like other physical resources, are terminations that are persistent as long as they are provisioned on a gateway. In contrast, RTP streams, which are created on demand, are *ephemeral* terminations. Terminations may come in a wide number of types. The MEGACO approach includes a mechanism to define them in separate *packages.*

A *context* is an association of a collection of terminations that defines the directions of flows, if any, between the terminations. Terminations can be *added* to or *removed* from a context. A context is created when the first termination is added and is destroyed when the last termination is removed. (Similarly, an ephemeral termination is created when it is added to a context and destroyed when it is removed from the context.) Terminations can also be moved from one context to another. In addition, their properties can be modified within a context. Terminations without any association belong to a special type of context called the *null context.* Such terminations usually represent physical resources. Adding these terminations to a normal context removes them from the null context; removing them from a normal context returns them to the null context. Figure 3.8 shows examples of contexts and terminations.

Based on the connection model, the MEGACO approach defines a set of *commands* for the overall purpose of call and connection control. Among them are the commands for direct manipulation of terminations and contexts, including addition of a termination to a context, removal of a termination from a context, modifying the properties of a termination, and moving a termination from one context to another. Other commands are for auditing of the current state of a termination and the range of the termination properties supported on the media gateway, event notification, and management of the association between the media gateway and the controller. Most of these commands are initiated by the media gateway controller and are sent to the media gateway under its control. The exceptions are the ones for event notification and association management. For notifying the controller of certain events (for example, off-hook and end-of-tone) received by the media gate-

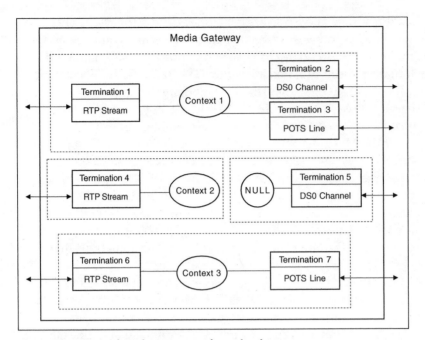

Figure 3.8 Examples of contexts and terminations.

way, the command for event notification is naturally initiated by the media gateway. In contrast, the command for association management can be initiated by either the media gateway or the controller. When initiated by the media gateway, it is used to notify the controller of the change of the availability status of terminations on the media gateway or the availability status of the gateway itself. When initiated by the controller, it is used to instruct the media gateway to establish an association with a new controller or to take certain terminations out of service.

Another important aspect of the MEGACO approach is its operational model, which recognizes *transactions* and *actions*. A transaction consists of one or more actions; an action is composed of a series of commands and is applicable only to a specific context. Invocation of transactions is done by way of messages. To reduce the load of the communications exchange between the media gateway and the controller, a message can hold multiple transactions. The transactions in a message are treated independently and can be processed in any order or concurrently. In contrast, commands within a transaction must be processed sequentially. When a command fails, the processing of the rest of the commands stops, unless the failed command is optional. Commands must be responded to upon completion. When a transaction takes a long time to complete, a provisional response should be sent periodically to its originator indicating that the transaction is being processed. Responses are sent also by way of messages. As expected, a message can hold multiple transaction responses, each of which consists of a series of action responses. An action response comprises the responses to the commands pertaining to the action.

An assumption of the MEGACO operational model is that messages are exchanged reliably over the network. For this reason, implementations must ensure that the media gateway and the controller use a reliable transport mechanism [such as *Transmission Control Protocol* (TCP)] for the relevant exchange.[5] When an unreliable transport [such as *User Datagram Protocol* (UDP)] is used, the mechanisms that eliminate message duplication and ensure in-sequence transmission of transactions must be used. In addition, it is important to have mechanisms that detect network congestion and respond to it by reducing the traffic. On the other hand, when a reliable transport is used, simple application-level timers may be all that is needed to guard against component failure and undesirable use of the network.

As you have probably noticed the MEGACO technology is somewhat closer to supporting the old-type telephones than true IP telephones, which can establish an end-to-end call without the network even being aware that the call is established. Doing so requires signaling protocols such as SIP and H.323.

Gateway Location

What we have touched on so far are the core gateway functions—signaling and media conversion. Yet, to support an IP telephony call end to end, other things need to be taken care of. One such thing is *gateway location.*

Suppose a call originated in (or was passed on to) an IP network, and the call needs to be terminated in the PSTN. There are many gateways that could do the job, but only a few may be suitable for a particular call. For instance, the gateway definitely should be chosen so as to terminate the call at the point in the PSTN as close to the called party as possible. In this case, terminating at the gateway that is connected to the called party's end office is clearly the optimal solution if other factors are not involved.

But other factors *are* typically involved, such as the load and capability of gateways in question, the IP network provider's and the end user's preferences, agreements with the PSTN service providers, and—to top it all—the costs to be incurred.

Thus, gateway location is an important activity that is bound to become more complex as more telephony gateways are built and deployed. A considerable amount of research on the subject has been done (Schulzrinne and Rosenberg, 1999) and more or less detailed proposals on that matter have been submitted to both ITU and the IETF [specifically, the IP Telephony (*iptel*) working group].

---

[5]A reliable transport mechanism that has received increasing attention is the protocol named Simple Control Transmission Protocol developed in the IETF *sigtran* working group.

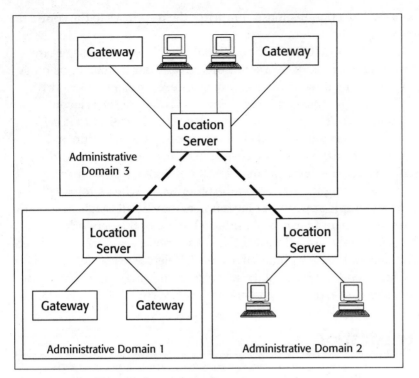

Figure 3.9   Architecture for gateway discovery.

As it happens, the Internet has had a similar problem with interdomain routing, which has been solved. It should come as no surprise, then, that many ideas of a specialized routing protocol [called *Border Gateway Protocol* (BGP) and described in Chapter 7] have been used to develop the gateway location technology.[6]

In the tradition of IP routing, the process is dynamic and the knowledge is built using distributed computation performed by the gateways. Before the decision can be made regarding which gateway to choose, the database of eligible cooperating gateways has to exist. This database is built in the act of gateway discovery. Figure 3.9 shows a representative architecture that spans several administrative domains. Each domain, which contains several gateways and some number of endpoints (for example, PCs), has at least a logical entity, called a *location server.* The main job of the location server is to learn about the gateways in its own administrative domain as well as in other domains and to construct the database of the gateways. In the intradomain case, this is usually achieved in a registration process. Each gateway signs on with the location server when started up and updates its availability status

---

[6]In Chapter 7, you will find that many Internet access issues are not unlike those of IP telephony gateways. In fact, the emerging gateway products are often built on the access server platform. You will also find that BGP is essential for the access products.

whenever necessary. The information is propagated by means of an intrado-main protocol, such as the Service Location Protocol.[7]

In comparison to the intradomain case, discovery of gateways in other domains is not as straightforward a process. Complicating the process is the need for a business agreement between the administrative domains for any exchange of gateway information or any use of the gateways by users in a different domain. A location server can only propagate to another location server the gateway information that is permitted by the agreement between the administrative domains to which they each belong. Similarly, synchro-nization of the database in one domain with that of another and selection of the route of a call are subject to the intradomain agreement and policy. As a result, there cannot be a single global database of gateways where a user can look up and select a gateway as desired. Instead, different databases may be available in different domains based on the respective business agreements and associated policies. The database contains the IP address of a gateway and a range of telephone numbers that the gateway can terminate. In addi-tion, it contains the attributes of the gateway, such as signaling protocols (for example, SIP and H.323), usage cost, and the provider's identification num-ber, which we have mentioned before. A location server uses the attributes to decide which gateways are to be used for terminating a call to a particular number or to be further advertised to other location servers.

Interdomain gateway discovery is carried out through an interdomain pro-tocol, such as the *Telephony Routing Information Protocol* (TRIP), which is under development in the IETF. As mentioned before, an inter-domain gate-way discovery protocol resembles a routing protocol. It also shows signifi-cant differences, however. The most important are that the inter-domain gateway discovery protocol runs at the application level and runs between location servers, which may not be adjacent and, unlike routers, do not for-ward IP packets.

As far as access to the gateway database is concerned, it is an activity that is independent of gateway discovery. There are several possible approaches for such database access using different protocols. One protocol is *Lightweight Directory Access Protocol* (LDAP), which, as its name suggests, is for access to any directory organized in a special tree structure. (You can find a summary of LDAP in Chapter 6.) When LDAP is used, the gateway database is orga-nized based on the LDAP data model. Another protocol is Service Location Protocol, which has been designed for locating a networked service based on service attributes rather than the name (or location) of the network host pro-viding the service. Logically, it can be used to find gateways given a set of user preferences. Yet another protocol is HTTP, the communications enabler of the World Wide Web. In this case, the gateway database has a Web front

---

[7]The *srvloc* working group in the IETF is responsible for developing the Service Location Proto-col. The initial SLP specifications can be found in RFC 2165, RFC 2608, and RFC 2609.

end, which allows a user to query it through Web-based forms. We should note that an inter-domain gateway discovery protocol is actually another possible candidate. Nothing prevents it from being used for retrieving information in the gateway database.

Address Translation

A subject that is often confused with gateway discovery is the translation of a telephone number into an IP address. Among the services that need such translation are phone-to-PC calls made from a PSTN telephone to a PC (or to any telephony-capable IP appliance) on the IP network. A way to accommodate such a call from the PSTN is to assign the PC a telephone number. This not only allows a PSTN operator to leverage its existing PSTN infrastructure to offer IP telephony services, but also makes it easy for the telephone user to place a call to a PC. Of course, telephone numbers for this purpose should adhere to a special numbering plan that is distinct from the ones used in traditional telephony services. Depending on its geographical scope, this special numbering plan is under the administration of ITU-T or the national (or regional) telephone numbering authority.

Another service in question is *Internet Call-Waiting*, with which an end user can be notified of an incoming call while using the telephone line for a dial-up connection to the Internet. Upon receipt of the notification, the user then has the option to reject or accept the call. Either way, there are further details on the disposition of the call, which we will describe in Chapter 9. What is relevant here is that the notification is delivered to the called party (identified by a telephone number) over the Internet. Ensuring instant notification of a call in waiting typically requires the knowledge of the IP address of the PC connecting to the Internet via the telephone line.

In general, any directory-like technology can support the type of translation in question. An example is a *domain name system*, which is best known for mapping a domain name (for example, www.lucent.com) to an IP address. Another example is LDAP, which is used to look up information (for example, John's e-mail address) in a directory that is organized in a special tree structure. A caveat is that whatever existing directory technology is used must be adapted to satisfy the special requirements posed by IP telephony. One such requirement is that the directory used must allow for frequent updates of its entries. This arises where an IP endpoint is assigned an IP address dynamically, as is often the case in dial-up connections. In contrast to the relatively static telephone number given to the IP endpoint, the IP address changes at each connection. Another special requirement has to do with the real-time performance need of IP telephony. The additional step for directory lookup must not introduce significant delay in the IP telephony setup procedure.

An immediate benefit of using the general directory technology for telephone-number-to-IP-address translation is that other attributes associated with the endpoint can also be obtained with the operation. Consider as an example Mary, who wishes to receive calls at her PC over the IP network only from her daughter between 5:00 and 6:00 P.M. every day. Such information can be stored in the directory. If so, a call to Mary could trigger a directory query whose response includes the IP address of Mary's PC as well as her preference for receiving calls. The additional information can then be used to process all calls to Mary. For instance, a call from a friend at 5:15 P.M. will result in no attempt at call setup inside the network. Instead, the call will be redirected to Mary's voice mail. If you find this scenario familiar, you are right. It is similar to an IN-supported service where the user's policy (or service logic) plays a part in the overall call processing and the policy is stored somewhere inside the network. This similarity again suggests that a networked repository for policies and dynamic information (for example, IP addresses) with simultaneous access from the PSTN and IP network is an effective device for supporting integrated services.

The subject of telephone number translation has been addressed in the IETF Telephone Number Mapping (*enum*) working group (www.ietf.org/html.charters/enum-charter.html), which has been chartered to "define a DNS-based architecture and protocols for mapping a telephone number to a set of attributes (for example, URLs) which can be used to contact a resource associated with that number."

Codecs

When speech is carried on the Internet, it is of course carried in digital form. Speech is also carried digitally through most portions of modern telephone networks (although in the PSTN, it is still normally converted to analog form on the last mile of transmission over analog telephone lines). Having the speech signals available digitally provides the opportunity to use digital speech processing techniques, and particularly speech coders, which can compress the digital bit stream to low bit rates—with trade-offs against increased delay, implementation complexity/cost, and quality. In this section, we will discuss motivations for speech compression, review the basics of coding, discuss some specific coders, and look at the trade-offs that must be understood to decide which kind of coding is appropriate for specific applications (and, in particular, whether compression is desirable).

Motivations for Speech Coding in Internet-Telephony Integration

Classically, speech compression techniques have been used in situations where bandwidth is limited or very expensive. For example, prior to the development of high-bandwidth digital fiber-optic undersea cables, undersea telephone trunks were carried on very expensive analog coaxial cable systems, and the utilization of these expensive trunks was increased by the use of *voice activity detection* (VAD) techniques. The technique used by these early systems, known as *time assignment speech interpolation* (TASI), was to detect when speech was present on a given channel and then, in real time, switch it through to one of a set of undersea cable trunks. When the channel went silent due to a pause in the conversation (typically caused by Party A pausing to listen to Party B's response—in normal, polite conversation, there are only short intervals when both parties talk simultaneously!), the channel would be disconnected and the trunk given over to another active speaker. Given the activity factor of normal conversation, these systems could achieve compression of about 2:1.

Another situation in which the need for speech compression seems obvious is that of wireless transmission—for example, in cellular telephony systems. Over-the-air bandwidth is limited both by government regulation and by the potential for multiple users of the free-space channel to interfere with each other. In addition, due to the tremendously high growth rate of cellular telephony, more and more callers seek to use the same limited bandwidth. As a result, modern cellular telephony standards do indeed provide speech coder options, which achieve various levels of compression and increased utilization of the scarce wireless bandwidth.

Turning to the subject of this book—the integration of the Internet and telephony—the situation is somewhat less clear. On the telephony side, if we are talking about wireline telephony, the cost of bandwidth is a relatively small part of the total cost of providing service (see Chapter 12 for a more extensive discussion of this point). On the Internet side, one of the defining characteristics of the explosive growth pattern that we have seen in recent years has been the utilization of higher- and higher-bandwidth channels to interconnect nodes in the Internet. To a great degree, this is caused by (and, in turn, enables) the running of multimedia applications over the Internet and especially the World Wide Web, involving the transfer of large image files, audio and video streams, and so on. With so much bandwidth, and with so many applications apparently using a larger average bandwidth than ordinary telephone speech, why would anyone want to compress speech on the Internet?

In fact, there are several possible reasons. One simple reason is that bandwidth for access to the Internet is often quite severely constrained, as is the case for consumers who dial up using modems with rates of 56 kbps or lower. In this case, voice and all other active applications have to share a bandwidth that is narrower than that normally provided in the telephone network for speech alone. Another motivation may be integration with wireless networks. As noted earlier, wireless voice typically uses coding for speech compression in order to conserve the scarce, expensive over-the-air bandwidth. So, wireless voice over IP may employ compression for exactly the same reason. Even in the case of an end-to-end path that is only partly wireless, keeping the voice encoded in a compressed format would avoid the degradation of voice quality that can come with repeated encoding and decoding (so-called tandem encoding).

Another whole class of applications for voice coding on the Internet may be revealed if we allow ourselves to step outside the traditional telephony definitions of 4 kHz, point-to-point, real-time voice. For example, integrated messaging applications require the storage of voice signals, and compression can then be important in reducing storage requirements.

Similarly, the flexibility afforded by an all-digital medium may be used to encode voice (or audio) for higher quality, including preserving more of the bandwidth of the input signal and employing multichannel communication techniques (for example, stereo). Applications include the creation of highly realistic teleconferences and the transmission of music. For these applications, efficient coding techniques may be used to keep the consumption of bandwidth by the high-quality service to reasonable levels.

Broadcast applications constitute another class whose needs differ from those of traditional point-to-point telephony. Broadcasting to *n* locations can consume *n* times the bandwidth of a point-to-point transmission, so there is a high motivation to code for compression. At the same time, broadcast applications typically are more tolerant of delay, which means that more sophisticated and complex coding algorithms may be used without introducing noticeable impairments.

Voice Coding Basics

Some specific references are given on the subject of voice coding in our bibliography. In this section, our goal is to provide some intuitive understanding of how coders work so that the material that follows makes sense to the general reader.

Everyone probably understands that voices and other sounds in general may differ in frequency (or, in musical terms, *pitch*). A woman's voice is usually higher in frequency (or pitch) than a man's, and a child's may be higher still. The music of a bassoon is lower in frequency than that of a piccolo. Also, complex sounds actually consist of more than one frequency. In music, the overtones of the saxophone differ from those of the oboe, so that these two instruments sound different even if both are playing the same note. Similarly, we can distinguish between the voices of two people whom we know, even if their voices are about equal in overall pitch, due to the complex structure of frequencies produced by the human voice, which differs in detail from individual to individual.

An idea that is quite fundamental to voice coding is that the range of important frequencies in a given sound (and, in particular, the sound of the human voice) is limited. We need only reproduce this range of frequencies for the transmitted sound to be recognizable and useful. It is true that the quality and naturalness of the sound will be better if more frequencies are transmitted. However, we are all familiar with an example in which very useful voice transmission is accomplished by using a quite limited range of frequencies: In telephone networks, frequencies higher than 4 kHz (4000 vibrations per second) are not transmitted, and, in fact, the actual range is probably closer to between 200 and 3400 Hz. Nonetheless, we can not only understand what is said, but usually we can recognize and distinguish familiar voices as well.

Digital coding starts with *sampling* the continuous-sound waveform at discrete intervals (see Figure 3.10). An important theorem states that the waveform may be completely reproduced from samples if the sampling rate is at least twice as great as the highest frequency that is contained in the sound. Now you can see why we were so concerned with the range of frequencies to be transmitted—this tells us what sampling rate is needed. For telephone speech that is limited to 4 kHz, the sampling rate is $2 \times 4000 = 8000$ samples per second.

Each of these samples is a measurement, typically of an electrical voltage somewhere inside the coding system. However, in order to be carried in packets on the Internet (or, indeed, on a digital telephone network), the output of the coder needs to be a string of bits. This is accomplished by *encoding* each voltage measurement sample as a binary number. Another critical parameter is how many bits will be used to encode each sample. Research done over 40 years ago showed that excellent speech reproduction could be achieved with 8 bits per sample. At 8 bits per sample and 8000 samples per second, this implies a bit rate out of the coder of 64,000 bits per second (64 kbps).

The system that we have just described is the most basic form of digital coder, called a *pulse-code modulation* (PCM) system. In practice, one additional step is taken to improve the performance of such coders and, in fact, to ensure that 8 bits per sample is sufficient to encode the samples. This is *companding,* in which the dynamic range (range between maximum and minimum values) is compressed at the coder and then decompressed (expanded) at the decoder. Telephone systems in the United States and some other places

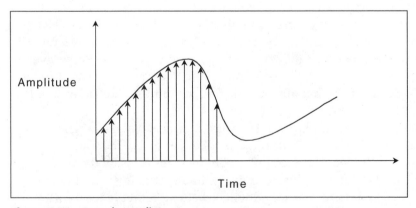

Figure 3.10   Sound sampling.

use a companding formula called μ-*law,* and those in Europe and some other places use a companding formula called *A-law,* leading to one of those troublesome international standards differences! Both the A- and μ-law systems have been standardized by ITU-T as G.711.

By the way, how does the decoder work? For PCM, it is relatively simple to describe. The sequence of 8-bit binary numbers is turned back into a string of voltage pulses, the magnitude of each pulse corresponding to the encoded voltage measurement. This string of pulses is then passed through a circuit called a *low-pass filter,* which interpolates between the pulses, producing a smooth signal. (In terms of frequency, the action of the low-pass filter is to remove irrelevant high-frequency components; in the case of standard telephony, everything above 4 kHz is removed.) What remains is a close reproduction of the original voice waveform with *quantization noise,* which represents the slightly inaccurate encoding of the voltage measurements as finite-length binary numbers.

Achieving a Lower Bit Rate

Very simply, the goal of compressed speech coding for telephony is to use less than 64 kbps of bandwidth while preserving desirable characteristics of the speech. Here we will briefly discuss some basic approaches to reducing the bit rate that is required for carrying digital speech below the nominal 64 kbps.

A simple variation of PCM that achieves a lower bit rate with still quite good quality is *differential PCM* (DPCM). In DPCM, information about the difference between succeeding samples is transmitted instead of their absolute value. This takes advantage of the fact that two succeeding samples will often be quite close in value. With a slightly more sophisticated variant, called *adaptive differential PCM* (ADPCM), it is easy to get quite excellent speech reproduction while using only half the bit rate of straight PCM (that is, using 32 kbps). ADPCM has been standardized by ITU-T as G.726.

To get lower bit rates, it is necessary to adopt much more sophisticated approaches. Some low-bit-rate coders attempt to take advantage of the fact that the input signal is known to be human speech. *Vocoding,* in which an electrical model of the human vocal tract is constructed and used as the basis of a low-bit-rate coder/decoder system, is a decades-old idea from speech research that has been made practical by advances in high-speed electronics. Besides vocoders, other types of very-low-bit-rate coders include *parametric coders* and *waveform interpolation coders.* The ITU-T has standardized a number of low-bit-rate coders, including the following:

- G.723.1, low-bit-rate coder for multimedia applications, 6.3 and 5.3 kbps

- G.728, 16-kbps low-delay code-excited linear prediction (LD-CELP) coder

- G.729, 8-kbps conjugate-structure algebraic-code-excited linear prediction (CS-ACELP)

For an excellent discussion of these low-bit-rate ITU coders, see Cox and Kroon (1996).

Since we are interested in integrating Internet and telephony, it is important to note that the coder bit rates we have quoted do not, of course, take into account various overheads that are introduced when voice is packetized, compared with circuit-switched voice. Packetization is quite a complex subject in its own right, and outside the scope of our present subject—speech coding. Suffice it to say that, depending on the specific choice of coder, packetization technique, and protocol stack, it is quite possible to use up most (or even all!) of the bandwidth gained in compression through packetization overhead. Other choices can result in a net bandwidth gain compared with uncompressed circuit-switched voice. Obviously, packetization is an area that requires careful attention if achieving actual bandwidth savings is important to the application.

Trade-offs

In spite of the truly impressive advances that have been made in the past few years both in developing more sophisticated algorithms for compression and in high-speed electronics to run them, the world of speech coding still provides many illustrations of the earthy adage: There's no such thing as a free lunch. In general, lower-bit-rate coders introduce more delay in the signal path, are more complex-expensive to implement, and involve more compromises to voice quality. This section discusses these trade-offs and is intended to help you decide whether you want to use voice compression for your application and, if so, how aggressive you can afford to be.

Delay

Voice communication can be highly sensitive to total end-to-end delay. Excessive delay interrupts the normal conversational pattern in which speakers reply to each other's utterances and also exacerbates the problem of echoes in communication circuits. Delay is the reason why links via geostationary satellites are, at present, only used on very thin traffic routes in the modern international telephone network. Even with echo cancellation systems in place, the hundreds of milliseconds of delay introduced by the trip up to the satellite and back is very disruptive to conversation, which you will notice immediately if you ever make a call over such a circuit. The strong preference is to use optical fiber routed over the earth's surface (or under the ocean) wherever it is feasible.

The most fundamental component of delay introduced by speech processing is called *algorithmic delay.* Algorithmic delay comes about because most speech coders work by doing an analysis on a batch of speech samples. Some minimum amount of speech is needed to do this analysis, and the time to accumulate this number of samples is an irreducible delay component—the algorithmic delay. Another component added by the coder is *processing delay*, the time for the coder hardware to analyze the speech and the decoder hardware to reproduce it. This component can be reduced by using faster hardware. Cox and Kroon (1996) state that for ease of communication, the total system delay, which includes these coder components plus the one-way communication delay, should be less than 200 ms. The algorithmic delay for G.729 and G.723.1 coders is 15 and 37.5 ms, respectively. Assuming typical processing delays and communication over a serial connection (such as a circuit-switched transport), operating at the bit rate of the coder, the total system delays will be 35 and 97.5 ms, respectively. If a packet network such as the Internet is involved, there may be an additional *packet filling delay*. For example, for G.729, the coder outputs 80 bits of compressed speech every 10 ms. If the packet size is 160 bits, this means we have to wait an additional 10 ms before we can transmit the packet, thereby increasing the overall system delay.

From an application point of view, you may want to avoid the use of aggressive low-bit-rate coding in situations where the quality of interaction counts for a lot—teleconferencing, for example, or calls that your salesforce makes to customers. By contrast, a one-way voice broadcast would not be much impaired by some extra delay. Another issue to look out for is added delay from other active electronics in the path.

Complexity

The issue of complexity is of direct concern to designers of equipment. The more demanding a speech processing algorithm is of processing power and memory, the bigger and more expensive the *digital signal processor* (DSP) or other specialized chip needs to be. For the purchaser of equipment, this primarily translates into an impact on price, but possibly to some other parameters of interest, such as power consumption in a wireless handset, which will determine how long you can talk before the battery runs out.

Quality

The tried-and-true method of measuring quality in voice communications, and the one that is still used to evaluate speech coders, is the subjective test of *mean opinion score* (MOS). This is a test in which people are asked to listen to the speech and rate its quality as bad, poor, fair, good, or excellent. Cox and Kroon (1996) have compiled the results of many MOS tests of ITU-T and other standardized coders.

Behind the seeming scientific nature of mean opinion score testing are many issues that are difficult to quantify. How do the coders perform in the presence of a variety of types of background noise? Can individual speakers be recognized by the sound of their voices? What if the sound is something other than voice (music, for example)? The best thing for a prospective system purchaser to do is listen, of course, and test the system in as close an approximation of the intended environment as possible.

The bottom line is that integration of the PSTN and the Internet presents opportunities to use very sophisticated, modern voice coding techniques, but it is up to you as the system developer or purchaser to decide whether the advantages are worth the cost and potential trade-offs in quality.

PART TWO

Standards

This part of the book provides you with an overview of the standardization efforts relative to interworking the PSTN and the Internet. This material can give only a snapshot of new standards projects and new forums that were initiated while we were writing. It is not even clear whether most of these new projects will produce tangible results. For this reason, we concentrate only on the core standards and established projects that are relevant to products and applications detailed in Part Three.

But even then, the amount of raw material comes to thousands of pages of specifications, and that fact alone thwarts any attempt to provide a specific technical survey of even a small subset of the standards mentioned in this book. Fortunately, books that cover many of the relevant standards exist, and we will reference those books here. In addition, we will provide references to key standards documents. We have tried to highlight the primary developments, direction, and status of standardization in the outlined areas, and to point out the compatibility and interdependence of the existing and developing standards.

We also tried to make each part of the book as self-contained as possible. For example, if you are only interested in products, you could skip this part altogether and proceed to Part Three. If you decide later that you need more technical information on a particular subject or would like to review standards a particular product is based on, you could read a corresponding chapter in this part. To make things easier, the following outline establishes some forward references to products and applications supported by their respective standards.

This part starts with the description of the relevant standards bodies. Chapter 4 covers the ITU-T standards on the ISDN, *common channel signaling*

(Signalling System No. 7), *Intelligent Network* (IN), and *computer-telephony integration* (CTI). Following that, Chapter 5 concentrates on IP telephony. In Chapter 6 we cover messaging, directory, and network management standards, in that order. Chapter 7, the last chapter in Part Two, is dedicated to the standards pertinent to remote dial-in access.

The Relevant Standards Bodies

Two major bodies have been involved in standards relevant to the subject of this book: the Internet Engineering Task Force (IETF) (www.ietf.org) and the International Telecommunications Union—Telecommunications Standardization Sector (ITU-T) (www.itu.int). ITU-T has also issued a set of data communications standards (the X-series) in collaboration with the International Organization for Standardization (ISO) (www.iso.ch). The ISO *Open Systems Interconnection* (OSI) suite has had much influence on the basic concepts and terminology presently used in the IETF, and many IETF protocols have the OSI genes.

Another important organization, formerly named the European Computer Manufacturers' Association, is now known only by its acronym, ECMA (www.ecma.ch/). ECMA is an international industry association chartered for standardizing information and communication systems.

The International Telecommunications Union (ITU), a specialized agency of the United Nations, has been standardizing everything related to traditional telephone networks since the time they first appeared—ITU began in the 1860s, standardizing telegraphy. Historically, almost all telephone networks were operated by government agencies, which explains the place of ITU in the United Nations. Membership in ITU is open to all governments that belong to the UN, while private sector network providers, equipment vendors, and other international organizations may hold individual memberships, as *Sector Members*, in one or more of the three Sectors of ITU: ITU-T (Telecommunication Standardization), ITU-R (Radiocommunication), and ITU-D (Telecommunication Development). The governments, or *Member States* as they are known in ITU, belong to the three ITU Sectors as a matter of right. In general, membership involves paying a membership fee.

For the period from 1997 to 2000, ITU-T has fourteen active *Study Groups*, each of which leads standardization in a particular area (e.g., transmission, operations and management, switching and signaling, multimedia, network management). Each Study Group further divides its work among Working Parties. Specific, focused studies are performed within the Working Parties in what are known as Questions.

Any member may submit ideas in a contribution to the relevant Study Group, and as work progresses and a draft standard is developed, it will be published in the official reports of the Study Group meetings. When the draft is determined to be sufficiently mature, it is sent to all Member States and Sector Members for final comment and then consideration for approval at a Study Group meeting. The results of this process are international standards called *ITU-T Recommendations.* This term reflects on the subtlety that the documents serve as Recommendations to Member States, which could (but do not have to) adopt them. With the role of the governments in standardizing telecommunications diminishing, the industry more and more views ITU-T Recommendations as standards. Although the process of preparing the Recommendations is based on the consensus of participants reached at the meetings, the Recommendations are presently approved by the Member States present at the Study Group meeting at which final text is considered for approval. When published by ITU-T, the Recommendations are available to anyone for a fee; however, the interim drafts and working documents are available free, but only to members.[1]

The Internet Engineering Task Force (IETF) [unlike its umbrella organization, the Internet Society (ISOC)] has no legal status and no defined membership. Nevertheless, for a nonexistent (at least legally) organization, the IETF has done a remarkable job in producing stable and widely implemented Internet standards. The IETF is divided into eight broad expertise areas: the Applications Area, Internet Area, Operations and Management Area, Routing Area, Transport Area, Security Area, User Services Area, and General Interest Area. Areas are in turn divided into working groups, which focus on specific subjects of standardization. The decisions are typically made online (by consensus—there is no voting in the IETF), and anyone with access to the Internet can participate in any working group and get hold of any IETF documents for free. The terminology involved in naming the IETF documents (as well as the conventions of referring to them in this book) requires some further elucidation.

A contribution to the IETF takes the form of an *Internet Draft.* Anyone can submit his or her ideas in such a document, which is published by the IETF upon request without prescreening for relevance or technical accuracy. The publication of an Internet Draft implies no IETF endorsement. The Internet

---

[1]It is high time to thank the International Telecommunications Union for generously granting us its authorization as a copyright holder for the reproduction of the ITU-T Recommendations material quoted in this chapter. Of course, the sole responsibility for selecting extracts for reproduction lies with us. ITU-T Recommendations can be obtained from:

International Telecommunications Union
General Secretariat—Sales and Marketing Services
Place des Nations
CH-1211 GENEVA 20 (Switzerland)
Telephone: +41 22 730 51 11   Telex: 421 000 uit ch
Telegram: ITU GENEVE   Fax: +41 22 730 51 94
X.400: S=Sales; P=itu; A=Arcom; C=ch   Internet: Sales@itu.ch

Drafts are working documents, which are stored by the IETF for a period of six months and then automatically removed. Some are working group documents, but many are just individual publications whose authors want the IETF to take a look at them. This book never refers to Internet Drafts. Such references are implicit: Whenever the work in progress is referred to, it always concerns a particular working group, whose IETF home page lists its all current Internet Drafts. The only IETF documents explicitly referred to in this book are called *Requests For Comments* (RFCs). RFCs are approved and published by the RFC editor (in many cases, the RFCs are developed by respective working groups and then approved by the IETF) and stored permanently under unique numbers.

The term *RFC*, however, can denote a nonstandard document (such an RFC can be either *informational* or *experimental*) as well as a standards track document. Unless otherwise specified, the RFCs referred to in this chapter are always the standards track ones. The maturity levels (based on the maturity of a specification, existence of interoperable implementations, and deployment) are *proposed standard*, *draft standard*, and *standard.* The criteria for assigning these levels (as part of the comprehensive specification of the Internet standards process) are published in RFC 2026. Finally, yet another subseries of the standards RFC is called *best current practice* (BCP), which, according to RFC 2026, is "designed to be a way to standardize practices and the results of community deliberations." RFC 2026, for example, is a BCP.

Although ITU-T had implicitly used (and referred to) IETF documents in the past, until recently it could not do so explicitly. Since 1996, however, cooperation between the two organizations has made progress, and as ISOC became a member of ITU-T, the official cross-group representation has been maintained on several projects. This cooperation has already resulted in reducing duplication of effort. For obvious reasons, in the area of the integrating Internet and telecommunications, this partnership is crucial to the success of future standards.

Other important standards bodies whose work is relevant to the subject of this book include:

- *The European Telecommunications Standards Institute* (ETSI) (www.etsi.org), which has played an important role both in developing telecommunications standards for the European Union and contributing to ITU-T. The ETSI Telecommunications and Internet Protocol Harmonization Over Networks (TIPHON) project has become an international effort dedicated to the architecture and protocol requirements in support of IP telephony.

- *The Institute of Electrical and Electronics Engineers, Inc.* (IEEE) (www.ieee.org). The IEEE has standardized local area network (LAN) protocols, among many other things.

being developed solely with the goal of supporting services (including ISDN supplementary services). The first IN standard was developed after Signalling System No. 7 was defined. The resulting protocol[2] uses the SS No. 7 switch-to-database[3] protocol as the transport mechanism.

In the United States, where IN implementation has long predated the standards, the American National Standards Institute (ANSI) version of the Transaction Capabilities Application Part (TCAP, later reduced by ITU-T to its current two-letter version, TC) contained the IN messages as part of the protocol. ITU-T, however, having realized that the generic transaction capabilities protocol has many uses (for example, mobility), spun off separate applications protocols (like INAP for IN). This is why ITU-T decided to change the acronym. The terminology confusion persists, but you can avoid confusion by always referring to the ITU-T terms. Since the ITU-T standards have been accepted by the United States as well as all other members of ITU, this decision is well justified.

Keep the preceding historical notes in mind as we delve into this somewhat overwhelming and convoluted subject matter. The history explains the order in which we chose to introduce the related standards: ISDN, SS No. 7, then IN. We start with the ISDN standards because they specify network services and access to networks and so deal more or less with the endpoints of the PSTN. The two latter topics, in contrast, deal with what is happening within the network.

The last section of this chapter addresses the standards relevant to the traditional enterprise telephone network. Namely, it deals with the "one-switch IN" standard, officially called *computer-telephony integration* (CTI), which is essential to the PBX products. The particular standard described there in some detail is called *Computer-Supported Telephony Applications* (CSTA).

Integrated Services Digital Network (ISDN)

Work on the ISDN standards was led by what was then Consultative Committee for International Telephony and Telegraphy (CCITT) Study Group XVIII (now ITU-T Study Group 13), with the services, operations and maintenance, accounting, and other specific topics dealt with by Study Groups competent in each specific subject. For example, the access signaling (call control) protocols[4] have been developed by Study Group 11, which published the Q-series Recommendations (hence the double naming scheme). There are several hundred ITU-T Recommendations on the ISDN. Table 4.1 contains a list of the I-series.

[2]Intelligent Network Application Part Protocol (INAP).
[3]Transaction Capabilities Application Part (TC).
[4]Specified in Recommendations I.450/Q.930–I.452/Q.931.

- *The ATM Forum* (www.atmforum.org) has had a major influence on the work on broadband ISDN in ITU-T and overall development of the concept and technology in support of quality of service.

- *The Telecommunications Industry Association* (TIA) (www.tiaonline.org) and T1 (www.t1.org). TIA and T1 have been developing American National Standards for wireless communications and the PSTN, respectively. Both have addressed interworking with IP networks.

ISDN, SS No. 7, IN, and CTI

This chapter is dedicated to the components of "traditional" telephony, that is, the standards on which the traditional PSTN and private enterprise telephone networks have been based. We start with sections dedicated to the ISDN and SS No. 7. [This material is essential to all three topics of the book—Internet access over dial-in lines, IP telephony support, and provision of the Internet-based services in the PSTN. In addition, this material is highly relevant to understanding the important work on tunneling of the ISDN access (Q.931) and Signalling System No. 7 messages within IP networks presently performed in the Signaling Transport (*sigtran*) working group of the IETF.]

As we noted in Chapter 2, common channel signaling predated the ISDN. (Common channel signaling, which is out-of-band signaling carried by a specialized data network, has replaced the in-band signaling carried by the voice circuits). As the ISDN services and access protocols were defined, the new standard for common channel signaling, called *Signalling System Number 7* (SS No. 7), was developed with the goal of supporting ISDN signaling. Among other things, SS No. 7 specified the switch-to-switch interface.[1] An umbrella set of standards known as *Intelligent Network* (IN), among other things, defines the protocols among the service control point, the intelligent peripheral, the external databases, and the switch—the basic elements of IN introduced in Chapter 2. The protocols are service independent, but they are

[1]ISDN user part (ISUP).

Table 4.1 The ISDN I-Series

RECOMMENDATION NUMBERS	FUNCTION
Recommendations I.110–I.199	Define the general structure of the ISDN (that is, terminology, description, modeling methods, and so on).
Recommendations I.200–I.299	Define service capabilities.
Recommendations I.310–I.399	Provide overall network aspects and functions (i.e., reference models; numbering, addressing, and routing; performance objectives; and requirements for protocols and network functions).
Recommendations I.420–I.699	Specify ISDN user-network interfaces.
Recommendations I.730–I.799	Specify Broadband ISDN (B-ISDN) equipment [i.e., Asynchronous Transfer Mode (ATM) equipment].

Some Recommendations in the series—or at least their original versions—have double numbers (for example, I.250/Q.930) to reflect numbering schemes of ITU-T study groups involved in the work. (In the preceding example, Q.930 is the SG 11 number.) Fortunately, there is a thorough book that addresses ISDN in great detail (see Stallings, 1989). For our purposes, only two aspects of the ISDN standards are important: a class of services now supported also by the IP-based systems (for example, IP PBXs), and signaling. In the following section we review only the relevant subset of ISDN standards.

As you may recall, with the ISDN the user can get several standardized channel types. The most important are:

B. 64-kbps digital channel for voice or data

D. 16- or 64-kbps digital for out-of-band signaling

Not all combinations of these channels are allowed by standards. The major regional agreements support two combinations:

- *Basic rate interface.* Includes two **B** channels and one **D** channel of 16 kbps. This combination is usually expressed as 2**B** + **D**.

- *Primary rate interface.* Includes 23 **B** channels and 1 **D** channel of 64 kbps. This combination is accordingly expressed as 23**B** + **D**, and it actually represents the primary rate in the United States and Japan. In Europe, it is 30**B** + **D**.

Again, the **B** channel can be used for both voice (for example, as a single channel with 8-bit samples made 8000 times a second) and data. The standard does not specify bandwidth breakup, nor does it specify any formatting.

The services are divided into three types:

1. *Bearer services.* The network transports only real-time voice or video stream.

2. *Teleservices.* The network combines the bearer services with information services, such as Yellow Pages.

3. *Supplementary services.* Cannot be used alone but only as add-ons to the two former groups.

Even though this service taxonomy was devised long ago, it is still fundamental in that it separates basic call circuit provision from service provision.[5]

In the PSTN, the signaling protocols that support these services are carried between two pairs of entities:

1. Station equipment and the network [between the customer premises equipment (CPE) and the ISDN switch].

2. The switches in the network.

Switches, as a network interface, are part of SS No. 7 (addressed in the next section). Here we concentrate on the CPE-to-switch network layer signaling protocol called *Digital Subscriber Signalling Number One* (DSS1), but much more often referred to as Q.931, by the name of the ITU-T Recommendation that specifies it.[6]

DSS1 specifies a call model and a set of messages grouped in the following categories according to the states of the call:

■ *Call establishment messages.* ALERTING, CALL PROCEEDING, CON-NECT, CONNECT ACKNOWLEDGE, PROGRESS, SETUP, and SETUP ACKNOWLEDGE.

■ *Call information phase messages.* SUSPEND, SUSPEND ACKNOWLEDGE, SUSPEND REJECT, RESUME, RESUME ACKNOWLEDGE, and RESUME REJECT.

■ *Call clearing messages.* DISCONNECT, RELEASE, and RELEASE COM-PLETE.

---

[5]In particular, the supplementary services addressed by ITU-T Recommendations I.250 through I.299 (seven groups of services) include direct dialing in, conference calling, and call-waiting, and can be provided independent of the bearer service. Mixing and matching the provision of bearer services of one type of network (for example, the PSTN or the Internet) with the provision of supplementary services by another type of network is the topic of this book.

[6]Actually, Recommendation Q.931 specifies the protocol for basic call control. Other relevant Recommendations in the series are Q.930 (on general aspects), Q.932 (on generic procedures for supplementary services), Q.933 (on specification for frame-mode control), Q.939 (on typical service indicator codes), and Q.950 (on structure and principles of supplementary services protocols).

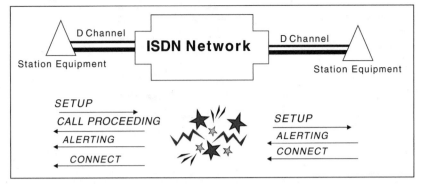

Figure 4.1 Example of the DSS1 (Q.931) call setup.

- *Miscellaneous messages.* (Generally speaking, these are not dependent on call state) *CONGESTION CONTROL, FACILITY, NOTIFY, STATUS,* and *STATUS ENQUIRY.*

Figure 4.1 demonstrates an example message exchange to set up a call.

Signalling System No. 7 (SS No. 7)

The SS No. 7 standards are essential to a wide range of convergence products for a number of reasons, of which we list three here. First, as mentioned in Chapter 2, Internet access servers need to access the PSTN signaling network by means of the SS7 gateways. Second, IP telephony gateways need to inter- act with the PSTN switches in order to establish PC-to-phone (or phone-to- PC) calls and IP trunking. Third, IP telephony gateways, soft switches, and access servers need to access the PSTN service control. For some of these pur- poses, SS No. 7 needs to be ported into the IP environment (that is, carried by IP-based networks), which, as mentioned before, is one activity carried by the IETF *sigtran* working group.

SS No. 7 was standardized (based on the common channel experience) in order to satisfy the need for a common signaling interface both within and across the national borders. Another benefit of standardization has been cost reduction through multivendor interoperability. As it happens, European and American SS No. 7 versions differ from one another, and even in the United States implementations in some interexchange carriers' networks differ from those of local exchange carriers. Nevertheless, signaling across networks works very well, at least as far as the provision of the basic call is concerned.

The overall objective of SS No. 7 is to provide a reliable means of informa- tion transfer in support of call control; remote control; and operations, man- agement, and administration. ITU also specifies SS No. 7 measurements and

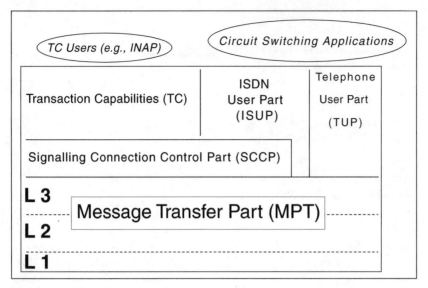

Figure 4.2   The SS No. 7 stack.

performance requirements. When printed double-sided and stacked one page on top of another, the SS No. 7 ITU-T Recommendations Series (Q.7xx—starting with Recommendation Q.700) is about a yard high. These Recommendations define all aspects of a four-layer protocol stack as depicted in Figure 4.2.

There are two types of SS No. 7 application users:

1. Applications that use service-related (but not circuit-related) transactions between the switches and network databases.

2. Switching applications that rely on the exchange of circuit-related information in order to set up, test, maintain, and tear down trunks.

Applications of the first type (for example, Intelligent Network) use the Transaction Capabilities Application Part protocol; applications of the second type use either the *Telephone User Part* (TUP) protocol[7] or *ISDN User Part* (ISUP), which has been the SS No. 7 response to the ISDN. Both TC and ISUP rely on the *Signalling Connection Control Part* (SCCP) protocol, which in turn runs on top of the *Message Transfer Part* (MTP), the lowest layer in the SS No. 7 stack. ISUP also uses MTP directly; TAP uses only MTP.[8]

The rest of this section sheds a bit more light on MTP, SCCP, TC, and ISUP, respectively.

---

[7]TUP predates the ISDN and is not further discussed in this book—for more information, please consult ITU-T Recommendations Q.721 through Q.725

[8]There are other users of SCCP [notably, the Operation, Maintenance, and Administration Part (OMAP)] as described in Recommendations Q.750 through Q.755, which are neither shown in Figure 4.2 nor discussed in this book.

Message Transfer Part (MTP)

As Figure 4.2 demonstrates, MTP[9] has three levels. The first two levels correspond to the physical and data link layers of the OSI model, respectively. The third level (Level 3) performs certain functions (such as routing and data delivery) of the OSI network and transport layers. In addition, MTP is responsible for the network management functions associated with the control of routing tables and other network configuration data.

Physically, MTP can be implemented in the endpoints (that is, switches, network databases, or operation and maintenance centers) or *service transfer points* (STPs), or both. The messages exchanged between any pair of these elements may traverse more than one intermediate STP. MTP does not guarantee in-sequence arrival and otherwise provides an unreliable connectionless transport mechanism to its users.

Each endpoint and each STP are identified by a unique *point code,* which is an exact equivalent of an IP address in the Internet. The MTP *routing label* contains three parts: the *originating point code* (OPC), *destination point code* (DPC), and *signaling link selection* (SLS). (The SLS field is used, among other things, for load sharing among STPs.) MTP can assign a specific hard link value [called *signaling link code* (SLC)] to an SLS, which is always done for MTP management information messages.

In order to recognize the user (for example, SCCP or ISUP) of the incoming message, MTP employs a combination of the *service indicator* (identifying the user) and a 2-bit-long *network indicator* (which, in combination with OPC and DPC, determines whether national or international signaling is involved) fields.

Note that MTP procedures include congestion control, of which MTP informs its users.

Signaling Connection Control Part (SCCP)

SCCP,[10] described in Recommendations Q.711 through Q.716, provides both connectionless and connection-oriented transport services. The services are grouped into the following four classes (enumerated from 0):

0 Basic connectionless class, which does not guarantee in-sequence delivery.

1 In-sequence-delivery connectionless class.

2 Basic connection-oriented class.

3 Flow-control connection-oriented class.

[9]MTP is defined in Recommendations Q.701 through Q.704, Q.706, and Q.707.
[10]SCCP is described in Recommendations Q.711 through Q.716.

SCCP peers address each other by the DPC–global title–*subsystem number* (SSN) triplet. *Global title* is defined in Recommendation Q.700 as a set of "dialled digits or another form of address that will not be recognized in the SS No. 7 network." The subsystem number identifies a user part (ISUP, for the purposes of this book) or TC application entities.

When the connection-oriented classes services are used, SCCP provides a reliable transport mechanism. During connection establishment, certain routing functions are provided by SCCP as well (in addition to those provided by MTP), as noted in Recommendation Q.711.

Transaction Capabilities (TC) Application Part

TC[11] is most typically used as a protocol between a switch and a network database, but it can also be used[12] between two network databases. For the purposes of this book, the primary user of TC is Intelligent Network, but there are other users (such as mobile service applications, administration of closed user groups, and transaction-oriented operations and maintenance applications). The main feature of all these applications is best defined through an affirmation—they are transaction-oriented—and a negation— they are not circuit-related.

The word *transaction-oriented* simply means that TC is designed to support the request/response type of communications, although in reality the protocol has evolved to support a dialogue of multiple requests and responses issued by either side of the communications link. Figure 4.3 depicts the place of TC in SS No. 7 and its structure.

First of all, TC has two sublayers: the *component sublayer* (CSL) and *transaction sublayer* (TSL). We don't concentrate on the TSL in this book, but we should describe the CSL, which provides the actual interface to the TC user. The CSL is responsible for:

1. Associating the user's requests (whose nature is discussed in a later section) with the responses.

2. Handling all abnormalities.

In a nutshell, the CSL provides the appearance of a (remote) procedure call to the user. In other words, CSL operations can be viewed (and implemented) by a programmer as procedure calls. To this end, TC is partially aligned with the capabilities of ITU-T Recommendations X.219 and X.229, developed jointly by ITU-T and the ISO. The CSL messaging unit is called a *component*. The user initiating a transaction issues an *INVOKE* component, which con-

---

[11]TC is described in ITU-T Recommendations Q.770 through Q.779.

[12]This use is noted in Recommendation Q.771.

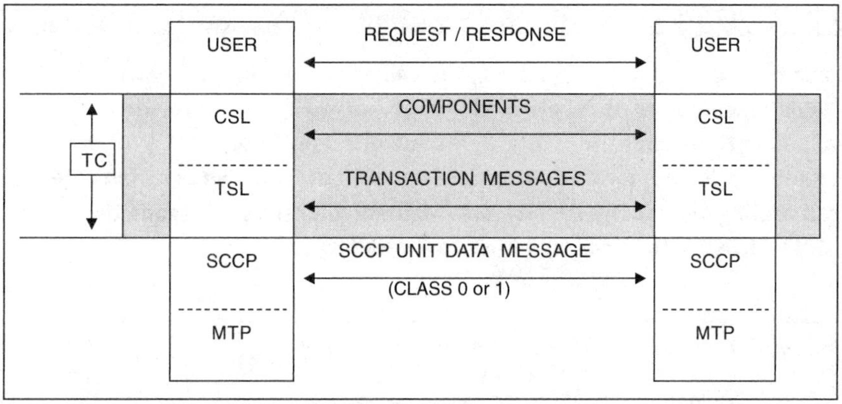

Figure 4.3   Transaction capabilities (TC) application part.

tains the *operation code* and arguments of the *operation*. Recommendation Q.771 defines four classes of operations in respect to the expected response:

1. Both success and failure are reported.
2. Only failure is reported.
3. Only success is reported.
4. Neither success nor failure is reported.

The response can also carry rejection to perform the requested operation. What is most interesting is that the responder may, in turn, send its own *INVOKE* component *before* returning a response, by means of *linking* the components into a dialogue. (A classical example of such dialogue is the *freephone* service. When a switch asks the service control point to translate a number, the latter requests that the switch connect to the device that plays announcement and collects digits. After the service control gets what it needs, it finally sends the response back to the switch.) The response components are:

- *RETURN RESULT NOT LAST.* Contains the list of parameters defining the result, and also indicates that other *RETURN* components are going to be issued (thus, the response may be *segmented*).

- *RETURN RESULT LAST.* Contains the list of parameters defining the result.

- *REJECT.* Contains the problem code (for example, malformed component).

- *ERROR.* Contains the error code (the error being the result of performing the operation).

TC is based *only* on the connectionless capabilities (that is, classes 0 and 1) of SCCP and uses the same addressing mechanism as SCCP.

ISDN END-TO-END CALL SETUP

In the example illustrated by Figure 4.4, the calling party terminal sends a Q.931 SETUP message to its local switch, which parses it, finds it correctly formed, and in turn sends the ISUP INITIAL ADDRESS MESSAGE (IAM) (of the forward setup category) to the appropriate transit (tandem) switch as indicated in its call routing table. Concurrently, the originating local switch sends the Q.931 CALL PROCEEDING message back to the calling party.

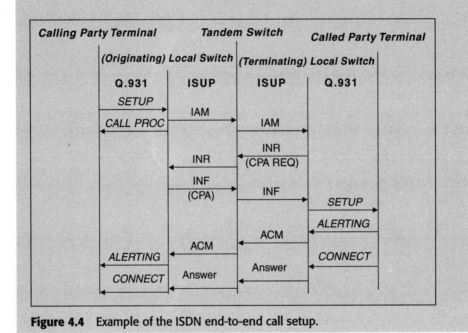

Figure 4.4 Example of the ISDN end-to-end call setup.

ISDN User Part (ISUP)

As mentioned, SS No. 7 was adapted to interworking with Q.931, and so became the system of choice for the ISDN network support for call management. Call management is in turn realized through switch-to-switch signaling. ISUP[13] is the protocol used for switch-to-switch signaling.

ISUP entities address each other with the MTP addressing scheme, augmented by *circuit identification,* which refers to a specific trunk.

The ISUP call model views three call phases:

1. Call setup.

2. Conversation (includes pure data exchange).

3. Call teardown.

---

[13]ISUP is described in ITU-T Recommendations Q.761 through Q.764 and Q.766.

Meanwhile, the tandem switch finds the terminating local switch in its routing table and forwards the IAM message to it. It so happens that the *calling party address* (CPA) is not sent as part of the IAM, but the terminating switch decides that it needs the CPA to complete the call. For this reason, the terminating switch sends the ISUP INFORMATION REQUEST (INR) message (of the general setup category) with the appropriate parameter (called a *request indicator*), indicating that the CPA is needed, back to the tandem switch, which passes it on to the originating switch.

The originating switch decides that it can comply with the request, and does so by issuing the ISUP INFORMATION message (also of the general setup category), which is propagated to the terminating local switch. The terminating switch sends the Q.931 SETUP message to the called party terminal, which responds with the Q.931 ALERTING message. The terminating switch also sends the ISUP ADDRESS COMPLETE MESSAGE (ACM) (of the backward setup category) on the backward path. When the originating switch receives this message, it informs the calling party that the alerting of the called party has begun by issuing the Q.931 ALERTING message in turn. By that time the path has been established.

When the calling party answers the call, its station sends the Q.931 CONNECT message to the terminating local switch, which follows up with the ISUP ANSWER message (of the call supervision category). The tandem switch does the same. Finally, the originating switch sends the Q.931 connect message back to the calling party terminal. The ISDN B-channel between the calling and called parties has now been established.

Accordingly, the ISUP messages are used to establish, maintain, and terminate different phases of a call. In addition, calls originating from ISDN terminals may be supplied with more detailed call progress information.

ISUP employs two methods—*link-by-link* (which passes messages through all intermediate exchanges, where they can be modified, hot-potato-style) and *end-to-end* messages that are exchanged between the ISUP endpoints (for example, local exchanges or international gateways). The end-to-end method typically employs either the connectionless or connection-oriented services of the SCCP; employing the latter makes things much simpler.

Unfortunately, there are too many ISUP messages to describe here. (Just the minimum internationally recognized set contains 29!) Instead, we list the basic message categories, followed by a call setup example:

- *Forward setup.* The messages in this category are involved in setting up a call with particular characteristics in the direction toward the called party.

- *Backward setup.* The messages in this category complete the call establishment (when it is possible) in the direction from the exchange containing the called party toward the calling party. Accounting and charging procedures belong in this category.

- *General setup.* The messages in this category carry additional call-related information needed to set up a call.

- *Call supervision.* The messages in this category are notifications of events like the call being answered, the circuit being released, or the need for an international operator intervention.

- *Circuit supervision.* The messages in this category are all kinds of notifications of the events related to circuits allocated for a call.

- *Circuit group supervision.* The messages (primarily of request/response type) in this category relate to circuit groups rather than individual circuits, and are used for network management purposes (for example, as preventive measures—such as call blocking on the indicated trunk groups, or circuit group status queries).

- *In-call modification.* The messages in this group support modification of the existing call characteristics (for example, a change from a voice call to a data call) or invoking a particular medium (facility).

- *End-to-end.* The messages in this group include user-to-user signaling independent of call control messages.

Intelligent Network

As we mentioned in Chapter 2 (and will further elaborate on in Part Three), the Intelligent Network technology is at the heart of PSTN service provision. The whole range of convergence products and services (such as Internet call-waiting, click-to-dial, and universal mailbox, just to mention a few) rely on and expand this technology.

The Intelligent Network standards are published by ITU in the Q.12*xy* series.[14] The IN architecture, in accordance with *open distributed processing*

[14]The index *x* indicates whether a Recommendation is of a general nature (that is, applicable to all versions of IN) or refers to a particular capability set (CS). The value 0 indicates that a particular Recommendation in the series is general; otherwise it indicates the specific CS. So far, CS-1 and CS-2 Recommendations have been published, CS-3 is scheduled for approval in 2000, and work on CS-4 is in progress. The index *y* specifies a specific topic of a Recommendation: *0* indicates that the Recommendation is an introduction to a series, and 1 denotes the subject of the principles of IN architecture. Thus, Recommendation Q.1201 is dedicated to general principles, Recommendation Q.1211- to CS-1-specific principles, and so on. The value of 9 is reserved for the IN User Guide. The remaining *y* values represent the relation of respective Recommendations to the IN architecture.

(ODP) principles, is viewed in terms of *planes:* the *service plane* is concerned only with the service description in terms of service features; the *global functional plane* deals with the *service-independent building blocks* (SIBs); the *distributed functional plane* addresses the elements of the architecture involved in the IN message exchange in terms of *functional entities* (FEs) (that is, the objects that are not associated with any *box*) and *information flows* (IFs), which model the message exchange among FEs; and the *physical plane* defines the actual boxes, called *physical entities* (PEs), and maps the FEs to PEs.[15]

As with most other ITU-T standards, the IN Recommendations are being adopted by regional standards bodies for use in their respective countries; however, we address only the ITU-T standards. You can find a detailed description of the IN standards up to CS-2 in Faynberg et al. (1997), but the text of the ITU-T Recommendations and their regional counterparts is, naturally, the ultimate reference.

Although the IN standards have provided in both IN CS-1 and CS-2 an effective model for service creation by specifying the so-called *service-independent building blocks* (SIBs),[16] the standardization of SIBs stopped after CS-2. Because standardization efforts ended, and the existing SIBs were not designed for interworking the PSTN and the Internet, we do not cover them.

The functional architecture and the mechanism for triggering the interactions between its elements are essential topics related to capability sets, addressed in the sections that follow. Figure 4.5 describes a subset of the presently standardized FEs and their interconnections.[17]

The IN FEs are grouped according to their role in supporting IN: FEs involved in service execution and FEs involved in service creation and management.

The service execution FEs are:

- *Call control agent function (CCAF).* Provides user access capabilities. It may be viewed as a proxy for a telephone (or ISDN terminal) through which a user interacts with the network.

- *Call control function (CCF).* Provides the basic switching capabilities available in any (IN or non-IN) switching system. These include the capabilities to establish, manipulate, and release calls and connections. It is the CCF that provides the trigger capabilities discussed in Chapter

---

[15]The topics of the IN Recommendations result in the rest of the values of index *y:* 2 for Service Plane Recommendations, 3 for the Global Functional Plane Recommendations, 4 for Distributed Functional Plane Recommendations, and 5 for the Physical Plane Recommendations. Finally, 8 denotes IN Application Part Protocol (INAP) Recommendations, which are what IN is ultimately all about.

[16]SIBs have been specified in ITU-T Recommendations Q.1203 (general aspects), Q.1213 (CS-1), and Q.1223 (CS-2).

[17]In the main text of Recommendation Q.1224, CS-2 adds the non-call-related FEs to those defined here, but they play no role in supporting interworking with the IP network.

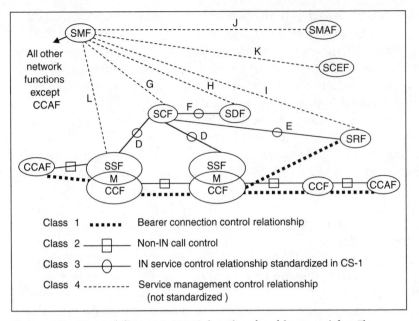

Figure 4.5 IN capability set 1 (CS-1) functional architecture (after Fig 3/Q.1211).

Source: ITU-T Recommendation Q.1211: Figure 3.

2; however, another object called the *service switching function* (SSF) is needed to support the recognition of triggers as well as interactions with the service control. The SSF and CCF are supposed to be colocated (that is, they cannot be placed in different PEs).

- *Service control function (SCF).* Executes service logic. It provides capabilities to influence call processing by requesting the SSF/CCF and other service execution FEs to perform specified actions. Implicitly, the SCF provides mechanisms for introducing new services and service features independent of switching systems. It is therefore the function that interworks (via applicable gateways) with the IP hosts in support of joint service control. Two main principles of both CS-1 and CS-2 standards are *single-endedness* (that is, the service logic is aware of only one relation with the SSF/CCF for the purpose of a given terminating or originating call process) and *single point of control* (that is, only one instance of service logic may be in contact with the SSF/CCF for the purpose of a given terminating or originating call process).

- *Specialized resource function (SRF).* Provides a set of real-time capabilities, which Recommendation Q.1204 calls *specialized*. These capabilities include playing announcements and collecting user input [either dual-tone-multi-frequency (DTMF) or voice, depending on the facilities]. The SRF is also responsible for conference bridging, fax support, and certain types of protocol conversion as well as text-to-speech (and vice versa) conversion. The SRF is crucial to supporting services like click-to-fax. To this end, the SRF also interworks with IP hosts, although—unlike the SCF—it supports the delivery of a service rather than the control of it.

- *Service data function (SDF).* Provides generic database capabilities to either the SCF or another SDF.

The following three service creation and management FEs are defined in ITU-T Recommendation Q.1204:

- *Service creation environment function (SCEF).* Responsible for developing (programming) and testing service logic, which is then sent to the *service management function* (SMF).

- *Service management function (SMF).* Deploys the service logic (originally developed within the SCEF) to the service execution FEs, and otherwise administers these FEs by supplying user-defined parameters for customization of the service and collecting from them the billing information and service execution statistics.

- *Service management agent function (SMAF).* Acts as a computer terminal that provides the user interface to the SMF.[18]

These entities serve to complete the architecture and reflect the industry development. No associated protocols have been defined by ITU-T.

As you may recall, the fundamental idea of IN is to open the basic switching process (run by switches) to external influence. This is done by defining and standardizing the call model.[19]

Figure 4.6 depicts the CS-2 *Basic Call State Model* (BCSM), which is the latest released standard. BCSM models both the originating and terminating basic call processes, which are depicted in Figures 4.6 and 4.7, respectively. In

---

[18]Because of the highly competitive nature of service creation, very little has been said about it in the standards documents. One natural question that arises is why there is a user interface agent (terminal) for service management (that is, SMAF), but none for service creation. Although a review of available IN-related products is outside of the scope of this book, at this point we observe that some vendors have separate systems for service creation and service management so that each system has a distinct user interface. Other vendors implement the service creation environment and service management environment within the same system, which requires only one user agent function. Although an architecture that supports the service creation environment agent function (SCEAF) had been accepted by ITU and the augmented architecture had been considered by the industry, this architecture has not yet been reflected in the text of any Recommendation. On the other hand, given that the user-interface-related issues of service creation and service management are outside the scope of standardization, the issue is moot, and neither the absence nor the presence of a function relevant to the user interface is significant.

[19]Recommendations Q.1204, Q.1214, and Q.1224 standardize the call model for the general case, CS-1, and CS-2, respectively.

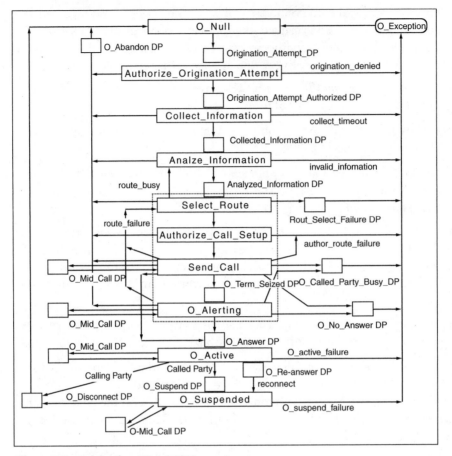

Figure 4.6   Originating CS-2 BCSM.

Source: ITU-T Recommendation Q.1224: Figure 4-4.

both processes, the primary states of calls as seen by a switch, depicted within rectangles are termed *points in call* (PICs). In addition, certain transitions lead to other states called *detection points* (DPs). It is at DPs that the switch may interrupt its processing by sending a message to the SCF. Each DP may be either *armed* or *unarmed*. As far as IN is concerned, being armed is the first essential prerequisite for being active, for only when a DP is armed is the external service logic (within the SCF) informed that the DP has been encountered.

A DP may be armed either *statically* (from the SMF, as the result of the service feature provisioning) or *dynamically* (by the SCF). If it is statically armed, the DP remains armed until the SMF disarms it—as long as the service that needs it is to be offered; if it is dynamically armed, the DP will remain armed for no longer than the duration of a particular SCF-to-SSF relationship. A statically armed DP is called a *trigger detection point* (TDP); a dynamically armed

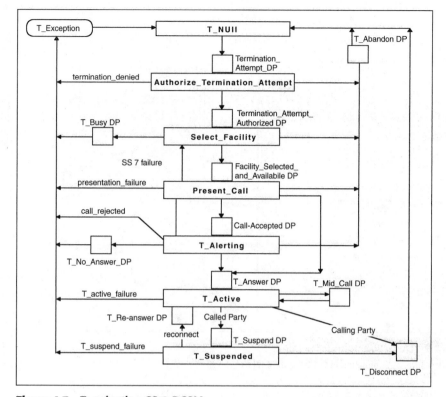

Figure 4.7 Terminating CS-2 BCSM.

Source: ITU-T Recommendation Q.1224: Figure 4-5.

DP is called an *event detection point* (EDP). The DP nomenclature is illustrated in Figure 4.8.

The DP nomenclature is essential for understanding how IN can interacts with the IP networks. When a service originates from the Internet, the DPs in the PSTN may be armed only dynamically. When, on the other hand, a service originates from the PSTN, all DPs that can invoke it must be armed beforehand (but other DPs can be armed dynamically in the process of service delivery). These cases are respectively addressed by the IETF PSTN/Internet INTernetworking (*pint*) working group (www.ietf.org/html .charters/pint-charter.html) and the Service in the PSTN/IN Requesting Internet Service (*spirits*) working group (www.ietf.org/html.charters/ spirits-charter.html) in cooperation with ITU-T SG 11.

Figure 4.9 depicts the distribution of the IN functional entities among the subset of physical entities in CS-1. (For purposes of our discussion, we have reduced this subset to the bare minimum.) The physical entities are:

- *Service switching point (SSP).* A switch that provides access to IN capabilities.

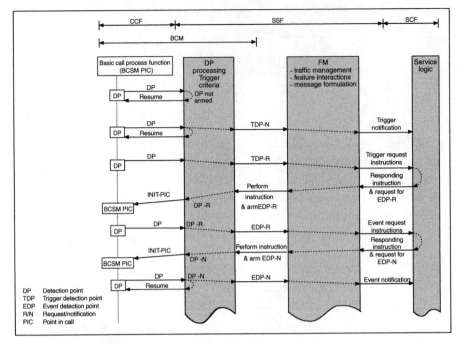

Figure 4.8 Detection point processing.

Source: ITU-T Recommendation Q.1214: Figure 4-[E]10.

- *Service control point (SCP).* A general-purpose computer that has access to the SS No. 7 network for communicating with SSPs and IPs.

- *Service data point (SDP).* Contains only the SDF. The SCP can access data in an SDP either directly or through a signaling network.

- *Intelligent peripheral (IP).* Its function is primarily to support the SRF. However, it may also include the SSF/CCF to provide external access to resources.

- *Adjunct (AD).* Functionally equivalent to an SCP, but connected to a single switch via a high-speed network, not the SS No. 7 network.

- *Service node (SN).* Similar to an AD, but in addition to performing a role of an SCP, it can perform the role of an IP. The SN connects to switches via the ISDN interface. (As you will see in Part Three, present implementations often include the SCP and small SSP as part of SN offers; however, those SCPs and SSPs act independently rather than as part of the group of standard SN functions.)

The Intelligent Network Application Part (INAP) protocol is defined[20] as a TC user.

---

[20]In Recommendations Q.1208, Q.1218, and Q.1228.

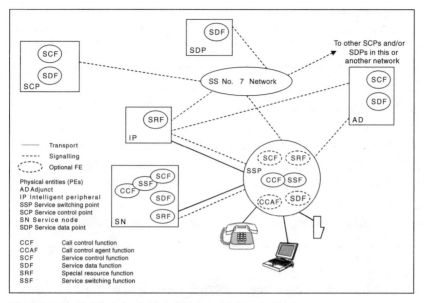

Figure 4.9 IN CS-1 physical architecture (after Q.1215).

Source: ITU-T Recommendation Q.1215: Figure 1.

Computer-Supported Telephony Applications (CSTA)

The standards of this section are relevant to the computer-telephony integration (CTI) technology, which is sometimes referred to as "one-switch IN." The basic goal of the technology is to provide the service platform to a PBX switch on a general-purpose computer and thus separate call and service control from connection control. The particular Computer-Supported Telephony Applications (CSTA) standards described here are the ones on which

Table 4.2 ISO CSTA Standards

ISO/IEC DIS 18051 (ECMA-269), Information Technology—Telecommunications And Information Exchange Between Systems—Services For Computer Supported Telecommunications Applications (CSTA) Phase III
ISO/IEC DIS 18052 (ECMA-285), Information Technology—Telecommunications And Information Exchange Between Systems—Protocol For Computer Supported Telecommunications Applications (CSTA) Phase III
ISO/IEC DIS 18053 (ECMA TR/72), Information Technology—Telecommunications And Information Exchange Between Systems—Glossary Of Definitions, And Terminology For Computer Supported Telecommunications Applications (CSTA) Phase III

Table 4.3 Pre-ISO CSTA Specifications

ECMA TR/52, Computer Supported Telecommunications Applications (CSTA), 1990
ECMA-179, Services for Computer Supported Telecommunications Applications (CSTA) Phase I, 1992
ECMA-180, Protocol for Computer Supported Telecommunications Applications (CSTA) Phase I, 1992
ECMA TR/68, Scenarios for Computer Supported Telecommunications Applications (CSTA) Phase II, 1994
ECMA-217, Services for Computer Supported Telecommunications Applications Phase II, 1994
ECMA-218, Protocol for Computer Supported Telecommunications Applications (CSTA) Phase II, 1994

the traditional PBX products have been based. As the PBXs migrate to IP platforms, the PBX switches are being replaced (by local area networks, for example), but the CSTA part remains the same. Adherence to CSTA standards remains an important requirement for the modern IP PBXs.

Computer-Supported Telephony Applications (CSTA) is a set of CTI standards initially developed by ECMA. The latest version of CSTA (Phase III) was also approved as an ISO international standard in July 1999. Table 4.2 lists the appropriate ISO standards.

Although these documents fully specify the CSTA services and protocol, the documents from the preceding phases (listed in Table 4.3) could be helpful in the process of learning CSTA.

There are other standards applicable to the CTI area. One of them, *Switch-Computer Application Interface* (SCAI), is thoroughly described in Grinberg (1995), which we highly recommend as excellent reading not only on SCAI but also on the subject of CTI in general.

CSTA achieves computer-telephony integration through an approach based on *open distributed processing* (ODP). ODP was developed jointly by the ISO and ITU-T and standardized in ITU-T Recommendations X.901 through X.904.

Table 4.4 Grouping of CSTA Operations

Capability Exchange	System	Monitoring
Snapshot	Call control	Call-associated features
Media attachment	Routing	Physical device features
Logical device features	Input-output	Data collection
Voice unit	Call detail record	Vendor-specific extensions

Table 4.5 Examples of CSTA Call Control Operations

CALL CONTROL OPERATION	FUNCTION
Alternate call	Places an existing call on hold and then retrieves a previously held or alerting call at the same device
Camp on call	Queues a call at a busy device until it becomes available
Clear connection	Releases a device from a call
Conference call	Merges a held call and an active call at a conferencing device
Dial digits	Dials digits for an initiated call
Make predictive call	Establishes a call between two devices and presents it to the calling device only after the called device is alerted or answers the call
Park call	Moves and queues a connected call to another device
Single-step conference call	Adds a device to an existing call

General functional entities—switching function, computing function, and special resource function (*specialized resource function* in IN parlance)—are defined to support services over a combination of computing and telecommunications networks. Normally auxiliary to switching or computing function, special resource function provides specialized capabilities such as voice response and fax. The functional entities and the relationship between them are then studied without regard to their physical realization. As a result, an application supported by these functions, such as call center, appears to the human or machine user as though it is integrated in a single network. (You may have noticed the resemblance of Intelligent Network to the CSTA approach and terminology. This is not surprising, because the concepts as well as the purposes of CSTA are very similar to those of IN. The difference between Intelligent Network and CSTA is in their respective target realization environments: IN is for PSTN service control; CSTA is for control of private branch exchanges.)

Table 4.6 Examples of CSTA Routing Operations

ROUTING OPERATION	FUNCTION
Route register	Registers a routing server
Route request	Requests the routing server to provide a destination for a call
Route reject	Indicates a call should be returned to the originating network for alternate routing

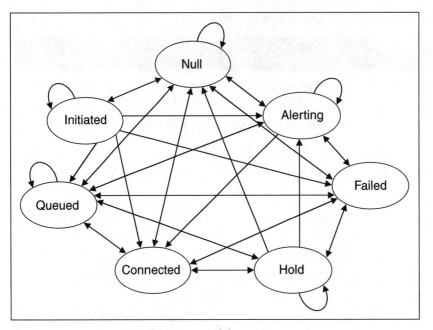

Figure 4.10   CSTA connection state model.
Source: ECMA-269: Figure 6-17.

CSTA defines a set of operations that a computer can request a switch to perform or vice versa. Based on Remote Operations,[21] these operations, performed at the OSI application layer, are of the request/response type. According to their functions, the CSTA operations are grouped as demonstrated in Table 4.4.

The number of operations in each group varies. Altogether, there are 25 call control operations and 9 routing ones. Some examples shown in Tables 4.5 and 4.6.

A basic concept of CSTA is *connection*, which is defined as a relationship between a CSTA device and a call in which the CSTA device is involved. (A *CSTA device* is an entity, such as button, line, or trunk group, used to access telecommunications services; a *call* is a switching function communications relationship, generally between two or more CSTA devices.) Transition from one connection state to another is caused by either a user action or a CSTA operation. State transitions can be observed by monitoring associated events or by requesting snapshot operations on the associated call or device. Figure 4.10 demonstrates the CSTA connection state model.

With that, we conclude the discussion of standards related to "traditional" telephony. Chapter 5 introduces the elements of the multimedia (primarily, IP telephony) standards.

---

[21]As defined in ITU-T Recommendation X.219.

IP Telephony-Related Standards

As its name suggests, this chapter deals with the standards that are related to multimedia technology. Of these, IP telephony is the technology that is most relevant to the subject of this book. We start with the IETF standards for the real-time transport. (Incidentally, these standards are used by both the IETF and ITU-T.) We proceed by addressing the ITU-T H.323 and T.120 protocol suites. Then, we return to the IETF standards on *Session Initiation Protocol* (SIP) and *Session Description Protocol* (SDP). These are especially important because SIP and SDP are used not only in IP telephony, but also to provide the Internet interface to the PSTN for service control (for example, for the PINT services or Internet call-waiting). The last section of this chapter addresses quality of service (QoS) standards in the IP world. We address QoS here because real-time applications in general—and IP telephony in particu-lar—are its primary applications; overall, the set of QoS applications is much larger than that.

Real-Time Transport

This section deals with the standards that are pertinent to the mechanisms of carrying voice and video over IP networks. These standards are essential to interworking with the PSTN because IP telephony gateways need to convert the IP voice and video payload into a form that is accepted by the PSTN and, conversely, translate the PSTN voice and video payload into a form that is accepted by IP networks. The gateways also need to reconstruct the original voice or video stream to be as close to the original as possible. Naturally, such reconstruction should retain the real-time properties of the original stream. In addition, an interactive application—such as a two-person voice call—also requires that the transport *service* itself be fast, reliable, and perceived as "free" of *jitter* (that is, high variation in delay) to maintain the perception of a real-time interaction.[1]

These real-time transport requirements explain why the protocol suite, developed by the Audio/Video Transport (*avt*) IETF working group (see www.ietf.org/html.charters/avt-charter.html) has been called *Real-Time Transport Protocol* (RTP) in RFC 1889 (Schulzrinne et al., 1996). RTP has been designed for multicast, as well as point-to-point, transmission and is accompanied by its quality control component, *Real-Time Control Protocol* (RTCP). Both protocols are carried by the User Datagram Protocol (UDP).

RTP specifies the header of the packets that carry streams of encoded audio or video samples. This encoding is performed by a device (or software module) called a *coder*; the subsequent decoding is performed by a *decoder*, but for full-duplex communications, both are usually combined in a *codec*. (See Chapter 3). RTP specifies the payload format, which, in turn, identifies a specific codec. (The *avt* working group has also developed a number of RFCs that deal with payload formats.) The codec header, which is appended to the RTP header, determines the format of the attached encoded data unit (called a *frame*).

Since UDP does not guarantee sequencing (that is, arrival of packets in the order they were sent), this function is assisted by RTP, which stipulates the inclusion of sequence numbers in packets. Sequence numbers are used at the receiver not only to reconstruct the original sequence, but also to keep count of lost packets (one of the quality of service statistics fed back to the sender via RTCP).

RTP deals with any jitter by time-stamping packets. At the receiving end, the play-out devices buffer the packets and then reconstruct the stream at the original rate. Another synchronization mechanism is the *marker* bit of the header, which, according to RFC 1889, "is intended to allow significant events such as frame boundaries to be marked in the packet stream."

The RTCP packets are sent to exactly the same addresses as the RTP ones, but on different ports. The primary function of RTCP is to carry, from receivers to senders, the statistics on the number of lost packets, jitter, and round-trip delays. RTCP carries sender reports in the opposite direction. The statistics are used by senders to adjust encoding rates (and, possibly, the

---

[1]We put the word "free" in quotes so as to indicate that it is only a perception that the network is free of jitter. To compensate for the jitter in the network, the time-stamped packets are saved in a small buffer in the receiver and then played back, as described later in this section.

choice of codecs) in order to use less bandwidth. In addition, the statistics are useful for network management as the mechanism to detect the type and location of network problems (such as congestion). In addition to supporting quality control, RTCP performs the following functions:

- Synchronization of video and audio streams

- Identification of session participants (by their full names, telephone numbers, and e-mail addresses)

- Session control (through indication that a user is leaving the session and user-to-user control messages)

Real-Time Streaming Protocol (RTSP), developed in the Multiparty Multimedia Session Control (*mmusic*) working group, is a network remote control for multimedia services, as defined in RFC 2326 (Schulzrinne et al., 1998). The main purpose of the protocol is to control a device for so-called stored media [for example, a compact disc (CD) player, tape recorder, and so on]. But the control here actually encompasses playing the device, which evolves the transfer of the stream across the network. The applicability of this protocol to the task of integrating the PSTN and the Internet can be found in the areas of voice and video messaging. Like SIP, RTSP is also a descendant of HTTP, but unlike SIP, RTSP maintains a virtual connection identifier by assigning a session identifier in the beginning of the session and then keeping it in all messages relevant to the session. RTSP defines its own URL in reference to the media servers. RTSP can also interwork with SIP, as explained in Schulzrinne and Rosenberg (1999).

H.323

To many people, the very term *H.323* has become a synonym for those of *IP telephony* and *multimedia*. Most products that implement the multimedia technologies described in Chapter 2—starting with PCs and extending to gatekeepers and media gateways—have implemented the set of standards commonly referred to as H.323. For this reason, the convergence products described in Chapter 10 refer to H.323 systematically.

ITU-T Recommendation H.323 specifies an umbrella standard for real-time multimedia communications over packet networks. The standard refers extensively to other ITU-T Recommendations for certain specifics while defining the relevant system components and how these components interact with each other. Most important among the referred ITU-T Recommendations are H.225.0 and H.245, which specify the protocols used between the H.323 components for call and media control.

H.323 was first developed by the ITU-T Study Group 15. As a result of the ITU-T reorganization in 1997 to consolidate multimedia-related work spread across multiple study groups, the work has been moved to newly formed Study Group 16 since then.

The initial H.323 Recommendation, entitled "Visual Telephone Systems and Equipment for Local Area Networks (LANs) that Do Not Provide Guaranteed Quality of Service (QoS)," was approved in 1996. As the title suggests, the Recommendation had a specific scope concerning a particular type of packet networks. Over the next two years, in response to the growing public interest in the Internet, the scope of H.323 was considerably extended to cover *metropolitan area networks, intranetworks,* and *internetworks.* Consequently, a new version (publicly know as version 2) of ITU-T Recommendation H.323 was approved in 1998. The Recommendation also received a new title—"Packet-Based Multimedia Communications Systems." The rest of the section describes the major aspects of this Recommendation.[2]

Call and Channel

H.323 draws on the constructs of *calls* and *channels* for modeling a communication session. A call is defined as point-to-point communications between two H.323 endpoints. (An endpoint can both call and be called. It can also send or receive—or both send and receive—media streams.) A typical call begins with a call initiation attempt issued by the calling endpoint to the called endpoint and ends with a termination request from either endpoint. Specifically, H.323 divides the life cycle of a call into the following phases:

- *Phase A.* Call setup (that is, initiation of a call).
- *Phase B.* Initial communication and capability exchange (that is, determination of capabilities supported by endpoints and the endpoint to serve as the master at times of conflicts).
- *Phase C.* Establishment of audiovisual communication.
- *Phase D.* Call services (for example, increase of bandwidth and addition of conferencing parties during the call).
- *Phase E.* Call termination.

Channels are used as building blocks for calls: A collection of channels between two endpoints makes up a call. Conceptually, channels (normally unidirectional) are used to transmit signaling messages and media streams. Channels can be either reliable or unreliable. Reliable channels (for example, TCP connections) are used to carry signaling messages (for example, H.225.0 and H.245 messages), and unreliable channels (for example, RTP sessions) are used to carry media streams.

---

[2]Since then, another version of H.323 was approved in late 1999. As far as IP telephony is concerned, the new version (version 3) differs little from the previous one.

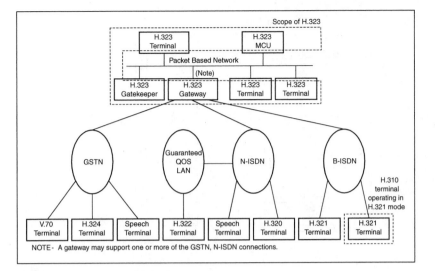

Figure 5.1   H.323 system.

Source: ITU-T Recommendation H.323: Figure 1.

System Components

Figure 5.1 depicts an H.323 system consisting of typical H.323 components, including the *terminal, multipoint control unit* (MCU), *gateway,* and *gatekeeper.* With the exception of the gatekeeper, these components can serve as endpoints. Before getting into the detail of the components, we should point out an important H.323 requirement: Its components must interwork with multimedia communications terminals for other types of network connections.[3]

This interworking consideration resulted in adoption of the Q.931 access protocol as the basis for the protocols of Recommendations H.225.0 and H.245.

Terminal

A terminal provides the real-time audio and, optionally, video and data communications capabilities for the direct use of users in a point-to-point call or multipoint conference. Figure 5.2 depicts the internals of a terminal. The H.323 Recommendation prescribes that a terminal include an audio codec unit, system control unit, H.225 layer, and network interface. It also defines each of those elements, with the exception of the network interface, which is noted as being out of the Recommendation's scope. We briefly summarize the defined elements here.

---

[3]Such as *plain old telephone service* (POTS) and *narrow-* and *broadband integrated service digital networks* (N-ISDN and B-ISDN).

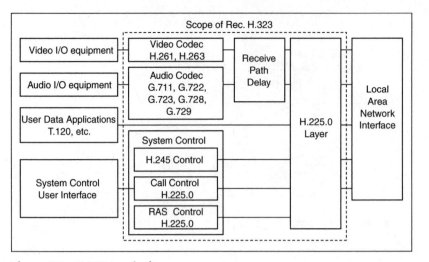

Figure 5.2   H.323 terminal.

Source: ITU-T Recommendation H.323: Figure 4.

As shown in Figure 5.2, several audio codec standards are specified in H.323. In particular, the G.711 codec[4] must be supported by any H.323 audio device. This support is prescribed for a good reason: G.711 is the coding scheme used in the PSTN for digitizing voice; it is considered the benchmark voice codec. Other coding schemes (such as G.723.1 and G.729) are optional, however.

The system control unit performs signaling operations that concern the communications between the terminal and other endpoints or gatekeepers. It provides for call control, capability exchange, logical channel control, and signaling of command and indications. As shown in Figure 5.2, these functions must use the mechanisms defined in Recommendations H.225.0 and H.245, which we discuss later in this section.

Finally comes the H.225.0 layer, which packs the media (a combination of audio, data, and video) streams and control messages for transmission and unpacks the received packets through the network interface. As the name of the layer implies, the specifics of packaging are defined in H.225.0. An important prescription is that RTP must be used to carry audio and video streams over unreliable logical channels. Another is that there must be no fragmentation of H.225.0 and H.245 signaling or control messages across transport packet data units.

Gateway

The gateway provides the functions that are required for interworking between an H.323 terminal on a packet network and an ISDN terminal or

---

[4]This codec has been standardized in CCITT (now, ITU-T) Recommendation "Pulse Code Modulation (PCM) of Voice Frequencies," published in 1988.

POTS telephone of the PSTN (as depicted in Figure 5.1). Through gateways, IP-based telephones are connected with a billion or so PSTN telephones. Specifically, the gateway provides a conversion function for the transmission format, as well as call control and logical channel control messages. It may have the characteristics of a terminal or an MCU, but the choice (terminal or MCU) is left to the manufacturer. The gateway communicates with other H.323 endpoints or gatekeepers using the same means as H.323 terminals. Its communications with PSTN terminals are beyond the scope of the H.323 Recommendation.[5]

Because it has an important role in IP telephony, the gateway issue is tackled by various standards bodies. Several new interfaces and protocols are being developed to support large-scale deployment of IP telephony services, as mentioned in Chapter 3.

Gatekeeper

The gatekeeper is optional in an H.323 system. Yet, when present, it plays an important role—as its name implies. The gatekeeper provides the following services:

- *Address translation.* Translates an alias address (for example, a telephone number or an e-mail address) to a network address (for example, an IP address). This function is particularly important in scenarios where a telephone on the PSTN is attempting to call a PC on an IP network. It is also important when determining the location of a gateway to the PSTN.

- *Admission control.* Authorizes network access using the *registration, admission,* and *status* (RAS) messages defined in H.225.0. The rules or policies for authorization are unspecified, however, so that they can be customized for a given situation. Examples: (1) admit all requests or (2) admit only requests from subscribers.

- *Bandwidth control.* Handles bandwidth change requests from an endpoint. The requests and responses must use the corresponding RAS messages. The H.323 Recommendation leaves open how bandwidth requests should be handled.

- *Zone management.* Manages a *zone,* the collection of all endpoints registered with and managed by one and only one gatekeeper. The gatekeeper, in turn, must support the registration and management of all endpoints registered in the zone. The H.323 Recommendation does not specify the rules governing the geographic or logical composition of a zone, nor does it specify how two gatekeepers communicate with each other across

---

[5]Those should follow procedures defined in ITU-T Recommendations such as H.320, H.324, and V.70.

zones. Related methods for communications between administrative domains can be found in a separate Recommendation—H.225.0 Annex G.

In addition, the gatekeeper may optionally provide the following services:

- *Call control signaling.* Call signaling messages between endpoints may be passed with or without the involvement of the gatekeeper, as illustrated in Figures 5.3 and 5.4. If the gatekeeper is involved (this case is called *gatekeeper-routed call signaling*), the call signaling messages are routed through the gatekeeper; otherwise, they are passed directly between the endpoints (this case is known as *direct endpoint call signaling*). The choice of the call signaling method belongs to the gatekeeper. In the response to an endpoint's admission request, the gatekeeper must indicate the call signaling method. Note that gatekeeper-routed call signaling is of particular relevance to service providers and enterprise network managers. The routing method supports collection of calling activities at a central place and provides an entry point for additional policy enforcement and service processing during a call, thereby enabling advanced resource management and services.

- *Call authorization.* The authorization policy (unspecified by the Recommendation) can be based on, for example, restricted access to a gateway, time of day, type of service subscription, and bandwidth availability.

- *Bandwidth management.* A call request or bandwidth request may be rejected because of bandwidth limitations. Theoretically, the gatekeeper could also instruct an ongoing call to reduce its bandwidth usage. The criteria for determining whether there is bandwidth available are outside the scope of H.323.

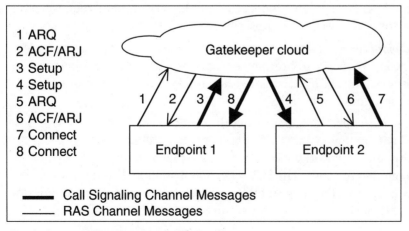

Figure 5.3   Gatekeeper-routed call signaling.
Source: ITU-T Recommendation H.323: Figure 9.

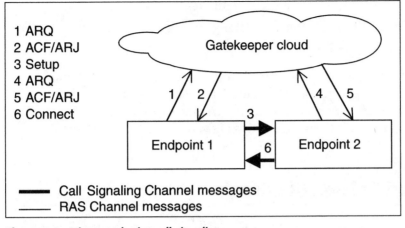

Figure 5.4   Direct endpoint call signaling.

Source: ITU-T Recommendation H.323: Figure 10.

- *Call management.* The gatekeeper may maintain a list of ongoing H.323 calls and provide call management based on the information. For example, for a call to a busy terminal, the gatekeeper can redirect the call or simply not make an attempt to establish the call.

Multipoint Control Unit (MCU)

The MCU provides control functions to support conferences of three or more endpoints. It manages conference resources and negotiates with the endpoints the modes of communications. Optionally, the MCU may also provide functions, such as mixing and switching, for processing the media streams it receives before distributing them to endpoints. *Mixing* is the operation for combining multiple-input media streams into one single output stream; *switching* is the operation for selecting an input media stream for output to an endpoint. The MCU uses H.245 messages and procedures for establishing multipoint communications between the endpoints.

Signaling Procedures

H.323 also stipulates the procedures the communicating endpoints should follow when exchanging signaling messages throughout a call. It specifies the sequencing of relevant H.225.0 (including RAS) and H.245 messages for every phase of a call in various scenarios. In particular, the call setup procedures cover the following scenarios concerning the role of gatekeepers:

- Neither of the endpoints is registered with a gatekeeper
- Both endpoints are registered with the same gatekeeper

- Each endpoint is registered with a different gatekeeper
- Only the calling endpoint is registered with a gatekeeper
- Only the called endpoint is registered with a gatekeeper

Note that the call setup procedures support a signaling method known as *fast connect,* which allows the establishment of media channels without the use of H.245 signaling. As a result, media channels can be opened for sending and receiving media information with as few as one round-trip signaling message exchange.

T.120 and Related Standards

Among the most promising multimedia applications to be delivered by the converging networks is *collaborative conferencing,* which supports such services as *telemedicine* and *distance learning.* You will find descriptions of these services in Chapter 9. Here, we concentrate on the T.120 standard, which is invariably supported by the top conferencing products [such as Multipoint Conferencing Units (MCUs)] addressed in Chapter 10.

The T.120 series of Recommendations has been developed by ITU-T Study Group 8; the work has subsequently moved to Study Group 16. The Recommendations in the series define multipoint communication services and protocols for use in multimedia conferencing environments. In contrast to traditional telephone services, in which the communications take place between two points (or *point-to-point*), the word *multipoint* refers to services that support group activities (such as teleconferencing). This set of standards is particularly relevant to the subject of this book because T.120 terminals (that is, endpoints) can be located in both the PSTN and LAN environments, and the interconnection between these two is achieved through the Internet.

The philosophy of the series is similar to IN in that T.120 has been based on three so-called independence principles: platform independence, network independence, and application independence. *Platform independence* means independence of the choice of an operating system (and, indeed, T.120 has been implemented in most leading commercial operating systems environments (see the *T.120 Primer* on www.databeam.com/ccts/t.120primer.html). *Network independence* implies the support of endpoints located in the PSTN (including both POTS and ISDN) and LANs. *Application independence* is achieved through definition of generic communications services that can be used by many applications (virtual reality and simulations, real-time news delivery, etc.) other than teleconferencing. It is important to note, however, that T.120 does not guarantee real-time delivery.

ITU-T Recommendation T.120, entitled "Data Protocols for Multimedia Conferencing" (approved in 1996), defines the T.120 architectural model and describes the rest of the Recommendations in the series as well as the rela-

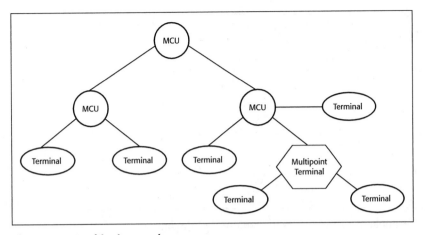

Figure 5.5   Multipoint topology.

Source: ITU-T Recommendation T.120: Figure 1.

tionships between them. First of all, in order to support multipoint communications, T.120 defines a special network element, the *multipoint control unit* (MCU). T.120 terminals may provide user access to the following media: audio (telephony); audio and data; audio and video; and audio, video, and data. MCUs, on the other hand, do not provide immediate user access to any medium; their role is to interconnect the terminals. Furthermore, T.120 by itself is not concerned with either voice or video; it deals only with signaling for synchronizing events over the network. As far as the subject of this book is concerned, MCU is the entity that interworks the PSTN and the Internet.

A special type of T.120 terminal with several connection ports (each port has an appropriate T.120 transport stack), a *multipoint terminal,* can also act as a bridge. The overall architecture (depicted in Figure 5.5) takes the form of a tree, in which T.120 terminals (and only they) form leaves; the rest of the nodes are MCUs and multipoint terminals. Figure 5.6 provides a useful example of mixed-network topology in which terminals located in an enterprise network and the PSTN are interconnected.

The T.120 protocol-related architecture is depicted in Figure 5.7. The following bulleted list describes architecture components, including user applications, application protocols, node controller, communications infrastructure, and networks:

- *User applications.* While Recommendation T.120 affirms that applications per se are not the subject of standardization in the T.120 series, it identifies a class of applications that use services of *generic conference control* (GCC)[6] and *multipoint communication service* (MCS)[7] and calls

[6]Defined in Recommendation T.124.

[7]Defined in Recommendations T.122 and T.125.

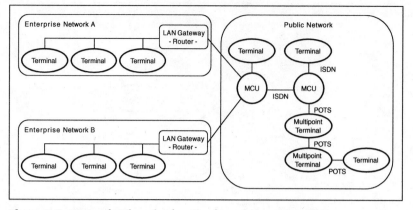

Figure 5.6 Example of a mixed-network conference topology.
Source: ITU-T Recommendation T.120: Figure 2.

those *user applications.* The T.120 environment explicitly supports resource allocation to multiple concurrent application processes. To guide the developers on the use of the T.120 infrastructure so that multiple application processes do not interfere with each other, Recommendation T.121 defines the generic application template.

- *Application protocols.* In the T.120 series, these include the *Multipoint Binary File Transfer* (MBFT) protocol (Recommendation T.127), and *Still*

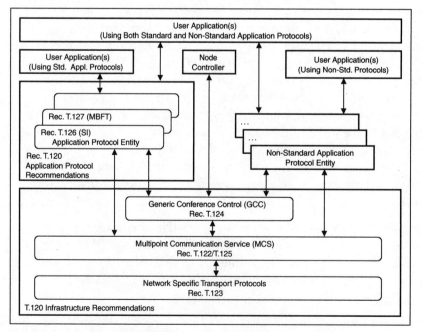

Figure 5.7 T.120 system model.
Source: ITU-T Recommendation T.120: Figure 3.

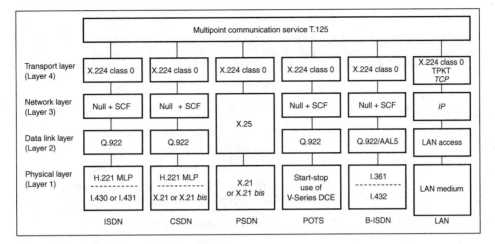

Figure 5.8 Basic structure of a profile.

Source: ITU-T Recommendation T.123: Figure 3.

Image (SI), also known as *Multipoint Still Image and Annotation* (MSIA), shared whiteboard, and facsimile.[8]

■ *Node controller.* A management entity that is responsible for starting and controlling the communication session by using the primitives of the generic conference control described hereafter.

■ *Communications infrastructure.* Consists of three standardized components: *generic conference control* (GCC), *multipoint communication service* (MCS), and *transport protocol profiles* (one for each type of network). GCC is accessed via primitives for setting up and managing the multipoint conference, and it provides access control and arbitration of capabilities. MCS is the facility for multipoint connection-oriented data services. MCS assembles *multipoint domains* from network nodes and point-to-point connections; the nodes in a domain are hierarchically organized, and there is an optional mechanism that ensures that data is received in the same sequence at all nodes. MCS acts as a monitor, controlling network resources (*channels*); it also coordinates application process events by issuing *tokens.*

■ *Networks.* The networks (or rather network types) over which the T.120 protocols operate include the ISDN, other (switched or permanent) *digital circuits* (CSDN), packed switched data networks based on Recommendation X.25, and PSTN (which is meant here in a narrow sense of POTS), as well as IP networks. It is interesting that the latter is referred to as LAN rather than IP. This naming convention is used because at the time of developing this Recommendation, the status of the IETF in ITU-T was unclear, and there was no procedure for referencing the

---

[8]Defined in Recommendation T.127.

Table 5.1   The ITU-T T.120 Recommendations

ITU-T RECOMMENDATION NUMBER	TITLE
T.120 (1996)	Data Protocols for Multimedia Conferencing
T.121 (1996)	Generic Application Template
T.122 (1998)	Multipoint Communication Service for Audio Graphics and Audiovisual Conferencing Service Definition
T.123 (1996)	Protocol Stacks for Audiographic and Audiovisual Teleconference Applications
T.124 (1998)	Generic Conference Control
T.125 (1998)	Multipoint Communication Service Protocol Specification
T.126 (1997)	Multipoint Still Image and Annotation Protocol
T.127 (1995)	Multipoint Binary File Transfer Protocol
T.128 (1998)	Multipoint Application Sharing

Internet standards. Nevertheless, clause 7.6, "LAN basic profile," of T.123 specifically refers to the TCP- and IP-related RFCs. To this end, the Recommendation addresses a problem over a fundamental difference between the TCP and ISO transport protocols (ITU-T Recommendation X.224) in that the former "conveys a continuous sequence of octets with no explicit boundaries between related groups of octets." The problem has been solved in RFC 1006, which defines an additional layer, and the solution was accepted in and cited by T.123. For each relevant network, the Recommendation defines a profile. The complete profile directory is summarized in Figure 5.8. Because the original figure neither mentions nor explicitly depicts TCP and IP layers (for the reasons already stated), the authors augmented it appropriately.

Table 5.1 lists all currently valid published ITU-T Recommendations in the T.120 series.

Session Initiation Protocol and Session Description Protocol

The two standard protocols that govern session control are the *Session Initiation Protocol* (SIP) and *Session Description Protocol* (SDP). These standards were originally intended for loosely controlled multimedia conferencing over the

Internet; however, they have developed into a functional alternative to the H.323 suite. In particular, the combination of SIP and SDP is functionally equivalent to that of H.225.0 and H.245.

SIP (see RFC 2543) was initially standardized by the Multiparty Multimedia Session Control (*mmusic*) (see www.ietf.org/html.charters/mmusic-charter .html) working group in the IETF Transport area. As the work had grown, a specialized SIP working group was created (see www.ietf.org/html.charters/ sip-charter.html).

SIP was designed to create and tear down multimedia sessions. In its syntax, SIP is similar to the Hypertext Transfer Protocol (HTTP)—defined in RFC 2616—and it reuses many HTTP header fields (such as authentication). Like HTTP, SIP is ASCII text encoded. Unlike HTTP, however, SIP was developed with the intention of addressing human users, for which reason the *uniform resource identifier* (URI) defined by SIP looks more like an e-mail address than the address of a World Wide Web page. For example, sip:hui-lan.lu@bell-labs.com is a SIP URI. For the purposes of integrating the PSTN and the Internet, it is important to note that SIP message headers can also carry other URIs (such as telephone URLs, defined by the IETF).

SIP is a client-server protocol: A client generates a request, to which a server sends one or more responses. A (potential) session participant can both generate and receive requests, which suggests that the end systems should have both the client and server capabilities. SIP also supports transaction capabilities. The RFC 2543 definition of a transaction is:

> A SIP transaction occurs between a client and a server and comprises all messages from the first request sent from the client to the server up to a final . . . response sent from the server to the client.

Transactions are assigned the *command sequence* (CSeq) numbers. The SIP nomenclature (similar to that of SNMP and HTTP) alludes to the object-oriented model by defining the following methods that are carried in SIP requests (one method per request):

- *INVITE.* Conveys the information about the call to invited participants. It is issued in order to set up a call, and once the call is set up, it can be issued by any party to the call in order to change the call parameters or to add another party.
- *BYE.* Terminates a connection.
- *OPTIONS.* Solicits information about a user's capabilities.
- *CANCEL.* Terminates the search for the user.
- *REGISTER.* Makes the user's location known to a SIP server.
- *ACK.* Invokes the reliable message exchange for invitations. (Note that SIP has its own mechanism for invitation exchange; thus, it can run on top of an unreliable transport layer protocol such as UDP.)

The invitation to a session is accompanied by the *Session Description Protocol* (SDP) defined in RFC 2327, also developed by the *mmusic* working group (WG). SDP provides the description format (*not* the protocol) of the multicast and unicast addresses, the number and types (that is, audio, video, data, control) of streams involved, the codecs involved (that is, the payload types to be carried by the transport protocol), the transport protocol itself (for example, RTP or H.320), the UDP port, the list of starting and stopping times of the session, encryption keys, and so on. Keep in mind that SDP is only one possible payload of SIP; SIP can also carry all Multipurpose Mail Extensions (MIME) types, for example.

In the following section, we discuss location of clients and servers. In a perfectly valid degenerated case, both a client and server can be located in the same host. The opposite extremity, which is strategic to network-wide applications of SIP, is when several SIP servers located in different hosts act as proxies. In this case, server A, after having received a request from a client, may consult a local directory (by using LDAP, for example), only to find out that there is another SIP server, server B, which is better suited to respond to the request. Server A forwards the request to server B, which, from now on, will route its responses through server A.

The proxies can form a routing chain of any length. Figure 5.9 demonstrates such a chain. You have probably noticed a striking similarity between this figure and Figure 4.5. This similarity is actually profound, and it has been among the major factors that have influenced the *pint* working group to adopt SIP as the foundation of the PINT Protocol. SIP also offers a natural

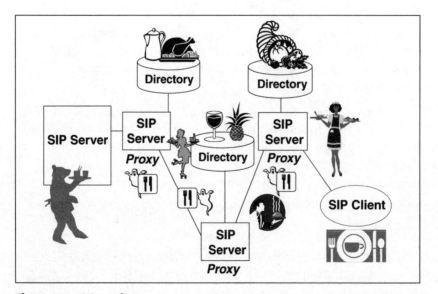

Figure 5.9 SIP routing.

solution to the problem of gateway discovery (addressed in Chapter 3), which is being worked on in the IP Telephony (*iptel*) working group (www.ietf.org/html.charters/iptel-charter.html).

The use and applications of SIP are growing. The present specification of SIP, however, as far as size is concerned, is about one-tenth of that of the H.323 suite. In some cases (for example, session control), the protocols seem to be working to solve the same problem; other aspects (for example, definition of network functional elements and their respective roles) are different. For a good comparison of H.323 and SIP, please see "A Comparison of SIP and H.323 for Internet Telephony" (Schulzrinne and Rosenberg, 1998).

Quality of Service (QoS)

As we pointed out in Chapter 3, QoS is the subject of ongoing active research and more or less active standardization.

ITU-T has done much work in relation to B-ISDN, in which it effectively relied on the output of the ATM Forum. To this end, ITU-T Recommendations I.356 and I.610, respectively, specify performance measurement methods and QoS objectives for end-to-end connections and define operations and management tools to monitor the QoS parameters. In addition, the B-ISDN signaling[9] specifies mechanisms for negotiating traffic parameters and QoS performance objectives.

Because of its connection-oriented, virtual-circuit approach to packet networking, it is more or less straightforward to deal with the QoS in the PSTN: The characteristics of the virtual circuit are what need to be negotiated among the participants of a session (and between each participant and the network). Given the inherently connectionless and stateless nature of the IP networks, guaranteeing end-to-end QoS is a much more complex matter. Consequently, standardization of relevant protocols is more complex, too. Virtually all QoS work that is related to routing (or, more precisely, forwarding) is performed in the IETF, and so, for the purposes of this book, we concentrate on the IETF developments (some of which are explicitly addressed by the documents issued by other standards bodies).

As mentioned in Chapter 3, there are two basic approaches to IP QoS:

1. Guaranteeing certain QoS on a per-flow basis.

2. Guaranteeing QoS on a per-packet basis (as designated by the packet's class of service).

---

[9]Standardized in the ITU-T Q.29xx Recommendation series.

The former approach is taken by the Integrated Services (*intserv*) and Resource Reservation Setup Protocol (*rsvp*) working groups, the latter by the Differentiated Services working group. In addition, the Multiprotocol Label Switching (*mpls*) working group is dealing with what effectively amounts to establishing virtual circuits for IP traffic, which makes it particularly suitable to interworking with the PSTN B-ISDN networks (such as ATM and Frame Relay networks). In the rest of this section, we address the respective standardization developments in that order.

Integrated Services (*intserv*)

The IETF Integrated Services (*intserv*) working group (www.ietf.org/html .charters/intserv-charter.html) has been chartered with the development of an abstract packet-forwarding model. The applications of the model to particular Layer 2 protocols (such as ATM) have been, and continue to be, developed in the Integrated Services over Specific Link Layers (*issll*) working group (www.ietf.org/html.charters/issll-charter.html), which has produced ATM-related RFCs and works on the following link layer protocols: PPP, IEEE 802.2 LAN, and *ISO High-Level Data Link Control* (HDLC).

The earlier informational RFC 1633 specified the reference model for the network elements, which sets basic functions and terminology (see Figure 5.10). In this model, an arriving packet passes the:

- *Classifier.* Maps the packet into a specific class (the class of the packet determines its treatment).

- *Packet scheduler.* Manages the forwarding of different packet streams using a set of queues and possibly other mechanisms, like timers.

- *Output* (first-in, first-out) *queue.*

In the upper part of the figure, the routing agent supports a specific routing protocol and maintains the routing database. The reservation setup agent supports a specific resource reservation protocol; after approval by admission control, the traffic control database (which is shared with the classifier and packet scheduler) is modified to reflect the desired QoS. The management agent can modify this database, too, on behalf of the network management requests, in order to arrange controlled link sharing and to set admission control policies.

Following the template defined in informational RFC 2216, two types of services—the *controlled-load service* and *guaranteed service*—and their respective network element behavior types are defined in RFC 2211 and RFC 2212, respectively, as follows:

Controlled-load service provides the client data flow with a quality of service closely approximating the QoS that same flow would receive from an unloaded

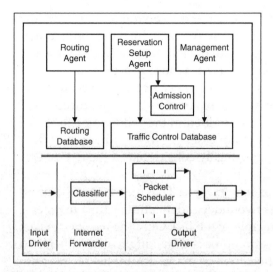

Figure 5.10 Implementation reference model for routers.

Source: RFC 1633.

network element, but uses capacity (admission) control to assure that this service is received even when the network element is overloaded.

Guaranteed service provides firm (mathematically provable) bounds on end-to-end datagram queuing delays.

To the application processes subscribing to the controlled-load service, the network appears to be unloaded. In other words, the packet loss, if any, will approximate that typical to the transmission medium. As for the delay, it is supposed to be nearly constant, dependent again on the transmission medium delay and the processing time delay in devices along the path. The application process specifies the controlled-load service by providing the *Token Bucket Specification* (Tspec, defined in RFC 2215). The application process specifies the guaranteed-load service by the same token bucket specification (*Tspec*) as well as the Reservation Specification (*Rspec*). Rspec is a pair of numbers that, respectively, specify the data rate (ranging from 1 to 40 TB/s) and the *slack term* (ranging from 0 to $2^{32} - 1$ μs). The slack term is used by any network element to reduce its reservation level (the updated slack term is then passed to the next network element in the chain). RFC 2211 and 2212, respectively, specify the actions of network elements for each of the two types of services.

One resource reservation protocol has been developed, in close cooperation with the intserv working group, by the Resource Reservation Protocol (*rsvp*) working group (www.ietf.org/html.charters/rsvp-charter.html) in the transport area of the IETF. The protocol is also called RSVP, and is published in RFC 2205.

RSVP is used by the application process at the receiving end of *flows* (that is, streams of data with the same QoS requirements, which are defined by the destination address related to a particular session) as well as by the network elements along the path among the hosts whose processes are involved in the session. (The protocol has been specifically designed for and used by the multicast sessions, which explains its major features—especially the reservation mechanism described in the following text.) Although choice of a transport layer is not essential to key function of the protocol, the transport layer ports specifically considered in the document are those of UDP and TCP.

The reservations are requested for *simplex flows*. That means that the protocol treats the receiver and sender as two independent entities (in a manner similar to the single-endedness principle of the IN). Only the receiver makes reservations. If there are two application processes talking to each other, two different and independent reservations will be made: one by the receiver in one process, and one by the receiver in the other.

Figure 5.11 demonstrates the place of RSVP in the integrated services architecture—in particular, to the interface between a host and a router. The host model is equivalent to that of the router, which underlines the principle that the QoS is defined at the edges by hosts with routers carrying out the requests. The *data path* (that is, the interface between the packet scheduler of the sender and classifier of the receiver) is clearly separated from that between the two RSVP processes, which explains why the "implementation of RSVP will typically execute in the background, not in the data forwarding path." (For this reason, following telephony terminology, the Internet community often refers to RSVP messages as the *out-of-band* signaling, although the difference between in-band and out-of-band is much more subtle here than in the case of the PSTN.) We should clarify, however, that RSVP is not an admission-control or packet-scheduled application, and its role is to reserve rather than provide the resources.

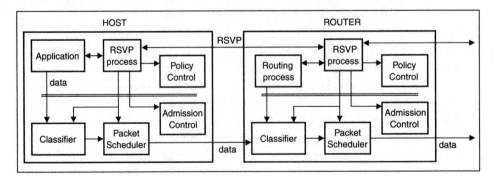

Figure 5.11   RSVP in hosts and routers.

Source: RFC 2205.

An RSVP reservation request uses a *flow descriptor,* which consists of *flowspec* (which may, in turn, include the service class, Tspec, and Rspec) and *filterspec.* The flowspec describes the QoS and is used by the packet scheduler; the filterspec defines the set of packets (that is, the flow) for the given QoS and is used by the packet classifier. Two-reservation options with respect to the treatment of different senders in the same session are supported: (1) establishing a distinct reservation for each sender and (2) making a single reservation shared among all senders. Other two-reservation options with respect to the selection of senders and, thus, the existence and number of filter specs provide (1) the explicit list of senders (with one filter spec for each sender) and (2) the so-called *wildcard* that explicitly selects all senders (and so eliminates the need for the filterspec).

Following is a description of how RSVP works. The sender transmits the *Path* message specifying the QoS request. As this message traverses network elements, it is stored in the *path state* in each of them. The receiver sends back along the same path *Resv* messages specifying the QoS for the reservation requests. The messages affect a *soft* (i.e., temporary) state: As the *Path* messages are periodically retransmitted, so the *Resv* messages are repeated to maintain this soft state for the duration of the session. These two messages are defined as fundamental by the RSVP standard (RFC 2205), which was designed to identify (via *Path* messages) all endpoints of a multicast flow. (The *Resv* messages from separate receivers can be combined into a single request at those points in the network where a flow's paths merge.) With these two messages, RSVP not only uses existing routing protocols to determine the path of the flow between source(s) and destination(s), but it also reacts to changes in the network topology. Retransmission of *Path/Resv* over a new path can be used to change a path of a reserved flow, while the absence of retransmissions can be detected by the routers so as to deallocate the QoS resources associated with a delinquent path.

RSVP also defines messages for optional confirmation, elimination of a reservation, and error reports. The RFCs in the *rsvp* group are listed in Table 5.2.

Differentiated Services (*diffserv*)

The effort of the Differentiated Services (*diffserv*) working group (www.ietf.org/html.charters/diffserv-charter.html) is directed toward the development of the mechanisms that support *aggregate* QoS services. In other words, *diffserv* is concerned with ordering (and treating accordingly to this order) traffic aggregates. The packets that end up in a particular aggregate are classified according to a certain behavior rather than according to a particular service. With the *intserv* model, the admission control considers only the available capacity in order to grant or deny the resource reservation request. Yet, a new set of admission criteria (such as the identity of users,

Table 5.2 RFCs in the RSVP Group

RFC 2205	Resource ReSerVation Protocol (RSVP)—Version 1 Functional Specification
RFC 2206	RSVP Management Information Base using SMIv2
RFC 2207	RSVP Extensions for IPSEC Data Flows
RFC 2208	Resource ReSerVation Protocol (RSVP)—Version 1 Applicability Statement Some Guidelines on Deployment
RFC 2209	Resource ReSerVation Protocol (RSVP)—Version 1 Message Processing Rules

security-related information, time of day, and day of the week) are becoming increasingly important in influencing admission policy.

These criteria, once specified at the network endpoints, are mapped into *differentiated services* (DS) codepoints to be carried in the IP packets and thus recognized by the network elements. Informational RFC 2475 explains the relevant architecture model and sets the terminology. To this end, RFC 2475 classifies existing models of service differentiation into five categories: (1) relative priority marking (including IP version 4 precedence marking), (2) service marking, (3) label switching, (4) integrated services/RSVP, and (5) static per-hop classification. The *diffserv* architecture can be considered as a refinement of the relative priority marking in that it "more clearly . . . [specifies] the role and importance of boundary nodes and traffic conditioners." As for the integrated services/RSVP model, which lacks state aggregation, the differentiated services mechanisms are expected to help by aggregating the RSVP state in the core of the network.

Among the key concepts of *diffserv* is that of *per-hop behavior* (PHB), defined as "a description of the externally observable forwarding behavior of a . . . node applied to a particular . . . behavior aggregate." (A *behavior aggregate* is a set of packets, marked with the same codepoint, that are moving in the same direction over a given link.) A simple example of a PHB is specification of a guaranteed minimal allocation of bandwidth to a link for a period of time. RFC 2475 further notes that PHBs may be specified in terms of their resources (for example, buffer or bandwidth), priority relative to other PHBs, or relative observable traffic characteristics (for example, delay or loss). PHBs shaped by a common constraint so that they can be specified (and subsequently implemented) together, form a *PHB group*. PHB groups are essential differentiated services building blocks, and their concept is central to defining other elements of the *diffserv* architecture.

A *differentiated services domain* (DS domain) is defined as a contiguous set of nodes "that operate with a common service provisioning policy and set of PHB groups implemented on each node." Nodes within a DS domain use the

DS codepoint of an IP packet to select a relevant PHB and to deal with the packet accordingly. Typically, a DS domain encompasses one or more networks under the same administration (that is, an enterprise network or an ISP). As illustrated in Figure 5.12, a DS domain consists of *DS boundary* nodes (interconnecting the DS domain with the outside world, which, in turn, consists of other DS domains as well as non-DS-capable nodes) and *DS interior* nodes. As Figure 5.12 points out, a host "may [but does not have to] act as a DS boundary node for traffic from applications running on that host . . ." Contiguous DS domains form a *DS region*. Note, however, that the domains within any given region are not required to have a common set of PHB groups or identical codepoint-to-PHB mappings.

In order to support the services that span across the domains, the peering domains establish a *service level agreement* (SLA). The *diffserv* architecture defines an SLA in terms of the things it may provide, including:

- Packet classification policy (that is, the criteria for selecting the subset of traffic that is to receive a differentiated service) and remarking rules.

- Specification of traffic profiles and actions to traffic streams that fit (or don't fit) these profiles. (A profile may, for example, assign to a particular codepoint the request to measure the traffic marked by it with a token bucket and provide the respective parameters.) Actually, the binary fit/don't-fit scheme may be insufficient; according to *diffserv* architecture, "multiple levels of conformance with a profile may be defined and enforced."

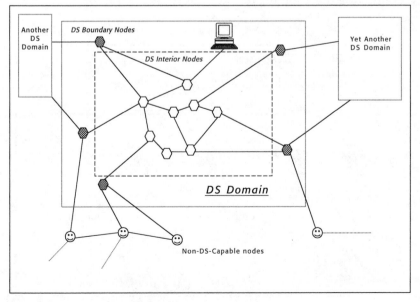

Figure 5.12 Classification of the DS domain nodes.

The ultimate product of the SLA is the *traffic conditioning agreement* (TCA). Here, the word *conditioning* means ensuring that the classified traffic complies with the profile; as the result of conditioning, certain packets may be dropped or delayed (delaying packets is one means of shaping the traffic). In addition, the packets' codepoints can be changed in the process of conditioning. The act of measuring the arriving traffic against the profiled temporal properties is called *metering*. RFC 2475 defines a TCA as "an agreement specifying classifier rules and any corresponding traffic profiles and metering, marking, discarding and/or shaping rules which are to apply to the traffic streams selected by the classifier. A TCA encompasses all of the traffic conditioning rules explicitly specified within a SLA along with all of the rules implicit from the relevant service requirements and/or from a DS domain's service provisioning policy."

The traffic enters a DS domain through a DS boundary node, which, in this case, is called (in complete analogy with the PSTN terminology) a *DS ingress* node; the traffic leaves the domain through a DS boundary node called a *DS egress* node. Figure 5.13 illustrates the role of these nodes in traffic conditioning and their relation to TCAs. Here, the downstream traffic is leaving DS domain X through a DS egress node bound by the X-to-Y TCA. The egress node must therefore ensure that the traffic to DS domain Y corresponds to this agreement; if it finds the input traffic in violation of the TCA, it conditions it appropriately. The peering DS ingress node of domain Y is responsible for checking (again, by possibly conditioning it) by the same agreement. Typically, "the SLA between the domains should specify which domain has responsibility for mapping traffic streams to DS behavior aggregates and conditioning those aggregates in conformance with the appropri-

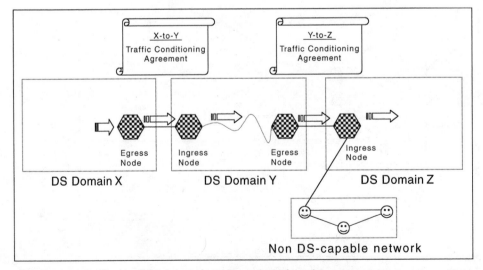

Figure 5.13   Traffic conditioning at the edges of DS domains.

ate TCA," but the DS ingress node is ultimately responsible for enforcing the TCA within its domain. The functions of the DS egress node of DS domain X and the DS ingress node of DS domain Y are similar with respect to the Y-to-Z TCA, but note that the (only depicted) ingress node of DS domain Z is also connected to the non-DS-capable network. In this case, the ingress node is responsible for traffic conditioning in accordance with the local policy (of the DS domain Z).

Figure 5.14 depicts the elements of the *diffserv* architecture relevant to the packet classification and traffic conditioning process. The first functional element of the architecture is the *packet classifier,* whose role is to sort the incoming packets based on some packet-related criteria. RFC 2475 defines two types of classifiers. The *behavior aggregate* (BA) classifiers look only at the DS codepoint; the *multifield* (MF) classifiers consider other packet header fields as well as additional information (for example, incoming interface). The packet classifier passes selected packets to the *marker* (which sets the DS field of each packet to a particular codepoint and adds it to a particular behavior aggregate) as well as to the *meter* (which measures the temporal properties of the traffic according to a particular profile and triggers specific actions for the in- and out-of-profile packets in the rest of the conditioning elements). Finally, the traffic streams end up in the *shaper/dropper,* whose role is to delay the traffic when it is necessary to bring it in compliance with a traffic profile. The delayed traffic is held in a buffer; when the buffer is full, certain packets (including those already in the buffer) may be dropped.

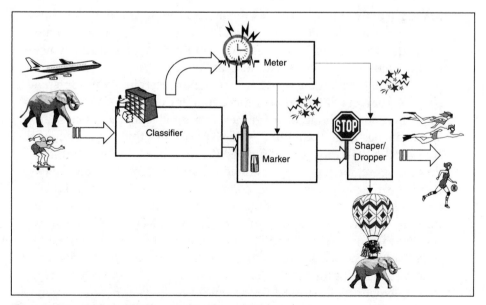

Figure 5.14 Packet classifiers and traffic conditioners.
Source: RFC 2475.

RFC 2475 also addresses a number of important topics (like security and tunneling considerations and PHB specification and guidelines) that are essential for complete understanding of the scope of differentiated services. The present *diffserv* standards-track documents have been published in RFC 2597 and RFC 2598.

RFC 2474 defines the DS field of the IP header for IP version 4 (IPv4)—where it replaces (or rather reinterprets) the *type of service* (TOS) octet—and version 6 (IPv6)—where it reinterprets the *class of service* (CoS) octet. Six bits (bits 0 through 5) of the field contain the DS codepoint; the last two bits are reserved. The document also addresses the existing ("historical") codepoint definitions and the resulting issue of backward compatibility. To ensure the backward compatibility, a set of codepoints (called the *class selector codepoints*) that meet minimum requirements of compatibility with the deployed forwarding treatments is reserved. The document also makes recommendations regarding PHB standardization guidelines and assignment of codepoints.

The last two RFCs, respectively, define the *assured forwarding* (AF) PHB group and the *expedited forwarding* (EF) PHB:

1. RFC 2597 defines the AF PHB group. The group contains four general-use AF classes; within each class there are three levels of *drop precedence*. Packets belonging to a specific AF class are forwarded independently from packets of any other class. The standard deals with short-term congestion by prescribing packet queuing. The long-term congestion is dealt with by dropping packets with higher drop precedence. RFC 2597 recommends specific codepoints for the 12 *class–drop precedence* pairs.

2. RFC 2598 defines the EF PHB as the mechanism for building low-loss, low-latency, and low-jitter end-to-end services through a DS domain. (Note that these qualities are especially important for real-time voice-over-IP delivery.) EF PHB is defined as "a forwarding treatment for a particular *diffserv* aggregate where the departure rate of the aggregate's packets from any *diffserv* node must equal or exceed a configurable rate." In order to eliminate (or reduce to a small size) the queues the aggregate has to go through, RFC 2598 postulates that the DS nodes that support the PHB must be configured (by network administrators), "so that the aggregate has a well-defined minimum departure rate." Furthermore, the aggregate is to be conditioned, "so that its arrival rate at any node is always less than that node's configured minimum departure rate." Conversely, to protect non-EF traffic, RFC 2598 postulates that the maximum EF rate and, when appropriate, burst size must also be settable by network administrators. The document recommends a specific codepoint for the EF PHB and provides example mechanisms for implementing the EF PHB. It also reports (in its appendix) on an implementation of the *Virtual Leased Line* (VLL) *Service*.

Multiprotocol Label Switching (MPLS)

The MPLS standards are being developed by the IETF Multiprotocol Label Switching (*mpls*) working group (www.ietf.org/html.charters/mpls-charter .html). The term *multiprotocol* has been chosen to stress that the method applies to all network layer protocols, not only IP. In fact, the method was brought to life by integrating the ATM or, for the purposes of this book, B-ISDN network layer with IP.

The MPLS architecture is described in [IETF MPLS WG, Rosen et al. (1999)]. We examine this document by first introducing a *forwarding equivalence class* (FEC). An FEC is a set of packets associated with a path starting at a given router, so that all packets in the FEC follow this path. (In reality, there are cases of multipath routing; in these cases, an FEC corresponds to a set of paths, and the packets that belong to the FEC then follow a path out of this set.) The job of the router is first to classify the incoming packets into FECs and, once this is done, to forward all packets within each FEC without making any further distinction.

You may recall from Chapter 3 that in non-MPLS routing, each packet is typically forwarded based on its IP destination address. The packets are considered equivalent (and thus belong to the same FEC) if the router's table contains an address prefix that is the longest match for each packet's destination address. Each router reclassifies the packets.

In contrast, with MPLS forwarding, each packet is assigned to an FEC only when it enters the network, at which point the FEC value (encoded as a fixed-length string called a *label*) is sent along with the packet. The routers traversed by such a packet ignore the IP header and instead use the label as an index into a table that specifies the next router to which the packet is to be sent and a new label, which replaces the old label. In other words, labels have, in general, only local significance. The forwarding operation itself (which includes looking up an incoming label; determining the outgoing label, outgoing port and other information; and replacing the incoming label with the outgoing label) is called a *label swap*. As far as the location of the label within a packet is concerned, it could reside within a specific encapsulation header or be placed within an existing data link or network layer header.

In the previous section, we discussed how the *diffserv* and *intserv* approaches support the prioritization of packets. Such prioritization defines the precedence (or class of service) of each packet so as to choose the pertinent discard threshold or scheduling. This prioritization can be preserved with MPLS: In this case, the label represents a combination of an FEC and the precedence or class of service. In fact, a label can be assigned to a union (*aggregate*) of FECs with similar properties rather than one FEC.

An MPLS-capable router is called a *label-switching router* (LSR). A hop (that is, link) between two routers, on which a labeled packet is forwarded, is called a *label-switched hop* (LSH). Different labels arriving at an LSR are replaced with one label through a procedure called *label merging*. A *merge*

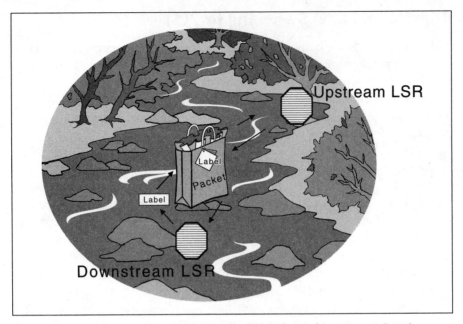

Figure 5.15   Label assignment and the roles of label-switching routers (LSRs).

point is the node at which the label merging is performed. When this procedure involves framed media, it is called *frame merge.*[10]

A contiguous set of LSRs in the same routing or administrative domain form an *MPLS domain*. A router that connects an MPLS domain with the node outside the domain is called an *MPLS edge node*. An MPLS edge is called an *MPLS ingress node* when it handles the traffic entering an MPLS domain; it is called an *MPLS egress node* when it handles the traffic exiting an MPLS domain. (These last two definitions refer to a role the same physical router plays in respect to the direction of the traffic that passes through it.)

The agreement between two LSRs on a forwarding path to use a given label for a given FEC is called *label binding*. The responsibility of ensuring that the binding is unique lies with each LSR receiving a packet. With respect to a given label, the LSR that sends the packet that contains it is called an *upstream* LSR, and the LSR that receives such a packet is called a *downstream* LSR (as depicted in Figure 5.15). These definitions are important because, in the MPLS architecture, the decision to bind a label to an FEC is made by the LSR that is downstream with respect to that binding. (The downstream LSR informs the upstream LSR of the binding.) Thus, labels are downstream assigned, and the binding is distributed in the upstream direction.

[10]Labels have been used in the ATM network to identify virtual circuits. *Virtual circuit* (VC) *merge* and *virtual path* (VP) *merge* apply, respectively, to the cases when label merging supports mapping multiple ATM VCs into a single VC or multiple VPs into one VP.

At this point, we can define the key concept and product of MPLS—the *Label Distribution Protocol* (LDP), a set of procedures by which one (downstream) LSR informs another (upstream) LSR of the label-to-FEC bindings it has made. The Label Distribution Protocol also includes the negotiations in which these LSRs (called *label distribution peers*) may engage in order to learn of each other's MPLS capabilities. There is no plan for a single LDP—several such protocols are being standardized (like MPLS-LDP and MPLS constraint-based LDP). The existing protocols that can be used for label distribution include RSVP and BGP.

One ingenious feature of MPLS is that it helps implement a network layer tunnel without using encapsulation. Because the traffic that flows along the *label-switched path* (LSP) is defined by the label received at the first LSP node, this path can be treated as a tunnel (called an *LSP tunnel*). By definition, such LSP tunnels are unicast. Tunneling for IP VPNs can be achieved by using a stack (that is, first-in-last-out data structure) of labels rather than a single label. Although forwarding is performed by an LSR always on a single label, the MPLS architecture provides that the labels may be stacked, with the stack carried in an IP packet. The set of packets to be sent through the LSP tunnel constitutes an FEC, and each LSR in the tunnel must assign a label to that FEC (that is, must assign a label to the tunnel). To put a packet into an LSP tunnel, the transmit tunnel endpoint pushes a label for the tunnel onto the label stack and sends the labeled packet to the next hop in the tunnel. The label stack is then popped by the penultimate LSR in the tunnel.

RSVP is being extended to establish unicast LSP tunnels in MPLS networks (with or without resource reservation). IP hosts and routers that support both RSVP and MPLS can associate labels with RSVP flows. (In this case, the flow corresponds to the LSP.) One important application of combining the RSVP and MPLS is that the LSP tunnels can be routed away from the points of network failure or congestion. Finally, we should note that the *mpls* working group has decided to define capability sets (similar to the ITU-T practice). All such capability sets [so far, 10 have been defined in IETF MPLS WG (Andersson et al., 1999)] support basic LDP; they differ in particular features and interwork with other protocols (for example, BGP).

CHAPTER 6

Messaging, Directory, and Network Management Standards

In this chapter, we first cover messaging standards, which are relevant to the support of the unified messaging service, perhaps the most striking application in the area of interworking IN and the Internet. Specifically, we address three messaging-related standards: *Simple Mail Transfer Protocol* (SMTP) and its extensions, *Multipurpose Mail Extensions* (MIME), and *Voice Profile for Internet Mail* (VPIM). After that, we cover the *Lightweight Directory Access Protocol* (LDAP) and *Simple Network Management Protocol* (SNMP), the standards that are used in virtually all products and applications mentioned in this book.

All these standards are defined by the IETF.

Simple Mail Transfer Protocol (SMTP) and Its Extensions

The standards described in this section are essential for products that implement a "four-star" converged network service—the unified messaging service (which was briefly mentioned in Chapter 2 and is described in detail in Chapter 9).

Especially important are SMTP extensions that support profiles for sending voice messages. In this section, we first explain the basic SMTP components before proceeding to the extended SMTP, known as ESMTP (RFC 1869).

The SMTP model (RFC 821) is based on distributed processing. It relies on a sender-SMTP process and a receiver-SMTP process working cooperatively to carry out the task of relaying e-mail. The sender-SMTP governs all communications with the receiver-SMTP. The sender-SMTP issues commands to initiate an SMTP session and transaction, while the receiver-SMTP receives commands, sends replies, and performs the specified operations. In particular, the receiver must respond to every command it receives and the sender must wait for the response before issuing more commands. Note that *session* and *transaction* are two distinct constructs in SMTP. A session denotes the set of exchanges that occur while the transmission channel is open; a transaction, contained in a session, is the set of orderly exchanges required for transmitting a message.

All SMTP exchanges (that is, commands and replies) are in the U.S. ASCII representation. Table 6.1 summarizes the mandatory SMTP commands. As described, every command must be responded to. Moreover, there should be exactly one response to the command to report success, failure, error, or provisional information. SMTP responses are devised to ensure the synchronization of requests and actions in the process of mail transfer and to guarantee that the sender-SMTP always knows the state of the receiver-SMTP.

Figure 6.1 shows an example of SMTP exchanges for sending mail from *Mary@mason.lucent.com* to *John@tao.yale.edu*. For simplicity, we assume that the host *mason.lucent.com* contacts the host *tao.yale.edu* directly. To initiate the session, the sender-SMTP at mason.lucent.com issues a HELO command after a connection to tao.yale.com has been established. With the command the sender host identifies itself and the receiver host specifies its identity in reply as well. The sender then sends the MAIL command, initiating the mail transaction and indicating Mary@mason.lucent.com as the originator of the e-mail. Prepared to accept the mail, the receiver sends a positive reply—250 OK.

Table 6.1   Mandatory SMTP Commands

COMMAND	DESCRIPTION
HELO	Begins a session.
MAIL	Initiates an e-mail transaction to deliver mail to one or more recipients.
RCPT	Identifies an individual recipient of the mail message.
DATA	Indicates to the receiver-SMTP that the following lines from the sender-SMTP are parts of the mail message encoded in the US ASCII representation. (Note that a new line containing just a period indicates the end of the mail message. SMTP includes a procedure to avoid interference with user's actual mail message.)
RSET	Aborts an e-mail transaction.
NOOP	Tests the conductivity of the transmission channel.
QUIT	Ends a session.

```
Receiver:    220 tao.yale.edu Simple Mail Transfer Service Ready
Sender:      HELO mason.lucent.com
Receiver:    250 tao.yale.edu

Sender:      MAIL FROM:<mary@mason.lucent.com>
Receiver:    250 OK

Sender:      RCPT TO:<john@tao.yale.edu>
Receiver:    250 OK

Sender:      DATA
Receiver:    354 Start mail input; end with <CRLF>.<CRLF>
Sender:      This is a test message.
Sender:      Do not respond.
Sender:      .
Receiver:    250 OK

Sender:      QUIT
Receiver:    221 tao.yale.edu Service closing transmission channel
```

Figure 6.1   Example SMTP exchange.

Upon receipt of the reply, the sender issues an RCPT command indicating John@tao.yale.edu as the recipient of the e-mail. The receiver can relay mail to the recipient, so it responds positively with 250 OK. The sender then sends a DATA command and, upon receiving the provisional reply 354, follows with the message as a series of ASCII lines. When the receiver receives the end of text—a line containing only a period—it responds with a 250 OK reply. (Note that it is possible that the end-of-text delimiter may interfere with the message text. SMTP includes a procedure to avoid such interference. Also, a mail transaction, once started, must be followed by one or more RCPT commands and a DATA command, in that order.) Finally, the sender issues a QUIT command to end the session and the receiver responds positively with a 221 reply. QUIT must be the last command in a session and cannot be used at any other time in a session.

Originally designed for relaying plaintext mail, SMTP lends itself to extensions to transfer other types of mail, such as audio and images, more efficiently. The framework defined in RFC 1869 allows all SMTP extensions to be built in a consistent way. A key component is EHLO, a new command that lets an extended SMTP server and receiver recognize each other as such. A sender-SMTP supporting SMTP service extensions should start an SMTP session with the EHLO instead of the HELO command. In response, the receiver-SMTP indicates the service extensions, if any, that it supports.

Naturally, the service extensions must be available to the public before they can be used. The framework includes procedures for defining extensions. The procedures require all service extensions to be defined in standard-track or experimental RFCs and to be registered with the Internet Assigned Number Authority (IANA).

The initial registered service extensions listed in RFC 1869 consist of those SMTP commands defined as optional in RFC 821. Subsequent RFCs have defined extensions for, for example, transmission of large amounts of binary data (RFC 1830), message size declaration (RFC 1870), and command piping (RFC 2197).

Also included in the ESMTP framework is the provision of additional parameters for the SMTP MAIL and RCPT commands. Service extensions can make use of these parameters to convey additional information pertinent to a mail transaction. For example, the message size declaration extension (RFC 1870) adds a SIZE parameter to the MAIL command so that an ESMTP sender can inform an ESMTP receiver of the size of the message to be sent. This is particularly useful for efficient transmission of large messages such as multiminute voice mail. Note that all new parameters should be defined and registered as part of the service extension procedures described previously.

Multipurpose Internet Mail Extensions (MIME)

Like SMTP and its extensions, MIME is another standard necessary for the implementation of the Unified Messaging platforms.

The widely deployed Internet mail standard RFC 822 (aka STD 11) defines the format of e-mail messages on the Internet. Designed in the early days of the Advanced Research Projects Agency Network (ARPANET), RFC 822 is ideal to support text messages written in English and coded in ASCII. It is, however, inadequate to support messages of different kinds—such as messages in Chinese and messages with multimedia content—which are common today. The extension of RFC 822 for support beyond simple text messages resulted in a set of IETF standards collectively called *Multipurpose Internet Mail Extensions* (MIME).

The basic idea of MIME is to add structure to the message body defined in RFC 822 and to supply encoding rules for non-ASCII messages. Because they do not deviate from RFC 822, MIME messages can be sent across the network using the existing e-mail systems. The result is an Internet message format that allows for:

- Textual header information in character sets other than U.S. ASCII
- Textual message bodies in character sets other than U.S. ASCII
- Multiple-part message bodies
- Message bodies of an extensible set of media types, such as audio, video, and image

---

THE LIST OF CURRENT RFCs SPECIFYING MIME

- RFC 2045, N. Freed and N. Borenstein, 1996. "Multipurpose Internet Mail Extensions (MIME) Part One: Format of Internet Message Bodies."
- RFC 2046, N. Freed and N. Borenstein, 1996. "Multipurpose Internet Mail Extensions (MIME) Part Two: Media Types."
- RFC 2047, K. Moore, 1996. "Multipurpose Internet Mail Extensions (MIME) Part Three: Message Header Extensions for Non-ASCII Text."
- RFC 2048, N. Freed, J. Klensin, and J. Postel, 1996. "Multipurpose Internet Mail Extensions (MIME) Part Four: Registration Procedures."
- RFC 2049, N. Freed and N. Borenstein, 1996. "Multipurpose Internet Mail Extensions (MIME) Part Five: Conformance Criteria and Examples."
- RFC 2231, N. Freed and K. Moore, 1997. "MIME Parameter Value and Encoded Word Extensions: Character Sets, Languages, and Continuations."
   RFC 2231 is not part of the original MIME-related RFC series; it provides updates to RFC 2045 and RFC 2047.

The MIME message format includes five new header fields, shown in Table 6.2. Of particular interest here is the Content-Type header field for specifying the nature of the data in the body of a message part. This is done through media type and subtype identifiers and auxiliary information that may be required for certain media types. The media type declares the general type of data (for example, image); the subtype declares a particular format for that type of data (for example, JPEG). Table 6.3 shows the initial set of MIME media types and subtypes defined in RFC 2045. Among the media types, the last two are specific for use with composite entities. *Multipart* indicates that the message contains more than one part, with the beginning and end of each part being clearly delimited; *message* indicates that the message encapsulates another message, such as in the case of forwarded e-mail. Note that the set of

Table 6.2 MIME Header Fields

HEADER FIELD	FUNCTION
MIME-Version:	Declares the MIME version in use.
Content-Transfer-Encoding:	Specifies how the message is encoded for transmission.
Content-Type:	Identifies the nature of the message.
Content-ID:	Declares the unique message identifier for reference by other messages.
Content-Description:	Describes the content of the message, typically in plaintext.

Table 6.3 MIME Media Types and Subtypes (RFC 2046)

MEDIA TYPE	MEDIA SUBTYPE	DESCRIPTION
Text	Plain	Unformatted text.
Image	Jpeg	Still picture in the JPEG format.
Audio	Basic	Single-channel audio encoded in PCM.
Video	Mpeg	Video in the MPEG format.
Application	Octet-stream	Arbitrary binary data.
	Postscript	Printable document in PostScript.
Message	Rfc822	Encapsulated RFC 822 message.
	Partial	Message split for transmission.
	External-body	Message included by reference.
Multipart	Mixed	Independent parts in the specified order.
	Alternative	Same information in different formats.
	Digest	Each part by default a RFC 822 message.
	Parallel	Parts to be viewed simultaneously.

MIME media types and subtypes is extensible. New media types and subtypes can be defined on an as-needed basis without any changes to the basic standards. Furthermore, a registration process is in place to allow this to be done in an open, orderly manner. MIME also has provisions to distinguish nonstandard media types and subtypes. These media types and subtypes should have the prefix X- and should be used for experimental or private purposes only.

Another interesting MIME header field is Content-Transfer-Encoding. Should the native representation of a message body happen to be unsupported by the message transport, encoding transformation is required to transform the message body into one that is supported. The Content-Transfer-Encoding header field is used for specifying the encoding transformation scheme as well as the domain of the transformation. MIME permits three encoding transformation schemes (*identity*, *quoted-printable*, and *base64*) and three domains (*7bit, 8bit,* and *binary*). The quoted-printable and base64 schemes are described in RFC 2045. Here we simply note that both schemes transform messages into the 7-bit representation, with the quoted-printable scheme for messages with just a few non-ASCII characters and the base64 scheme for binary messages. The 7-bit representation is the most suitable representation for data to be transported over the 7-bit text-oriented Internet mail protocol SMTP. Specifically, data in the 7-bit representation, according to RFC 2045, is described as:

". . . relatively short lines with 998 octets or less between CRLF line separation sequences. No octets with decimal values greater than 127 are allowed and neither are NULs (octets with decimal value 0). CR (decimal value 13) and LF (decimal value 10) octets only occur as part of CRLF line separation sequences."

The 8-bit representation has a similar definition. The only difference is that octets with decimal values greater than 127 may be used. Finally comes the binary representation, which permits any sequence of octets.

Voice Profile for Internet Mail (VPIM)

Voice Profile for Internet Mail (VPIM) is a specification for the exchange of voice and fax messages between messaging servers over an IP network. As such, it characterizes (similarly to SMTP and MIME) another essential component of unified messaging. VPIM defines the format of the messages as well as the way to transport the messages across the network. In particular, VPIM specifies a restricted profile of MIME and ESMTP (RFC 1869) (see the preceding sections.) The basis of the major Internet messaging standards explains why the various versions of VPIM have also been submitted to and reviewed by the IETF, even though they were originally developed by the *Electronic Messaging Association* (EMA) (www.ema.org). The IETF has approved VPIM Version 2 as a Proposed Standard (RFC 2421).

VPIM enables Internet mail systems to be used to transport voice and fax messages, even though these messages may have originated or terminated in the PSTN. In addition, the user can be given access to voice and fax messages from an Internet mail application (see Chapter 9). The rest of this section summarizes key components of VPIM V2, including addressing scheme, message body format, and message transport.

The VPIM addressing scheme provides for the unique identification of the sender (or recipient) of a VPIM message, whose access device may be a simple telephone. It is composed of two parts: the host part for server identification and the local part for user or mailbox identifier. Specifically, the host part is based on the domain name system (DNS) (RFC1035) and the local part on ITU-T Recommendation E.164. The purpose of restriction to a numerical local part is to maintain compatibility with traditional messaging servers tailored to a single type of access device—telephones. An example of a VPIM address is +17329490321@lucent.com.

Regarding the format of the message body, VPIM supports a profile of MIME. Using the extension mechanism of MIME, VPIM adds a new content type—multipart/voice-message. In most cases, this content type is declared in the top-level header of a VPIM message, which is typically composed of multiple parts containing content such as the spoken name, spoken subject, voice message (or fax message), and electronic business card of the originator. Each of the multiple parts also carries a content type. VPIM V2 only supports certain content types. In particular, Audio/32KADPCM is the content type that must be used for parts carrying voice information; 32KADPCM denotes the 32-kbps ADPCM voice encoding standard (as defined in the IUT-T Recommendation G.726) according to which the voice must be encoded. Image/Tiff, on the other hand, is the content type that must be used for parts carrying fax messages. Moreover, the F profile of Tag Image File Format (RFC 2306) must be used for fax encoding.

VPIM V2 also specifies how the entire message should be encoded for transporting. If binary transport is available, voice and fax parts are to be sent in binary format (RFC 2045). Otherwise, they are to be encoded in base64. In order to meet MIME requirements and to preserve interoperability with the fullest range of possible devices, the detection and decoding of *Quoted-Printable, 7bit, and 8bit* is also mandatory in VPIM V2.

Another key issue addressed by VPIM V2 is how messages should be transported between messaging systems. ESMTP (RFC 1869) is the mechanism selected for message transporting.[1]

VPIM V2 does not interfere with desktop delivery protocols [such as Internet Message Access Protocol (IMAP) (RFC 2060) or Post Office Protocol Version 3 (POP3) (RFC 1939)]. The user can employ IMAP (or POP) to retrieve VPIM messages from a remote mailbox just like regular text e-mail messages.

POP3 is a simple protocol used for fetching e-mail from a remote mailbox and storing it on the user's local machine to be read later. It has commands for the user to log in, log out, fetch messages, and delete messages. Encoded as U.S. ASCII text, it has some flavor of SMTP. Compared with POP3, IMAP is a more sophisticated delivery protocol. Its key objective is to let the e-mail server maintain a central mailbox to which the user can have access from any computer, such as a workstation in the office, a PC at home, or a laptop on the road. As a result, unlike POP3, IMAP does not copy e-mail to the user's personal machine. In addition, IMAP has advanced features such as addressing mail not simply by arrival sequence but by attributes like subject and sender.

Lightweight Directory Access Protocol (LDAP)

As a general mechanism of the IP-based network for retrieval of the directory information, LDAP is uniformly supported by all products (IP PBXs, multiservice modules, and universal messaging platforms, to name just a few) that require directory access.

The *Lightweight Directory Access Protocol* (LDAP) was designed by the IETF for accessing directories based on the X.500 data model and directory service.

---

[1]In particular, the following ESMTP commands, keywords, and parameters must be supported: HELO, MAIL, RCPT, DATA, QUIT, RSET, EHLO, SIZE (RFC 1870), DSN (RFC 1894), and NOTIFY (RFC 1891).

It is a less complex alternative to the Directory Access Protocol defined by the ITU-T for the same purpose. At the time of this writing, the third version of the LDAP specification RFC 2251 has been approved by the IETF as a Proposed Standard.

Before describing LDAP, we should review its foundation: the X.500 data model and directory service. The X.500 data model is hierarchical; the information in the directory is arranged in the form of a tree, called the *directory information tree* (DIT), where the vertices denote entries representing objects in the real world. An entry is composed of attributes, each with a type and one or more values. Normally, one of the attributes is special in the way it has to assume a unique value for each of the sibling entries (that is, those descending from the same vertex) in the DIT. As a result, the attribute and value pair, called the *relative distinguished name* (RDN), unambiguously distinguishes an entry from its siblings. The concatenation of the RDN of an entry and the RDNs of all its superior nodes (in descending order) further forms the *distinguished name*, which uniquely identifies the entry in the entire DIT.

The X.500 directory is a logical concept and is normally distributed across many directories in practice. According to ITU-T Recommendation X.500, the directory provides the directory service upon the requests of users. The requests, subject to security measures such as authentication and access control, are typically to interrogate or modify the directory entries. The directory always reports the outcome of a request, whether the operation succeeds or not. In particular, X.500 permits the directory to return a referral, which suggests an alternative access point where the user can make the request.

In support of the X.500 data model and directory service, LDAP is designed as a client-server protocol, which assumes a reliable connection-oriented underlying transport, such as *Transmission Control Protocol/Internet Protocol* (TCP/IP). A client sends a server a request describing the operation desired on the X.500 directory. The server performs the operation and then returns one or more responses indicating the results of the operation. RFC 2251 specifies the following LDAP requests:

- *BindRequest.* Starts an LDAP protocol session; allows authentication information to be exchanged between the client and server.

- *UnbindRequest.* Terminates an LDAP protocol session.

- *SearchRequest.* Requests a search based on specified criteria within the directory.

- *AddRequest.* Adds an entry into the directory.

- *ModifyRequest.* Modifies an entry in the directory.

- *DelRequest.* Removes an entry from the directory.

- *ModifyDNRequest.* Changes the leftmost component of the name of an entry or moves a subtree of entries to a new location in the directory.

- *CompareRequest.* Compares an assertion against the attributes of an entry in the directory.
- *AbandonRequest.* Abandons an outstanding operation.

For each of the preceding requests, a matching response is defined.

A notable aspect of LDAP Version 3 is its support of operations defined elsewhere using a special request, *ExtendedRequest,* which serves as the envelope for foreign operations. The results of the operations are returned in the response to *ExtendedRequest.* This special request feature enables development of dynamic directory services, which are particularly relevant to services such as IP telephony and Internet call waiting. Dynamic directory services are concerned with the directory entries that exist only for a certain period of time. Such an entry is associated with a *time-to-live,* which is set upon creation and can be reset as needed. After being set or reset, the *time-to-live* decreases with each clock tick. When it reaches zero, the entry is removed. An example of dynamic entries is the description of an online user; naturally it exists only for as long as the user stays online. RFC 2598 defines an operation to be used within *ExtendedRequest* to refresh the time-to-live of a dynamic entry by a client, typically the creator of the entry. In addition, it defines the schema extensions required for representing dynamic entries.

RFC 2251 defines the LDAP syntax in Abstract Syntax Notation One (ASN.1). In addition, it prescribes that ASN.1 Basic Encoding Rules (BER) be used to encode the protocol elements for transfer. Certain restrictions apply to avoid the high overhead associated with BER.

Network Management

As we stressed in Chapters 2 and 3, network management is an indispensable part of operations of both the telecommunications and data networks. In STN, the *operations support system* (OSS) products (specialized for every application) predated the development of the standards in this area. Once the products were developed and successfully deployed, the change toward the standardized framework came about rather slowly. In the Internet, on the other hand—due to its relative youth—there was a base set of OSI standards by the time the need for network management became critical. Since that time, the products and standards have been evolving in conjunction.

The PSTN network management standards *Telecommunications Management Network* (TMN) and *Common Management Identification Protocol* (CMIP) were developed jointly by the ISO and ITU-T Study Group 4 and standardized in ITU-T Recommendation M.3010. The Internet standard developed in the operations and management area of the IETF is called *Simple Network Management Protocol* (SNMP).

Both TMN/CMIP and SNMP were made out of the rib of the OSI framework, sharing the basic concepts [such as *managed objects* and *management information base* (MIB)] as well as the language for their specification (ASN.1). RFC 1157 gives an interesting historical overview of the subject and notes that the first two relevant IETF RFCs were designed to be compatible with both SNMP and the OSI network management framework. In fact, the eventual transition to OSI-based network management *was* part of the SNMP strategy, but, as RFC 1109 reports, the requirement of compatibility with OSI was lifted in 1989 because needs of the Internet had become different from those of the OSI. Since then, the development of SNMP has proceeded on its own, resulting in several full-blown Internet standards (for example, RFC 1155). There is also a specification for SNMP over OSI, specified by RFC 1418.

Because the network management products described in Chapter 9 are invariably based on SNMP, we will consider only SNMP for network management from this point forward. Much has been written about SNMP. Perhaps the best book is Rose and McCloghrie (1994), which is authored by active participants in the IETF work who also wrote several fundamental SNMP-related RFCs. If you would like to follow up by reading RFCs, we recommend RFC 1157 as the first one to read. The (informational) RFC 2570 is an excellent reference to the latest SNMP version—SNMP v3.

RFC 1157 describes an early model of a managed network, which *is* in fact simple. The physical entities involved (illustrated in Figure 6.2) are *management stations*, which execute specialized management applications, and *network elements*, which are managed by the management stations. A network element can be any device, as long as it is attached to the IP network; examples include hosts, gateways, and terminal servers, as shown in Figure 6.2. The actual exchange of *management information* takes place between the application processes.

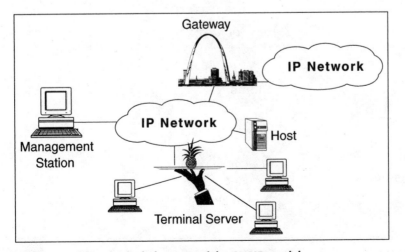

Figure 6.2 The physical elements of the SNMP model.

As Figure 6.3 demonstrates, the management process (executed by the management station) communicates via SNMP with the *managed agent* processes (which are executed by network elements) and *SNMP proxies.* The latter are processes that act as managed agents on behalf of non-SNMP-compliant devices. The role of an SNMP proxy is to translate the SNMP messages into something equivalent but understandable to the device represented by the proxy, and, conversely, to translate the information obtained from such a device into something the management station can understand. The messages between a proxy and its device are typically carried by a proprietary protocol. In general, management stations are attached to an IP network, but SNMP can also run over protocol stacks other than the Internet.

The main purpose of SNMP is to carry requests from management stations to the network elements in order to (1) provide the device state information (which is sent back to the management stations in matching responses) or (2) change the state to a certain (supplied) value. The state of a network element is represented by the set of the values of predefined data structures (called *objects*); the full collection of the objects pertinent to a device and ordered lexicographically is called the network element's *management information base* (MIB). The same term also applies to the state associated in a network element with executing a particular protocol. (For this reason, many IETF groups specify MIB documents related to protocols they are working on.)

RFC 2570 summarizes the basic structure of the Internet standard management framework common to all versions of SNMP in a somewhat different language, referring to the following four components: (1) several managed nodes, each with an SNMP entity that provides remote access to management instrumentation; (2) at least one SNMP entity with management applications;

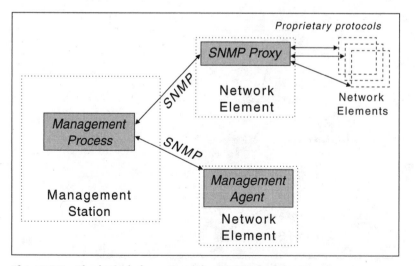

Figure 6.3 The logical elements of the SNMP model.

(3) management information; and (4) the management protocol to carry it among the entities.

Just to give a few simple examples, we describe several (but by no means *all*) operations of the early two versions of SMNP. The management station sends the following protocol data units (PDUs): *get-request*, *get-next-request* (for the value of the next variable in the MIB), *get-bulk-request* (for large data structures—an SNMP version 2 efficiency improvement), and *set-request*. These PDUs contain the methods to be invoked on the network elements' objects.

The management agent (or SNMP proxy) responds with the *get-response* PDU. SNMP also allows network elements to send unsolicited messages (that is, messages that are not responses to *get-request*) that inform the management station about certain events, such as cold or warm start, change of link state (up or down), and authentication failure (see RFC 1157). Unsolicited event messages are carried in *trap* PDUs.

Although SNMP can run on several protocol stacks, in the IP world its messages are typically carried by UDP. Thus a specific UDP port (UDP port 161) has been prescribed for the reception of all SMNP PDUs except the *trap* ones by both the management station and the managed agent (or SMNP proxy). UDP port 162 has been assigned for the reception of *trap* PDUs by the management station.

The precise format and layout of the MIB objects and PDUs is specified using a simplified version of the ASN.1 language. The ASN.1 specifications are typically compiled to produce the encoding and decoding processes. As in the case of LDAP, the encoding is performed using BER.

At the time of SNMPv1, Internet security was not much of an issue. RFC 1155, for example, does not even contain the word *security*, although it does deal with authentication—performed by carrying the "community strings" in all messages.

The second version of SNMP (SNMP v2) improved on SNMP v1 by expanding data types, improving efficiency, and adding confirmed event notification and error handling, just to list a few significant changes. Nevertheless, the so-called "commercial-grade" security still was not quite there, nor was what RFC 1570 identifies as "suitable remote configuration and administration capabilities."

The latest version of SNMP (SNMP v3) has a significantly more extensible SNMP framework developed by the IETF SNMP Version 3 (*snmpv3*) working group (www.ietf.org/html.charters/snmpv3-charter.html). The appropriate definition of security and administration has been identified as the single most critical need of SNMP.

RFC 2571 describes the overall architecture of SNMP v3 (and its relation to earlier versions) and provides an abstract and systematic approach to SNMP standardization. Figure 6.4 (after RFC 2571) demonstrates the SNMP documents classification. Note an emphasis on the coexistence of different ver-

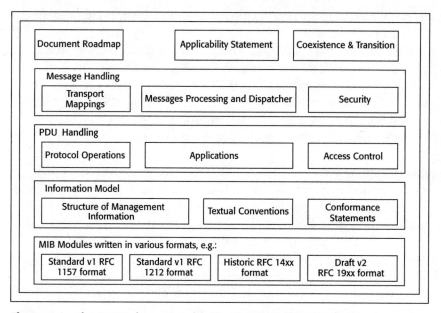

Figure 6.4   The SNMP document classification (after RFC 2571).
Source: RFC 2571.

sions and the design that supports smooth transition from an earlier version to a later one. Another essential design decision is support of different transport mechanisms; the transport mappings specifications map SNP to specific transport mechanisms.

The present SNMP v3 documents define a new SNMP message format, remote configuration of SNMP parameters, message security (both authentication and privacy), and access control.

With this rather brief discussion of the network management discussion, we conclude Chapter 6. Our next topic is standards related to remote access.

Remote-Access-Related Standards

In this chapter we address access to IP networks over the PSTN lines with IP riding on top of PSTN circuits, which is relevant to technologies in both the PSTN and the Internet. We have already discussed PSTN signaling standards (for the purpose of Internet offloading); the related Internet standards fall into the following categories:

- Point-to-point interactions over the PSTN
- Authentication, authorization, and accounting (AAA)
- Internet Protocol security
- Multihoming (that is, maintenance of connections to multiple Internet service providers)

We address each *category* in its own section.

Point-to-Point Interactions over the PSTN

As Figure 7.1 demonstrates, point-to-point lines are used either to provide connections to end users over dialed-up lines or to interconnect two routers (in which case the connections may be leased from a telephone company). Naturally, certain difficult problems (like authentication, authorization, and

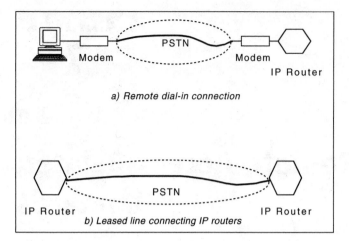

Figure 7.1   Two types of point-to-point connections over the
PSTN: (*a*) remote dial-in connection; (*b*) leased line connecting
IP routers.

accounting) are more pertinent to the former case, in which the end users'
PCs dial into an ISP or enterprise network.[1]

A typical telephone line, attached to a modem at either end, provides a
serial (that is, one bit at a time) stream of bits to the entities interfacing the
modems. In order to move IP packets (and consequently everything running
on top of IP), a link layer protocol is needed. An earlier link layer protocol for
point-to-point communications called *Serial Line IP* (SLIP) (RFC 1055) has
become widely deployed, although it is being phased out. SLIP has a number
of drawbacks: it monopolizes the telephone line for carrying IP only, and it
merely provides framing, leaving error correction (and even detection) to
transport or application layers. Leaving error detection to higher-layer protocols is acceptable in local area networks, but serial lines have a higher error
rate, and this may cause problems—especially in the case depicted in Figure
7.1, where hosts in the networks on either side of the serial line must retrans-
mit transport layer messages through *all* involved networks just because of
problems on *one* link. Yet another problem with SLIP is that each end must
know the IP address of its interlocutor. For additional discussion of SLIP, see
Tanenbaum (1996) or Stevens (1994).

Running teletype terminal applications (which require that every byte
transmitted by a terminal be echoed by the host) over TCP/IP/SLIP stack
produces an overhead of 40 (!) bytes for each byte carried across the line.
Implementation of the header compression mechanism of RFC 1144, which
effectively moves awareness of the TCP connection state into the link layer,
causes reduction of the header overhead by about an order of magnitude. A

---

[1]Strictly speaking, dialing in does not happen with the digital subscriber lines (DSL) described
in Chapter 2. In this case, end users effectively get permanent connections.

similar compression mechanism combined with a number of features (for example, error detection and support of multiple protocols on a single line) that eliminates SLIP deficiencies results in a new link layer protocol—or rather interworking family of protocols—called *Point-to-Point Protocol* (PPP). RFC 1661 defines the three components of PPP as:

1. "A method for encapsulating multiprotocol datagrams.

2. "A link control protocol (LCP) for establishing, configuring, and testing the data link connection.

3. "A family of network control protocols (NCPs) for establishing and configuring different network layer protocols."

To this end, the PPP RFC (RFC 1661) describes the first two components. By design, each network layer protocol needs a separate NCP. For the purposes of this book, RFC 1332 is most important in that it defines the IP NCP (IPCP), which configures, enables, and disables the IP protocol modules on both ends of the point-to-point link and handles the IP address assignment dynamically. The IPCP also specifies the Van Jacobson TCP/IP header compression of RFC 1144 for PPP. The IPCP is effectively an extension of the LCP, which restricts the use of the latter's fields and temporal procedures.

Overall, PPP has eliminated all SLIP deficiencies. Specifically, it detects errors and supports multiple protocols on a single serial line, as well as dynamic setting of IP addresses (through the IPCP). The importance of the latter feature is hard to overestimate; for one thing, it eliminates the enterprises' need to own an IP address for each PC. On a grander scale, the ability to assign the IP addresses only for the duration of a session (and, in fact, more than once) is a key enabler of *virtual private network* (VPN) services. PPP (namely, the LCP) also allows negotiation of a protocol to authenticate peers (we cover specific protocols in a later section).

In fact, since the PPP was defined, its extensions to PPP have mushroomed. The IETF PPP Extensions working group (www.ietf.org/html.charters/pppext-charter.html) lists more than 50 RFCs. Obvious reasons prevent us from merely listing all of these RFCs, let alone going into any level of detail of even a sizable fraction of this rich set. For the purposes of this book, RFC 1618 is important because it specifies the use of PPP over the ISDN B and D channels.

Terminating a dial-in connection at an entity within the network one dials can be quite expensive. Conversely, as discussed in Chapter 2, the PSTN needs to offload data calls as soon as possible. The IETF PPP Extensions WG solved this problem by specifying the *Layer Two Tunneling Protocol* (L2TP) in RFC 2661. With this solution, the PPP packets terminating at an access concentrator (which can be located as close to the local telephone switch as needed) are *tunneled* (that is, carried as the payload by higher layers so as to be transparent to the underlying network) over the Internet (or any other IP network) to the *network access server* located in the destination network. L2TP is the protocol that performs the Layer 2 tunneling.

Figure 7.2 demonstrates the architecture for point-to-point connections over the PSTN. In order to maintain a seamless point-to-point connection between the remote system and the home network, the *L2TP access concentrator* (LAC) terminates the dial-in connection and passes the PPP frames between the remote system and the *L2TP network server* (LNS) of the home network.

Figure 7.3 is an example of flow across protocol layers, in which the SMTP client on the remote system communicates with the SMTP server on the host in the home network. In this example, the PPP frames received over the ISDN B-channel are encapsulated in L2TP frames, which are then sent over UDP/IP/LAN and over the Internet (note that L2TP acts as transport layer in this case) to the LNS. The LNS extracts the PPP payload (that is, IP packets) and sends it over the LAN to the SMTP server. The SMTP server sends the response traffic in exactly the reverse order.

As RFC 2661 points out, not only the access concentrator but any host running the LAC client software can participate in this particular tunneling scheme. Note that the remote-system-to-LAC link is a "real" point-to-point link, which means that the exact IP addresses involved in the exchange (in particular, the IP address of the remote system) are not essential as far as this particular link is concerned. Nor is the IP address of the remote system of any relevance (or even visible) to the Internet part of the path. That means the IP address of the remote system does not have to come from the (quickly decreasing) pool of available registered IPv4 addresses but could be assigned by the home network. In fact, it could be assigned temporarily for every session. The general issue of interconnecting private networks (which may use

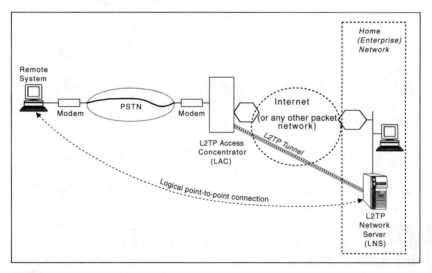

Figure 7.2   L2TP Architecture.

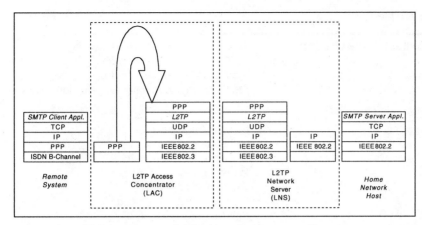

Figure 7.3 Layer-by-layer arrangement example.

unregistered IP addresses) with the Internet is presently addressed in the IETF Network Address Translators (*nat*) working group (www.ietf.org/html .charters/nat-charter.html).

L2TP uses control messages to establish, maintain, and clear tunnels and calls; it uses data messages to carry the PPP frames. Control messages employ sequence numbers and other mechanisms that ensure their reliable delivery, but data messages are transmitted over unreliable channels. Both types of messages are transmitted over UDP if the IP networks are tunneled; the use of UDP port 1701 is prescribed for the L2TP traffic. RFC 2661 also defines the encoding scheme, which hides (that is, encrypts) the values of certain attributes. Examples of such attributes are *challenge* and *challenge response*, which are used for the authentication of the channel endpoints as discussed later in this chapter. The L2TP control messages (listed in Table 7.1) fall into four categories—control connection management, call management, error reporting, and PPP session control.

The L2TP tunnel can be started by either the LAC or LNS. The names of the control connection messages are self-explanatory, except for Hello, which is a "keep-alive" message intended to ensure that a tunnel that has had no traffic for a while is still active. Within a tunnel, call-related *sessions* are established. Calls can be incoming (for example, really *dial-in*), in which case the respective request messages are originated by the LAC, or outgoing, in which case the requests are originated by the LNS. Keeping track of the dial-up connections is coupled with the DSS1. In fact, the values of certain attributes— namely the *Cause Code* and *Cause messages* (such as *DISCONNECT*)—are encoded as specified in ITU-T Recommendation Q.931. RFC 2661 specifies state machines for both the tunnel-related and session-related protocols, which clearly define sequencing of relevant messages.

Of course, tunneling can be (and, in fact, is) performed at the layers other than Layer 2. In Chapter 3 we discussed Layer 3 tunneling with MPLS.

Table 7.1   L2TP Messages

Control connection management	Start-Control-Connection-Request
	Start-Control-Connection-Reply
	Start-Control-Connection-Connected
	Stop-Control-Connection-Notification
	Hello
Call management	Outgoing-Call-Request
	Outgoing-Call-Reply
	Outgoing-Call-Connected
	Incoming-Call-Request
	Incoming-Call-Reply
	Incoming-Call-Connected
	Call-Disconnect-Notify
Error reporting	WAN-Error-Notify
PPP session control	Set-Link-Info

Another Layer 3 tunneling technique (that is, encapsulation of IP messages within IP), which will be further addressed in the section on IP security, is systematically used in support of VPNs. This type of tunneling is standardized in RFC 2003 as the means of altering "the normal IP routing for datagrams, by delivering them to an intermediate destination that would otherwise not be selected by the (network part of the) IP Destination Address field in the original IP header."

Authentication, Authorization, and Accounting (AAA)

Authentication, authorization, and accounting have become so important that the IETF has started a separate working group (www.ietf.org/html .charters/aaa-charter.html) that is focusing on a general AAA architecture for the Internet in order to "create a set of base protocols applicable to a number of specific AAA applications." The applications include IP telephony and access server AAA. Note that the IETF does not get involved in the issues of business models or billing; the first two As were standardized as part of *Remote Authentication Dial-In User Service* (*RADIUS*), defined in RFC 2138, while the accounting part is published in the informational RFC 2139. RADIUS has been implemented and deployed in remote access servers (see Chapter 10); the *aaa* working group was created as a follow-up to RADIUS.

Authentication of an entity can be done via a *Password Authentication Protocol* (PAP), which sends the request for password and then verifies the response, or a *Challenge Handshake Authentication Protocol* (CHAP), which "challenges" the entity to be authenticated by sending it a random string *S*.

The entity uses a function f (identified by a secret key, which may otherwise be known only to the authenticator) to compute $f(S)$. The computed value is sent to the authenticator, who computes the same function on the same string, checks the response, and confirms or fails the entity depending on whether the computed and received values are equal. In a communication session, this process can repeat at random intervals.

PPP CHAP is standardized in RFC 1994, which, among other things, provides a thorough review of its advantages and disadvantages (there are some) as well as some practical considerations. RFC 1994 specifies four messages: *Challenge, Response, Success,* and *Failure. Challenge* is sent during the authentication phase (but it may be sent at other times, too); it is sent again and again until a satisfactory *Response* message is received (or an optional counter exceeds a specified value). The *Failure* message is sent if the *Response* value is unsatisfactory; otherwise, naturally, the *Success* message is sent.

Although authentication is performed in only one direction, the processes on the both ends of the PPP link can use it to authenticate each other. RFC 1994 effectively requires that Message Digest Algorithm Five (MD5) (RFC 1321) be supported for hashing with CHAP. In practice, either specialized hardware (typically, a card) or software is employed to compute the challenge. Although we don't cover cryptography in detail, it is worth at least explaining why the words *message digest* are used in the name of the algorithm. This happens because the algorithm, which takes a message M of any length as an input, produces as the output a string $MD5(M)$, whose length is fixed. Computing this string is much faster than encrypting the whole message. For more information on cryptography, see Tanenbaum (1996).

RFC 2138 defines RADIUS as a client-server protocol. One client of the RADIUS server is the *Network Access Server* (NAS), which can perform the LAC or LNS function (or both). In turn, a RADIUS server may also act as a proxy client to other RADIUS or (non-RADIUS) authenticating servers. When a user requests a connection, the NAS makes a corresponding request to an appropriate RADIUS server, which then attempts to authenticate the users. If the authentication is successful, the RADIUS server sends to the NAS the configuration information pertinent to the user in order to establish the requested connection and otherwise provide all services that the user is entitled to. Specifically, RADIUS server queries the user database, whose entries include lists of requirements (such as password verification) to be met in order to establish the connection. The user database entries may contain specific resources (for example, servers) that a particular user may access as well as specific port numbers.

All transactions between the client and server are authenticated through the use of the *shared secret*, which is never sent over the network. (The users' passwords, however, *are* sent to RADIUS servers over the network, but they are always encrypted before they are sent.) The shared secret is put through the MD5 algorithm to create a 16-octet-long digest value used to authenticate messages between the RADIUS client and RADIUS server. Before we continue our discussion of the RADIUS messages, note that ultimately it is the NAS that is responsible for authenticating the end user (with or without RADIUS). Thus the NAS is the first entity to receive the user's password. (This is done by either prompting the user or employing the information that arrived in the PPP authentication packets.)

Once the NAS has the password, it may submit it to a RADIUS server in the *Access-Request* message, whose attributes include the user's ID and password (hidden using the MD5 algorithm). The RADIUS server considers such a request valid only if it shares a secret with the client. All invalid *Access-Request* messages are discarded; every valid *Access-Request* message is responded to (after a lookup in the user database) with one of the following three messages:

- *Access-Reject.* This message is issued if the requirements pertinent to the user requesting access are not met.

- *Access-Accept.* This message is issued if such requirements are met.

- *Access-Challenge.* This message is issued if the user is to be authenticated via the challenge mechanism.

The latter message may include the text (typically obtained from an external server) to be displayed to the user (for example, *Challenge 90778976. Please respond at the prompt =>*). The NAS issues the request to the user, collects the response, encrypts it, and sends it back to the RADIUS server in the password field of yet another *Access-Request* message. The RADIUS server may then issue another challenge or reply with either *Access-Reject* or *Access-Accept*, depending on whether the user's response to the challenge matches the expected response.

For the cases where PAP and CHAP are employed by the NAS, RFC 2138 specifies interworking with these protocols, which in most cases amounts to one-to-one mapping of respective attributes. In some cases, however, the RADIUS server may be unable to perform the requested CHAP-compliant authentication. In the example given in RFC 2138, the user password may be unknown to the RADIUS server in cleartext. Since CHAP needs the cleartext password value in order to encrypt the CHAP challenge, RADIUS cannot perform the authentication. RFC 2138 leaves no ambiguity, however, by requesting that the RADIUS server send *Access-Reject* when it cannot go through with authentication.

The remaining RADIUS messages are:

- *Accounting Request* and *Accounting Response.* Described in the informational RADIUS RFC (2139), although their codes are assigned by RFC 2138.

- *Status-Server* and *Status-Client.* Designated *experimental* by RFC 2138.

All the RADIUS messages are assigned codes specified in RFC 2138. In addition, one RADIUS message code is reserved for the future.

RFC 2138 has deliberately chosen UDP as the transport layer for RADIUS messages. Four reasons for doing so include:

1. Presence of alternative servers.
2. Timing requirements.
3. Stateless nature of the protocol.
4. Simplification of server implementation.

Internet Protocol Security (IPsec)

The work on the *IP security suite protocol* (IPsec) is carried out in the *ipsec* working group (www.ietf.org/html.charters/ipsec-charter.html) in the security area of the IETF. We strongly recommend Kaufman and Newman (1999) if you would like a detailed treatment of the subject and its business applications.

RFC 2401 defines the design goal of the IP security (IPsec) protocol as the means to provision interoperable, high-quality, cryptography-based security for both versions of IP protocol—IPv4 and IPv6. In a nutshell, the IPsec suite provides privacy (through encryption) and authentication services at the IP layer (which, among other things, means that application and transport security as well as data link layer security are outside of the scope of the IPsec suite). The services provided by the suite include access control, connectionless integrity, confidentiality, and protection against replays (that is, reuse of snooped messages).

To provide these services, first, two traffic security protocols are defined:

- *Authentication Header (AH) (RFC 2402)*. Provides connectionless integrity, data origin authentication, and an (optional) antireplay service.

- *Encapsulating Security Payload (ESP) (RFC 2406)*. Provides one of the two sets of services:

  1. Confidentiality and limited traffic flow confidentiality.
  2. Integrity, data origin authentication, and an antireplay service.

Each of these protocols can be used in either *transport mode* (where transport protocols are protected) or *tunnel mode* (where the IP itself is protected). Tunnel mode is particularly important to VPN services in connection with IPIP (RFC 2003).

Second, algorithms for encryption and authentication as well as automatic key management schemes (such as RFC 2408 and RFC 2409) are defined, each in a separate RFC. The informational RFC 2411 provides guidelines for specifying new encryption and authentication algorithms and explains the interrelationship of all the protocols and algorithms in the IPsec suite.

The interrelationship of the elements of the IPsec architecture is demonstrated in Figure 7.4. The ESP and AH protocol documents cover the packet format and general issues of these protocols. They also define the default and mandatory values (as, for example, specified in RFC 2407) that are fed into the *domain of interpretation* (DOI) document, which deals with assigned values. The ESP protocols can use various encryption algorithms (for example, those specified by RFC 2405 and RFC 2451) as well as authentication algorithms (for example, those specified by RFC 2403 and RFC 2404). The authentication algorithms are also used by the AH protocol.

Both the encryption and authentication algorithms may also specify values for the DOI (for example, the values that identify these algorithms). Finally, the key management documents specify the IETF standards-track key management schemes, which also define the values for DOI. The IPsec DOI also supports negotiation of IP compression (as specified in RFC 2393); this function may be necessary because the encryption of IP payload prevents compression at lower layers. For example, a message containing a string of 50 octets filled with 0s could have been successfully compressed to something much smaller than 50 octets had it not been for the encryption, which—by design—not only changed 0s to other values but also eliminated the pattern.

Overall, IPsec provides security services at the IP layer by selecting (1) appropriate security protocols, (2) algorithms to be used with these protocols, and (3) appropriate cryptographic keys. The major function of the Internet Key Exchange (IKE) protocol (RFC 2409) is to establish and manage *security associations* (SAs), a function supported by both AH and ESP.

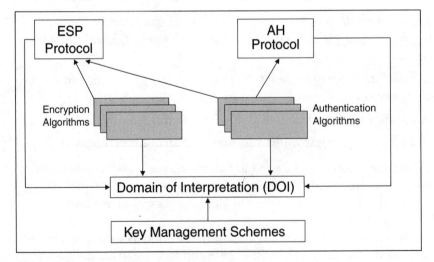

Figure 7.4   IPsec architecture.
Source: RFC 2411.

The concept of SAs is fundamental to IPsec. RFC 2401 defines an SA as a simplex connection that affords security services to the traffic carried by it. These services can be afforded by either AH or ESP, but in the case where both are to be employed, two SAs need to be established. An SA is uniquely identified by the following triplet:

1. Security parameter index (SPI).

2. IP destination address. Although this can in principle also be a broadcast or multicast address, only the unicast address is presently supported by the IPsec management mechanism.

3. Security protocol identifier (that is, AH or ESP).

RFC 2401 defines two types of SAs—*transport mode* SA and *tunnel mode* SA—to support the AH and ESP modes of operation, respectively. As Figure 7.5 demonstrates, the transport mode SA is an association between two hosts. The double arrows are used only to indicate the nodes between which the SAs are established, not to imply by any means that that the SAs are duplex! The tunnel mode SA, however, may be established between:

- Two security gateways. A security gateway is defined in RFC 2401 as an intermediate system that acts as the communications interface between two networks.

- A host and a security gateway.

- Two hosts.

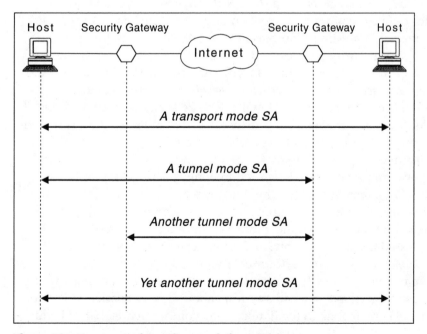

Figure 7.5 Two types of security associations (SAs).

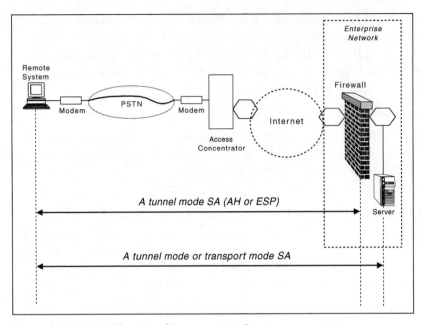

Figure 7.6   Remote host reaching an enterprise server.
Source: RFC 2401, Case 4.

Any SA that supports tunneling (that is, an SA between a host and a security gateway or two security gateways) must be a tunnel mode SA, but an SA between two hosts may be either a transport mode SA or tunnel mode SA. The modes define the order and selection of appropriate headers. RFC 2401 provides several interesting examples of how SAs can be combined to satisfy complex, *nesting* security policies, and introduces into the model the notions of the *security policy database* (which specifies the policies that determine the disposition of IP traffic) and the *security association database* (which specifies the parameters of each active SA). Finally, RFC 2401 studies four cases of security associations, of which the fourth—depicted in Figure 7.6—is specifically relevant to the topic of dial-in access to an enterprise network. The situation is effectively equivalent to that presented in Figure 7.2. There Layer 2 tunneling was employed; here Layer 3 tunneling is used with IPsec.

In Figure 7.6, a remote host (dialing into an access concentrator) uses the Internet to reach an enterprise's firewall (a security gateway) and then a particular host (a server). Only tunnel mode is required for an SA between the remote host and the firewall, while an SA between the remote host and the server can be either a transport or tunnel mode SA.

We have mentioned how IPsec standards relate to access and, particularly, VPNs, but so far we have not said anything about IPsec's relation to IP telephony. The general feeling in the IP telephony community[2] is that AH and

---

[2]We are grateful to J. Rosenberg for this communication.

ESP can be used in a standalone IP telephone, but the complexities of key exchange through IKE and the Internet Security Association and Key Management Protocol (ISAKMP) are too much to be handled by a client in a small standalone telephone.

Kaufman and Newman (1999) report that "early generations of IPsec products have proven to be suboptimal for many VoIP installations" and recommend deploying IPsec and voice over Internet Protocol (VoIP) separately and "experiment[ing] with integration only when you have debugged both installations." In addition to technical reasons, the same monograph brings up an important regulatory consideration: In some circumstances, there are regulations that restrict voice encryption.

Multihoming

One important detail affecting the design of access servers (which, for example, may contain the LAC function) is that their routers are typically located at the borders of enterprise or ISP networks. The servers then act as gateways to their respective networks. Three applications pertinent to this book—remote dial-in, VPN, and IP telephony—deal with the IP packets that can traverse more than one network. For this reason, the remote access products that support the VPN service and IP telephony gateways benefit from the implementation of *Border Gateway Protocol* (BGP) version 4 (RFC 1771).

Although the subject of routing algorithms is outside of the scope of this book, a short discussion of BGP is warranted. You may notice that some issues (such as *policing*) inherent in BGP are very similar to—and, in some cases, even the same as—those pertinent to the QoS standards addressed in Chapter 5. BGP is the means of realizing multihoming (that is, maintenance of connections to multiple ISPs or enterprise networks). Thus, BGP is of considerable importance to dial-in access and VPN applications. The IETF has paid much attention to the BGP development, which dates back to ARPANET and then was pursued in the Inter-Domain Routing (*idr*) working group (www.ietf.org/html.charters/idr-charter.html) over several years. Four versions of BGP have been released. In the latest series of RFCs, RFCs 1771 and 1772 have achieved the status of Draft Standards. Informational RFCs 1773 and 1774, respectively, document experiences with BGP-4 and provide an analysis.

RFC 1771 defines an *autonomous system* (AS) as "a set of routers under a single technical administration, using an interior gateway protocol and common metrics to route packets within the AS, and using an exterior gateway protocol to route packets to other ASs." ISPs and enterprise networks are two typical examples of ASs.

Whereas interior nodes are concerned with making the best effort at delivering IP packets, exterior nodes have to deal with many other tasks. One task is to decide whether certain packets should be admitted to the AS; the other is to maintain the appearance of a coherent interior routing plan (which is not necessarily the case in practice). As RFC 1771 says: "The use of the term Autonomous System here stresses the fact that, even when multiple IGPs and metrics are used, the administration of an AS appears to other ASs to have a single coherent interior routing plan and presents a consistent picture of what destinations are reachable through it."

There are two aspects to packet admission: Some packets may actually be destined to terminate in the AS, whereas others should be allowed to traverse it in order to get to other ASs.

In the world of the exterior nodes, which is significantly cozier than the world of all routers—if only because it is much smaller—the ASs are somewhat selfishly viewed as the means of connecting the exterior nodes. As far as transit through ASs is concerned, BGP provides the following taxonomy (illustrated in Figure 7.7):

- *Stub AS.* An AS that has only a single connection to one other AS. Naturally, a stub AS only carries local traffic.

- *Multihomed AS.* An AS that has connections to more than one other AS, but refuses to carry transit traffic.

- *Transit AS.* An AS that has connections to more than one other AS and is designed (under certain policy restrictions) to carry both transit and local traffic.

Stub and multihomed ASs do not need to employ BGP at their border nodes, but transit ASs do. The responsibilities of the border gateways involve, among other things, policing the incoming traffic.

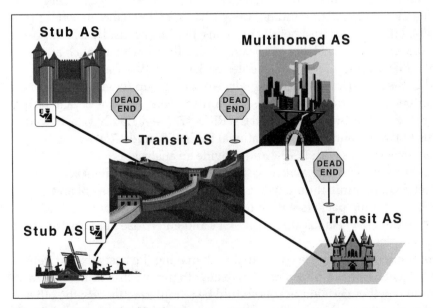

Figure 7.7 The AS classification.

This situation is strikingly similar to what used to happen at the borders of the Iron Curtain countries in Europe before the fall of the Curtain. In particular, the German Democratic Republic—the former East Germany—which had a piece of the free world (West Berlin) within its territory, was well equipped for dealing with transit traffic at its borders, where the cars queued up amid many uniformed men and women with automatic rifles and barking dogs. Unless all present in a car were citizens of East Germany or had prearranged visas for visiting specific places in the country, they were issued—for a fee— time-stamped transit visas that indicated a particular border point at which the car had to exit the country. The choice of destination border point belonged to the driver, but could not be changed once it was written in the visa. Furthermore, the car was supposed to reach its destination border point by (1) always staying on the East German highway network, (2) following the shortest path through this network, and (3) obeying all the laws of the country, which in this case were of course effectively reduced to the traffic laws. With that, the car was virtually *tunneled* through the country, its passengers seeing not much more than other cars and trucks—including many police cars—and vast fields on both sides of the highway. At the destination border checkpoint, more armed men and women with dogs were waiting. One of the many checks they performed was that of the initial time stamp. If the elapsed time indicated that the car had clearly spent more time in the country than it would have had it taken the shortest path, some specific policies applied, with the actual consequences (fines? imprisonment?) fortunately unknown to these authors. Another—and, alas, often unexpected—effect of time-stamping was discovered by those drivers whose traveling time was too *short* for the distance, which was a clear proof of speeding. The offense was punished by a large on-the-spot fine to be paid in cash *and* in hard currency. The latter policy example, however, is more illustrative of QoS rather than border gateway policies.

Policy-based routing is an essential job of the routers that serve as border gateways. Policy specification is a job of network administrators rather than of the protocol itself, but BGP routers do make routing decisions based on these policies.

In a deviation from other Internet routing protocols, BGP uses TCP (instead of a link layer protocol) as a reliable data transport for routing messages. The actual routing algorithm belongs to the so-called *distance vector routing* family, which operates by maintaining within each router a table of distances (*costs*) to all reachable routers and exchanging this information with other routers. The most lamented deficiency of the distance vector routing is that the "bad news," (that is, loss of a link between two routers or router flop) propagates through the network extremely slowly. BGP differs from other distance vector routing protocols in that the routers maintain—and share with one another—full paths to the nodes reachable from them. That fixes the problem of spreading the bad news, because the routers notice all the nodes disappearing from neighbors' paths as soon as they get the change information. Note that being reachable is not simply a matter of connectivity but also of active policies.

In an example of RFC 1772, a multihomed AS may actually act as a transit AS for some ASs by advertising to them paths to foreign gateways; on the other hand, a transit AS may restrict access to some ASs by never advertising paths to them (that is, declaring them unreachable). In the example of Figure 7.8, AS *D* is reachable to AS *A* through AS *C*, but AS *B* is not.

Initially, a BGP router sends its whole routing table to its neighbors, which are supposed to keep it until the connection is closed because from now on they will receive only incremental updates. Even though TCP is used for transport, BGP still uses its own *KeepAlive* messages to ensure that the connection is open. The connection is closed whenever an error condition (such as nonreception of *KeepAlive* messages) is encountered. In addition to incremental updates, BGP-4 has added the concept of *route aggregation* so that information about groups of networks may be represented as a single entity.

BGP-4 has also addressed the problems of (1) the exhaustion of class B address space and (2) threatening growth of the routing tables. In listing the differences between BGP-4 and previous versions of BGP, RFC 1771 notes: "BGP-4 is capable of operating in an environment where a set of reachable destinations may be expressed via a single IP prefix. The concept of network

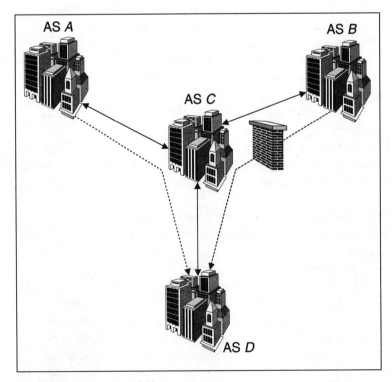

Figure 7.8   Access restriction.

classes, or subnetting, is foreign to BGP-4. . . . New text has been added to define semantics associated with IP prefixes."

This concludes the discussion of BGP, which is also the last standardization topic. We are ready to move to Part Three, which deals with the real-world products and services that use the standards discussed in this part.

Choosing Products and Services

In this part of the book we walk you through steps that will show you how to benefit from the spectrum of existing and emerging products and services. First, we help you map your business and its needs to determine how Internet and telecommunications integration can help you succeed. Second, we survey the categories of available products and services. Finally, we help you match features and characteristics of products to your application requirements.

CHAPTER 8

Identifying Your Environments

Who are you? Presumably, you already know that you are, for example, the CIO of XYZ LLP, responsible for delivering an ever increasing quality of local and remote voice and data networking services to your firm's professional employees within the constraints of an ever tightening budget. Step back and spend a little time thinking about your business environment, both in itself and in how it compares to other business environments. This exercise will have two benefits: (1) it will help you distill requirements for Internet and telecommunications integration (an essential step), and (2) it will aid you in gaining knowledge of where you fit in the vendors' categories of customer environments, which will help you communicate with vendors and avoid inappropriate choices.

Following are descriptions of some of these customer environment categories, based on current terminology. We present these categories to give some structure to a very broad and complex space by naming some regions within it. You may feel that you belong in several of these places, or somewhere not precisely captured here. You may also use different terms or encounter vendors who use different terms. Nevertheless, please view these categories in the spirit of the maps drawn by early European explorers of the New World—accurate enough to show the major landmasses, though not all the details of the interior.

Table 8.1 introduces the specific network environment taxonomy we will use.

Table 8.1 Network Environments

Enterprise Networks	Small office/home office
	Medium to large business—single building or campus
	Medium to large business—multiple campuses
	Medium to large business—single or multiple campuses with small remote locations
	Interenterprise networks and extranets
Public Networks	Internet service provider
	Long distance and international carrier
	New carrier
	Incumbent national carrier
	Incumbent local exchange carrier (United States)
	Competitive LEC
	Cellular/wireless
	Cable network

Enterprise Networks

Enterprise networks are used by businesses to accomplish the everyday functions essential to their success. They are characterized by requirements for features, functionality, and scale that go far beyond typical consumer needs for telecommunications services. Enterprise networks can be very large, spanning the entire globe and operating with multimillion-dollar annual budgets, or they can be much more modest in scale, conforming to the needs of a small business operating in a distinct geographical area.

No matter how large or small, one defining characteristic of an enterprise network is that in almost all cases it is a means to another end. That is, the company that pays for and supports the network is not primarily in the communications business, but rather is in some other business supported by the network. Salespeople make calls to customers and to the home office. Product planners on opposite sides of a continent or an ocean hold weekly conference calls supported by high-quality graphics. A call center takes customer orders or provides support to users of the firm's products. Remote workers dial in to the company network for e-mail and voice mail. All of these activities are essential to conducting the firm's business, and some may place critical and demanding requirements on the network, but they are not in themselves the reason why the firm is in business or the sources of its revenue.

The degree to which the network is managed and operated by the firm itself, or to which these functions are outsourced to another company, varies from firm to firm. In the one case, you as the network manager may have a staff of employees that you hire, compensate, and coach in performing tasks to keep the network up and running and expand and extend it to keep pace with user demand. In the other case, you may be primarily responsible for managing the relationship with an outsourcing vendor who in turn performs these tasks. Either way, one of your central concerns is likely to be the costs of network operations, and managing these costs within a budget may be a major function of your job.

Enterprise networks often differ in scale and geographical scope, as mentioned previously. You must consider size and scale when you evaluate your Internet and telecommunications integration needs. Since cost savings is an important goal, it is essential to understand how scale and geographical scope can affect IP telephony costs, including the effects of government regulation in different jurisdictions.

The following sections introduce some possible enterprise network environments. As noted previously, you may find that your own environment is some combination of these, or that it is somewhat different from any of them. Nonetheless, they should provide a framework for thinking about the applicability of Internet and telecommunications integration to your business.

Small Office/Home Office (SOHO)

A SOHO environment can be a small office in a business location, a small office located in a private home, or even a home office setup designed primarily to support a remote worker for a large business. There may be several workers in the office with voice and data communication needs, or there may be just one. In either case, needs for communication within the office are likely to be minimal; the most demanding need is for communication outside the office with customers and suppliers, and, in the remote worker case, with other employees and centralized facilities of the large business. Depending on the nature of the business, the scope of communication may be local, regional, national, or international.

To support voice communications, the most readily available traditional options will be based on switched telephone service from the local telephony provider, possibly augmented by relatively simple premises telephone equipment (an electronic key system or the like) to help manage multiple lines. Connections to *Internet service providers* (ISPs) or the internal network of a large business can also most readily be supported on a dial-up basis. Depending on the locality, you may have other options such as cable modems or *digital subscriber line* (DSL) technology.

Medium to Large Business—
Single Building or Campus

The medium to large business with a single building or campus category can span locations with less than a dozen to more than 1000 employees. A defining characteristic is a significant need to provide communication among the colocated employees (for example, at an R&D site or large professional office) and/or to manage high-volume incoming or outgoing communications (as at a call center).

Traditionally, voice communications for a single campus location would be handled by a digital *private branch exchange* (PBX) supported by a substantial in-building twisted pair wiring infrastructure. In a minority of cases (usually governmental organizations or other institutions with a limited ability to raise capital for buying things like PBXs), the same functions may be provided by Centrex service from a telephone company. For call center operations, a special feature of PBX called *automatic call distribution* (ACD) may be in use, possibly along with computer telephony (CT) capabilities to optimize the flow of calls and connect agents with customer information databases and other information systems. Data communications would be provided by *local area network* (LAN) technology, probably running over the same twisted pair infrastructure as the telephone system, using networking technology like switches and routers. Depending on the scale of the operation, you may have a hierarchy of departmental and backbone LANs.

Communications outside the building or campus may use a combination of local, regional, national, and international services, depending on the nature of the business. If the building or campus is part of a larger business, a substantial amount of off-premises voice and data traffic may flow over private facilities such as leased circuits or specialized carrier services like software defined networks (primarily for voice) or frame relay service (traditionally for data). Switched business lines from the local telephony provider are available as the ultimate default.

Medium to Large Business—
Multiple Campuses

The medium to large business with more than one campus is a generalization of the preceding category. All of the same characteristics are present. The new factor is that there are substantial traffic flows between two or more buildings/campuses. As a result, there will often be significant use of private facilities or specialized carrier services to connect the multiple large locations. Distances between pairs of buildings/campuses, of course, can vary enormously, from a few miles/kilometers to intercontinental distances, and may have a great impact on the specific services available for interconnection as well as on the relative economics of different options.

Medium to Large Business—
Single or Multiple Campuses
with Small Remote Locations

Many medium to large organizations fall in the category of medium to large businesses with single or multiple campuses with small remote locations. Not only are there possibly multiple large buildings or campuses with substantial traffic flows among them, but there are very important communication flows to and from a relatively large number of small locations. These small locations may be similar in character to the small office/home office environments described previously, or they may be a bit larger, more like the lower end of the single-campus category. All of the communication options described in the preceding two categories may be in place, and in addition the small remote offices present important communication requirements that may need to be satisfied by a combination of switched business lines, specialized carrier services, and, if traffic densities are high enough and the economics work out, leased lines like T1s or cable-based circuits.

The limiting case of the small remote office is probably the single nomadic worker who needs to stay in touch with the business through whatever combination of e-mail, voice mail, and fax he or she can manage. Communications options for this increasingly important case are typically based on dial-up from wired or wireless telephones into corporate voice networks and/or remote access servers for corporate data networks.

Interenterprise Networks
and Extranets

All of the preceding categories include some amount of communication between the enterprise in question and other businesses, including suppliers, distributors, and business customers. The default communication mechanism for such communication flows is the public telephone network, whether employed for voice or fax transmission, or maybe the post office, or, in a small but growing number of instances, the public Internet. However, for high-volume transactions between companies that are regular, long-term partners, intercompany private networks or industry-wide jointly managed networks are sometimes employed. Examples are the use of *electronic data interchange* (EDI) for functions like ordering and invoicing, and electronic funds transfers in the banking industry. Internet technology is often adapted to interenterprise uses in the form of an *extranet*—an IP-based network that is neither public nor strictly private and that is used by two or more businesses with a long-term relationship.

Providers of Public Networks

Now we will change gears to describe networks of an entirely different kind. Enterprise networks, covered in the preceding sections, are one factor—possibly a critical one—in the success of a business whose primary purpose is something other than networking. For a public carrier network, the network *is* the business—sales of network services are the primary source of revenue and the reason why everybody from the CEO to the cable splicer goes to work in the morning. The most obvious effect of this different focus is to considerably raise the stakes as far as network reliability and service quality are concerned. While there are arguably a number of other businesses that rely on telecommunications so directly that their reliability requirements may actually be similar, for a public carrier there is no denying the fact that if the network stops, the inflow of revenue stops too. It's not possible to just spend an hour cleaning out your inbox while the phones are down! Quality is a sensitive matter as well, because along with price, customer relations, and a few other factors, it inevitably constitutes one of the basic dimensions of competition.

Reliability and quality requirements are among the characteristics that make public network providers stand apart, but they are not the only ones. For the largest public carriers, including the former national monopolies and their largest competitors, scale is obviously another consideration. Public networks may have hundreds or thousands of times as many end users as the very largest enterprise networks. Large scale determines the optimum choice of network architecture as well as approaches to operations and network management.

Regulatory requirements also come into play for public networks. In many places, in spite of deregulation, there may be specific government-imposed metrics of service quality. Government rules may require that carriers implement certain features, and may prohibit certain classes of carriers from implementing other features. The path to deregulation itself, for example as followed in the United States, has created perhaps arcane-seeming rules about which carriers are allowed to handle which types of calls and what charges may or may not apply to them for purposes such as supporting universal service. Government efforts to open the telecommunications business to competition and foster interconnection have resulted in requirements to support specific types of open interfaces.

Stepping beyond technical requirements and looking at the businesses as a whole, one of the defining characteristics of public carriers as opposed to enterprise networks is that the public carriers have to incur extremely large expenditures in order to convince customers to use their services. Costs may include mass television advertising to consumers or support of large sales forces to stay in touch with the needs of business customers. An effect of these large sales and marketing expenditures is that the cost of the network and its technology, while never unimportant, may figure less in the business decisions of a public carrier than you might think. (We'll revisit in Chapter 12 the point that the cost of the network and technology does not always determine the business decisions of public carriers.)

At one time there was just one public network provider in each country or major geographical region. Much has changed, of course, and in some places there are hundreds or even thousands of public network providers with the right to compete for business. Technology and changing government regulations have also created different types of carriers, which the following sections attempt to categorize. If you are a planner for a public carrier interested in Internet and telecommunications integration, your company should fit in one or more of the following groups loosely if not perfectly. We hope the discussion will help you think about characteristics of a public network provider that should influence your decision about whether and how to integrate Internet and telecommunications technologies.

Internet Service Provider (ISP)

We will begin our survey of public network providers with one of the newest categories: Internet service providers (ISPs). The Internet service provider industry arose in the early 1990s when the U.S. government began a phased withdrawal of its direct support for the Internet and encouraged commercialization. ISP at the moment is a broad and rapidly evolving category, embracing thousands of firms ranging in size from mom-and-pop operations to some of the largest communications businesses in existence. All ISPs, however, offer services related to the Internet. Most ISPs offer points of presence for flat-rate dialup access to the Internet over local telephone lines, but services may also include providing high-speed private line access, hosting and creation of Web content, caching of Web pages, and providing a variety of proprietary information services.

ISPs tend to arrange themselves into a hierarchy depending on their geographic scope. Local ISPs specialize as the primary point of contact for end-user customers, deliver services, and bill customers. Backbone ISPs haul traffic across continents and around the world. In between there are levels of regional and national ISPs. These categories overlap and combine in all possible ways. For example, backbone providers often have large retail businesses and function as local ISPs as well. Consolidation in the ISP industry seems inevitable and appears to be happening, but it is not clear whether the rate of destruction yet exceeds the rate of creation of new firms.

The interest of ISPs in Internet and telecommunications integration comes from two different directions. Local ISPs are critically dependent on the local public telephone network to support dial access for their consumer business. So local ISPs need products to optimize the use of the telephone network for remote access, and technology that provides alternatives to circuit-switched access. ISPs may also be direct providers of IP telephony services. In this role, they may need to provide differentiated *quality of service* (QoS) over the Internet for telephony applications, and the ability to interconnect the *voice over IP* (VoIP) traffic with the public telephone network.

Long Distance and International Carrier

By law, custom, or choice, some carriers focus on national long-distance or international traffic. This category includes the U.S. long distance industry created by the breakup of the Bell System some 15 years ago (carriers include AT&T, MCI WorldCom, and Sprint) as well as some others such as KDD, the traditional international carrier of Japan. Regulatory liberalization and business mergers continue to blur boundaries, so these carriers now have local telecommunications interests—some of them quite substantial. Nonetheless, to the degree that they remain focused on long distance and/or international telecommunications, they have common characteristics that shape their needs for Internet and telecommunications integration.

The economics of voice over IP can be tricky (see Chapter 12), but, at least in the near term, the economic payoff is more obviously positive for long distance—and particularly international—traffic than for local calls—due mostly to the artificially high level of some international voice tariffs and the consequent opportunities for arbitrage. The relative lack of local infrastructure also gives these carriers an incentive to seek out new ways of establishing relationships with customers. Offering Internet-based services with less direct dependence on local telephone infrastructures is one way to attract customers. Also, the reduced embedded infrastructure per customer allows long-distance telecom companies flexibility to contemplate radical changes in technology (like using ATM or IP-based networks).

A final characteristic is that the U.S.-based long distance companies have been in a highly competitive environment for a long time now and attempt to differentiate themselves by developing a wide set of IN-supported vertical services on top of the basic telephone call. Many of these services have been implemented in some form of intelligent network technology—often a proprietary flavor that does not correspond exactly to either the international standards or Telcordia requirements for IN. For carriers with a large embedded base of IN, integration of the Internet with IN is a primary challenge.

New Carrier

New carriers constitute another broad and flexible category. Here the term refers to carriers whose idea of the path to fortune for their investors is to take a clean sheet of paper and design a completely new network using the latest technology. Often these carriers intend to focus, at least as a first order

of business, on long distance and international instead of local telecommunications. This focus has the advantage of reducing somewhat the enormous
capital expenditures involved in building a network from scratch. Examples
of such carriers are the U.S.-based firms Qwest and Level 3. Similar carriers
are developing in Europe as competitors to the former national monopoly
providers. Since they are open to the use of new technology, and in fact use it
as a key differentiating factor, these carriers actively engage in integrating
Internet and telecommunications, including use of such technology as large-
scale circuit-to-packet voice gateways.

Incumbent National Carrier

Incumbent national carriers include most of the very large embedded telecommunications providers of the world. In most of the places where competition
is being introduced into the telecommunications service industry (though not
the United States—see the following sections), the former national monopoly
carrier is more or less intact as an entity, though often privatized in the sense
that its shares are traded on the stock market and its finances are no longer
part of the national budget. This description includes giants such as Deutsche
Telekom, France Telecom, and British Telecom. (It probably includes NTT of
Japan as well, although the regulators in that country have made a half-
hearted attempt to separate NTT into two regional subsidiaries for local service plus a long distance subsidiary.)

Generally, these incumbent national carriers are highly aware of the Internet as both opportunity and threat, and may be interested in integrating
Internet and telecommunications for a number of reasons. First, most have
either established or acquired ISPs, and so have the same interests as other
ISPs (see the preceding ISP discussion) in efficient dial-up access as well as
potential direct provision of IP telephony. Second, most are studying options
for evolving part or all of their network infrastructure to be based on IP. Any
such evolution, of course, would demand implementations that could operate at extreme scale and deliver services with differentiated QoS characteristics. Although not to the degree of the U.S. long distance carriers, these
national carriers typically have implemented value-added services using IN,
making the interworking of this IN infrastructure with VoIP an important
consideration.

Incumbent Local Exchange Carrier (United States)

While incumbent local exchange carriers are a unique product of the path
taken by regulation and deregulation in the United States, this category
includes a number of very large companies, namely the regional Bell operating companies (RBOCs) like Bell Atlantic, SBC, BellSouth, and USWest

and, in a rather different regulatory position, GTE. All of these companies have their assets heavily concentrated in local telecommunications, and, in the case of the RBOCs, they are currently still legally restricted in their ability to offer long distance, having just barely begun to overcome the legal hurdles defined in the Telecom Act of 1996. Nonetheless, they are all developing plans for eventual long distance services, and it is partly as potential deployers of substantial amounts of new long distance infrastructure that they loom large in the picture of Internet and telecommunications integration.

On the more traditional end of their business—local access—*local exchange carriers* (LECs) are also interested in providing dial-up access to ISPs. Here, the unusual traffic characteristics presented by dial-up (large volumes of long-holding-time calls, where ISPs serve almost exclusively as terminators rather than originators of calls) have caused the LECs to reengineer their networks, purchase and deploy capacity upgrades to their existing circuit-switched infrastructures sooner than anticipated, and actively seek more technologically advanced solutions. IN interworking with VoIP is also a concern of the LECs; the larger LECs have made significant investments in IN infrastructure, even though a smaller percentage of calls access an IN SCP compared to calls in a U.S. long distance provider's network.

Competitive LEC

CLECs are the new carriers of the LEC market. What makes them different from the new carriers described earlier is a focus on the local (as opposed to long distance and international) market. Because CLECs are deployers of new infrastructure and competitors in search of a technological edge over the incumbent LECs, integrating Internet and telecommunication has great appeal, although competitive LECs should take a hard look at costs relative to more traditional solutions in their environment.

Cellular/Wireless

Providers of cellular and wireless communications are having their own experience of spectacular growth, which seems to be continuing unabated. A commonly held belief is that a crossover of wired and wireless access will occur early in the twenty-first century. This means that much VoIP traffic will be wireless voice over IP, which makes wireless a big factor in the integration of Internet and telecommunications technologies. In addition, there is strong interest from consumers and service providers in enabling wireless access to the Internet for Web, e-mail, and similar applications, so that IP voice in a wireless environment is likely to be one component of a multimedia mix.

Cable Network

Cable TV networks have long been recognized as a potential alternative means of access for consumers to communications services that go beyond one-way transmission of TV signals. This potential is finally being actualized due to developments such as the upgrading of cable systems with two-way fiber trunks and the deployment of cable modems. Business moves such as the acquisition of TCI by AT&T are also accelerating developments in this sector. Since second-line voice and Internet access are both key components of the service mix being contemplated by the cable companies, interest in integrating the Internet and telecommunications is natural.

CHAPTER 9

Identifying Your Applications

This chapter lists applications that use both the PSTN and IP networks and that work across these networks. Our goal here is to highlight the generic types of applications (or services) that exist today and that may serve as building blocks for creating new applications. Our list of applications is by no means exhaustive, since the infrastructure integrating the two types of networks is developing, and the capabilities of applications and newly invented business models seem to be limited only by inventors' imaginations. In addition, not all aspects of the applications described here have found their way into implementations, and some of those that have been implemented have not reached levels of maturity and stability equal to those of *plain old telephone service* (POTS) calls. Among those described, the unified messaging application is perhaps the most mature, and IP telephony is the most fashionable.

We describe the applications from an end-user point of view, avoiding references to the underlying technologies or types of products that implement them; however, we highlight the behavior and high-level functions within networks as much as is necessary to demonstrate the principles of the PSTN and Internet interactions. We examine relevant products in detail in Chapter 10.

We start by describing a somewhat static service (compared with real-time communications) in which messages are expressed in different media (native to either the PSTN or IP networks) and are delivered by both the PSTN and IP networks: the *unified messaging* service.

We continue with the real-time basic services by addressing an IP telephony call and IP telephony fax as services. With basic services as the prerequisite, we proceed to more complex multimedia conferencing and data collaboration services. Next, we focus on services that use the Web as the means of control, signaling, and customization; to this end, we deal with the Web-based conference control, Internet call center, Internet call-waiting, the PINT services, and Web-based service customization. Finally, having dealt with the voice-over-data issues, we address the reverse data-over-voice case, in which the PSTN is used for IP transport (i.e., remote dial-in access applications such as Internet access and telecommuting). Especially in connection with telecommuting, we address the concept of *virtual private networks* (VPNs).

Unified Messaging

Messaging refers to non-real-time communications by way of voice mail, e-mail, fax, and the like. Of these, voice messaging and fax have traditionally been provided by voice networks and e-mail by the Internet. Until recently, each form of messaging required separate storage, access, and management; neither the applications nor the specialized devices worked with each other.

Unified messaging is positioned to eliminate the boundaries across these different forms of messaging.[1] As a result, users can create, send, and retrieve any type of message with any type of terminal anytime, anywhere (Figure 9.1).

Users are given access to any type of message from a number of devices that themselves belong to different types of networks. They have the following options for retrieving messages:

- Receiving notification of incoming messages (regardless of type) on a combination of devices such as telephone, PC, and *personal digital assistant* (PDA).

- Using a PC (or PDA) to retrieve voice-mail messages. Depending on the technology and device available, this option provides two further possibilities:

  1. Playing the messages on the PC (or PDA), if it is equipped with a speaker.

  2. Reading the voice messages (converted to text) on the PC (or PDA).

---

[1] As an introductory example of a crude mechanism of establishing something that approximates a telephone conversation (and is available to all owners of multimedia PCs connected to the Internet), consider the following exchange. A person speaks a phrase or two into the PC microphone and saves this message as a file (preferably in a compressed format). That file is then sent via e-mail to another person, who receives it (typically, in a matter of seconds), plays it, and produces a response in exactly the same manner. The conversation can go on like this indefinitely, and, if the files are not too large, this poor man's IP telephony can be surprisingly efficient. This simple example vividly illustrates the potential of unified messaging.

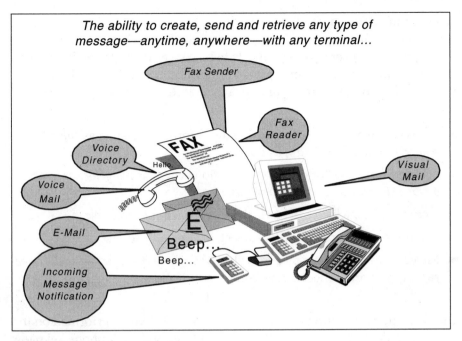

The ability to create, send and retrieve any type of message—anytime, anywhere—with any terminal...

Figure 9.1   Unified messaging.
(Courtesy of Jackie Orr.)

- Using a telephone to retrieve e-mail messages. The e-mail messages can be delivered to the user as voice-mail messages with the help of the text-to-speech technology. Alternatively, the messages can be delivered via facsimile to a fax machine that the user specifies, after the user listens to the converted message headers.

- Using a PC (or PDA) to retrieve fax messages, or requesting that the fax messages be delivered to a specific fax machine.

- Using a telephone to retrieve fax messages and listen to them (here the messages are first converted to text—involving a character recognition application—and then to speech), or requesting that the fax messages be delivered to a specific fax machine.

The user has various options for sending messages as well. You can mix the means for both creating and delivering messages. For example, the user can create a voice message using the telephone over the PSTN and have the voice message delivered to the recipient as a voice attachment (or just as a plaintext message with the help of the voice-to-text technology) via e-mail over the Internet.

Behind unified messaging is the concept of the *universal mailbox* (see Figure 9.2), which holds messages of all types in a single logical location. With a universal mailbox, the user no longer needs to be concerned with the location of messages. In addition, the user is given numerous options for handling messages, regardless of their format and means of access. For example, the messages can be:

- Sorted by using any part of the header information (such as *subject*, *date*, *sender*, *length*, and *priority*) as the key.

- Selected from a list of common operations (such as *reply*, *forward*, *save*, *delete*, *skip*, *rewind*, and *fast-forward*).

- Stored in files, which can be further organized into folders.

- Filtered according to priority, subject, sender, and so on.

- Mixed with other messages (possibly of various types, so an audio message and a spreadsheet can be combined into one message) and sent to another user.

Today, unified messaging operations are most effectively performed on the computer. As the limited (and limiting) capabilities of the telephone keypad are being augmented by voice-controlled applications, telephones are on their way to becoming as effective.

Figure 9.2 Universal mailbox. (Courtesy of Jackie Orr.)

A closer look at unified messaging reveals its essence: the use of the e-mail paradigm by voice mail. The universal mailbox is connected to networks of different types and acts as a voice portal for voice-controlled services.

The immediate improvement in services that has resulted from the application of the e-mail paradigm is best illustrated in a relatively new voice messaging application called *call sender with rebound*. An annoying feature of yesterday's voice mail was that you could not return a call pertinent to a particular message without leaving the mailbox. You had to either write down on a piece of paper all the numbers while listening to all the messages (and risk forgetting in the process what some of the calls to be returned were about) or keep calling the mailbox back after each call returned. Clearly, this is not how e-mail works; e-mail is more flexible and user friendly. The *call sender with rebound* feature available in today's top products works just like e-mail: It allows the recipient of the message to call back and, after having completed the call, to return to retrieving the messages starting just at the point where he or she left off. The procedure of calling back (using traditional telephone) was also adopted from the e-mail paradigm: You can call back by pushing a single button on a telephone keypad or giving a voice command. In addition, the return addresses of voice messages delivered by the PSTN (that is, telephone numbers) can be stored in and retrieved for redial from personal address books. Similarly, the voice confirmation of (voice) message delivery is a very convenient e-mail-like feature, and so are the abilities to send messages to groups and to specify delivery options.

Another interesting application called *reply-to-telephone* answering enables messaging replies to telephone callers. Through access to an IN database, the contact options of the calling party are captured and presented to the called party, who has a choice of returning a call, sending a voice message to the caller's voice mailbox, or sending a voice message via a store-and-forward network.

To access voice messaging from the computer, the *visual mail* application, convenient for small-office/home-office (SOHO) subscribers, provides end users with the ability to see (and edit) complete lists of their incoming or stored voice-mail and fax messages. The messages can be replied to by using the microphone of a multimedia computer; they can be forwarded, copied, and so on, in exactly the same manner as e-mail. Voice messages can be played using specialized player interfaces with controls that allow you to replay specific portions of a message. Callers often leave their numbers only at the end of their messages after they have been warned that only a few seconds of recording time are left—which, in turn, makes them rush when leaving numbers. As a result, the recipient of a message has to listen to it several times in order to write down the number. This visual-mail application comes in two flavors: Web visual mail and PC visual mail. With the former, users access and manage their mailboxes at a Web site using standard browsers; with the latter, subscribers use a standard Internet mail agent to access their mailboxes.

Even without the full set of visual-mail capabilities, the following two simple unified messaging features explore the duality of the vocal versus visual access:

1. *Bridging.* Telephone numbers are converted into e-mail addresses and vice versa. Voice-mail users can send their messages to the Internet; e-mail users can send voice messages to the PSTN.

2. *Cross notification.* Voice-mail users are notified of their e-mail reception; e-mail users are notified of PSTN calls.

Support of multiple languages is typical for advanced implementations of messaging, but one important language supported by the voice-mail part of the application is designed specifically for the deaf. The *telecommunications device for the deaf* (TDD) converts tones to alphanumeric characters and vice versa. TDDs have been used for communications with the deaf over PSTN lines, but now they can be naturally integrated with messaging.

IP Telephony Calls

As we noted in Chapter 3, the pure form of IP telephony that is supported over only IP networks without involving any circuit telephony equipment (as depicted in Figure 9.3) has not spread outside of enterprise networks. What is prevalent is the kind of IP telephony that is delivered over hybrid networks involving IP networks as well as the PSTN.

This situation has been shaped by the technological and economic developments as follows:

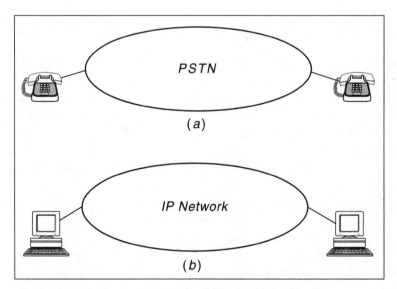

Figure 9.3 (*a*) Circuit telephony and (*b*) pure IP telephony.

- IP networks and the Internet were initially designed to deal with data communications traffic. This traffic, as predicted in the 1970s, was for communications among programs rather than people. File transfer and, later, electronic mail and remote terminal access (*telnet*)—which do involve humans on one side of the communications channel—were the driver applications. As a result, IP networks were engineered to deal with the bursty patterns typical of the data traffic. Whether the packets carrying parts of a file arrive in or out of the order in which they were sent is pretty much irrelevant, as long as the file can ultimately be assembled correctly. For the same reason, variation in the rate at which these packets arrive (versus the rate at which they are sent) naturally has no effect on the result. On the other hand, the loss of even a single packet renders the result meaningless unless the packet can be successfully retransmitted.

    Antithetically, in order for the voice-call application to work, the packets that carry voice must arrive in the order they were sent and at about the same rate at which they were transmitted. Dissimilarity of the voice traffic requirements with those of data traffic is visible in the area of tolerating packet loss, too: Occasional loss of packets has little or no effect on the quality of a call, while the delay of a stream of packets caused by the retransmission of the lost one is simply unacceptable. So, support of voice calls requires significant reengineering of the IP networks with many paradigm changes. Nevertheless, once the transport of the voice has been taken care of, service creation and management are the matter of data communications, and the Internet has already proven to be extremely efficient in this respect.

- Telephone calls (especially emergencies—such as 911 in the United States) must be given priority, and the originating locations of the calls must be identifiable, for which presently there are no standard mechanisms in pure IP networks.

- With the PSTN paradigm of a circuit established between the two parties to the call, the accounting is fairly straightforward (and even then devilishly complex!). The Internet, however, has not been designed with accounting for its services in mind. Accounting is further complicated by services like freephone (800 service in the United States), which require that a third party pay for the call.

- With the current telecommunications tariff regulations, the Internet (or IP networks in general) can be effectively employed to bypass those parts of the PSTN used in long-distance calls (thus eliminating long-distance call charges). There is much effort in both the existing and newly formed companies to explore this arbitrage advantage of IP networks in general and the Internet in particular.

When delivered over hybrid networks, IP telephony can be further classified into four types according to the use of the endpoint devices involved in the call: (1) when both devices are traditional telephones, the service is called *phone-to-phone*; (2) when the originating device is a properly equipped PC (or an IP phone) and the terminating one is a traditional telephone, the service is called *PC-to-phone*; (3) in the case of the same pair of endpoints but reversed roles in the call, the service is called *phone-to-PC*; and, finally, (4) when both devices are PCs (or IP phones), the service is called *PC-to-PC*.

Before proceeding with reviewing these cases, let's reflect on the various arrangements for pure IP telephony. (Even though it is somewhat outside the scope of the book, it will help to shape the border of the topic.) The arrangements in question are differentiated by the level of the network servers' involvement:

- *End-to-end.* End devices exchange signaling information with one another directly from the beginning to the end of a voice-over-IP call—there is no network server involved. Consequently, there is no network-based user location, authentication, admission control, capability negotiation, or any form of central call management. For this to work, naturally, there should be a prior agreement between the end devices on at least the signaling method (for example, H.323 or SIP).

- *Lightweight network services.* End devices may rely on network servers (for example, gatekeepers or SIP proxies) for user location services. The network servers maintain access to a directory of end users and all the associated information that allows end users to be reached for real-time voice conversations. The information can be relatively static (such as the capabilities of the end users' devices), or it can be dynamic (such as IP addresses or states of the devices).

- *Heavyweight network services.* End devices only have the minimum capabilities required for initiating or receiving a voice-over-IP call. Replicating in a way the traditional PSTN architecture, soft switches (or similar devices) do everything—from user location to advanced call management.

Phone-to-Phone

Phone-to-phone calls originate and terminate in the PSTN. In most cases, the goal of this service is toll bypass: All of the calls are local as far as the PSTN is concerned. As Figure 9.4 shows, only a part of the voice path belongs to the PSTN; an IP network interconnects the PSTN portions by means of generic gateways, called *telephony gateways.*

A variation of the phone-to-phone case is depicted in Figure 9.5, where the PSTN is replaced with an enterprise circuit-switched network that has its own numbering plan, but otherwise operates in the same way as the PSTN.

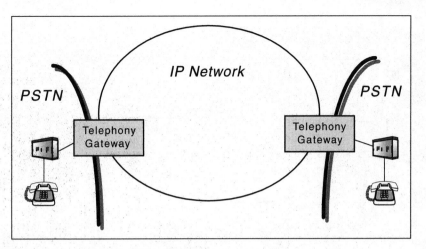

Figure 9.4   Phone-to-phone IP telephony.

Still another variation on phone-to-phone telephony is achieved by replacing just the access or egress portion of the PSTN with an enterprise circuit-switched network (as in Figure 9.6).

Depending on the accounting arrangement, the calling party may dial the destination telephone number in one or two stages. With two-stage dialing (typical for the case depicted in Figure 9.4), the caller normally pays for the call by a credit card or prepays the call by purchasing a special type of calling card. The prepaid card is issued for a specific amount of time, and it provides a personal identification number (PIN). In addition, the caller may be provided with a unique user identification and password. (These can take different forms; sometimes the telephone number from which the caller is to dial becomes his or her user identification, and the PIN serves as a password). To make the call with a prepaid or credit card, the caller takes the following three steps:

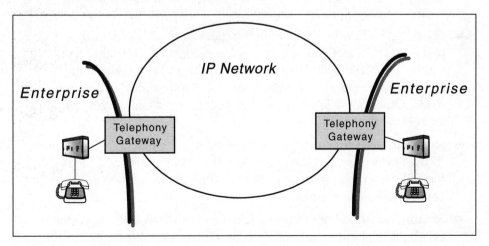

Figure 9.5   A variation of phone-to-phone IP telephony.

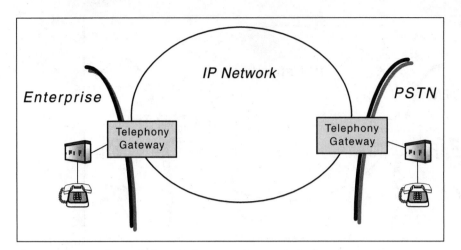

Figure 9.6 Another variation of phone-to-phone IP telephony.

1. Dial the telephone number (local or a freephone service call) of the selected service provider for IP telephony.

2. Enter the user identification and password (or just PIN), if the call is prepaid; or enter the credit card number if the call is to be paid by a credit card.

3. Enter the destination telephone number as prompted.

With step 1, the subscriber is connected via the PSTN to a service provider's telephony gateway. This originating server performs the following functions:

- Verifying if the caller is authorized to use the service. A general way to do this is based on the user identification and password. A less general way is based on the origination number, which allows the caller to call only from a telephone line that is preregistered with the service provider.

- Selecting the terminating telephony gateway that is to complete the call to the destination. (Various criteria are used in selecting the terminating server. The most typical criterion is that the server be within the minimum distance from the destination so that only a local call will be made. Other possible criteria include (1) the best overall voice quality and (2) the least load.

- Signaling the terminating server to establish the call to the destination. (If the line is busy, the server informs the calling party and disconnects the call. Otherwise, it waits until the called party answers or the calling party disconnects the call.)

- Starting transmission of voice packets in both directions when the called party answers. (Transmission involves possible digitalization and always special encoding—an essential function.)

- Keeping track of time and periodically informing the calling party about the time left for the call; disconnecting the call when the time is up if a prepaid card is used.

With one-stage dialing, a calling party simply dials the destination telephone number. Whereas with a two-stage call, any telephone may be used, here the calling party may use only a telephone that is registered with the service provider. (There is a deviation from this rule in the case when the enterprise network on-premises switch selects the IP path, as described in the PBX section of Chapter 10. As far as the end user is concerned, there is no difference from traditional telephony, including dialing.) All calls from the registered telephone number are routed to the service provider telephony gateway; there may be no fallback to the PSTN-only calls. The telephony gateways record the time of calls and take care of the billing.

Dialing procedure aside, the involvement of the IP network in these types of calls should be largely transparent to users, particularly if there is no obvious voice degradation or unusually long postdialing delay. The callers still have access to the services and features available in the PSTN (for example, *freephone, follow me, call-waiting,* or *call-forwarding,* as well as the emergency and operator assistance calls).

PC-to-Phone

In a PC-to-phone model, a call originates from a multimedia PC or from a specialized appliance called an *IP phone* (or a *packet phone*) and terminates at a traditional telephone in the PSTN. The configuration is depicted in Figure 9.7. A typical PC making the call would be equipped with a microphone, speakers, and IP telephony software (for example, Microsoft NetMeeting). In addition, a telephony server is introduced in the IP network to provide cer-

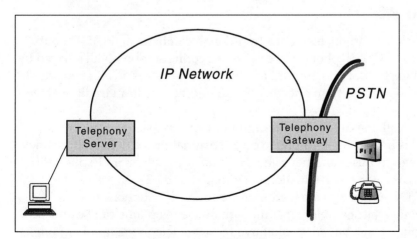

Figure 9.7 PC-to-phone IP telephony and vice versa.

tain functions such as authentication and call control. Theoretically, it is possible for the telephony server and the telephony gateway to be colocated; however, gateway and server locations have no impact on our application-level discussion.

To make a call, a caller using an IP phone simply dials the destination telephone number. In contrast, a caller using a PC must take the following three steps:

1. Invoke the IP telephony application supported by the service provider.

2. Establish a session with the originating telephony server.

3. Enter the user identification, password, and destination telephone number.

As the result, a properly authenticated caller is connected to the originating server and is authorized to use the IP telephony service. The originating server performs the authentication, authorization, and terminating gateway selection functions in much the same way as the originating gateway described in the phone-to-phone case. A great difference with the gateway is that the originating telephone server may be used only for these functions; the ultimate voice path may not pass through it. The only requirement for the IP portion of the voice path is that it connect the originating PC and the terminating telephony gateway.

One serious disadvantage to the caller is that advanced services and features (like freephone) are generally unavailable for PC-to-phone service. Many regulatory and technology issues still need to be resolved before advanced services become available. A straightforward solution is to implement IN in servers for access to the PSTN service control points; however, this solution covers only the technology side—regulatory and economical issues are still unresolved.

Phone-to-PC

A phone-to-PC call originates from a traditional telephone in the PSTN but terminates at a PC or IP phone. Otherwise, the configuration is still covered by Figure 9.7. One typical phone-to-PC application example is an all-enterprise IP telephony system; calls from outside (typically) originate from traditional telephones.

To make a call, the caller goes through the same one-stage or two-stage procedures as in the phone-to-phone case. Terminating a call to an IP phone (or PC), however, raises another issue: How do you address an IP phone? In other words, what is the destination telephone number?

In the PSTN, telephones are identified through the telephone lines to which they are attached. (Note that more than one telephone can be attached to one telephone line, but all would have the same telephone number.) A telephone number is assigned to a particular telephone line when a subscriber requests the telephone service from a service provider. Once assigned, this number remains until the subscriber cancels the service.

The number assignment is quite different in IP networks. Here, it is the IP terminals (that is, PCs or IP phones) themselves—not the lines attaching them to the network—that are assigned addresses. Another difference is that the IP addresses are not necessarily static. An IP terminal may connect to an IP network on demand, and so may be assigned an IP address only when the connection is established. The address is valid only for the duration of the connection; after that, it can be assigned to another terminal. It is therefore impossible for a person to make his or her IP address known and to be associated with the terminal ahead of time. A new way must be found to bind the person to the terminal, which, in turn, will define what digits a caller should dial when placing a call to an IP terminal.

Presently, there is no standard way of addressing an IP phone, but the industry may be moving toward a directory-driven solution in which a person is assigned an identifier. Then, the IP address of the IP phone at which the called party is to be reached can be looked up in the directory. This method works in two stages as follows:

1. *Personal registration.* The user of the IP phone registers with the IP telephony directory service, at which point he or she is assigned a unique identifier.

2. *Terminal registration.* The person's IP phone also registers its IP address with the directory whenever it is connected to an IP network and deregisters when it is disconnected from the network. (Note that terminal registration takes place frequently, while personal registration is typically a one-time affair.)

The format of the personal identifier determines what a caller enters as the destination number when placing a call to an IP terminal. There are several proposals including personal names, e-mail addresses, traditional telephone numbers, domain names, and so on. The case is presently being made for using traditional telephone numbering schemes because most calls originate at traditional telephones, which can enter only numbers anyway. The numbers-only argument, of course, protects the interests of traditional telephone users who may not want to (and, in some cases, cannot) switch to computers or IP phones. At the same time, the numbers-only scheme can reuse much of the existing telephony software and databases.

PC-to-PC

A PC-to-PC call originates and terminates in an IP network between two IP telephony terminals, such as multimedia PCs. The voice path traverses a combination of the IP networks and the PSTN where the PSTN connects the two IP networks (Figure 9.8).

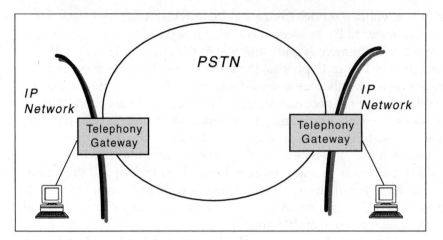

Figure 9.8   PC-to-PC IP telephony.

The PC-to-PC configuration does not seem to make much sense at first. The two PCs should be able to communicate over IP networks alone, so the involvement of the PSTN appears unnecessary and costly. The following two considerations explain the advantages of using the PSTN arrangement:

1. In some circumstances, IP networks can serve as a means of accessing the long-distance networks. This model is a mirror image of the phone-to-phone case (where the long-distance instead of local network is bypassed). Interexchange carriers would discount such calls because they do not incur costly local access charges.

2. An enterprise with several fast and reliable local IP networks (possibly just LANs) quite suitable for voice over IP can now expand to an all-enterprise network covering all locations. The enterprise network can fully utilize the strength of the PSTN in guaranteeing call quality and security for long-distance calls.

PSTN involvement in a PC-to-PC call is transparent to the user. Following are three typical PC-to-PC call steps:

1. Invoke the IP telephony application.

2. Establish a session with the originating gateway.

3. Select the called party from the IP telephony directory, or enter the e-mail address of the called party or the domain name or IP address of the called party's PC, whichever is accepted directly by the gateway.

Calling from a packet phone is simpler. Step 1 is eliminated by design; in a sense, a packet phone is just an ever running IP telephony application. In addition, step 2 may be as easy as lifting the phone off the hook.

IP Fax

Fax has traditionally been treated as a telephony application because it is sent over the telephone network. In reality, it is a data application that results in transmitting scanned document images from one facsimile terminal (fax machine) to another. The wide availability of the Internet has created an environment that allows the fax application to return to its true identity as a pure data service. If the real-time delivery of fax is not a requirement (and more often than not it is not), the image of a scanned document can be sent over the Internet in a way that is similar to sending e-mail.

For integrating the PSTN and the Internet, the following three scenarios are relevant:

1. A traditional fax machine sends a document to another one by way of an IP network. (A configuration is depicted in Figure 9.9.)

2. A traditional fax machine sends a document to an IP fax machine. (See Figure 9.10.)

3. An IP fax machine sends a document to a traditional fax machine. (See Figure 9.10.)

Note that an IP fax machine is an appliance, typically a PC, that can be connected directly to an IP network. Because it is necessary to establish a phone call in order to interoperate with the traditional fax machine, the steps involved in making fax calls repeat those already discussed in the IP telephony-call scenarios.

The IP fax operation can take place in two modes: real-time and non-real-time. In the real-time mode, IP fax emulates the behavior of a traditional facsimile over the PSTN. The sequence of events, such as capability negotiation

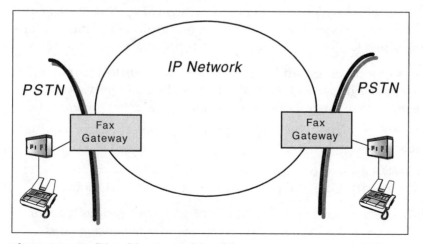

Figure 9.9   Traditional fax–to–traditional fax.

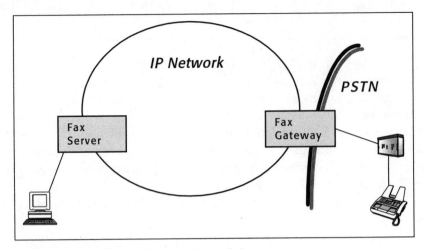

Figure 9.10 Traditional fax–to–IP fax and vice versa.

and confirmation of receipt by the endpoints in a traditional facsimile session, are largely preserved.

In the non-real-time mode, IP fax operates much like e-mail, relying on the store-and-forward process. The fax is stored at a staging point before being transmitted to the next staging point. The end-to-end transmission of the facsimile may involve several staging points with an unpredictable delay.

Multimedia Conferencing and Data Collaboration

Multimedia conferencing services support real-time communications among users at multiple (usually more than three) locations. The communications use a combination of various types of media such as voice, video, text, graphics, and still pictures. Following is a list of common forms of multimedia conferencing services:

- *Audio-graphic conference.* Adds nonvideo data exchange to a normal audio conference. Participants of the conference can, for example, view the same presentation slide as the presenter during his or her presentation.

- *Video conference.* Uses video and voice for communications for a virtual face-to-face meeting.

- *Data collaboration.* Allows the participants not only to share, but also to edit documents (like word processor files or spreadsheets) jointly.

Multimedia conferencing services can be provided over various types of networks. Figure 9.11 depicts a scenario where audio conferencing takes place over the PSTN while data conferencing takes place over the Internet.

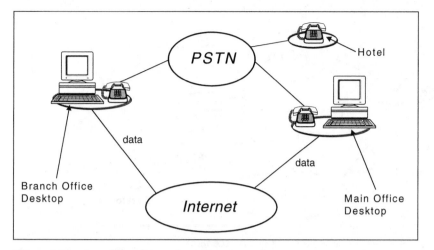

Figure 9.11   A multimedia conferencing scenario.

Naturally, the conference participants need both voice access to the PSTN (via a telephone terminal) and data access to the Internet (via a PC). This access could be achieved in several ways:

- With two POTS lines
- With a modem that splits a POTS line into voice and data channels
- With an ISDN line
- With an xDSL line (as described in Chapter 2)
- With a cable or power line, or wireless or enterprise LAN connection for the Internet access

Figure 9.12 depicts another scenario where audio conferencing takes place over the PSTN as well as an IP network, while data and video conferencing take place over just the IP network.

Regardless of network configuration, conference control and management (or operation) of the conference resources (like media and bandwidth) are important aspects of the multimedia conferencing services. Conference control provides the means for a conference to proceed in a certain order, as determined by a designated *conference chairman.* The chairman of the conference can give the floor to a conference participant to speak, or grant permission to a participant to transmit supporting media. A participant making a presentation naturally should be given the right to speak as well as transmit and control the visual information. The chairman may also mute a speaker, normally for quick intervention with an important message. The chairman may also organize a private subconference (or side conversation) meant to proceed undetected by the excluded participants.

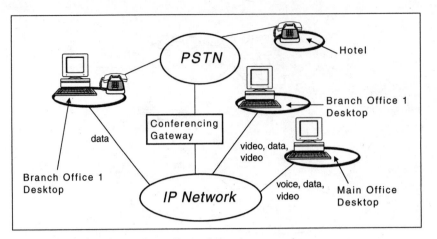

Figure 9.12 Another multimedia conferencing scenario.

In addition to the conference chairman, conference control also recognizes the role of the *conference controller* (both roles are often given to the same person, associated with one terminal). The conference controller can perform the following functions:

- Add or drop a party (terminal)
- Split the conference or merge a split conference
- Extend or terminate the conference

For a video conference, the controller may also be able to change the composition of the video screen displaying images from various locations during the conference.

Conference functions are limited by the capabilities of the terminal equipment. Unlike the telephone sets, which have more or less standard capabilities, multimedia terminals are quite dissimilar. For example, one terminal may handle just audio; another terminal audio, video, and fax; and yet another may handle audio and video capabilities, but with inferior quality. The resource management aspect of multimedia conferencing services must accommodate the varying capabilities of different terminals. There are mechanisms for terminals to negotiate capabilities when joining the conference. These capabilities can be renegotiated while the conference is in progress. Following are three common ways to handle differences in terminal capabilities:

1. All terminals operate in the mode supported by the least capable terminal.

2. Each terminal operates in its own mode, rejecting or ignoring input beyond its capabilities.

3. Specialized conference equipment mediates communications so that each terminal receives and transmits only what it can handle. (This

mediation may involve transcoding if the media formats supported by the terminals are incompatible.)

In addition to capability mediation, the conference equipment manages resources by performing the following three actions:

1. Establishing, modifying, and releasing connections to the terminals.
2. Monitoring the activities over each connection and tracking the status of each terminal.
3. Handling media streams received and sent through each connection; switching, distributing, multiplexing, and mixing them as necessary.

Note that conferencing service requirements have been studied by the industry for several years and have been standardized by ITU-T. However, it is beyond the scope of this book to describe all the relevant standards. For more details on the generic multimedia conferencing service and features, consult ITU-T Recommendations F.700 and F.702. Collaborative conferencing is an application that can be further subdivided into broad categories in which the same features are used for different ends. Categories include *executive meetings* (the model for the introduction and discussion of the major conferencing features), *distance learning,* and *telemedicine.*

With distance learning, university classrooms can be brought to corporate locations and even homes. It is less important for the professor to see his or her students than the other way around, so video broadcasting is a viable option for distance learning. As the student works, the professor can access and evaluate the assignment and provide feedback in real time. As a result, the student may actually receive more personal attention than a typical classroom student. Organizations that encourage employees to take distance learning classes save both tuition and commuting time.

Telemedicine also includes meetings of doctors and continuing education (required of physicians by law in many countries), but its more ingenious and often life-saving use is in remote diagnosis, consultation, and patient prescreening. With distance diagnosis, the services of the best physicians can be rendered to patients in the remote geographic areas where treatment is not readily available. The transmission of both static (still) images (e.g., X-rays, electrocardiograms, and biopsy images) and dynamic ones (e.g., ultrasound images or patients' movements) is possible. In special cases where several variously located specialists must all examine a patient virtually, all features of collaborative conferences can be used. Special features include the ability for doctors to make comments unheard by the patient. The savings due to elimination of travel for both doctors and patients is obvious, but the chief advantage of telemedicine is that it can bring health care services of the highest quality to areas where they were previously unavailable.

Web-Based Conference Control

Web-based conference control, as its name implies, provides the basic user interface for conference control through the World Wide Web. The lack of a friendly user interface for conference control has long made it an awkward task for conference chairpersons and administrators. If you have even the most basic experience with audio conference calls, you realize how difficult it can be at times to identify the speaker. The conference chairperson faces the more difficult problem of trying to determine who wishes to speak next: The traditional method of raising one's hand clearly does not work in voice conferencing. Keeping track of attendees is not much easier—participants can join and leave as they wish, often without an audible announcement. When the application includes an audible notification, the same chime sounds for both arrival and departure of a participant. The Web-based conference control service allows the chairman of an audio conference to control data over the Web. It may also provide a way for conference participants to retrieve information pertaining to the conference. Data about conference participants and the active speaker is readily available to all participants. Identification is simple because each participant's terminal is associated with the participant. Conference reservations can also be made using the Web tools.

Because of the proprietary nature of most business conferences, the Web-based conference control applications normally support security for authentication and authorization of participants. Access control to any conference information is guarded via a password, and often, data transported over the Internet are encrypted.

Internet Call Center

A *call center* is a system that allows a group of people (agents) either to make calls to or take calls from customers. The system usually provides the following functions:

- *Queuing of incoming calls.* A typical queuing discipline is first-come, first-served, but often large-volume customers are given priority.

- *Call distribution.* Incoming calls are typically distributed based on the agents' availability. With the feature known as *automatic call distribution* (ACD), any given call is routed to the agent who has not received calls for the longest period of time. With another feature, that call can be routed to the agent who can best deal with the caller's problem. For best-agent calls, the caller is first connected to the voice response system, which prompts the caller to make a choice from a list of options, and then is transferred to the appropriate agent.

- *Agent monitoring.* The system tracks the time each agent spends actually responding to a call, the duration of each call, and other statistics that report on the load and efficiency of agents.

The Internet call center augments the capabilities of a traditional call center with the access to the Internet in general and to the World Wide Web in particular. In some cases, it also enables agents to use IP telephony in addition to the PSTN. In all cases, it gives the agent access to e-mail, text chat, and escorted Web browsing. These services are used to improve the information exchange between the customer and the agent. For example, voice communication may also be supplemented by IP-based information services. With escorted Web browsing, the agent can guide a customer through a set of Web pages, viewing the same pages as the customer.

Internet Call-Waiting

Call-waiting is a familiar service in the PSTN world. With this service, a subscriber who participates in a telephone call is notified when another call comes in over the same telephone line. Then it is up to the subscriber to place the party on hold and accept the incoming call, or to ignore the incoming call. After accepting the new call, the subscriber can also toggle between the two calls.

As the number of data calls grew, the telephone companies realized that they needed to provide the means for temporarily disabling call-waiting. Subscribers invariably use the cancel waiting feature when they go on-line; if they did not, the tones that indicate the arrival of a new call would interfere with the operation of the modem and could result in loss of the connection. Until the *Internet call-waiting* (ICW) service was introduced, subscribers could not eat their cake and have it, too.

The ICW service typically works as follows:

- When the subscriber logs onto the Internet via a dial-up connection, the IP address of his or her PC is recorded.

- When the network detects an incoming call destined to the subscriber, a dialog box pops up on the subscriber's screen. The dialog box presents the caller's telephone number or name, if available, and a set of options for call treatment. The options may include the following: accept as an IP voice call, accept as a PSTN voice call, route to another telephone number, or route to voice mail.

- After obtaining the subscriber's response, the network implements the option chosen.

Unlike its PSTN counterpart, the ICW service does not always support toggling between the calls. In the case where the incoming call is accepted as an IP voice call, toggling between calls is just toggling between applications, which makes it simple to support. But the case where the incoming call is accepted as a PSTN voice call, toggling between the PSTN call and the data call is not currently supported.

The ICW service can be enriched with many useful features. For example, the subscriber may be given the option of setting up a list of telephone numbers from which all originating calls are to be blocked, keeping a log of calls not answered, and returning calls by automatic dial-out. In addition, the idea behind the ICW automatically extends to "Internetization" of a large set of IN-supported services (such as *call-forwarding, personal number,* or *follow-me*).

It is obvious how the ICW service benefits Internet users. It also benefits service providers by increasing the number of completed calls.

PINT Services

The basic PSTN/Internet Internetworking (PINT) services (RFC 2458) include click-to-dial-back, click-to-fax, click-to-fax-back, and voice-access-to-content. The common denominator of PINT services is that they combine the Internet applications and PSTN telecommunications services in such a way that Internet applications can request the PSTN telecommunications services. Further, the Internet is used for nonvoice interactions, while voice (and fax) is carried entirely over the PSTN. An example of such a service is the combination of a Web-based Yellow Pages service with the ability to initiate a PSTN call between a customer and a supplier in the manner described later. Note that the word *click* in some of these services should not be taken literally and construed as a prescribed way for invoking the services. It is rather used to underline that service initiation takes place on the Internet, where pointing and clicking are the most prevalent user actions.

Click-to-Dial-Back

With the click-to-dial-back service, a user requests (through an IP host) that the PSTN call be established with another party. As in several other examples of PSTN/Internet hybrid services, an important prerequisite for using this service is that the user have both voice access to the PSTN (via a telephone terminal) and data access to the Internet (via a PC).

A typical example application of this service is online shopping: A user browsing through an online catalog clicks a button, thus inviting a call from a sales representative. Note that (as is the case with the all-PSTN freephone), flexible billing arrangements can be implemented on behalf of the service provider. In addition, the PSTN can route the call depending on the time of day, day of week, availability of agents in different locations, and so on.

Click-to-Fax

With click-to-fax service, a user at an IP host requests that a fax be sent to a particular fax number. This service is especially meaningful when the fax is to be sent to someone who has only a fax machine but no access to the Internet. Consider as an example a service scenario in which a Web user makes a reservation for a hotel room in Beijing from a travel service page containing hotel information for major cities around the world. Suppose a specific Beijing hotel chosen by the user does not have an Internet connection but has a fax machine. The user fills out the hotel reservation form and then clicks a button to send the form to the service provider, whose equipment then generates a fax request and sends it together with the hotel reservation form to a PSTN node. Upon receiving the request and the associated data, the PSTN translates the data into the proper fax format and delivers it to the Beijing hotel.

Click-to-Fax-Back

With click-to-fax-back service, a user at an IP host can request that a fax be sent to him or her. Now the traveler of the previous example can request confirmation from the Beijing hotel. Another useful application of the service is when the size of the information that a user needs to retrieve is so large that downloading it to the user's PC over the Internet would require a long time and too much disk space.

Voice-Access-to-Content

With voice-access-to-content service, a user at an IP host requests that certain information on the Internet be accessible (and delivered) in an audio form over the PSTN, using the telephone as an informational appliance. One application of this service is providing Web access to the blind. (This may require special resources—available in the PSTN—to convert the Web data into speech.) A variant of this service is that the telephone is used to initiate as well as to retrieve the content. In other words, the user requests through the telephone with voice commands that certain information on the Internet be delivered in an audio form over the PSTN and heard on the telephone.

Web-Based Service Customization

Service customization is the activity through which a subscriber to a communications service can change a subset of parameters. These parameters typically define the runtime behavior of the service. For example, for the freephone service, subscribers should (at minimum) be able to set the following parameters:

- The time of day when the calls are to be directed to a particular destination number
- The day of the week when the calls are to be directed to a particular destination number
- The destination number where the calls from a certain area code should terminate

Another example is the *follow-me service,* where customers can prescribe how they wish incoming calls to be directed according to their schedule and availability (by using similar parameters).

Traditionally, to customize a communications service, particularly one that is delivered over the PSTN, a subscriber would need to have a special networking arrangement with his or her service provider to receive direct, secure access to customer records. Before the proliferation of the Internet, there simply was no infrastructure that would allow small customers to access such information. Now, telecommunications companies can move the customizable parameters to (properly secured) IP hosts that are accessible by subscribers.

When it is easy for subscribers to customize the services so that they can be called when they wish, the telephone companies that serve them naturally complete more calls and thereby improve profits. Since services offered are Web-based, the potential customer base extends worldwide.

Remote Dial-in Access Applications and Virtual Private Networks

Remote dial-in access (or simply *remote access*) is the way many users access the Internet. It is also used in the *telecommuting* service whereby corporate road warriors and those who work at home access corporate IP networks. On the surface, both types of access look the same. In fact, the very procedure (dialing a number and entering a password) and the end-user equipment necessary (a telephone line and a modem) to accesses the network are identical. At least one important piece of the underlying technology pertinent to this book—carrying IP packets over PSTN lines—is also present in both types of services. There are significant differences as well, with underlying issues, between accessing the Internet privately (through an ISP) and accessing corporate networks. We treat remote dial-in access simply as part of VPNs, discussed in a section that follows.

One problem inherent to data access from home via a telephone line is that the line will be busy for the duration of the data access session. The busy line has posed a number of problems for households with only one telephone line. One solution, perhaps most typical for many American households, is to have two lines. Another is to have ISDN installed (which is still rather expensive). Yet another solution is to use a special modem that splits the line into data and voice. Then, of course, there are service solutions (such as the Internet call-waiting service). As it becomes more available, the xDSL technology described in Chapter 2 will eliminate the need to dial at all!

With remote access, in its oldest form (See Figure 9.13), a user simply established a point-to-point link between a terminal (connected to a modem) and a remote computer (also connected to a modem).

As PCs became household appliances, the terminals virtually disappeared. PCs are presently used both as terminals (with so-called *shell accounts*, provided by both ISPs and corporations) and IP hosts. Even with the shell accounts, users get access to the Internet (including the Web) through a host. However, with shell accounts, the graphical interface that has made the World Wide Web so popular is not available.

To act as a host, a PC typically dials in the *remote access server* (RAS) of an IP network (as depicted in Figure 9.14, where the PSTN path happens to traverse three telephone switches). Access servers are discussed in Chapter 10, but we will answer here one basic question: What actually distinguishes a host equipped with a set of modems from an access server? The answer is simple: A RAS is an IP router equipped with a set of modems or digital signal processors capable of terminating a call. Remote access servers are sometimes called *remote access concentrators.* Although both terms are used interchangeably, some people use the latter term only when referring to large *multiservice modules,* which have access to asynchronous transfer mode (ATM) networks, X.25-based public data networks (PDNs), and other non-IP networks (hence the term *multiservice*). Clearly, any analysis of multiservice module functions is outside of the scope of this book, but we will refer to the capabilities in Chapter 10.

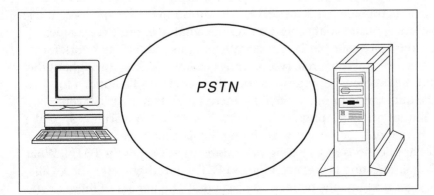

Figure 9.13 Terminal-to-host dial-in access.

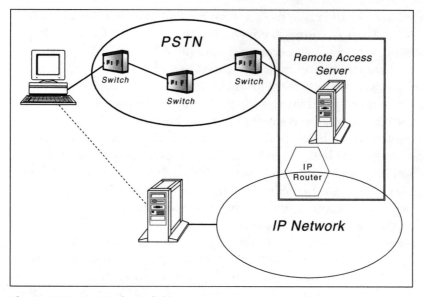

Figure 9.14   Host-to-host dial-in access.

Having just defined a RAS, we should note that the data network access may be not so remote. First of all, an enterprise or ISP can place several access servers (see Figure 9.15) so that users in different geographic areas can call local numbers. Second, remote access can also be outsourced. A *remote access outsourcing application* uses the existing network infrastructure of a larger service provider to offer remote access termination service to enterprise customers. Then, with the *Internet offload application* (also called *Internet call diversion*), the very edge (that is, the central office switch) of the PSTN can recognize the call (based on the dialed number, for example) as a data call, and terminate it at a colocated or even internal access server. From there the call is passed to the appropriate ISP (or enterprise) network (Figure 9.15).

As mentioned in Chapter 2, the Internet offloading application has been created out of urgency. The ever increasing use of Internet access has manifested a serious problem with the PSTN: The duration (or *holding time*, in telephony parlance) of such data calls far exceeds what telephone companies expected from voice calls (and consequently engineered their network for). As a result, more and more real (voice) calls became blocked throughout the PSTN, and the problem became so serious that specialized solutions to offload the data traffic from telephone switches to data networks, were urgently requested by telephone companies. The problem warrants special attention here if only because it was among the first instances where data-over-voice applications required significant restructuring of the PSTN. What is especially interesting is that even the old PSTN paradigm—the more calls and the longer they are, the better—has changed! The danger of these long data calls blocking voice traffic became so serious that the telephone compa-

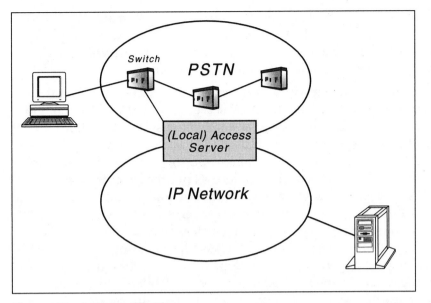

Figure 9.15   Internet offload.

nies decided they did not want data calls in the voice network. This conflict has created a classic example of PSTN-Internet integration by necessity.

Security

There are two essential security issues with remote access: authentication of the user, and the user's authorization to use particular services. One old and proven way of authorizing dial-in is *call-back.* In a call-back authorization, the caller dials into a remote access server and enters a log-in name and password. The remote access server then hangs up the modem connection and searches its database to authenticate the user. If the user is authenticated, the access server calls the user back at a predefined number. This method can work for a telecommuter who always works at home, but naturally fails if the worker travels.

Although call-back could be improved (for example, the access server could be reprogrammed to dial a specific hotel telephone based on a preapproved travel itinerary), the industry has agreed on a much more versatile security application: The *Remote Authentication Dial-In User Service* (RADIUS) (see the discussion of RFC 2138 in Chapter 7). RADIUS is an important application by itself; the following example describes how it works:

1. Using a modem, the user's PC dials in to a modem that is connected to a remote access server.

2. Once this connection is completed, the user is prompted for the log-in name and password.

3. The access server encrypts log-in and password information and sends it to a centralized RADIUS server, which decrypts the data and passes it on to the appropriate security system module. (The encryption and decryption steps are omitted in some networks.)

4. The security system module authenticates (or rejects) the caller; if the caller is authenticated, the RADIUS server checks its database to find out which services the caller is authorized to use. [This includes specific protocols supported by the user's PC, such as *Point-to-Point Protocol* (PPP) or *Serial Line Internet Protocol* (SLIP), protocols described in Chapter 7.] If the authentication process fails, the caller is denied access to the network. Otherwise, the authorization and specifics of the applicable services are sent to the access server. The RADIUS server may also send policing information (such as the data rate for carrying user data) to the access server, as well as filtering information, which limits the caller's access to the enterprise network resources (for example, the caller may be allowed to access e-mail, but not to change or even copy the contents of files). To ensure that requests are not responded to by unauthorized sources, the RADIUS server sends an authentication key identifying itself to the RAS.

Some networks may require multiple levels of passwords for resource access, in which case RADIUS may be involved in authorizing relevant access.

In the preceding description, the seemingly unnecessary references to the security system module (why would RADIUS itself not do that?) are actually essential to understanding of the service: Support of any specific security mechanism is not a function of RADIUS per se; instead, RADIUS interworks with security mechanisms.

Telecommuting

Telecommuting is a work arrangement that allows an enterprise employee to work from a location other than the company premises on a regular or temporary basis. The employee may travel, work from home, or work from a leased office. The telecommuting application provides a secure means for the employee to reach the company IP network and to access all the network resources and IP services in the same way they would be accessed in the office. Mail servers, file servers, Web servers, databases, and print servers are common examples of network resources; e-mail, the World Wide Web, FTP file transfer, and telnet (that is, virtual terminal) are common IP applications that access these resources. The telecommuter's computer connects to the enterprise network as an IP host and is treated as though it is located on the enterprise premises (and is connected to the company network by a dedicated link).

As noted before, the telecommuting service is typically provided by way of the dial-up access through the PSTN. (Although the use of cable networks to reach the enterprise networks is an important and interesting alternative, it is outside the scope of the book.)

To support telecommuting, an enterprise may set up dedicated remote access servers and operate, manage, and administer them like other customer premises equipment. Alternatively, it can rely on remote access outsourcing to ISPs or the PSTN employing access servers. The motivation for outsourcing is to allow the enterprise to avoid the capital cost of the servers and to avoid having to retain a dedicated staff to maintain the equipment. The enterprise may also share the servers with other companies to further cut costs. Whatever the actual arrangement for supporting telecommuting, security is by far the most important corporate requirement. A telecommuter must be authenticated before he or she is authorized to have access to the network.

Accounting is another essential application. In this case, accounting actually refers to the collection of resource consumption data. This information is useful for capacity and trend analysis, cost allocation, auditing, and billing.

Telecommuting is further complicated by the increasing mobility of telecommuters and their geographic impermanence. A global enterprise typically has its employees calling in from different parts of the world at any given time of the day. If they all dial in to a remote access server in the same country, the expenses can quickly mount to cosmic proportions. If, on the other hand, they dial in to local access servers, dedicated connections of these servers with the local company can be prohibitively expensive, too. Finally, the requirement to provide telecommuters with the same services as employees working in the enterprise office brings up both security and traffic policing issues (addressed by the VPN service).

VPNs

As a general definition, *virtual private network* (VPN) refers to a class of applications that use public or shared network resources to emulate the characteristics of private or dedicated network resources. We need such a general definition since the term has been used by both the PSTN and VPN to designate different services.

In the PSTN parlance, the term *VPN* usually denotes a service by which an enterprise is given its own numbering plan as well as other PBX-like (but network-based) features. [*Software-defined network* (SDN) is sometimes used in place of VPN.] Initially, corporations leased dedicated permanent switched circuits (reserved by telephone switches) in order to provide to their employees the look and feel of the dedicated private networks. Subsequently, as telephone switches became programmable, the need for the permanency disappeared; the circuits were established on demand. However, all involved switches had to be programmed to support the corporations' numbering plans, dialing restrictions, and so on. Furthermore, switches have to be reprogrammed every time something changes. Finally, with the advance of IN solutions, establishment and maintenance of the VPN features can be done in only one place—a network database.

With each of these steps, VPN costs were further lowered without any visible impact on the quality of services provided. The IN mechanism is totally independent from the transport mechanism of voice (that is, IP or PSTN lines and trunks); thus, all the PSTN VPN features can be supported with the same mechanism in the IP environment. In a joint PSTN/IP environment, the control of VPN (a classic IN application) can partially reside on an IP host, making the actual service delivery (for example, number translation or administration of restrictions) much more effective compared with the case in which the control belongs only within the PSTN.

In the IP world, the historical use of the term *VPN* is similar, except that the items being replaced are dedicated private data communications (rather than telephone) lines. With dedicated private data lines, the Internet can be used to transport corporate data. Definitions of the term vary. We will use the one given in Kosiur (1998): "A virtual private network is a network of virtual circuits for carrying private traffic," where the virtual circuit is defined as "a connection . . . between a sender and a receiver in which both the route for session and bandwidth . . . [are] allocated dynamically."

The performance, reliability, security, and quality of service of a successfully implemented VPN are comparable with those of dedicated network solutions. The costs of VPNs, however, are at least 50 percent lower than those of dedicated solutions. In the data environment, the VPN supports private IP addresses, differential treatments of traffic inside and outside a particular private network, and management of the firewalls that separate the private network from external networks. [By far, the best book on firewalls is Cheswick and Bellovin (1998); we recommend it.] The VPN interconnects enterprise networks via a public data network and provides remote on-demand connection to enterprise networks through the PSTN.

We concentrate only on remote on-demand connection to enterprise networks through the PSTN. It is important to stress, however, that regardless of the initial connection (for example, the PSTN dial-in), VPN solutions may allow user traffic to pass through the Internet. Again, the transport of data over a public medium makes security the central issue when providing VPN service. Authorization and authentication are clearly not enough: Data traveling in IP packets over the Internet can be intercepted. As you may remember from Chapter 2, one existing scheme, called *tunneling*, hides the network infrastructure from the VPN application by establishing gateways at borders with the Internet to encapsulate the IP packets destined for travel over the Internet into point-to-point (that is, gateway-to-gateway) protocol packets as shown in Figure 9.16. The figure depicts the enterprise network connections

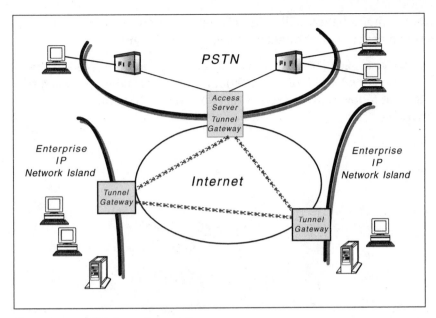

Figure 9.16 VPN through tunneling.

(via VPN), but the same configuration applies to ISPs. This mechanism demonstrates how remote users (and separate so-called islands of a private IP network) can be connected into one network. Another important attribute of this solution is that it aids in management of the ever decreasing IP address space in the following two ways:

1. The dial-in users can be assigned their IP addresses dynamically.

2. Only gateways need unique IP addresses (as far as the Internet is concerned); the rest of the VPN IP endpoints can be assigned private IP addresses, which are unique only for that VPN. (The numbers could duplicate the addresses used in any other network, including the Internet.)

Tunneling itself supports several applications, a few of which have already been mentioned, including:

- *Remote access outsourcing.* A larger service provider offers remote access termination services to customers, with data traveling through tunnels. The customer requires much less equipment (and less capital investment), which, in turn, would allow more focused specialization in services.

- *Feature services.* Tunneling enables the delivery of value-added services (such as IP multicasting and low-latency IP service classes), and so supports applications like video conferencing.

- *Business-to-business services.* Tunneling facilitates content hosting for intranets and extranets. With the public key infrastructure in place, support of nonrepudiation will definitely help electronic commerce by making merchants confident about selling over the Internet.

IP VPN service is peculiar to IP networks, and is beyond the scope of this book; see Kosiur (1998) and Huston (1999) for more information on this topic. The chapter that follows covers aspects of VPNs in which dialing in is directly involved.

CHAPTER 10

PSTN-Internet Interworking Products

In this chapter we review types of products available to support PSTN-Internet interworking applications; then we discuss the criteria (for example, features, legacy support, capacity, reliability, and so on) for product selection. We intended this section to be self-contained: In cases where the function of a product is not clear without some knowledge of relevant technologies or standards, we reintroduce and briefly explain the concepts that we have already elaborated on in previous chapters.

PSTN-Internet Interworking Product Types

We have deliberately avoided reviewing specific vendor products. Instead, we outline generic families of existing products, describing their features, major parameters, and—whenever applicable—criteria for interworking with other products. Because new products emerge constantly and existing products are updated frequently, you should expect the product capabilities listed here to change.

You should obtain the latest descriptions from the product vendors for details like prices and performance characteristics. The product families we focus on correspond to the three categories of PSTN-Internet interworking:

1. *Carrying voice across both the IP networks and the PSTN.* Products include IP telephony gateways [usually called *voice-over-IP* (VoIP) gateways in the trade], gatekeepers, multipoint conferencing units, and *private branch exchanges* (PBXs).

2. *Combining PSTN transport and the Internet access to PSTN services.* Products include intelligent network service nodes and intelligent peripherals. The messaging platforms that support unified messaging also fit here, because a central feature is that they rely on IN control. Note: You could argue that multimedia support by these products justifies including them in the previous item, while access support warrants placing them in the next list item.

3. *Carrying data over PSTN lines on the way to IP networks.* Products that support remote access and VPN applications include access servers, Signalling System No. 7 gateways, and class 5 (that is, local) switches with multiservice capabilities. (As you may remember from Chapter 2, the term *multiservice* designates the capability to support connections to multiple types of networks—PSTN, frame relay, ATM, and IP networks in particular.)

VoIP Gateways

The range of products in the VoIP gateway area starts with small PC-compatible boards with a few ports, which accommodate one to four analog telephone lines, and extends to large carrier-grade devices that can be used by both telephone companies and Internet service providers. Toward the high end of such products, the functions of a gateway per se are often integrated with gatekeepers into standalone products (IP telephony servers) that have many additional functions, as described in the next section.

At the heart of any gateway is the capability of converting a stream of voice-carrying signals (either analog or digital) from a telephone line or trunk into a stream of RTP packets (transmitted over a shared channel, which in general should be expected to have a much lower bandwidth). Part of such a conversion involves compression, which compensates for bandwidth reduction. Conversely, every gateway has the capability of converting a stream of RTP packets (and possibly decompressing the data) into a stream of signals acceptable by existing traditional telephony systems. The conversion is performed by coder/decoder modules, or *codecs*, which can be purchased separately and subsequently integrated into gateways. The role of codecs is central to the basic function of any gateway, because their performance affects crispness and clarity of sound. Other important gateway capabilities that affect the quality of sound are echo cancellation and compression. Overall, it is a legitimate requirement in today's market that the audio capabilities of gateways enable full-duplex conversations. Another important requirement is that gateways used by the switches (for example, PBXs) for toll saving monitor the quality of IP-transmitted sound (by employing RTCP, for example) and generate an appropriate signal to the switches when sound quality falls below a customer-set threshold. Upon reception of a poor-quality signal, the switches can automatically select a PSTN trunk to continue the call.

Chapter 3 gives an introduction to codec technology and alludes to major codec standards. We have not addressed codec standards in detail because much literature on the subject is available (see Minoli and Minoli, 1998b) and such a treatment is beyond the scope of this book. We will provide recommendations on what to expect (and request) of vendors. The role of codec standards is hard to overestimate because, in principle, gateways cannot interoperate if they do not support the same sets of codecs. Thus, compliance with codec standards is an essential factor when evaluating gateways purchased from different manufacturers.

As we have said before, major codec standards are produced by ITU-T in its G Series of Recommendations. First of all, the G.711 standard (for ISDN voice channels; yields 64 kbps of digital audio) must be supported by any gateway. In connection with regional standards, all gateways that interoperate with the North American telephone system must support the *μ-law* scheme; all gateways that interoperate with the European telephone system must support the *A-law* scheme. In addition, advanced gateways may support low-bandwidth connections with G.723.1 or G.729A codecs. In that case, the support of transporting DTMF tones using a non-RTP path is important because the low-bandwidth codecs are not designed to reliably pass DTMF tones as part of a compressed voice stream. This feature allows the regeneration of the DTMF tones at the receiving gateway and improves overall call performance, in particular for applications (for example, voice mail) that require correct detection of DTMF tones.

Voice compression makes it difficult, if not impossible, to *transcode* (that is, translate from one encoding scheme to another). Transcoding is well understood for the compression schemes defined in the G.729 and G.729A standards. Thus, if compression is supported, it should adhere to these standards. Some gateway products attempt to realize much-needed bandwidth savings by monitoring sound activity. When silence is detected by the transmitting gateway, it stops the sound transmission and informs the receiving gateway about the background noise. Then the receiving gateway emits *comfort noise* to create the perception of uninterrupted transmission. Unfortunately, this feature always seems to affect voice quality negatively—much more research is needed to develop the necessary heuristics. G.729 and G.729A are two codec standards that support some degree of implementation of this feature, but there are so many incompatible solutions among current products that it is essential to require any products that support this feature to provide a means to turn it off. Finally, when this feature is implemented for G.729 or G.729A, the G.729B standard should be complied with.

Another essential aspect of all gateway products is their ability to use signaling (for call establishment rather than voice transport) at the appropriate level of interconnection. For example, a two-stage gateway that provides a toll bypass (or trunk replacement) service described in Chapter 9 must support call establishment signaling (in most cases, SS No. 7 ISUP) with the access switch. Similarly, a one-stage enterprise gateway that connects to a PBX must support access (typically Q.931) signaling. Even the lowest-end gateway products— one-port residential gateways that interconnect analog telephones with the Internet—must still comply with the standard in-band signaling (that is, provision of dial tone, acceptance of dialed tones, and recognition of on-hook/off-hook events) in order to work with the telephone. Thus, on the traditional telephony side, gateway products destined for a particular function must support appropriate in-band signaling. On the IP side, gateway products should support (and all advertised products invariably do support) the H.323 family of standards. In particular, at the time of this writing, H.323 version 2 is supported by leading products. In addition, some products also support the SIP protocol as an add-on, since several providers—especially those integrating cable networks—require SIP compliance. To this end, industry attention to SIP is growing steadily at the moment of this writing.

One function, already mentioned in Chapter 3 and present in several products, is gateway *self-discovery*. This is a novel feature particularly relevant to the gateways at the edge of the PSTN. For a phone-to-phone toll bypass service, calling party access to a (local) gateway is achieved through a local telephone call. For the service to be cost effective, the called party must also be dialed from its local exchange, so the local terminating gateway must be the endpoint for the IP-carried part of the call. The IP addresses of the gateways (relative to the local PSTN numbers they serve best) are currently hard-coded, but products that support dynamic discovery of the gateway are emerging. (Note that, as an alternative, gatekeepers could perform self-discovery.) To handle the case in which a local terminating gateway cannot be reached (because of network congestion, gateway overload, or network server failure), advanced gateways often support *PSTN fallback*. This feature allows a phone-to-phone toll bypass call that otherwise cannot be completed to be completed entirely over the PSTN.

Gateway products fall into three general categories:

1. *Small (branch office or residential) gateway products.* One- to four-port interfaces to which POTS telephones are connected.

2. *Enterprise-grade (access gateway) gateway products.* Support up to a thousand ports. On the traditional telephony side, enterprise-grade gateway products typically interface with a PBX (and employ Q.931 signaling) and are usually located on the enterprise premises. As an exception, they can be located at an ISP or LEC, but with the sole purpose of providing PBX-emulating *Centrex* services to a particular enterprise that

does not own a PBX. Enterprise gateways support one-stage dialing: PBXs divert voice-over-IP traffic based on either a specific number or an algorithm computed by the PBX.

3. *Carrier-grade (trunking gateway) gateway products.* Support up to 10,000 ports located on the premises of IP telephony providers (for example, ISPs, IXCs, and LECs). The connection (and, therefore, the signaling arrangements with the PSTN) requires the use of Signalling System No. 7 (SS No. 7) ISUP. If the SS No. 7 *transaction capabilities* (TC) are supported, then the VoIP gateways equipped with the application supporting the *Intelligent Network Application Protocol* (INAP) can also benefit from using Intelligent Network. To get the SS No. 7 support, the VoIP gateways can be paired with the SS7 gateways described later in this chapter.

The rest of this section deals with carrier- and enterprise-grade gateway products.

The gateway hardware invariably consists of line modules (cards) mounted on a rack and a management board that is responsible for the control of line modules. Communications among the line modules and the management card are carried through fast-switching fabric, such as an asynchronous transfer mode (ATM) cell backplane, at a high rate (100 to 200 Mbps in the case of the ATM fabric). Switching fabric components are augmented by Ethernet cards and ports (and necessary wiring) as well as the cooling system (typically fans). Cooling is important because of the highly CPU-bound nature of codec software, which necessitates the employment of multiple digital signal processors (DSPs). In fact, the two major limitation factors for scalability of gateways are heat and space. The system is administered via the operator console, which may (but does not have to) be part of a particular offering; however, console ports are provided on the gateway chassis. In high-end products, the line modules are *hot-swappable:* Any line card can be replaced by another one without the need for reconfiguration—it will automatically load its configuration from the management board once it is in the slot.

As you may recall, the ISDN *primary rate interface* (PRI) service provides bandwidths of 1.544 Mbps for T1 lines in the United States and 2.048 Mbps over E1 lines in Europe. This translates to twenty-three and thirty 64-kbps bearer (B) channels, respectively, augmented by a 64-kbps data (D) channel. In high-end gateway products, the capacity is measured in *quad-T1* and *tri-E1*, corresponding to four T1 and three E1 circuits, respectively—the capacity of one card. Cards can be added to a system, and systems can be stacked on top of each other.

In addition to PRI, a number of other trunking services (which we do not cover) are supported by the high-end products. Note that ISDN is a typical and widely deployed use of trunking services; while a T1 line is normally associated with a single telephone number, when it is set up for ISDN B channels, each can be assigned a separate number. The lines can be configured for both inbound and combined inbound and outbound calling. Another configuration option is alternating circuit-switched voice and data, which permits modem calls.

As far as software is concerned, each line module's *central processing unit* (CPU) executes the gateway operating system independently. The operating systems themselves are often proprietary. High-end products provide both command-line and graphical user interfaces for monitoring, maintenance, and operations of the gateway via the console or *telnet* connection. In addition, most systems support *Simple Network Management Protocol* (SNMP) for the same purposes. To this end, an important feature of a gateway is provision of SNMP alarms for a number of causes, including power failure and overheating. Another important feature is automatic turn-off of the overheated or otherwise problematic line modules by the management board.

An important function of gateway software is billing. Gateways should generate *call detail records,* whose attributes are described in more detail in the next section, and then pass them to the gatekeeper responsible for billing. Part of the software is libraries that provide the application programmer's interface (API) that allows the use of third-party billing software in support of various paying methods, such as prepaid calling cards or credit cards. (A key feature of a prepaid billing system is to send a *call drop* request to the originating gateway when the caller runs out of prepaid funds.) Billing is of course inseparable from authentication. In two-stage calling, the user is identified by a *personal identification number* (PIN); the *Automatic Number Identification* (ANI) parameter passed from the PSTN is also used for authentication. Again, the authentication may be performed by gatekeepers.

Proprietary coding and compression techniques often make gateways from different vendors noninteroperable. While enterprise network managers can solve this problem by purchasing a matching set of gateways from a single vendor or ensuring that the gateways from selected vendors do interoperate, neither ISPs nor telephone companies can presently ensure that calls originating or terminating in another ISP's or telephone company's network can be successfully handled by the receiving gateway. This interoperability issue is one reason (QoS is the second) why the quality of voice-over-IP calls has been reported to be high in the enterprise networks, but remains problematic over the Internet.

Finally, it is important to note that distributed implementations of VoIP gateways are emerging. These implementations are generally associated with so-called soft switches and media gateways, as described in Chapter 3. Soft switches provide call control and signaling interworking, while media gateways handle the transcoding of voice streams tailored for different networks. The aim is to make distributed VoIP gateways more scalable and programmable than their monolithic cousins and ultimately to ease the introduction of new services.

Multipoint Conferencing Units
(MCUs)

MCUs provide a means of implementing the multimedia conferencing services described in Chapter 9. The products come in several grades, depending on the number of ports and features they support. On the switching side, MCUs can be connected to PBXs, central offices, or toll switches via trunks; the rest of the connections are to the endpoints, a gatekeeper, or other MCUs for cascading, as described in Chapter 5. MCUs may also provide a connection to an external computer (server) that actually runs the conferencing application software. In the latter case, more than one MCU is typically connected to the server.

MCU hardware arrives in cabinets hosting multiple circuit packs with video and audio codecs that are connected internally via a fast switch. In essence, MCUs are specialized multimedia gateways augmented by conferencing capabilities. In high-end products, the packs are equipped with clearly visible green, yellow, and red *light-emitting diodes* (LEDs) that indicate real-time status. The LEDs can be easily removed (via the turn of a single screw) and replaced without powering down the whole system.

At the time of this writing, MCUs support from 4 to 20 video ports in low-end products, up to 42 in medium-end products, and up to 64 in high-end products. Other parameters include the number and supported types of audio ports, the total number of conference participants, the total number of conferences per MCU, and the number of MCUs that can be connected for cascading—an important indicator of scalability. Overall, one large MCU is typically less expensive than several smaller MCUs with the same total capacity; the maintenance and operations costs are also lower if only one MCU is employed.

High-end MCUs also support *bonding* (that is, the capability of aggregating independent 56/64-kbps calls) to achieve high-bandwidth conferences. For example, ten 64-kbps calls from one endpoint can be bonded for a 640-kbps conference. Currently, high-end products support up to 24 T.120 multipoint data conferencing ports, H.320 ports, and active conferences per MCU, and can interconnect with up to 50 MCUs for cascading.

Support of video, audio, and data conferencing standards is essential, although high-end products invariably support proprietary codecs (and provide transcoding when necessary).[1]

---

[1]The imperative standards are ITU-T H.221 (frame structure); H.230 (control capabilities); H.231 (multipoint control units); H.242 (establishing multipoint connections); H.261 and H.263 (video coding); and H.320 (terminal specifications). The data standards supported include the T.122–T.125 sequence discussed in Chapter 5 (T.123 is a standard that addresses IP networks). G.711, G.722, and G.728 audio standards make up the typical set required in all products.

Some existing high-end products support all of the following features:

Chair control.   As discussed in Chapter 9, the conference chairperson can request or relinquish control of the conference, choose the broadcaster, and drop a site or a conference.

Continuous presence.   Several images (up to 25 in high-end products) can be maintained on a participant's screen simultaneously. For example, a picture composed of images taken from several participating sites is composed and maintained at video rates from 56 to 768 kbps and 30 frames per second. Another example is display of *panoramic view* (derived by maintaining several simultaneous images of a conference site).

Broadcast with autoscan.   Participants can see the speaker all the time, but the speaker sees the participants on a rotating basis.

Voice activation.   The MCU automatically switches the video display when the speaker changes. It is important to test voice activation, because unexpected switching of the display can occur due to background or other accidental noise. High-quality products switch the display only in reaction to the human voice.

Full-duplex audio.   This is present only in high-end products because it requires rather sophisticated software control of the DSPs. Every conference participant can talk and hear what others are saying at the same time. Full-duplex audio is important for highly interactive conferences, especially to those who are participating as audio only.

Presentation mode.   Participants can see the presenter at all times, but the presenter can see only the person who is asking questions.

Terminal naming.   Conference participants are identified by strings of characters associated with their terminals (typically the names of participants, but sometimes titles or geographic locations). The name is displayed when a person associated with the terminal speaks. For terminal naming to work, the terminals must support the H.243 standard.

Speed match.   Participants can join the conference at different transfer rates (varying from 56 to 768 kbps). In particular, low-speed endpoints can still be admitted to higher-speed conferences for audio only.

Still image transfer.   Still images can be transmitted at 4 times the quality of moving images. The images are transmitted using the H.320 video channel (rather than data channels, which are endpoint dependent); the endpoints must support Annex D of ITU-T Recommendation H.261 for still image transfer to work.

Data conferencing.   Participants can share data in real time. Spreadsheet applications, word processors, and file transfer applications are typically supported.

Universal control. The conference parameters (for example, composition of the screen) can be controlled by a device as primitive as a touch-tone telephone or as sophisticated as a highly specialized real-time graphical user interface application (often part of a product offering) running on a PC.

Conference mobility. Useful for trouble isolation as well as some advanced services, such as meet and greet. Conference participants can be temporarily moved from one conference to another.

Audio mode selection. The codec to be used for the conference can be selected at the time of reservation.

Dial-in (meet me) conferencing. Conference participants dial into the conference. High-end products support a variation called *one-number access*, which allows participants to dial the same number (regardless of the number of cascaded MCUs) to enter the conference.

Dial-out conferencing. The MCU itself dials the participants of a conference. Dial-out conferencing is essential when the conference participants are spread around the world and the MCU is located in the United States, since international calls tend to be cheaper in the United States than in rest of the world. Another important benefit of dial-out conferencing is that it automatically results in one bill. The same billing can be achieved with dial-in conferences.

Web-based reservations. A conference host can schedule a conference by accessing a Web page on the enterprise intranet. Once the conference is scheduled, records can be updated by the person who has scheduled it. In some implementations, a password is maintained for each conference schedule. This password is made known only to conference participants, who are prompted for it when they join the conference.

The preceding features are used by conference participants. There are features pertinent to system management that do not affect conference participants directly. Faultless system management and fast troubleshooting are essential to the perception of high-quality service, and so are its enabling features, as follows:

Active serviceability. Available only in high-end products, this feature allows the hot-swapping of port circuit packs without any disruption to active conferences. Using hot-swapping, you can change a circuit packet without powering off and on, so it is not necessary to reboot the system. Furthermore, advanced products support automatic self-diagnostics and self-monitoring as well as customer-programmable fault isolation procedures. For example, ISDN interfaces can be programmed to filter and display specific ISDN messages based on trigger conditions (such as channel number or calling or called party numbers) and keep a trace of them as well as H.320 signaling exchanges. Error and event logs are time-stamped and kept for real-time and postconference analysis. Service administrators (who should be able to log in remotely) are provided with a large number of commands for testing the resources and modifying the runtime parameters if necessary. The administrators can also decide which conditions should trigger problem alerts as well as choose a particular form of alert. Typical available forms of alerts include dialing out the alarm collection center, lighting an LED on the maintenance telephone, and a range of other audible and visible alerts communicated to specialized network management centers.

Conference monitoring. Systems administrators can request that a snapshot of any conference in progress be provided on the MCU console screen. With some products, the administrator can further request that this snapshot be updated at a given frequency (for example, every 30 seconds). Another feature is roll call, which allows the conference administrator to view and hear every endpoint participating in the conference.

Service flag. Reservation agents can enhance endpoint compliance. Based on the historical information of an endpoint, the agents can manually activate a flag that would allow that endpoint to enter a conference with only a subset of supported services. The subset is determined on the basis of historical compliance information; access to services that require stronger compliance than the endpoint is capable of would be prevented.

Software control of dial-in numbers. A single number can be used at different times of day for different dial-in capacities (a bonded call, an H.320 call, and so on), as requested by conference reservations. (The alternative, still employed in some products that maintain a static association of hardware to the dialed number, is manual reconfiguration of boards in the cabinet.) The dynamic association significantly simplifies maintenance of MCUs and at the same time reduces the total number of network addresses required and improves the reliability of the system. To appreciate the network address reduction point, note that the dynamic association of a number with a particular hardware resource actually takes place only at the start of a call. Thus, the resources are pooled and acquired by hunting. Consequently, a malfunctioning resource has no effect on service until all good resources have been used. (With static association, however, a malfunctioning board simply prevents calls to the number associated with it, so the number may not be used.)

Cascading. Multiple MCUs can be linked to create a single conference. This allows a significant increase in the number of endpoints on one conference when necessary. Naturally, the maximum number of MCUs that can be cascaded is an indication of the scalability of a particular make of MCU. High-end products also offer many features that contribute to a secure conference. H.320 password protection is almost invariably supported; audio conferencing passwords can be entered by using a telephone's dial buttons.

H.323 Gatekeepers

While VoIP gateways are effectively switches that cross the border between the PSTN and IP networks, endpoint management and service control on the IP side are performed by gatekeepers. In many implementations, gatekeepers are responsible for call routing, billing, security (particularly user authentication and authorization), QoS reservations, and—depending on the implementation—any other functions that deal with executing user applications that control gateways. Just as is the case with the SCPs (or switch adjuncts), the gatekeepers are general-purpose computers, which means that they can potentially execute any application. On the other hand, there are functions that all gatekeepers must execute according to the H.323 family of standards. Thus, the first things to do when selecting a gatekeeper are to ask whether the current version of the H.323 standard (in late 1999, version 2) is supported and to assess the degree to which it is supported by going through a checklist of standard requirements.

Figure 10.1 depicts the interconnection of the gatekeeper with other network entities. First, note that the entities (that is, gateways and other H.323 clients) are placed into zones. (You may remember from Chapter 5 that a *zone*, as defined by H.323, is an area administered by one gatekeeper.) In high-end products, a zone supports up to 2000 concurrent active calls at the arrival rate of 30 calls per second for small systems. The number of gateways in a zone is determined solely by the preceding parameters. There is only one gatekeeper in a zone, but gatekeepers do interact with each other across zones. Gatekeepers also interact with gateways across IP networks; however,

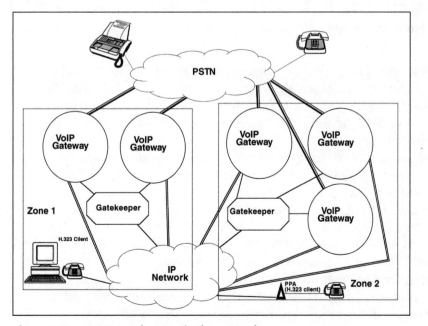

Figure 10.1 H.323 gatekeepers in the network.

PSTN-INTERNET INTEGRATION AT THE EDGE OF A NETWORK

The telephone shown in Zone 2 of Figure 10.1 is a normal POTS telephone, not an H.323 entity. It is connected to a *packet phone adapter* (PPA), which *is* an H.323 entity (specifically, a gateway) connected to the IP network. (The PPA function is implemented in residential gateways, as described in Chapter 3, and lately the terms *PPA* and *residential gateway* have been used interchangeably.) Telephones, fax machines, and personal computers with telephone modems can be supported by PPAs. PPAs can connect via cable modems to *multisystem operators* (MSOs). Thus, MSOs can offer telephony services to cable subscribers. To PSTN devices, PPAs provide dial tone and otherwise behave exactly like the PSTN; the PPAs communicate with IP gatekeepers to set up a call.

as Figure 10.1 demonstrates, it often makes sense (especially in the enterprise environment) to interconnect the gatekeeper directly with the gateways in its zone, for example, via a LAN.

As hardware components, gatekeepers are no more than general computers, although high-end models presently run on top-of-the-line servers with fast CPUs, local (cache) memory, gigabits of *random access memory* (RAM), and several hot-swappable disk drives and power supplies. The hardware itself typically supports several levels of system diagnostics. Together these features ensure both high-speed processing and necessary fault tolerance. In some systems, the gatekeeper hardware is augmented by a database server running on a separate machine. The defining element of a gatekeeper, however, is software, and in fact some vendors' products are software only.

The features of leading enterprise-grade gatekeepers provide the following functions:

Call routing. The gatekeepers determine by using the destination number whether the originating gateway can terminate the call. If so, the gateway is instructed to complete the call. Otherwise, the gatekeeper must find the IP address of the terminating gateway and pass it to the originating gateway.

One element of the call-routing capabilities provided by advanced gatekeepers employed in multigateway zones is *load balancing*. Based on the load within a zone, the gatekeeper selects the VoIP gateway with the least load at the moment. Location of the appropriate terminating gateways (assuming there is more than one) is based on data stored in routing tables and the current status of possible termination gateways. If the call setup to a chosen gateway fails, the next available gateway is selected, and so on, until the list of gateways is exhausted or a preconfigured number of attempts is reached. When either limit is reached, the gatekeeper notifies the originating gateway of the failure.

H.323 endpoint management.   The mandatory H.323-prescribed capabilities include terminal registration, zone management, admission control, address translation, and bandwidth control. Gatekeepers accept a registration request from a terminal, MCU, or gateway joining the zone and respond with confirmation or rejection; these entities can also unregister with a corresponding message.

Authentication and authorization.   *Authentication* is the process by which a gatekeeper establishes whether a user can make a call; *authorization* ensures that users have access only to services to which they are subscribed. PSTN users are authenticated with a user identification and PIN (for two-stage dialing) and originating telephone number [*automatic number identification* (ANI) in North America or *calling line identification* (CLI) in Europe]. Authentication information is collected by the gateway and then transferred to the gatekeeper in an authentication query. IP users are authenticated at the time the respective endpoints register with the gatekeeper. Gatekeepers may perform authentication themselves (often during endpoint registration) or they can query external authority databases. An example of such an external database is a *prepay billing server*, which is typically used with prepaid two-stage calls. In either case, gateways maintain the subscriber authorization and authentication table described later in this section. The same table contains information about services to which users have subscribed, which is used by the gatekeeper in the process of authorization.

Accounting.   If authorization is successful, the gatekeeper creates a record [a *call detail record* (CDR)], which contains information about the call, including all endpoint addresses (IP address in the case of IP endpoints, or ANI/CLI or destination number in the case of PSTN endpoints), packet transmission information, numbers of bytes and packets received, termination causes, and other data that vary from one product to another. [Note that CDRs are established for both originating (ingress) and terminating (egress) calls. Naturally, their formats differ.] The information in and disposition of a CDR depends on whether the call is prepaid or billable.

For prepaid calls, CDRs are issued once every *pulse* (predefined period of time). Multiple CDRs pertinent to a single call are linked by the *call reference value*, which the gatekeeper assigns to each call and subsequently stores in all relevant CDRs. These CDRs are usually shipped to a server associated with a prepaid service. (There can be several such servers for a given gatekeeper.) The responsible server actually performs the authentication and authorization and ultimately takes care of accounting. This server also notifies the gatekeeper when to disconnect the call. Usually, there is a provision for polite handling of the end of a call. When little time remains on the call (say 30 seconds), the gatekeeper, via signaling to the gateway, interrupts the call and makes an announcement warning of pending disconnection.

Subsequently, the gatekeeper reestablishes the call, which lasts until it is either disconnected by one of the parties or the call time is up, in which case it is disconnected on the request of the gatekeeper.

For billable calls, CDRs are issued once per call (in which case they contain the call setup and disconnect times) and then accumulated until billing software processes them. Experience has demonstrated that CDRs require extensive disk space, which makes it important to ensure that the gatekeeper (or relevant servers) have enough space to operate for at least 24 hours. The estimated volume of disk space required for a sustained rate of 30 calls per second is close to 2 GB.

System security.   Authentication and authorization addresses the issue of *call* security. *System-level* security is achieved through a network-wide shared configurable *control string* to prevent unauthorized access over the network, maintenance of access control lists (where all admissible gatekeepers and gateways are identified), and enforcement of access control. The mechanisms that log and process failed access attempts are also present in most products. Configurable automata that disable user accounts (for example, after a wrong password has been entered several times) constitute another effective security mechanism that can be easily implemented by a customer as long as the product provides SNMP alarms for corresponding events.

Administration.   Administration packages are effectively database management systems tuned to administer a database. A specific (but still representative) example of the administered tables is as follows:

- *System elements table.* Stores the information required for routing, signaling, and monitoring. Such information typically includes unique identifiers of the gatekeeper subcomponents responsible for call routing (in products that include gateways as part of the offering, relevant gateway information); the IP address of and signaling port for each managed element (in some products, the RAS signaling port and call signaling ports are different); a secret key for security (to be used, for example, in H.323 tokens); zone identification; and status (in or out of service). Some products include a separate managing entity program running on a different processor than that used for the gatekeeper; in such products, the information pertaining to this managing entity is also included.

- *Authorization and authentication table.* Stores the gatekeeper identifiers; lists of identifiers of those users to whom a specific authorization or authentication procedure applies, as well as the address of the designated external authorization if the authorization is to be performed locally; and the recovery mechanism for the case when the external server is unreachable. The recovery mechanism, in order to maintain the customer-friendly perception of the overall service for two-stage dialing systems, is often implemented in a surprisingly straightforward way. The caller is allowed to proceed with the call for some minimum time (during which the gatekeeper is supposed to reach the external server); if the server cannot be reached within this time, the call allotment is again increased by the prescribed minimum, and so on.

- *PSTN user table.* For each user, stores a unique ID, a PIN, the status of the user account (in service or disabled), a set of services subscribed for by a particular user, and other user-specific information.

- *Intrazone routing table.* Stores the information needed to map a destination telephone number to a specific gateway within the zone. Each entry in the table is associated with a particular gateway and includes the prefix (a string of digits from 0 to 9) so that all numbers that start with this prefix are to be routed to a specific gateway; the numbering plan (private or public); and the gateway identifier. In addition, advanced products provide entries for a list of prefixes to which calls may *not* be made. Another useful entry provided in large gatekeepers specifies (via an integer number, typically 1 byte long) the *preference indicator* for terminating a call on that specific gateway; if several gateway entries contain the same prefix, the one with the largest preference indicator is selected. Thus, for example, algorithms that monitor the load of gateways may automatically update this field to achieve load balancing.

- *Configuration parameters table.* Stores the values of low-level runtime product-specific parameters.

Fault and performance management are typically performed, using the SNMP protocol, by an SNMP-based management system, which is included in some offerings. The management system is a necessary part of a telephony server, which typically combines a gatekeeper, gateway, and network manager. The network manager should be expected to scale so as to support multiple gatekeepers (that is, multiple administrative zones). At the time of writing, the SNMP versions 1 and 2 were supported by advanced products.

Private Branch Exchange Systems (PBXs)

Traditionally, a PBX has been a small telephone switch located on the customer (that is, enterprise) premises. Its evolution from a mere switching board operated manually by a receptionist to the versatile digital system it is today has closely followed the evolution of the PSTN. The two major aspects of the function of a PBX have remained unchanged, however: First, it is responsible for supporting telecommunications within the enterprise; and second, it is responsible for connecting the enterprise to the outside world (which has been traditionally done via the PSTN). Ultimately, a large enterprise dispersed over several geographical locations would have several PBXs, which should—in cooperation with the PSTN—behave as one virtual PBX. The perception of virtuality is created by supporting one numbering system and otherwise providing identical services throughout the enterprise so that communications across different locations appear to the user to be exactly the same as communications within any particular location.

Migration to IP-based voice and data delivery can be achieved in different stages by mixing and matching the existing and new technologies through a series of architectures and product types, described in this section. The enterprise manager may choose to totally replace existing PBXs with IP-based systems, or to invoke alternative solutions in which new systems are used as an add-on to the existing technology. The choice typically depends on the features of the system that are essential to the enterprise; cost is another factor. For this reason, we begin by listing generic PBX characteristics and features as a set of criteria for an enterprise manager comparing traditional and IP-based products. We then describe IP-based products and interconnection architectures. Note that it is still only the correct operation of the main features that can determine whether systems integrated from different types of products will work as expected.

Generic PBX Characteristics and Features

Three important PBX characteristics that are essential for the first-order comparison of existing products are:

1. Number of local extensions.
2. Number of outside connections (lines or trunks).
3. Number of busy hour call completions.

A traditional PBX can support from 2 to up to 100,000 telephone lines internally; the number of outside trunks is typically one order of magnitude smaller. Externally, digital PBXs have traditionally been connected to the PSTN via the ISDN PRI using digital T1 or E1 circuits. T1 lines operate at 1.544 Mbps, the equivalent of 24 analog voice lines, and E1 circuits operate at 2.048 Mbps, equivalent to 30 lines. When available, T1 or E1 lines cost much less than a set of analog lines with the same bandwidth. Note also that PBXs can be connected not only to central offices, but also directly to *interexchange carrier* (IXC) switches. The PSTN supports a single-numbering plan for multilocation enterprises as well as a number of important routing features, such as call distribution based on time of day or call queuing, via IN-supported *virtual private network* (VPN) service.

If the PBX switches are located in nearby buildings, they are often interconnected directly (via so-called *tie* lines) rather than through a PSTN virtual private network. Traditional PBX-PSTN interconnection is depicted in Figure 10.2. Separation of switching fabric (switches) from call control, service control, and administration and management performed by the communications software running on servers is a feature of *computer-telecom integration* (CTI) that has made the current generation of PBXs very versatile. Depending on the type and size of PBX products, such servers are sometimes standalone computers connected to switching modules via a LAN or dedicated point-to-point connection. On the other end of the spectrum, the server can be a PC that has one or more switching boards inside, so the PC *is* the PBX.

Note: High-end PBXs built for medium to large enterprises can provide, in addition to PSTN trunks, connections to frame relay networks to support *voice over frame relay* (VoFR), connections to ATM switches to support *voice-over-ATM* (VoATM), or both as a mechanism for toll bypass; the use of this technology and related products, however, is outside of the scope of this book. Three good references for the related information are Minoli and Minoli (1998a,b) and Davis (1999).

The services of traditional PBX combine the delivery of voice, fax, and data with special call features of the ISDN. The provision of these specialized features is of central importance to the enterprise. Some of the most essential features are:

Caller ID. Displays the telephone number (and often even the name) of the calling party. With integrated computer-telephony applications, this fea-

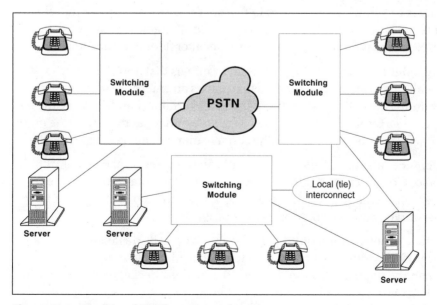

Figure 10.2 Traditional PBX interconnection.

ture can come in many flavors, including opening and presentation to the called party of a file associated with the calling party (for example, a customer file). Incidentally, even in its simplest form this feature can be provided in different ways that benefit customers. The most straightforward way of implementing caller ID is to support the ISDN *automatic number identification* (ANI) [or *calling line identification* (CLI) in Europe]; however, caller ID can also use the in-band ANI and *dialed number identification service* (DNIS) information delivery via DTMF signaling over incoming trunks. Some enterprise managers find that the latter option is less expensive than paying for ISDN ANI. The availability and pricing of the in-band ANI, however, depends on the telephone company to which the PBX is connected.

Dial-by-name.   A call can be placed by spelling the name of a called party. (A more sophisticated version of the same feature allows a user to place a call by typing in or simply clicking on a name in a directory accessible through a computer terminal or monitor.)

Call-forwarding.   A call is automatically forwarded to an internal extension or external telephone number. (To prevent potential abuse, control of this feature is needed to restrict it only to internal forwarding for most users.)

Call transfer.   A called party may transfer a call to an internal extension or external telephone number. (As with call-forwarding, this feature must often be restricted to use within the enterprise.)

Paging.   A call from an extension (usually that of a manager) rings all the telephones in a pre-configured group. Often, the same name is also used to refer to a much more elaborate feature by which enterprise individual employees or their entire groups can be simultaneously reached (through speakerphones or computer speakers) for announcements.

Group listen.   Enabled through special terminals that are often a part of the overall PBX system offer, group listen allows an enterprise employee to communicate with a distant party using the terminal handset while the terminal speakerphone operates in listen mode only, thereby permitting other employees in the room to hear the conversation but not participate in it.

Conference calling.   A party to the call can merge several existing calls into one conference call. In the advanced implementations of this feature, so-called *legs* of conference calls can be muted or deleted and new ones can be added as the conference progresses.

Call pick-up.   An authorized party can pick up calls destined to another party. One widespread use of this feature is allowing a secretary to screen the originating caller ID and then make a decision on whether to pick up the boss's call.

Call distribution.   A family of features that allow calls to be routed by a PBX in order to balance the load of all the enterprise employees within a particular group. For example, a PBX can route an incoming call to the first nonbusy extension in the group; if none of the extensions is busy, the PBX can chose the terminating extension based on a round-robin scheme or select the extension that has handled the least number of calls during the given day. Calls can also be routed based on time of day. For example, night calls could be routed to a guard desk or another PBX within the enterprise.

Call-waiting.   When the called party is occupied with another call, he or she is informed (by a distinctive sound or a message on the computer terminal screen) about an incoming call, at which point the called party may respond by putting the active call on hold. Toggling between calls or even switching between several waiting calls are other functional capabilities associated with call-waiting.

Whisper page.   A sophisticated variation on call-waiting that can be used to permit a secretary to interrupt a manager's call for an announcement. The manager is alerted by an audible signal that is heard by all parties to the call, but the subsequent message from the secretary is private.

Toll restriction/outside call blocking.   Certain enterprise extensions are restricted from making toll calls, receiving calls from outside of the enterprise, or both.

Message or music on hold.   Music or messages (usually promoting the enterprise's products) are played for the caller on hold.

Distinctive ring.   Incoming calls from predefined addresses can be introduced with unique ringing patterns.

Voice messaging.   Each extension has a voice-mail box where incoming voice messages are stored. The owner of the extension can typically administer his or her outgoing announcements and even schedule different ones to be played to a caller depending on the time of day or whether the line is busy. Traditional features include the ability to broadcast messages to a list of extensions, forward messages, and respond to messages (the latter can also be achieved by either dialing the extension from which the message came or recording and sending a response message—possibly with an attachment—to the originating extension). If voice messaging is already supported by the existing system at the time the decision is made about purchasing hardware and software for this set of features, an important criterion to apply is whether the add-on really interworks with the existing system. Confirmation of compatibility may require thorough checking of interworking of all features.

Unified messaging. Integrates voice messaging with e-mail and fax and provides a straightforward, uniform way of handling all aspects of messages arriving from different media.

Message waiting indicator. The telephone terminal's message waiting light is lit when a voice-mail message is waiting. (A message can appear when a call is redirected to voice mail because the called party is busy; alternatively, it can simply be sent via voice mail.) After the message has been retrieved, the light is deactivated.

The preceding features are normally required by enterprises of all sizes. Large enterprises, however, may need additional sophisticated features for private networking enhancements:

Trunk optimization. Because of feature interactions that arise from dialing out or transferring calls while using voice mail, the path for the new call may be selected inefficiently. Highly sophisticated PBX products optimize trunk use on rerouting.

Call-independent signaling. Supports passing of supplementary service information over signaling links, independent of any active call.

Call completion. Ensures the completion of a call to a busy called party or an unanswered call by retrying after the calling party hangs up, and subsequently establishes the call the moment the called party is available.

In addition to features for PBX users, there are a number of features designed for people in the enterprise who maintain and administer the PBX systems. By far, the most important feature is *application builders* (that is, software tools for building new PBX service applications as well as customizing existing ones). Others include the presence and ease of use of the configuration manager and diagnostics software, real-time status monitoring (including the capability of monitoring remote PBX switches), administration and security mechanisms, and the capability of installing hot-swappable hardware.

While on the one hand a rich set of features is essential to the efficiency and productivity of the enterprise, on the other hand, unrestricted access to such features may result in abuse of company resources. For example, an unscrupulous employee may use the conference calling or call transfer feature (described later) to arrange a two-party long-distance call between his or her friends at the enterprise's expense. For this reason, PBX products are equipped with restrictive control of the features they provide. The existing systems may differ in their restrictive capabilities as much as they differ in their main features, for which reason the restrictive capabilities are indeed an essential factor in product evaluation. The following is a list of the most important restrictive features and associated tasks used by PBX administrators:

- Configuring an extension so that it cannot be used to dial out. Such extensions are called *local-use-only* extensions. Note, however, that the definition of *dialing out* varies from enterprise to enterprise. For example, when the enterprise is spread over several geographic locations so that the PBX function itself becomes distributed (as depicted in Figure 10.2), calls within the enterprise are in many cases considered local even though they may leave an enterprise PBX and go through the PSTN before they return to another enterprise PBX. The problem of distinguishing intraenterprise calls that involve dialing through the PSTN from other nonlocal calls is easily solved by establishing an enterprise-wide numbering plan so that the PBX recognizes all enterprise-specific numbers as local (for restriction purposes) even though it will access the PSTN for all nonlocal numbers. Subsequently, the PSTN (typically by means of the IN-supported VPN) translates the enterprise-specific numbers and routes calls to their respective destinations. Alternatively, the involved PBXs can provide the translation of the enterprise extensions to the PSTN numbers and perform the following functions.

- Disabling the use of pay-for-access area codes (such as 900 in the United States) from an extension.

- Disabling call pickup to certain extensions (usually by configuring call pickup groups in which only the extensions in the group can pick up calls from other extensions).

- Disabling conference calling for local-use-only extensions.

- Configuring certain restrictions on call transfer (for example, transfer of an outside call to an outside number).

- Disabling paging in all but authorized extensions, and configuring paging groups.

The need for and significance of the restrictive capabilities grows with the size of a PBX. In addition, large PBXs require network management capabilities. To this end, the most important products address fault management and performance management:

- *Fault management systems.* Give customers tools to monitor all elements of the enterprise network and produce a variety of robust traffic and alarm reports. Typically, the systems provide a real-time graphical map of the enterprise network configuration and fault status. The administrator can see an on-screen hierarchical view of the layers of the network.

- *Performance management systems.* Enable customers to poll traffic data and generate a variety of performance reports that cover the switch traffic and statistics of activities (such as automatic call distribution).

There are products on the market that offer unified network management software to enable customers to centralize the management of voice, data, and mixed-media environments for the enterprise. These products automate consolidated alarm handling as well as management of network topology configurations spanning multiple locations and are capable of working with the products of multiple vendors. Unified network management products are uniformly based on the Simple Network Management Protocol (SNMP) standards.

IP-Capable PBXs

As mentioned, high-end PBX products include toll bypass features that can route calls over data networks. Until very recently, only circuit-based mechanisms (such as frame relay or ATM) have been employed, but now IP-capable PBX products are available and can send voice over the Internet or private IP networks. Such systems (depicted in Figure 10.3) comprise a traditional PBX, voice-over-IP gateway, and IP router. Though integrating such a system may appear simple, it is a major feat to pull it together from random components, and the communications software is the most essential glue. IP-capable PBXs from single vendors emerged in response to customer pleas. Another important advantage of procuring (rather than integrating) an IP-capable PBX is that vendors can ensure that PBXs in different locations can use IPs as tie lines: A call originating in a PBX in one location can be routed over an IP network to another PBX extension in the same enterprise with absolute transparency to both the calling and called parties.

Following is a list of hardware and software components that come as part of a PBX product in general, and an IP-capable PBX product in particular. We start with hardware features:

Switching modules (or switches).   Can be large cabinets, or—for very small PBXs (typically, under 10 trunks and 20 extensions)—PC boards that can be

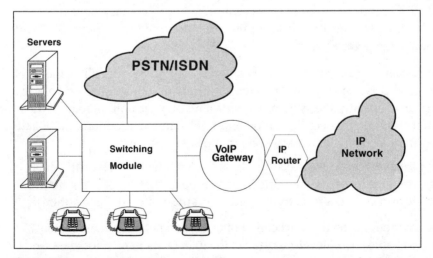

Figure 10.3   IP-capable PBX.

inserted into desktops or servers. (In the case of the latter, current products typically allow fewer than 10 boards per server.) In the PBX nomenclature, connections to PBXs are called *ports*, and it is number of ports that defines the number of external lines/trunks and internal extensions. The total number of ports is less than the sum of the latter two numbers because some ports are used for connection to the console and servers.

Console. In newer systems, the console is usually a PC (although it can be a dumb terminal) attached to the switch directly or to a network management server (if included in the offering) through which the system is administered.

Product line of specialized telephone terminals. Includes an LED display (to present calling number or name, among other data) and specialized buttons for activating the PBX features, selecting lines, administering messages, and so on. Other displays (such as a message waiting indicator) are often also included. The terminals differ in the number of lines supported; three is a typical minimum for ISDN terminals. Additional terminal equipment includes speakerphones (with a mute button) and headsets. Often the terminals have buttons associated with special features; typically, there is a set of buttons for speed dialing preassigned numbers, auto callback, call-forwarding, and telephone directory access. The terminals operate with either two-wire or four-wire circuit packs.

Wiring. Includes cables and connectors for connecting telephone terminals to switching modules; cables and connectors [such as the *Network Terminating Device* 1 (NT1)] for connecting to the ISDN, although in most cases this specific connector is provided by the carrier; wires for analog PSTN lines (for fax machines and analog telephone terminals); PBX connectors; and, when there are additional servers as described in the following, appropriate LAN connectors.

Analog line interface. Comes in the form of circuit packs with multiple ports for analog telephone lines.

Voice-over-IP (VoIP) gateways. Boards or chassis that can be colocated with the switching boards in a single compartment; alternatively, they can come in a standalone unit.

IP routers. Similar to gateways, these may come on a board for smaller routers, or in a standalone unit.

Servers. Standalone computers, in most cases attached to the PBX switch proper via a LAN (typically Ethernet), although direct digital links are also used (and some product offerings allow customers to chose between Ethernet and direct connections), especially when only one server is involved in the offering. It is the servers that keep and execute most of the critical software (for example, administration, network management, security, or call control); the servers also act as gateways and mediators for a mix-and-match approach, especially for building systems (described later) that combine existing and new products. One typical product example is *net messaging interchange*, a hub-and-spoke topology that connects currently nonnetworked messaging systems or complements the alternative point-to-point networks that exist for messaging systems. The interchange, a specialized server, acts as a post office (that is, a store-and-forward device) to which multiple messaging systems are interconnected. The interchange provides transcoding from analog to digital (and vice versa), thus reducing the cost of connecting nodes to networks. For such systems, a *Point-to-Point Protocol* (PPP) server acts as the base for remote user access. Specifically for the purposes of unified messaging, some products use one server for each type of messaging medium (for example, one for e-mail, one for fax, one for voice mail, and so on). Even though access is unified from the user's point of view, the system is fault tolerant in that the machine failure of one server cannot result in a total information blackout. However, such systems are more difficult to administer because of the necessity of replicating databases on different servers; hence the single-server messaging products are often preferred by a large segment of enterprises. In most products, NT servers are used because of the rich set of software building blocks provided, although Unix-based servers are also included in offers. Overall, the messaging platforms are most versatile, and they play an especially important part in integration of PSTN and the Internet, for which reason they will be addressed in more detail later in this chapter.

Typical software features include:

Call control.   The software for this function, which implements most of the real-time call control PBX features, is often based on *computer-telephony integration* (CTI) technology and typically runs on the CTI server. The presence of *telephony application programmer interface* (TAPI) [and particularly *Java API* (JTAPI)] libraries, which are available in many products, should be an important product differentiator: Experience has demonstrated that all enterprises, no matter how small, need to customize call control features or add new ones at certain points in time. To this end, application testing and debugging tools are offered with virtually all high-end products. With IP-capable PBXs, two especially important features that are pertinent to the use of IP are:

1. *Virtual tie lines.* The feature by which a PBX extension in one enterprise location is connected to an extension on a PBX in another enterprise location through the IP network, but with full transparency as far as users of either extension are concerned.

2. *Toll bypass.* The feature by which the call control software determines whether a particular call should be routed over the PSTN or IP net-

work. Some factors for making such a decision are quite obvious (for example, if a terminating location cannot be dialed through an IP network, the call cannot be routed only over the PSTN), but there are factors (for example, trunk availability, the cost of a call at a given time, or current availability of the QoS in the given IP network) that are time specific, and they can produce significant cost saving if the feature is present in the product.

Systems administration.   In addition to the usual knobs and buttons, invariably delivered via a graphical user interface package, the software for this function also comes as a modular Windows-based suite designed to help administrators by providing the means to program, schedule, and process transactions that update user records. The switch management packages provide the means for extracting reports on switch data and changing these data. High-end products also offer software that helps optimize the performance of the switch.

Messaging.   The messaging software available is typically compatible with the hardware (servers) described previously. Voice and fax messaging are available with a set of networking choices. For IP-enabled PBXs, LDAP-based multilocation directory databases make up an essential part of the offered software. Messaging is one important application used not only by the PBX extensions, but also by remote users, who can dial into a server in order to retrieve the messages stored in their mailboxes. Once inside the server, such users can have access to most of the PBX features; they can, for example, dial the extension of the message's originator.

Security.   Software is usually tightly coupled with hardware in order to protect the access of mobile telephone users and remote-site staff. In addition to the software for toll fraud prevention that has been part of traditional PBXs for years, IP-capable PBXs include software that enforces the registration process for the endpoints to authenticate the user.

While the IP-capable PBX products are successfully entering the market for medium to large enterprises, smaller enterprises now have a choice of either going with traditional small PBXs or going directly to purely IP-based systems (which in turn can connect to the PSTN).

Interconnection Architectures

One successful implementation of voice over IP for small enterprises (that is, one-location businesses with fewer than 100 extensions) has been demonstrated by *local area network* (LAN)-based PBXs. Figure 10.4 depicts a simple LAN-based PBX, where the LAN performs the physical switching function among H.323 terminals while the calls are administered by a *control unit*. The latter contains a gatekeeper at a minimum, and—in some products—a T.120 MCU. Other

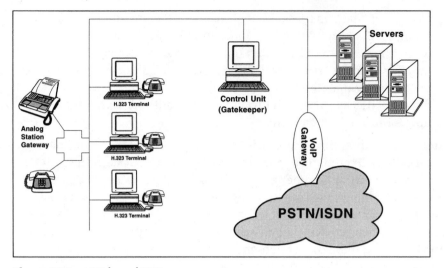

Figure 10.4   LAN-based PBX.

products postulate a more modular approach by which multimedia features are offered on a separate server. Such multimedia servers are separate products that can be integrated with LAN-based PBXs offered by different vendors. These servers support conferencing with multipoint collaboration, application sharing, and other conferencing services. Still other servers—for messaging, for example—can be integrated into the LAN-based PBX.

Connections to the PSTN (as well as to traditional PBXs and non-IP voice messaging systems in a LAN-based PBX) are achieved by integrating a *reverse* VoIP gateway. Note that the role of the gateway mirrors that in Figure 10.3. There, the role of the gateway was to connect a traditional PBX to the IP network; here, it is to connect what is effectively an IP network to the PSTN. This is an important example of duality manifested in the old PSTN and new IP converging products.

Except for a few especially sophisticated features (for example, whisper paging), the leading LAN-based PBX products support all traditional PBX features. The minimal list of such features includes call-forwarding, call transfer, call-waiting, calling party ID, conferencing, and support of multiple lines on one extension.

A LAN-based PBX can be distributed over several locations or even the whole enterprise network by adding routers, as depicted in Figure 10.5, thus creating a full-blown IP PBX.

The hardware of a typical IP PBX offer includes the following components:

■ H.323 or SIP terminals, which may look and feel (with their many buttons, the number of which determines their pricing) like traditional PBX multiple-line telephones

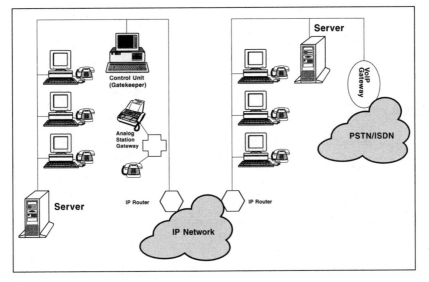

Figure 10.5   IP PBX.

- VoIP gateways to access the PSTN and other (non-IP) PBXs (number of ports varies)
- Analog station gateways for connecting fax devices and traditional (POTS) telephones
- Control unit (includes the gatekeeper at a minimum)
- All the necessary connectors, LAN hubs, and cables
- Servers for multimedia conferencing, unified messaging, administration, and other functions

Software is, of course, the most versatile part of the IP PBX. Its key enabling component, almost invariably called a *call manager*, resides in the control unit. In addition to provision and control of the PBX features, the call manager is responsible for gatekeeper-like functions, including registration of the H.323 or SIP terminals, admission control, guaranteeing QoS to participants (a significant function if the IP PBX spans several LANs), and, when necessary, cooperation with the software on the servers. Again, the presence of *telephony application programmer interface* (TAPI) and *Java TAPI* (JTAPI) libraries should be an important product differentiator, because these libraries allow you both to modify many service applications already provided by the vendor and to develop your own services. Theoretically, with a single control unit, the whole IP network can be turned into a PBX of sorts.

If different LAN-connected parts of an enterprise each have their own control units, as depicted in Figure 10.6 (such a configuration can often speed up and otherwise improve both communications and network management), the

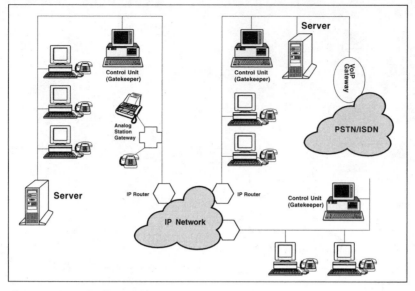

Figure 10.6   Distributed IP PBX.

PBX is called *distributed.* Note that what actually is distributed (compared to the configuration of Figure 10.5) is the function of call manager software. In this case, support of a form of signaling among the control units that aids in negotiating QoS and optimizing the use of servers is also required.

Finally, we should demonstrate what may already be obvious to you: Despite the introduction of IP PBXs, legacy non-IP PBXs can still be used. Figures 10.7 and 10.8 depict two ways of integrating IP and non-IP PBXs: (1) through the IP network and (2) through the PSTN. Both cases demand tailoring of the original software (one more reason to emphasize the importance of software tool kits!), but in the latter case the PSTN (through IN, with the SCPs as servers) will cooperate in or even do the whole job of supporting features such as call distribution and single numbering plans.

Service Nodes and Intelligent Peripherals

The standard *service node* (SN) (based on the IN standard described in the previous chapter) is a versatile system that has often been referred to as an intelligent network in a box. Indeed, the SN combines the functions of service control, circuit switching, and intelligent peripherals in one box. The ingenuity of the SN concept is manifested in the way the SN accesses the PSTN: As Figure 10.9 demonstrates, the SN is connected to the switched network through a local (or toll, or wireless) switch as the ISDN endpoint [versus the SS No. 7 endpoint, such as a *service control point* (SCP)]. Because of that, the

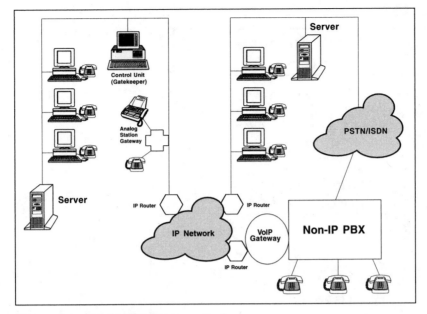

Figure 10.7   Hybrid PBX (IP connection).

SN—even when it is part of the PSTN—behaves as an edge-of-the-network entity. As such, it needs no triggers provisioned; nor do the switches need to do anything more than straightforward call termination in order to pass control of the call to the SN. Finally, the edge position of the SN makes it a natural gateway to the Internet.

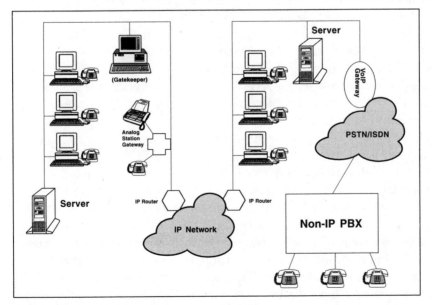

Figure 10.8   Hybrid PBX (PSTN connection).

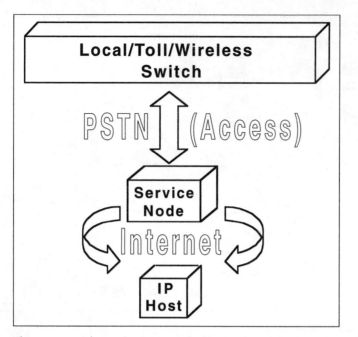

Figure 10.9   The SN interconnection for service control.

Later in this section, we will review examples of using the SN for supporting PSTN and Internet service interworking, but now we should emphasize another role of the SN—that of a pure intelligent peripheral. Although most digital switches now have built-in intelligent peripherals as part of their standard capabilities (for example, conversion from text to speech and vice versa), there are still switches that either do not have such capabilities or require for some calls certain rare and expensive additional capabilities that are implemented only in specialized intelligent peripherals. The IN standards specify the protocol necessary for accessing remote intelligent peripherals. As we mentioned in Chapter 4, this protocol (between the specialized resource and service control functions) is a part of the *Intelligent Network Application Part* (INAP) protocol. When the SN has to perform purely the function of an intelligent peripheral, it must be able to connect to the SCP through SS No. 7 and support the relevant subset of INAP. Figure 10.10 reflects this point.

The essential features supported by SNs include *voice dialing, personal number, audio calling name delivery, paging message delivery, voice announcement/digit collection, interactive voice response, text-to-speech conversion,* and *voice/fax mailbox* (a feature of universal messaging). Various service features can be mixed and matched in the SN to suit particular market demands. For example, one might install features like voice/fax mailbox and personal number to target a business district, and—in the same SN—voice dialing and voice mailbox to target residential areas. All told, the capabilities of the

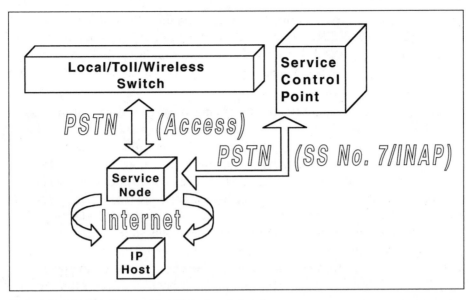

Figure 10.10   The SN as an intelligent peripheral.

SN products are naturally derived from the fundamental capabilities of its three components:

1. *Switching*. Capabilities include (1) establishment of a call *leg* from the SN to any party (by requesting a connection from the PSTN or responding to a request from the PSTN) and joining the legs into a multiparty call (although it is two-party calls that dominate the services scene) and (2) rearranging the legs as needed [for example, tearing down connections between parties *A* and *B*, releasing (disconnecting) *B*, and connecting *A* with *C*]. Note that a *party* to a call may be a device (specialized resource) within the SN. The legs are established using access protocols (typically, Q.931). Although this is not explicitly required by the IN standards, the most sophisticated products have the SS No. 7 ISDN User Part (ISUP) protocol, which allows the SN switching module to establish trunks to the switches.

2. *Specialized resources*. Capabilities include playing announcements and collecting digits (found in all products); converting text to speech; recognizing speech (in high-end products) and converting it to text; converting received faxes to text (using the optical character recognition technologies available in high-end products); and performing other intramedia conversions by chaining the preceding functions (that is, converting fax to speech by first converting it to text and then converting the text to speech). Another set of capabilities deals with communicating the results of conversions. Those that end up in speech are

naturally communicated over the voice lines; thus, the resources involved must be able to act as endpoints in telephone calls. Conversion to text (or encoded digits, as is the case with digit collection) is carried via data communications (to the SCP via SS No. 7) or to an IP host (via the Internet or a private IP network).

3. *Service control.* Capabilities are those of a general-purpose computer. To this end, the switching and specialized resources can be considered the peripheral input/output (I/O) devices of this computer. It is the *service logic* (that is, the program that implements a particular service) that makes the capabilities of service control devices available to end users. Service control is software function; service logic *is* software that is highly specialized to deal with the IN-supported services. The software is developed within the framework of a *service creation environment* (SCE). The output of the SCE is *provisioned* by the IN service management systems (SMSs) to all IN entities in the network. The SCE platforms typically run on the same machines that execute SMSs, but they may also run on separate processors. Because of their universal role (they are applicable to all IN physical entities), the SMS processors and software are usually sold separately from SNs. The SNs, however, must support the interface to service management, as reflected in Figure 10.11, which presents the full set of the SN interconnection with other network entities.

As we mentioned in the section on IN standards, the ITU-T standard for service creation is rather schematic in that only general building block capabilities

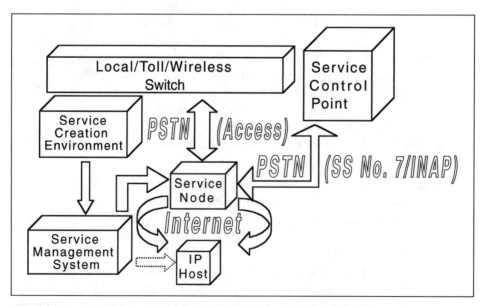

Figure 10.11   Connection to service creation environment and service management system.

have been standardized. Consequently, while most products are fully compliant with the standard, the compliance itself manifests only support of the capabilities rather than interoperability of SCEs and SNs [or *service control points* (SCPs)] from different vendors—in general, they are not interoperable. An important question to ask when evaluating a specific vendor is whether the SCE that interworks with the SN is the same as the one that interworks with the SCP. If the answer is yes, then the service logic developed for (and tested on) the SN can also run on the SCPs; otherwise, service development and maintenance are likely to be a nightmare. Finally, as in the case of the switching module, some implementations support the INAP interface to switches. This interface is not required by a standard. Its introduction, of course, makes the SN a full-blown SCP. This, paired with the standard SN capabilities, makes an augmented SN into a powerful and versatile IN engine.

SNs have been employed in PSTN-Internet interworking since 1995. We refer to the type of interworking where the PSTN services are accessed and, in part, controlled from the Internet, while the voice endpoints are connected to the PSTN. The PINT services and a notification version of *Internet call-waiting* (ICW) service described in Chapter 9 are typical examples of services easily supported by SNs.

Consider the operation of the click-to-call-back service described earlier in this chapter. (This example is illustrated in Figure 10.12.) Party A decides to receive a call from a sales agent (as offered on the Web page that A is presently looking at) and clicks on an appropriate button. (Without loss of generality, we can assume that A has already registered with the service provider and thus can be properly

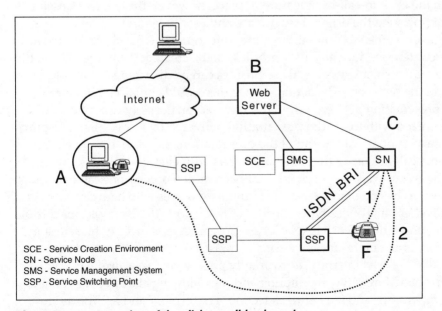

Figure 10.12 Operation of the click-to-call-back service.

authenticated.) The Internet carries the request to the Web server B, which generates a corresponding request to the service node C. The request results in the execution of C's service logic responsible for this particular service. As directed by the service logic, C, which has the ISDN basic rate interface (BRI) connection in this particular example to a local switch, first creates call leg 1 to the sales agent F, then call leg 2 to A, and finally merges these two legs in a two-party call: Now A and F are connected. The service management system is responsible for (1) passing the service-creation-environment-developed service logic to the service node and (2) provisioning the service-related parameters to both the Web server and the service node.

Now, click-to-call-back service could be further augmented to the full function of a call center. The service node could, for example, select agent F based on the time of day, day of week, agent F's availability and, if available, load relative to other available agents, and so on. For a report on relevant implementation experiences, see RFC 2458. A service like click-to-call-back is in fact a service feature that can be used as a building block to develop other services. Recently, there has been much interest in applying the Web business model (free access to customers subsidized by advertisers) to basic telephony service. Several telephone companies have tried a service offering a free-of-charge telephone call for customers who agreed to listen to several minutes of advertisements. This rather remarkable idea seemed to work, although advertisers complained that the purely audio commercial advertisements were not quite effective. Another problem with the advertisement was that end users had no control over (and, more importantly, no ability to request) the types of advertised information.

With the click-to-call-back feature in place, however, the creative possibilities of improving the original service are endless. To begin with, end users can register on the Web and at the same time indicate what types of products they are interested in. Thus, user profiles can be created. (With the help of the service management systems, these profiles can be distributed to all service nodes in the network.) The actual service then could contain an interactive video presentation delivered from the Web server, possibly combined and synchronized with the audio presentation delivered by a specialized resource of the service node. At the end of the presentation, the service node would create the call in exactly the same manner as with click-to-call-back.

As far as hardware is concerned, the SNs typically occupy one cabinet. They are powered by one or more fast CPUs and hard drives with high capacity. As with all other units of this type, one to six RS-232 ports (for example, for console support) and a 10/100-MB LAN port are present. A tape drive (which, in some cases, serves as a more efficient means of transferring the SMS output than an optional X.25-based interface) is invariably present, and so is firmware, which supports hardware sanity monitoring and the following alarms: over voltage, over temperature, and fan failure detection. The SS No. 7 and X.25 ports are usually optional.

Typically, the media service circuits and network interface come as *enhanced industry system architecture* (EISA) cards plugged into appropriate buses [such as a *pulse-code modulation* (PCM) bus]. The number of slots differs from 10 to over 100. Initially, large products (with over 100 slots) were popular, but recently the industry has set the requirement for an order of magnitude smaller (often called *compact*) SNs. (This requirement is quite reasonable: In diverse telecommunications networks it makes more sense to place more smaller and cheaper SNs in more places.) Different cards support different numbers of voice ports, T1 or E1 trunks, and so on, and configurations naturally differ among the products offered in and outside of the United States.

On average, a compact SN can terminate about 300 voice lines, all of which can be simultaneously married to the same number of resource circuits (text-to-speech and digit collectors). The supported resources can play and record voice (using the 32-kbps PCM format); detect dual-tone-multi-frequency (DTMF) and multifrequency (MF) tones; generate standard tones (*busy, dial, audible, reorder,* and *receiver off hook*); recognize digits pronounced in English, Italian, Spanish, German, Dutch, and French; and synthesize voice (both male and female) from text. Advanced products are also equipped with the grammar-based automatic speech recognition (ASR) capable of recognizing customer-defined names (for example, "Call Mom!") and user-trainable entries. Fax capabilities include Group 3 fax record and transmission, ASCII-to-fax conversion, and fax store and forward. The conferencing control (usually performed by one card) parameters vary from one vendor to another; advanced products support close to 100 conferences with a maximum of 256 conference participants.

The software platforms, including choices of operating systems, vary among vendors. Some solutions include support of real-time databases, which we consider an essential feature. Overall, it is the programmability (rather than one or another internal software solution) that is essential for this particular product: The easier it is to create or change a service, the faster the service can be delivered. To this end, it is important to ask a question: Who is the user really involved with programming the services? As far as SNs are concerned, a number of parameters (called *recent change data*) should be changeable by service subscribers. In the very near future, this change will be done via the Internet, but for now it is generally done with the help of the SMS; nevertheless, some products provide access to the SNs themselves for the purposes of administration. Similarly, *customization* (that is, modification of the high-level service logic programs) can also be done directly on the SN in some cases. Customization is straightforward when it is programmed via a graphical user interface with the use of a palette of service-independent building blocks (SIBs), each of which implements, at this level, an atomic capability (play an announcement, put a call on queue, merge call legs, and so on), and which are connected into graphs representing the logic of a program.

The creation of the original service logic programs must be done in the SCE, which in most product offerings is not part of the SN. As mentioned before, there is currently no service creation standard that would allow interworking of an SCE from one vendor and SNs (or SCPs) from another. Thus, your choice of an SN provider should coincide with that of the SCE; conversely, the convenience and versatility of service creation is an important factor in choosing the SN. As you may recall from Chapter 4, *service-independent building blocks* (SIBs) were standardized by ITU-T only for the purpose of modeling; however, the industry picked up on the idea and many vendors have provided SIB-like palettes with which one can quickly develop services by simply building decision trees (more precisely, graphs) simply by mixing and matching appropriate SIBs (such as *queue, play announcement, collect digits,* and so forth). Thus, with SIBs, a service designer could build and test a service in no time without much help from an expert programmer whose services would be required if the work needed to be done from scratch. It is fair to say then that the support of the SIB-like graphical user interface has proven to be an essential programmability feature.

Another issue to consider is other programming levels available in products. The service creation platforms of advanced products offer several layers of programming, in increasing complexity, of which the graphical user interface is the first. The second layer typically includes more complex (and, therefore, more versatile) specification tools such as state machines [for example, the ITU-T *Specification and Description Language* (SDL)], and the third layer supports programming with the high-level systems programming languages (for example, C++). No standard format exists for the output of service creation environment. In some cases it is direct object code in the native machine language of the SN or SCP; in others it is a script to be interpreted by a service control process; and there are cases in which it is a combination of both.

Messaging Platforms

Similarly to the SNs (which also provide messaging features), messaging platforms are effectively integrated products that combine switching modules with high-capacity storage and mechanisms for accessing both the PSTN and Internet databases. Unlike the SNs, however, messaging systems concentrate on near-real-time message manipulation rather than real-time call control. Until very recently, messaging systems had to be integrated within the enterprise with PBXs, as described earlier in this chapter. Some vendors, in fact, sell only software.

New platforms are emerging that are built specifically for unified messaging (as described in Chapter 9) for both PSTN carriers and enterprises. Platforms start with single boxes that support from 2 to 50 T1 ports; they can be further integrated into distributed systems that include a Web server and a firewall. Single boxes are typically built around the open-standard high-capacity backplane media bus (H.110) and dual 10/100-Mbps LANs. Hot-swappable E1/T1 boards, speech signal processing (SSP) modules, text-to-speech (TTS) conversion modules (multilingual in advanced products), alarm modules (monitoring temperature, voltages, and fans), control processor boards, and storage devices are mounted on the rack. Naturally, a dial-in modem pool is part of the box. You should also expect such a box to have connections to local and remote management consoles. The Web servers (which, in some cases, come on dedicated cards) support the graphical user interface access to visual mailboxes. High-end products support up to 30,000 mailboxes with about 100 sessions, each of which can be either voice or e-mail. To enable the transport of voice messages over the Internet, high-end products also support the *Voice Profile for Internet Mail* (VPIM) protocol. That way both POP3 and IMAP can be used for retrieving VPIM messages in the same way they are used to retrieve nonvoice e-mail messages. (See Chapter 6 for description of POP3, IMAP, and VPIM.) The number of sessions that require text-to-speech conversion varies between 10 and 100. The hardware boxes can, in some cases, be clustered together to build larger systems.

Unified messaging is a 24/7 application (that is, an application that is expected to function 24 hours a day, seven days a week). For this reason, nearly every architecture that implements unified messaging provides fault tolerance mechanisms (achieved through redundancy) for (1) power suppliers, (2) CPUs (in some cases), and (3) storage. Specifically, the *redundant array of inexpensive disks* (RAID) architecture, in which a single file is broken into blocks of data distributed across an array of disks, seems to be the architecture of choice. In this architecture, one designated extra disk keeps a certain function [*exclusive OR* (XOR), to be specific] of the blocks on other disks, so that if any disk fails, the blocks it contained will be immediately recovered. In addition to fault tolerance, the architecture provides simultaneous access to all the disks in the array, which speeds up data access by as many times as there are disks in the array and makes the array especially useful for real-time message playing.

An important component of the messaging platform concerns the management of the platform itself. Most messaging products today implement the management component based on SNMP. In addition to local alarm indicators, the SNMP agent for remote alarm monitoring runs as part of the systems software. Advanced products run similar agents for other features of the *remote access and diagnostics* (RAD) capabilities (such as remote reboot and password administration).

Other functional capabilities of the operations and management software include configuration management for platform administration and subscriber provisioning (through a management console) and support of LDAP API for external provisioning. Call detail records, which are essential for billing, are usually accessible through the *File Transfer Protocol* (FTP). As always, support of billing is a key differentiating criterion in choosing a particular product. While it is relatively straightforward to offer with the use of IN platform services like call sender with rebound (described in Chapter 9), provision of adequate billing requires much work. Advanced products solve this problem by carefully supporting as many scenarios as possible. For example, to support call sender with rebound, the calls returned from users' mailboxes must be appropriately logged. High-end products also provide software tool kits that allow you to build not only new services but also new capabilities.

An important product differentiator is the number of supported languages. Advanced products provide multilingual capabilities (up to 22 languages) as well as the support for *Telecommunications Device for the Deaf* (TDD) (treated as another language). (In some cases, customers who purchase TDD-compatible messaging systems may be entitled to a tax credit under the United States Americans with Disabilities Act.)

In the messaging platforms, the enablers of the voice capabilities are the same as in SNs; similarly, connection to the SS No. 7 network provides full access to IN and wireless signaling protocols. Figure 10.13 illustrates the entities to which unified messaging platforms are connected. In the PSTN, those entities include both IN SCPs and (typically central office) switches. In the wireless networks, messaging platforms are connected to *mobile switching centers* (MSCs) and *home location registers* (HLRs). To support the enterprise (premises-based) telephony, the unified messaging platforms must also maintain connections to PBXs. SNMP-based access to remote operations systems is

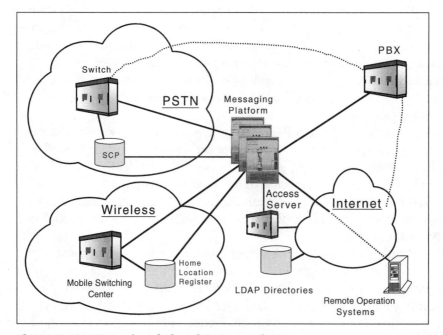

Figure 10.13 Messaging platform interconnections.

achieved through the Internet. The connections to access servers (discussed in the next section) are needed for the purposes of IP telephony. Because the unified messaging platforms also function as SCPs, their use of LDAP is very similar to the IN mechanisms for accessing external databases [called service data functions (SDFs)], which store subscriber-specific information. Naturally, these directories are accessed through the Internet.

Messaging platforms provided by one vendor may also work with switches manufactured by different vendors. Interoperability with other vendors' switches is achieved by carefully supporting multiple SS No. 7 ISUP options. Similarly, some messaging platform products can interwork with like platforms built by other vendors.

Remote Access Servers

The available remote access products range from very small secure Ethernet-to-ISDN bridges/routers that give SOHO users the flexibility to use digital technology without abandoning the PSTN lines to large multiservice systems destined for large enterprise networks, ISPs, or local exchange carriers.

At the heart of high-end access servers is the support for V.90, K.56flex, and V.34 modems (with speeds of up to 56 kbps downstream and 33.6 kbps (V.34) upstream) that can self-configure and provide real-time diagnostics. Advanced modems are DSP driven, with purely digital circuitry. Another important feature of access servers is support of data compression for the ISDN or leased-line connection, which can increase the bandwidth by a factor of 4.

In a nutshell, a medium-size remote access server—suited for high-density *wide area network* (WAN) service pooling and point-of-presence applications—consists of a pool of V.90 modems, a router, and a server on a single chassis. Such a chassis can support from 10 to about 200 modems. These units may also support frame relay communications (not discussed here). The scalability of an access server can often be increased by stacking multiple hardware chassis and interconnecting them via a LAN. To work as one unit, the product must ensure that a single user's ISDN connection of 128 kbps (2×64 kbps) can span multiple chassis. In addition, the product may allow all port resources of these multiple chassis to be pooled and available to all services.

Two important features of access servers are *dynamic port allocation* and *single incoming telephone number.* With the dynamic port allocation feature, the ports are pooled and made available for a call as required by incoming traffic. When the call is terminated, the freed port is returned to the pool. With the single incoming telephone number feature, a single number can be offered for different dial-in services, such as the ISDN and POTS. The access server recognizes whether an incoming call is made via an ISDN or analog (or channelized T1 or E1) line. When a call arrives on a PRI line, the access server checks to see if framing is present. If it is, the access server processes the ISDN call; if it is not, the DSP processor is brought up to execute the modem handshake.

Security solutions in high-end products allow network managers to configure and modify hierarchical security schemes. In some products, RADIUS software (which usually also supports accounting) is included in the offer, but RADIUS itself has to interwork with authentication software. Authentication via the *Password Authentication Protocol* (PAP) and *Challenge Handshake Authentication Protocol* (CHAP)—described in Chapter 7—as well as encrypted administrative passwords are examples of acceptable security solutions present in today's products. Support of call-back and firewall packet filtering are other important product differentiators for security. In addition, the PSTN information, such as *calling line identification* (CLI), is sometimes used in combination with the IP security mechanisms.

The requirements of emerging technologies (such as DSL) and the need to interconnect with the ATM networks has resulted in the emergence of carrier-grade access servers (also called *remote access concentrators*), which are suitable for large ISPs and enterprise networks.

An example hardware configuration of a high-end carrier-grade server is a multislot chassis connected by a fast switching fabric (such as 5-Gbps ATM). (Sometimes time division multiplexer buses are used, but they are inferior to the ATM cell switching fabric, which eliminates any congestion or arbitration delays as well as single points of failure.) The switching fabric, which provides a highly reliable cross-connect matrix, is combined with the passive backplane for redundancy. With the backplane so powerful, a single slot can be provided with a dedicated line whose bandwidth may range from 155 to 622 Mbps, which results in supporting of at least three T3 lines. A single high-end server may support over 800 simultaneous modem sessions (or leased line connections). Those servers can be stacked to support over 4000 modem sessions simultaneously. Systems of this class have highly reliable redundant power supplies, advanced power distribution, and efficient thermal design (typically with hot-swappable cooling fans to dissipate the vast amount of heat created by modem integrated circuits). Another redundancy is achieved by having more modems in the pool than there are possible connections. Thus, a malfunctioning modem can be immediately replaced by an extra modem, even at full capacity.

The capabilities of high-end access servers are attractive to local telephone companies that plan to offer advanced remote access services such as *virtual private network* (VPN) services. Two IETF-standardized mechanisms addressed in the previous chapter—L2TP and IPsec—are essential for provision of secure VPN.

Layer Two Tunneling Protocol (L2TP), described in Chapter 7, allows the (possibly encrypted) point-to-point protocol frames to be encapsulated in an IP packet and tunneled over any IP-based network. Two devices are used for the L2TP tunnel: the *L2TP access concentrator* (LAC) and the *L2TP network server* (LNS). (Figure 10.14 depicts the relevant architecture.) LAC encapsulates point-to-point protocol frames within L2TP packets and passes them to one or more

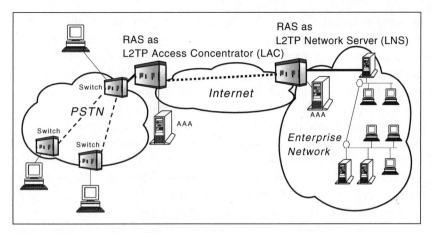

Figure 10.14 L2TP tunneling with RASs.

L2TP network servers over any IP-based transport (which includes frame relay and ATM networks). The LNS deencapsulates the L2TP packets, processes PPP frames, and routes them over the enterprise network.

Advanced remote access products implement both the LAC and LNS functions, thus supporting over 800 simultaneous L2TP tunnels. The routing software on the LAC side benefits from the implementation of the *Border Gateway Protocol* (BGP) by realizing multihoming (that is, maintenance of connections to multiple Internet service providers). On the LNS side, the challenge is that terminating L2TP tunnels is highly CPU intensive. For this reason, hardware solutions (such as LNS cards, which can be inserted into chassis slots) are necessary to ensure linear scalability. Some existing LNS cards can support up to 500 L2TP sessions each; however, interworking with the (invariably proprietary) software of RASs may actually reduce the number of active simultaneous sessions.

As in the case of the LNS, the software-only IPsec solutions are deemed neither to scale nor meet the performance requirements of typical networks. Optional IPsec encryption cards are supplied with advanced offers. Such cards can deliver near-wire speeds (that is, 1 to 1.5 Mbps, depending on the packet size) while supporting the 56-bit *Data Encryption Standard* (DES) or 168-bit Triple DES with MD-5 Authentication in *Encapsulated Security Payload* (ESP) mode.

RADIUS servers implement the authentication, authorization, and accounting (AAA) solution for the time being. The essence of the existing products [largely based on RFC 2138 (addressed in Chapter 7) and reported in the informational RFC 2139] is that they are software based. The problem itself does not require computationally intensive solutions; instead, platform independence and extensible plug-in capabilities are important requirements.

Platform independence is best achieved by providing software that can be executed in most environments. Presently, the Java programming environment is the environment of choice from this point of view. With the core RADIUS software developed by one vendor, plug-ins for support of user directories, data analysis tools, security, and billing services can be developed by other vendors or even customers. The key product differentiator is support of construction and management of specific policies that guard access to services. For example, leading products enable network managers to construct configuration files that specify AAA processing paths for unique policies executed in conjunction with external data sources. The feature sets so provided enable the support of applications starting with simple enterprise (or Internet) access and finishing with remote access outsourcing. For example, a built-in session control limits the number of sessions permitted on a per-user or per-realm basis. In support of remote access outsourcing, RADIUS servers enforce group limits and manage loading of logical ports and modem groups. As far as the accounting goes, it is again a matter of plug-in software, which can be supplied by the RADIUS vendors or developed independently. The RADIUS software interacts with that of the accounting plug-in by means of billing events.

Remote access servers typically support SNMP and *telnet* for network management. There are multiple network management applications with graphic interfaces that come with products.

The last, but not least important, feature of the leading remote access servers is support of SS No. 7 and, in some cases, DSSI (Q.931) between the access servers and central office, which enables the Internet offloading application. The ISP or enterprise can take a data call at the access server and route it through the Internet to the main facilities (which otherwise would need to terminate PSTN calls). As we mentioned in Chapter 2, with this feature an ISP can connect to a *local exchange carrier* (LEC) as a *competitive LEC* (CLEC) via a particular trunking arrangement. The calls are then routed to the ISP's access number so the ISP looks like a competing local carrier serving a single customer—the ISP access server. [For a detailed description, see Kozik et al. (1998).] The feature usually employs the SS7 gateway products (*SS7*, a shorter and simpler abbreviation than standard *SS No. 7*), described in the next section.

SS7 Gateways

The SS7 gateways, which are used for Internet offloading in conjunction with the remote access servers, also serve as building blocks for delivering voice and fax over IP.

Figure 10.15 depicts the interconnection of an SS7 gateway with the rest of the PSTN and IP entities. On the PSTN side, local switches and *service control point* (SCP) are interconnected, as far as signaling is concerned, through *signaling transfer points* (STPs). The SS7 gateway is connected (via SS No. 7 A links, depicted by dotted lines) to STPs, too, thus becoming an SS No. 7 net-

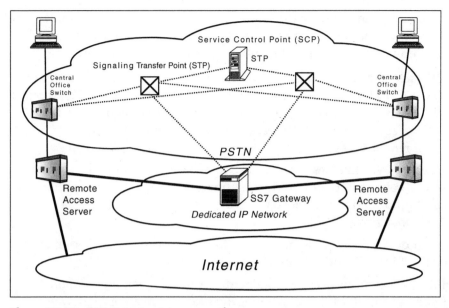

Figure 10.15   SS7 Gateway Interconnections.

work element. In addition to direct connection to the signaling network, an SS7 gateway is connected to a dedicated IP network, which it shares with the remote access servers it supports. When Internet users make data calls, central office switches route these calls to appropriate RASs' ports. The SS7 gateway (which acts on behalf of the RASs it supports) emulates a telephone switch on the switch-to-switch trunk setup interface exchanging ISUP messages with the real switches. The SS7 gateway also emulates a switch on the switch-to-SCP interface, exchanging INAP messages with the SCP. Thus, only the originating switches need to keep their lines occupied with the Internet calls; the rest of the PSTN is bypassed, so the valuable voice circuits are left for what they were intended for in the first place—voice. As we mentioned before, not only the PSTN benefits from this solution. ISPs can choose to leave the access service business to telephone carriers and concentrate on e-mail, World Wide Web hosting, and other services relevant to their customers' needs; ditto for enterprise networks.

The leading SS7 gateway products that combine both hardware and software are available in configurations that range from 10,000 to 200,000 ports and can work in the enterprise, ISP, and central office environments. The key requirement of such products—essentially high-powered (0.5 to 1 GB of memory) fault-tolerant computers—is effectively 100 percent availability (advertised as 99.999 percent). Typically, duplication of hardware components (so that all computations, including those that support all I/O operations, run in parallel) is sufficient for achieving total availability, but it is also important that hardware have self-checking logic to monitor the components in order to detect and remove the faulty one (while passing control to its double) at once. Self-monitoring is an important feature to look for in high-end products. Important software differentiating features are as follows:

Multistack SS No. 7 option.   Allows several processes, each executing the SS No. 7 stack with a different point code (that is, the SS No. 7 endpoint address), to execute concurrently on a single system. Thus a single system can emulate several different switches (in support of the same number of remote access servers or VoIP gateways) in ISUP dialogues.

Support of IN.   Enables communication of SS7 gateways with external service control. Top-end products support both the U.S. (DP-specific) and European (DP-generic) options of the ITU-T *Intelligent Network Application Part* (INAP).

Support of ISDN access signaling.   Allows processing of calls originating on the ISDN BRI and PRI lines.

Online provisioning and management.   Allows a customer to monitor (typically, via SNMP) and dynamically reconfigure an SS7 gateway.

In some implementations, the SS7 gateway has features of the so-called *soft switch* described in Chapter 3. In other words, the SS7 gateway not only acts as a telecommunications switch on the line and trunk setup interface, but also provides for the operational interface functions (such as circuit queries and blocking) as well as a full call state model, which maintains for each call the state of the path between voice and IP networks. To this end, call events are recorded automatically and call event records are generated for billing.

As you may have noticed, there is a striking similarity—as far as the interconnection architecture is concerned—between the carrier-grade VoIP gateways and remote access servers: Both need to support SS No. 7—best achieved today by pairing with the SS7 gateways. Both also advocate the need for IP trunking so as to interconnect with LECs' telephone switches. This subject is discussed in the section that follows.

Class 5 Switches with IP Trunks

As you may recall from Chapter 2, the number 5 in reference to telecommunications switches remains from predivestiture times when the U.S. telephone network had a hierarchical model in which five classes (according to their respective functions) of switches were employed. Specifically, class 5 was reserved for the central office switches. Although the name endures, the actual capabilities of some of today's large class 5 switches allow them to be configured for tandem, government, and other specialized applications. Furthermore, those class 5 switches that are equipped with appropriate signaling gateways are sometimes used as gateways to foreign networks. On the other end of the spectrum are smaller class 5 switches that are sometimes employed by large enterprises as PBXs.

Large class 5 switches (with about 200,000 access lines and 100,000 trunks) support metropolitan and urban areas; smaller ones (with about 40,000 access lines and 20,000 trunks) support rural areas; and the smallest ones (with about 20,000 access lines and 10,000 trunks) typically support small towns. Advanced switches provide ISDN (PRI and BRI) and ADSL access, and they invariably support SS No. 7 signaling and its applications (such as Intelligent Network) as well as the interfaces to telecommunications network traffic management platforms, billing systems, and other operations systems.

There are very few vendors of telecommunications switches; their products are so complex and so dissimilar—insofar as their architecture, hardware, and software are concerned—that each warrants a separate book. We do not attempt to review the existing hardware and software solutions, nor do we describe the resulting IP services or mechanisms that support them. Our review of VoIP gateways, gatekeepers, remote access servers, and SS7 gateways, whose functions are combined in the new switches, covers the IP services and mechanisms. We do report on the emerging solutions for IP connectivity (often combined with support for sending voice over ATM and frame relay networks—thus justifying the name *multiservice switching* used in the industry to describe these capabilities), which effectively make the telephony switches into packet switches.

Such switching solutions unite traditional call processing with the support of modem pooling and remote access, thus allowing ISPs (or enterprises) to terminate calls directly at the multiservice switch. All the features of remote access servers described in the preceding text are supported. In addition, the VoIP gateways and gatekeepers are also part of the multiservice switch, so the PSTN voice service is converted to voice over IP as close to the source as possible. Note that because class 5 switches already support SS No. 7 and its applications, support of the PSTN signaling and, in particular, use of Intelligent Network—which immediately solves the issues of supporting services and number portability, as well as the use of the end-to-end PSTN operations and management—come automatically with the product. Again, all the relevant IP telephony and remote access capabilities (including out-of-band signaling over IP) described earlier in this chapter are supported, but since they are supported at the switch itself, no front-end boxes for performing interconnections and conversions are needed. Telephone companies or enterprises that plan to replace their existing switches should replace them with the emerging multiservice switches; in many cases the costs of upgrade and integration of all the products needed to provide such functions are below the cost of an appropriate multiservice switch.

Typically, the features supported by the multiservice switches (in addition to over 3000 voice-related features inherent from the PSTN) come in feature groups called *bundles* in PSTN parlance. To date, the following bundles are available:

- Residential
- SOHO
- Large enterprise
- Multienterprise
- Virtual telco

Bundling eliminates the need to buy unnecessary features; each bundle costs less than an all-or-nothing package.

One more application of IP trunking is offloading the signaling network. Messages between the SS No. 7 endpoints (network elements) can be tunneled through the IP network. The IETF *sigtran* working group is presently developing the transport layer standard protocol for such tunneling; for the moment, there are several proprietary solutions. Here again an important and interesting duality can be observed: While the IP endpoints (such as SS7 gateways) adapt to the PSTN in order to connect to its signaling network, the PSTN switches use IP to tunnel the PSTN signaling.

This concludes the description of the available types of products. We are ready to proceed with the criteria for choosing those that best suit your applications.

chapter 11

Choosing the Right Products
for Your Applications

By reading the preceding chapters of Part Three, you have probably already formed at the intuitive level a pretty good notion of whether the integration of the Internet and telecommunications is right for you and, if so, what types of products may be helpful in your particular situation. That is, you have meditated on the environments in which your networks live, thought about the applications that are critical to your business, and obtained a feeling for the kinds of products available. What remains is to perform a structured analysis that leads to a conclusion or at least narrows your choices to a few.

There are many possible ways to choose products. You may feel comfortable doing it on your own, or you may prefer to seek the help of a consultant. You may produce documentation for your own use as you interact with vendor representatives, or you may write a formal Request for Proposal and circulate it to potential suppliers. In any case, an essential step is to assemble your requirements in a way that permits comparison with product capabilities. This section provides a checklist of possible requirements categories and a few suggestions about what kinds of information to include in each.

Features

Anything purporting to be a telecommunications product presumably supports some mechanism for one user to place a voice call to another. Beyond the support of basic calls, feature requirements and feature support by products can vary widely, so it is important to be explicit about each feature you need, confirm that it is supported by the products under consideration, and verify exactly how it works and how it is perceived by users.

Features may be categorized in several ways. One way is to distinguish between *line-oriented* features, which primarily affect the way an individual user interacts with the system, and *network* features, which provide capabilities to all users across a network of interconnected systems. Classic line-oriented features used in most business environments include call hold, transfer, call-forwarding, and conferencing calling. Network features include things like private dialing plans and full-blown virtual private networks. Centrex, which allows the switch to emulate the functions of a *private branch exchange* (PBX), constitutes an important group of business customer features for central office switches.

High-end PBXs support literally hundreds of different features, as do class 5 switches designed for central office environments. If you are replacing an existing system, you will probably want to check what features it supports and, if possible, determine which are actually utilized. A survey of the user population to determine the most popular and essential features may also be worthwhile. If you are planning for a new environment, blocking out some scenarios to capture the ways in which people with different work functions will use the telecommunications system may provide the right insights.

The kinds of features we have mentioned so far are traditional telephony features. In addition, you may be interested in new types of features that are made possible by the integration of the Internet and telecommunications. Examples of these include Internet call-waiting and text-to-speech conversion.

Ease of Use

Related to feature support is ease of use. The classic example of a set of features that are underutilized due to poor ease of use are those that require setting the correct time on a VCR. By contrast, almost everyone finds ordinary consumer telephone service easy to use. Standard business telephone services are somewhere in between. How often have you asked someone to transfer your call, only to be told, "Okay, but here is the number you want in case you are cut off"? This represents not an expectation that the switching system will capriciously terminate the call, but a lack of confidence on the part of the called party in his or her ability to make the call transfer feature work as desired.

Services based on the integration of the Internet and telecommunications have the capacity to go either way—that is, in the VCR direction toward unnecessarily complex interfaces for simple functions, or in the consumer telephone direction toward easy and natural use. An example on the positive side is the Web-based conference control described earlier in this book, which has the potential to eliminate a lot of the fumbling and uncertainty involved with setting up and conducting voice conference calls. A negative example would be any voice-over-IP service that requires users to dial a lot more digits or wait significantly more time for call setup than they are accustomed to with standard consumer phone service today.

The ease of use category is somewhat subjective, of course. Without an extensive human factors study of your user population and its ability to interact with specific product features, the best approach might be to map out typical application scenarios for your environment, determine which features of the system apply to each, and put yourself in the users' place as the scenarios unfold. A test drive might also be a good idea, and you may want to involve some representative users in this exercise if possible.

Billing/Accounting

The ability to record billable events, aggregate billing data, apply rating algorithms, and calculate, print, and deliver individual detailed bills, all at a sufficiently low cost to be feasible when billing for services that themselves cost only pennies a minute, is a hallmark of public telephone service. If you are a public network operator, you will already have a set of detailed requirements for voice telephone service billing capabilities and the reliability and security of the associated systems. New issues for you to consider when integrating Internet and telecommunications technologies include how services (especially integrated and nonvoice services) are to be priced and the impact of this on billing requirements.

Managers of enterprise networks face a different set of choices. While full-scale billing in the sense of public telephone service may not be a requirement, enterprises often *charge back* the cost of providing telecommunications service to specific units of the enterprise. To charge back, you must collect usage statistics on the basis of categories such as originating location, department, work group, project, or person; you may also need to generate an electronic or paper bill for distribution within the company. On the other hand, depending on size and usage patterns, some enterprises may find that sufficient cost control can be achieved by tracking more general usage statistics, without the need to generate individual or department-level bills.

Legacy Support

Unless you are building a completely new network from scratch, you will need to deal in one way or another with providing support for legacy systems. This support can take many forms and have a wide variety of implications, depending on the size, configuration, and technical generation of your existing network elements and end-user systems.

When integrating Internet services into an existing telecommunications network environment, you will need to interconnect with the transmission formats and signaling standards of the legacy systems. These formats and standards include things like analog and ISDN lines, loop start, ground start, and digital trunks, and, in a central office environment, out-of-band SS No. 7 and possibly in-band signaling carried on designated bits within the digital transmission systems as well as multifrequency tones. Converting this multiplicity of transport and signaling interfaces to formats that can be carried over an IP network is the job of gateway systems. To be sure you get the gateway system you need, it is important to identify all the necessary legacy interfaces and their properties and include them in your requirements.

Besides transmission and signaling interfaces, there may be other characteristics of the legacy environment that translate into requirements for new system procurement. For example, depending on the size and sophistication of the existing network, there may be in place an extensive operations environment whose proper functioning is essential to maintain the quality of service experienced by users of the network, as well as to control operations costs by centralizing and automating functions. You must exercise care and creativity when formulating appropriate requirements. On the one hand, you will want to preserve the desirable properties of a well-functioning operations environment (if you already have one) and may want to preserve things like the human interfaces to technicians to minimize retraining costs. On the other hand (as we will see in Chapter 12), integrating telecommunications and the Internet has the potential to reduce operations costs through network consolidation, so you will want to be flexible enough in your requirements to take advantage of potential savings.

From the user point of view, another important aspect of legacy support is *feature transparency*. This term means that features—including their subtle details—must operate in exactly the same way between new and legacy systems. User expectations for feature transparency tend to be quite high in the telecommunications environment, though it can be a difficult goal to achieve. Maintaining feature transparency requires a highly disciplined approach to feature software development and extensive testing on the part of the vendor.

You as the customer have the right either to require a high degree of feature transparency or to deliberately forgo it in the pursuit of other, possibly conflicting goals such as the deployment of new applications.

Standards Compliance

Telecommunications by its nature is a standards-intensive business, and the Internet owes its awesome success to the widespread acceptance of certain protocol standards. Compliance with specific standards is therefore a crucial (and possibly difficult) issue in the procurement of any system for integrating telecommunications and Internet. The difficulty of compliance with standards is compounded by the fact that, while some important standards (H.323 comes to mind) are published and have achieved a certain stability, others are still being crafted in various standards bodies.

Part Two of this book should provide a good source for developing requirements on standards compliance. Areas in which standards compliance may be important, depending on the application and type of product, include:

- Telephone line and trunk interfaces, including signaling
- ISDN
- Digital subscriber line standards
- Optical and electrical transmission system interfaces
- Basic voice-over-IP standards
- Standards for gateways and gatekeepers, including media gateway control
- Multimedia conferencing
- QoS mechanisms
- Computer-telephony integration (CTI) standards
- Intelligent network standards
- Network management
- Directory
- Security

Again, the specific standards that apply in each of these areas are discussed in Part Two. Some things to think about when constructing your requirements for standards compliance include the following.

Recall the discussion at the beginning of Chapter 8 about the environments in which your system must operate. Especially for telecommunications, it is often the case that different standards apply to private networks than to public networks, and different standards apply in different regions of the world. For example, the leading body setting telecommunications standards for North America is Committee T1, and its standards often differ from those promulgated for Europe by the *European Telecommunications Standards Institute* (ETSI). Differences exist between North America and Europe on such fundamentals as the number of channels in digital carrier systems. In some areas, such as SS No. 7 signaling, there are even important national differences in standards. Other standards in telecommunications are more universal, especially those developed by the International Telecommunications Union—*Telecommunications Standardization Sector* (ITU-T).

Some of the same bodies that develop standards for public telecommunications networks are also active in developing specifications that apply to private networks (for example, PBXs), though in this field some others are also important, notably ECMA. Regional standards differences are also common in the private network field.

The implication of standards compliance issues is that in formulating your requirements, you need to state in which geographical environments the network is intended to function and name specific applicable standards to the extent that you are aware of them.

On the Internet side, we are fortunate that IP and the related suite of protocols developed by the *Internet Engineering Task Force* (IETF) apply across a wide variety of underlying network types and are truly international in acceptance. However, even in this area, when different protocol choices present themselves on the Internet side, it may make quite a bit of difference whether your network is large or small in scale and whether it is entirely private (that is, an intranet) or whether it makes use of the public Internet. For example, a requirement for use of *IP Security* (IPsec) may exist if some traffic is routed over the public Internet, but may not if the network is a physically secure private network.

Another question to consider when formulating standards requirements is: Are you mainly looking for a general assurance that the system operates in accord with the latest industry directions, or do you have a much more specific objective in mind, such as enabling the interoperation of equipment from multiple vendors? If the latter, you may need to ask for more than a statement of compliance with the standard. Because most standards include a variety of options, leave certain details up to the discretion of the implementor, and may even be ambiguous in places, if assurance of interoperation is required you may need to ask the vendor for a more detailed implementation agreement or require evidence of successful interoperability testing. There are a number of groups that sponsor or facilitate interoperability testing. In the field of voice over IP, one established testing body is iNOW (which stands for interoperability now), sponsored by the *International Multimedia Teleconferencing Consortium* (IMTC).

Regulatory/Mandatory Standards

Various government regulations apply to the operation of electronic equipment in general and to telecommunications products in particular. These requirements are also called *mandatory standards*, since compliance with them is required by law. In contrast, standards discussed in the preceding section are generally termed *voluntary*, meaning that, however important they may be from a business view, there is no law that mandates their use.

Regulations and mandatory standards exist for things like electromagnetic compatibility (to prevent electronic equipment from radiating excessively strong signals, which can interfere with other electronic equipment and with radio and television transmission) and safety against such dangers as electrical shock, fire, and stray laser radiation. In the telecommunications field, government regulations such as the well-known FCC Part 68 in the United States place special requirements on the interface between network systems and customer premises equipment. While various efforts are under way to achieve more global uniformity on mandatory standards, at present they do vary from country to country. You should take care to require that equipment you purchase complies with the relevant regulations in the countries where it will operate.

Capacity

Specifying required system capacities may be an easy thing for a small, standalone system—or, for large networks, it may be a very complex matter involving multiple engineering trade-offs. For example, is it better to have a few large, centralized switches with a lot of transmission backhaul, or do the economics work out more favorably with small, distributed systems? The only way to gain a solid understanding of how these trade-offs play out for your network is to do some comparisons of alternative network designs. You can do this yourself if you have access to and understand how to use appropriate network design tools, or you can engage a consultant. You may also find that larger vendors will offer network design as a service. In any case, an important set of inputs will be the actual and projected number of users and the traffic they generate, expressed as a location-by-location traffic matrix or the equivalent. If you run an existing network, you probably have a lot of data of this kind. If you are working with a blank slate, your vendor or consultant can help you make estimates.

Specific capacity parameters for various product categories were discussed in Chapter 10. When specifying capacity requirements or interpreting vendor statements about capacity, keep in mind that capacity parameters may not necessarily be independent of each other. For example, if a system terminates 1000 physical telephone lines but the call processing engine can only handle 500 calls per hour, the system will not reach its maximum physical termination capacity if the average line generates 1 call per hour in the busy hour.

When evaluating vendor statements about capacity, it is also important to know what assumptions are made about background loads from other tasks.

Also, consider the possibility that the limiting capacity parameter could be something only indirectly related to the number of lines or calls—for example, the number or capacity of SS No. 7 signaling links or, for a system with large, frequently changing customer records, such as an *Intelligent Network Service Control Point* (INSCP), the customer record update capacity.

Scalability

Closely related to capacity is *scalability*. Requirements for scalability are critically important in networks that are expected to experience rapid growth. Things to look for include the following: Is the basic technology for integrating the Internet and telecommunications on which the vendor bases its products scaleable across the size range corresponding to your needs? If the vendor covers the capacity range with multiple products, are there any gaps? Is a smooth migration across the size range possible, with protection of your initial product investments, or are forklift upgrades required?

Extensibility

Another quality important to networks with changing needs is extensibility. This refers not to the ability to grow the physical size of the network, but to the ability to grow its capabilities. For example, you may have decided that you are comfortable with equipping a certain remote branch office with only basic calling features, but you know that if the contract with the XYZ Corporation comes through, the branch office will need to be upgraded to a full-scale sales office. Can the telecommunications system be easily extended in feature set as well as capacity, or must it be junked and replaced with another?

One way of making a product extensible, which you may require if your needs demand it, is the support of an interface to third-party feature developers. This is typically a software interface that allows software developers other than the original manufacturer to add new features to the system.

Quality of Service (QoS)

Voice quality is a well-known hot button in the world of telephony. Public telephone networks traditionally strove to provide a uniform level of voice quality that, while surprisingly limited in the dimension of bandwidth (the nominal 4 kHz being less than 25 percent of a normal young adult's perceptible frequency range) was overall quite good. By the 1960s, the standard for toll (long-distance) connections in the United States was that 95 percent of users should rate them good or better on a subjective poor-fair-good-excellent scale with respect to key impairments such as circuit noise. With the rapid deployment of long-haul digital fiber systems in the 1980s, users became accustomed to essentially noiseless telephone calls, even to overseas points. Echo cancelers employing digital signal processing cleaned up echoes on long circuits without introducing the other impairments characteristic of cruder echo suppression techniques. After bad user reaction to the 500-ms round trip delay, satellite circuits were banished to those parts of the international network too lightly loaded to justify undersea fiber cables. Most fundamentally, the basic technologies of circuit switching combined with *pulse-code modulation* (PCM) encoding essentially guarantee that whatever waveform enters one end of the network comes out the other side with very little modification.

Users have shown a definite willingness to tolerate lower voice quality in exchange for convenience—hands-free operation with speakerphones, mobility with cordless phones and cellular services. However, as long as wireline telephone companies manage to continue delivering standard quality in combination with attractive calling plans, there does not seem to be much margin for services with lower quality and no compensating convenience factors. It remains to be seen whether the ability to talk into your computer will turn out to be viewed as a convenience factor.

So, the best advice is to be very cautious about specifying or allowing lower voice quality, except perhaps in specific enterprise network situations where there is a well-quantified economic benefit and the business function being supported by the service does not involve, for example, customer contact.

Vendors may state that they support toll quality voice or make some quantitative statements about quality. However, given the crucial role of voice quality in voice networks, rather than trying to interpret these statements by themselves, you should also do the following:

1. Be sure you understand the voice coding scheme being employed. If it includes compression, you are making a trade-off against quality; and, depending on how aggressive a compression technique is employed, the quality difference may be perceptible under certain conditions.

2. Review one of the many published reports of *bake-off* events, in which voice quality is always one of the key system properties tested.

Quality of service in telecommunications networks in fact has many dimensions other than voice quality per se. Other commonly specified parameters include dial tone delay, postdial call setup time, and percent blocking. Standard objectives for these parameters for public networks are published by ITU and by Telcordia (formerly Bellcore, and at one time the joint R&D arm of the U.S. RBOCs). The ITU standards tend to be on the liberal side to allow for the significant variation in public network standards among various countries of the world.

Other quality of service parameters apply to traditional data networks. These include the probability of dropped, duplicated, or misrouted packets, as well as the statistics of packet delay. In an integrated system employing Internet technology to deliver telecommunications applications, these parameters may not be directly observable by the users, but will instead influence other quality parameters such as voice quality, call setup time, and blocking.

An important fact to keep in mind about quality is that in general there is a trade-off against cost. If you want a higher-quality system, you may expect to pay for that. If you are looking for the ultimate in low cost, you may need to compromise on various quality parameters.

Reliability

Reliability has been not just a hot button but maybe even an obsession with public telecommunications carriers, expressed in famous formulations such as the requirement that switching systems experience no more than two hours of downtime in a 40-year service life (or, in a slightly more modern-sounding twist, 3 minutes per year). Whatever the historical roots of this strong commitment to reliability (and it does seem to be linked somehow to the former status of these carriers as legal monopolies entrusted with providing a public service), high reliability is so integral to the value proposition of these companies to their customers that compromise remains largely unthinkable.

In some enterprises, telecommunications—or at least a portion of the firm's telecommunications network—is so critical to revenue generation that reliability requirements are at least equal to public network standards. In others, or for noncritical business functions, more relaxed requirements will be possible. In formulating requirements for reliability, try to think in terms of the business functions supported by the network and whether they can tolerate only negligible downtime or whether some downtime for system maintenance, upgrades, software crashes, and hardware failures is acceptable. If high reliability is essential, specific system features such as fault tolerance, sparing, hot-swappable boards, and the ability to maintain stable calls under noncatastrophic failure conditions may be specified.

Maintainability

Once you've built a network, you have to run it. As we will see when we take a look at network economics in Chapter 12, it may well be that the expenses of operating the network exceed the amortized cost of the network equipment itself. This provides a powerful motivation to specify maintainability requirements in order to minimize operational cost as well as to allow speedy repair of any problems and thus support overall high system availability.

Standards for network management are one important aspect of maintainability. (See Part Two for a more complete discussion of standards.) One challenge you must face when planning for integration of the Internet and telecommunications is that the telecommunications and data networking worlds have developed separate standards universes for network management in general, including maintenance. Depending on what sort of Internet-telecommunications system you are implementing, you may need to support standards from both the traditional telecommunications side and the traditional data networking side.

The maintenance capabilities of the system you are purchasing should also fit within your existing or planned operational environment. If you are planning to run a national network with a staff of 5 located in Minneapolis, you should verify that this is feasible with the contemplated system and that you will not be compelled to station 95 more people within an hour's drive of each remote unit to handle problems that cannot be managed centrally.

You should also understand what support the vendor will offer in the case of system or subsystem failure. What are the sources of replacement parts? Does the vendor provide a repair service or a telephone hand-holding service? What are the costs of these services? Exactly what is covered under the vendor's warranty?

Finally, the system you are purchasing should have specific features or capabilities intended to mitigate the effect of failures and ease repair. For example, the product may offer the ability to remove and replace failed boards while the rest of the system keeps running and processing calls. Your need for specific features of this kind will depend on your overall requirements for system availability.

Security

Security requirements will clearly differ depending on your applications and operating environments. Specialized requirements will apply to public networks and to applications requiring, for example, encrypted voice. Also, if any use of the public Internet is contemplated, Internet security becomes essential. However, attention to security requirements and the security features of vendor products will be important in almost any purchase. You will at least want to know, for example, how the vendor addresses classic telecommunications security holes such as the potential for PBX capabilities to be hijacked by someone posing as a remote user.

In general, if there are special features intended to be accessed only by certain users, either local or remote, you will need adequate capabilities to authenticate users (i.e., to verify that they are who they say they are) and authorize the use of specific resources. If you are purchasing a network supported by operations systems for maintenance and network configuration, it will be important to know that these operations systems have adequate security safeguards to prevent unauthorized people from accessing and using them. You may want to know if specialized software is available to alert network managers to suspicious activity patterns, such as an unusual number of calls to or from a specific number or the simultaneous use of an authorization code in two different geographic areas.

Especially if your network is intended to be accessible by the public, you need to know what protections the vendor provides against denial-of-service attacks (e.g., flooding your system with phony requests) as well as theft of service.

Disaster Recovery

If your network is essential to the operation of your business, you need to know what options are available to recover from disasters such as a fire or weather emergency that could take out an entire network site. Disaster recovery capabilities may be designed into your network by providing redundant equipment and geographical diversity of nodes and links. Of course, providing the required level of protection solely within your own network environment may be quite costly. Alternatively, you may be able to purchase disaster recovery services from firms specializing in this or from local telecommunications providers. No matter how the required backup is provided, you will want to understand how quickly service can be restored and the impact on your users and customers.

Vendor Services

Besides repairing failed units and advising on the use of their products, there are a variety of other services that vendors may provide. You may want to inquire about the possible availability and cost of such services when you interact with the vendor or when you draft your Request for Information/Request for Proposal. Examples include:

Training.   Many vendors provide training courses that can give your operations personnel helpful background on product architectures and specific guidance on product configuration and maintenance.

Engineering/configuration/network planning.   Some vendors may have the ability (probably for a price) to engineer (dimension) your network based on information about your traffic demand or user base, and to help you figure out how to minimize costs by planning the locations of nodes, trunk connectivity, and so on.

Network operation.   Some vendors may offer the option of operating your entire network on an ongoing basis, including administering and maintaining network elements from remote operations centers.

Given the wide scope of services offered by some vendors, it is really possible for you to outsource as much or as little of the work involved in planning, building, and running the network as you like, depending on your particular needs and where you would like to focus your own resources.

Life Cycle Cost

Life cycle cost (also called *total cost of ownership*) is an extremely important topic, because it goes directly to the bottom line in a literal sense. Also, for most organizations, accounting for the total cost of owning and operating the system over its lifetime is the appropriate way to judge its true cost impact. (There may be some exceptions, such as institutions that must live within hard constraints on capital spending, or start-up businesses for whom what happens in the next six months is more important than the long term.)

Vendors often make claims about life cycle cost, and it is important to be able to evaluate these claims. For example, if a vendor states that the somewhat higher initial cost of its product is offset by low operating cost due to excellent network management capabilities and high product reliability, the vendor might be (1) giving you some very valuable information that will enable you to embark on a successful network project and will benefit your business financially or (2) creating a smokescreen around a product with a cost problem. It's obviously important to be able to tell (1) from (2)!

Ideally, you should conduct your own economic study comparing the costs of purchasing and operating systems from different vendors over a consistent period of time. Teaching you how to do this is beyond the scope of this book, but it is not that difficult for someone with a background in engineering or accounting to learn the basic techniques of engineering economics.

At the very least, you should carefully study and evaluate statements by the vendor about life cycle cost, checking, for example, to see whether the key assumptions are realistic and valid for your own circumstances.

Price/Performance

Another way to view cost (or price) is in relation to performance. If a box from vendor X costs $800 and handles 500 calls per hour, while an equivalent box from vendor Y costs $1000 but handles 2000 calls per hour, the vendor Y box is superior in this measure of price/performance by a factor of about 3. Of course, this may be meaningless if, in your network, this particular box never needs to handle more than 300 calls per hour. Comparisons of price in relation to performance are thus useful in getting a handle on the robustness of product designs and what you are getting for your money, but are not sufficient to provide an overall economic evaluation. For that, you need full-scale analysis of the life cycle costs of actual network designs.

Future Proofing

Earlier we discussed extensibility; *future proofing* is a somewhat different concept that expresses the desire of network managers for products that provide them with some degree of insulation from or adaptability to major changes in the technology of networks. As an example: If a particular voice-over-IP system today employs an ATM layer as the currently feasible mechanism for ensuring quality of service, how readily might it be adapted to do without the ATM layer when purely IP-based QoS mechanisms being worked on in the IETF are mature and available? It doesn't hurt to ask vendors questions like this. The answers may be revealing.

Summary

By conducting a structured analysis of your environment and applications and using the results to distill the essential requirements across key dimensions, you will put yourself in an excellent position to interact with vendors and ultimately choose the right products.

PART

Four

Conclusion and
Reference Material

CHAPTER 12

The Technology Is Relevant

So far, we have surveyed standards and technology, discussed customer environments and applications, and talked about how to match these to the range of product technologies currently available in the realm of Internet and telecommunications integration. If you have made it to this point and have discovered some product categories that address one or more of your pressing needs, you may already be a believer and need no further convincing that the technology is relevant. There is, however, quite an active debate in the industry about the degree to which all of the telecommunications applications that are currently satisfied by circuit-switching technology will migrate to the Internet as some form of voice over IP (VoIP).

Some in the industry take the visionary approach and cite a few stark facts that seem to get to a conclusion in shortcut fashion. The simplest analysis relies on comparing the amount of network traffic (by some consistent measure) that represents conventional voice with that which represents IP data. IP data traffic is growing very quickly, and conventional voice traffic is growing relatively slowly, implying an eventual crossover in traffic volumes. Some large carriers are able to estimate, based on their own measurements and customer information, when the crossover will occur for them. WorldCom, for example, has said it should occur some time during 2001 in the long-distance network it operates.

The reasoning proceeds as follows: Since IP data will eventually represent the larger traffic volume, it will be more economical to convert voice to IP and carry it that way, just as it made sense to carry data over the telephone network when the volume of data traffic was small compared with the volume of voice traffic (and, going back to our history lessons in Chapter 1, just as it made sense in the mid-twentieth century to multiplex the diminishing quantity of telegraph traffic onto telephone carrier circuits).

This reasoning appears fundamentally sound, and, if you are the CEO of a large traditional telephone carrier, it certainly provides enough motivation to get your research and long-range planning departments to take a hard look at migration to an IP-based infrastructure.

However, in reality, nothing is quite this simple—certainly not the economics of the carrier industry. Also, the very idea that all forms of communication will converge on one infrastructure that is based on one protocol, whether IP or anything else, sounds a bit naive when said aloud without the aid of a full-color animated PowerPoint presentation. After all, it's never happened before. Even the telephone network, at the height of its monopolistic, government-owned-and-regulated powers, did not succeed in eliminating all other forms of communications technology. How likely is it then to happen in a market-oriented environment driven by customer choice, where there will be ample rewards for a technology that provides even a small but customer-perceptible advantage over IP for a given application set?

It appears, therefore, that there may be a few more things to be said about whether the technology of the integration of the Internet and telecommunications is relevant, or to whom or for what or for how long. These considerations will be the subject of our concluding chapter. Among the topics to be discussed are the following:

- The cost structure of the carrier business—which elements are sensitive to protocol differences at the IP voice layer, and which are perhaps not sensitive to this at all?

- Life cycle costs from the end-users' viewpoint.

- Regulation—local, national, and international.

- The impact of multimedia.

- The requirements of specialized applications.

Economics of the Integration of the Internet and Telecommunications

Carriers and enterprise networks differ to some degree in the way in which they are affected by network integration economics. Accordingly, in the following sections, we will begin by treating carriers and enterprise networks separately, and then follow up by looking at some joint effects.

Carrier Viewpoint

To understand the economics of the integration of the Internet and telecommunications from the carrier point of view, it is necessary to delve into the cost structure of the carrier business and then to attempt to determine how it is impacted by the opportunities for integration at either the service or the infrastructure level. It should be said at the outset that although today one can find any number of articles in both trade journals and scholarly publications that discuss the economics of, for instance, Internet telephony, any such analysis is actually fraught with various fundamental difficulties. To begin with, the sources of information are necessarily somewhat indirect. Essentially, any carrier that has a very good understanding of its own cost structure will usually treat the details of this information as a closely guarded competitive secret; any carrier that does not understand its own cost structure is not going to be of much help. Public record information, such as that contained in annual reports and reports to the FCC, includes only gross-level cost breakdowns. Also, there are inherent uncertainties in estimating the costs of new types of networks that have not yet been built. These include not only uncertainties in the costs of new hardware and software, but also, perhaps more important, an unknown impact on operational costs.

Perhaps we can truncate our list of caveats and warnings here. You get the idea; the answers are not going to be obvious, and, indeed, this is part of what makes the industry so interesting and dynamic at the present time.

First, let us clarify that we are talking about *costs* to the carrier. There is, of course, an economic theory that says that prices are equal to marginal costs, but that theory assumes an ideal free-market environment rather different from the collection of regulated, unregulated, deregulated, competitive, monopolistic, government-owned, and private ISPs, CLECs, ILECs, IXCs, MSOs, Post, Telegraph, and Telephone (PTTs), former PTTs, and second, third, and fourth operators that constitute the carrier industry today. Differences in pricing, which are solely or primarily driven by regulation, will be the subject of a later section. Here we are trying to get at the impact (if any) of Internet-telecommunications technology itself on underlying costs as seen by the carriers.

A first step (and possibly the most helpful one of all) is to understand the categories of costs seen by a carrier providing voice, data, or multimedia services.

Table 12.1, for example, shows the *AT&T Annual Report* for 1997 (a year that happened to be relatively free of extraordinary charges for restructuring or whatnot), which reveals the following breakdown of that U.S. interexchange carrier's operating expenses.

What is bundled into these categories? What effect could the integration of the Internet and telecommunications possibly have upon them? Let's take these four components in descending order of size.

Table 12.1 Components of Operating Expense

CATEGORY	PERCENT
Access and other interconnection	36.5
Network and other communication services	21.8
Depreciation and amortization	8.9
Selling, general, and administrative	32.8

Source: Derived from *AT&T Annual Report,* 1997.

1. *Access and other interconnection* is mainly what AT&T pays to U.S. local exchange carriers (LECs) for the services of originating and completing the calls of end-user customers and for similar services such as providing the local ends of long-distance private-line circuits. Recall that AT&T's main business (and even more purely so in 1997, before its recent forays into the cable television market) has been providing the long-distance portion of phone calls and private line circuits. Listing this very large expense as a separate line item is, in part, AT&T's way of highlighting what a large fraction of its costs are actually determined by the LECs and the federal regulators who approve the level of carrier access charges. This expense category is unique in that it is not directly affected by technical changes to the network, such as the integration of Internet and telecommunications from a network or equipment perspective. Rather, it is determined by regulatory treatment. At the moment, if AT&T acts as an ISP in providing a service, access charges do not apply. A very interesting question is whether this regulatory treatment would change if such an ISP began handling large volumes of telephone traffic as voice over IP.

2. *Selling, general, and administrative (SG&A)* expense bundles together most of the corporation's activities, other than running the network itself. Much of this has to do with the very high expenses associated with sales and marketing in the highly competitive U.S. long-distance telecommunications market. This includes paying for sales staffs to maintain relationships with large business customers and for advertising campaigns to woo smaller business customers and consumers. It is hard to foresee a direct, near-term impact on these costs from integrating telecommunications and the Internet. To the extent that the technology is used to provide the same services by another means, SG&A costs should remain about the same. To the extent that the integration of the Internet and telecommunications creates new and more complex service options, sales costs could increase somewhat in the near term.

3. *Network and other communications services* expense finally begins to get close to the network itself. Mainly, services are the cost of paying people to run the network. These people do things like testing and repairing switching

and transmission equipment and performing the administrative tasks that are necessary when new equipment is added to the network, when new routes are established, or when new customer services are turned up.

What additional impact the integration of the Internet and telecommunications will have on these network operating costs is a very interesting and important question, but a tough one to answer. The mainstream thinking seems to be that network operational costs for an embedded carrier with an existing circuit-switched network will go up initially as its Internet business grows, since the carrier will have to run an extra network in addition to the ones it already owns, but that it will then go down (possibly significantly) as it becomes possible to carry all services over a common IP network. However, there are a number of uncertainties associated with this scenario.

To begin with, the operational cost differences between circuit-switched voice networks and IP networks applied to multiple services, including telephony, are not well understood. Telephone companies today operate their circuit-switched networks with the aid of *operations support systems* (OSSs), which are either supplied by the telecom equipment manufacturers, developed in house, or developed by third parties such as Telcordia. Some of these systems support administration and maintenance of network elements, such as switches, transmission systems (terminals, multiplexers, line systems), and the signal transfer points of the SS7 networks. Other systems support service-level functions, such as loading data into switches and service control points as customers subscribe to services as simple as call-forwarding or as complex as a nationwide or international toll-free service or virtual private networks.

At the network element level, a voice-over-IP service would involve operations support for new network elements. In addition to IP routers, these would include the packet voice gateway systems, which convert voice from circuit to packet form. Whether configuring such systems is simpler or less costly overall than performing the equivalent functions for circuit switches is, therefore, a key issue.

Operations experts who have studied proposals for large voice-over-IP networks have concluded that there are substantial opportunities for savings at the network management level due to easier bandwidth management (use of virtual trunk groups in place of physical trunk groups) and a probable reduction in the total number of network nodes. These effects are illustrated in Figures 12.1 and 12.2, which show trunking patterns in an interexchange carrier before and after the application of packet gateways. [The figures are highly simplified to make the point; an actual U.S. interexchange carrier, depending on its size, may have many more circuit switches (at least one per metropolitan area), and may or may not have full trunk group interconnection, depending on what circuit-switched routing algorithms are employed by the switches.]

At the service management level, differences may be fewer. Indeed, there may be incentives to utilize the same Intelligent Network infrastructure to pro-

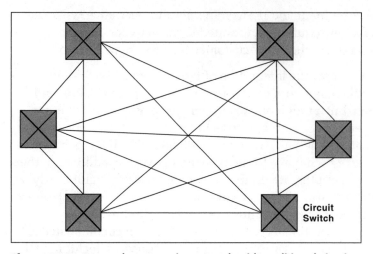

Figure 12.1   Interexchange carrier network with traditional circuit switches and physical trunk groups.

vide, for example, toll-free services over an IP-based infrastructure, in which case the service management costs are probably identical in the two cases.

The real opportunity for dramatic operations costs savings with an IP-based infrastructure is, therefore, linked to the possibility of network consolidation. Telecommunications companies today typically operate several networks that are not fully integrated. There is the circuit-switched voice network. There is a private-line network, which shares the same transmission infrastructure but not the circuit switches, instead relying on digital cross-connect systems to manage connectivity. There may be multiple data net-

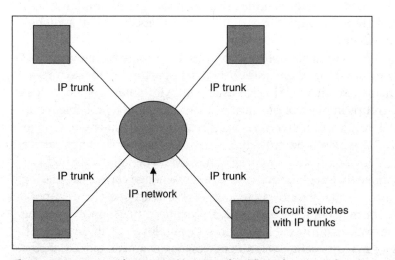

Figure 12.2   Interexchange carrier network with packet core, showing reduction in number of switches and virtual trunking.

works providing ATM, frame relay, and IP services. Each of these networks, in turn, has its own unique set of OSSs and operations workforces.

Because circuit switching does not seem to be up to the job of handling the data side, it has seemed clear for some time that some form of packet technology would be needed as the basis if consolidation of these networks were undertaken. From the late 1980s through the mid-1990s, there was a strong consensus in the telecommunications industry that ATM would eventually enable consolidation. Even before this, in the early 1980s, AT&T devoted a considerable amount of study to an internally developed technology called *wideband packet* (a form of high-speed frame relay), in which potentially large operational savings from network consolidation were identified. The reason these earlier visions did not materialize is that faith in the operations savings studies was not strong enough to support the massive investment costs of an infrastructure change-out. What may be different about IP is that the very high growth rate of IP-based services may reduce the need for leaps of faith—a large IP-based network will come into being in any case, and it can then be used as the basis for integration.

4. *Depreciation and amortization* at last gets down to the tangible things that make up the network—the costs of hardware for switching and transmission. At 8.9 percent, it is the smallest of the operating expense categories, but 8.9 percent is certainly not a negligible portion of total expense. There are several ways in which the integration of the Internet and telecommunications may save on hardware costs:

- Savings from overall network consolidation
- Voice compression
- More favorable switch port costs

Network consolidation savings are the hardware equivalent of the potential operations savings for the converged networks described previously. To a great extent, these derive from the principle that larger networks are more efficient. When all traffic types are put on one switched network, instead of being split among multiple separate networks, the hardware elements of the network are, in general, utilized more efficiently. The exact magnitude of these savings will vary greatly from carrier to carrier, depending on their overall size and the number and kind of legacy networks they are supporting. The added cost of gateway equipment to convert all traffic to IP must also be taken into account when calculating net savings.

The magnitude of hardware savings from network consolidation (or whether there are, in fact, savings at all) also depends on some effects that are quite familiar to students of engineering economics but that may not be obvious to more casual observers. One is the principle of *sunk cost*. If you have already made the capital investment in an older network technology, simply changing it out for a newer, more efficient technology may well result in an *increase* in overall capital cost, because the original expenditure is sunk and can't be made to go away. This concept underlines the crucial importance of operational cost reductions with new technology, because if these cost reductions are large enough, they can pay for any near-term increase in hardware capital costs. Sometimes there is another way out of the dilemma if the older equipment can be resold or reused to displace other investments, or if it is simply near the end of its book life and tax life.

Voice compression is possible with circuit-switched networks and has been done selectively (for example, on expensive intercontinental trunks) for many years. Today, it is widely applied in circuit-switched wireless networks. However, voice compression has not been broadly used in wireline circuit-switched public voice networks. Carriers have shown reluctance to invest in compression since it affects a relatively small part of the overall cost picture; and, on the downside, they are concerned about the impact on voice quality. Voice on IP may be an enabler for voice compression in the PSTN, since VoIP systems typically come with a choice of codecs, some of which offer compression at various levels.

Relatively conservative approaches with minimum impact on voice quality include the 2× compression available with *adaptive differential pulse code modulation* (G.726) and the additional 2× or so (for a combined 4× effect) from silence suppression. If one is willing to tolerate some degradation effects, standards are available for coders with bit rates of 8 kbps or even less (compared with uncompressed digital telephony at 64 kbps). The actual savings, compared with circuit-switched voice, are reduced somewhat due to protocol overhead; the exact values depend on which options are chosen for things like header compression and carrying IP packets over ATM, and unfortunate choices of these parameters can actually result in negative savings (i.e., *increased* costs). Within the portion of the network where compression is enabled, savings can be realized both in the transmission systems that interconnect switches and in the costs of switch ports themselves.

However, there are additional complications in the public network environment because of its multicarrier nature. Due to the regulatory situation in the United States, most U.S. long-distance calls cross two network boundaries. With deregulation, this kind of scenario is becoming increasingly common in other countries. Also, calls between countries usually cross at least one network boundary. At the present time, carriers planning for packet-based compressed voice generally assume that voice will be decompressed and returned to circuit format at the network boundary. This extra step, of course, adds to cost. It also creates the danger of *tandem encoding*, in which the same traffic is compressed more than once, possibly leading to a significant quality degradation and an increased delay of the voice signal. Eventually, we may see agreements between carriers to hand off voice in compressed form, which will increase the opportunities for savings and avoid the tandem encoding problem. This handoff scenario will require stable, detailed standards, not only for voice compression itself, but also for signaling and associated network management functions. It will also require good, mutually advantageous business relationships between the involved carriers. These differing scenarios for voice compression are shown in Figures 12.3 through 12.5.

Switch port costs are an interesting category. Apart from compression effects, one can try to compare the costs of terminations on a circuit switch and a packet switch that are doing something equivalent, such as handling the same number of bits per second. The packet switch usually wins, and prospects are for the gap to widen, since circuit switching is the older technology and thus is further along on its experience curve. From a fundamental point of view, it is not quite clear why this should be so. Why should the hardware be so sensitive to whether it is handling, at the same bit rate, the fixed-length groups of bits typically seen in the internals of a time-division circuit switch, the fixed-length groups of bits plus small headers of ATM switches, or the variable-length groups of bits (packets with headers) of an IP router? In part, the answer may simply be that the enterprise market where packet switching has grown up involves more intense price competition than the market for public carrier equipment, so the vendors have been forced to build it cheaper.

The most significant switch hardware cost difference, however, appears to stem from the fact that higher port speeds are actually available on packet switches than on traditional telephony circuit switches. This reduces the cost

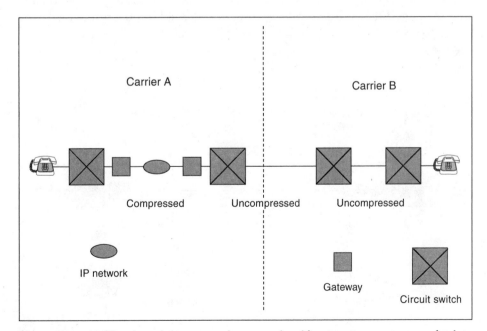

Figure 12.3 Multicarrier voice compression scenario with return to uncompressed voice at network boundary.

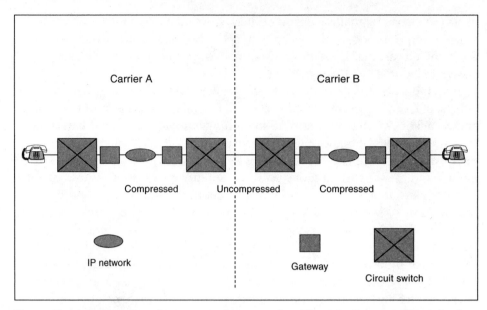

Figure 12.4   Multicarrier voice compression scenario with return to uncompressed voice at boundary and tandem encoding.

per bit per second at the switch interface, and also reduces the need for inter-mediate multiplexing equipment to get up to the speed of high-capacity opti-cal transmission systems.

Another aspect of switching cost is software cost. The costs of software are either recovered through separate charges or included in port prices by

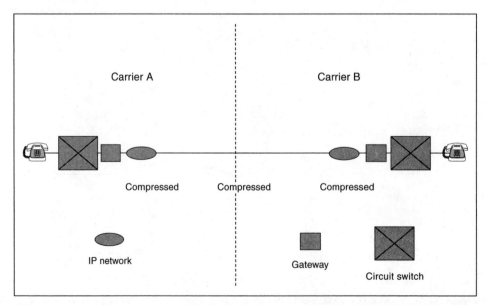

Figure 12.5   Multicarrier voice compression scenario with intercarrier VoIP interface.

switch manufacturers. Circuit switches for public voice networks typically come bundled with a large set of voice feature software. The cost of creating this software is related not only to the functionality of the features themselves, but also to the high standards for quality and ease of use that prevail in the public network industry. Thus, considerable effort is expended not only in testing and integrating features so that they do not have undesirable interactions with each other but function in precisely the same way from one release of the product to another. More than one observer has noted that expectations are very different in the desktop computing industry. This can be amusing to think about, but it really does point to a kind of cultural divide between the traditional telecommunications and information technology industries, which, in turn, is manifested in things like the relative cost of switch software.

So, what is the bottom line? Moving from qualitative discussion to actual dollar figures requires engineering and costing out some specific network configurations. W. R. Byrne of Lucent Technologies Bell Labs kindly shared some data with the authors from a recent study comparing circuit-switched with packet-switched infrastructures for new and incumbent U.S. interexchange carriers. (The packet technology in the study was actually ATM, but to the first order we can expect similar results for IP.) Results were that a new entrant using packet technology experienced a 15 percent reduction in depreciation and operations costs (about a 3 percent reduction in total costs, including access charges and SG&A) compared with an incumbent carrier using circuit switching. Savings for the packet-based new entrant came primarily from the following:

- Use of fewer but larger switches, resulting in operations support savings

- Additional operations savings from replacement of trunk group administration with link-based bandwidth management

- Small transport savings due to better packing of voice and data on one network, and higher interface speeds

To summarize this survey of interexchange carrier costs and their implications for the future of the integration of the Internet and telecommunications: The best prospects for actual cost savings appear to be in the area of operations costs for consolidated networks, and if IP-based services continue on their meteoric trajectory, this may provide the carriers with a path to get there. However, there will be many uncertainties and challenges along the road.

By the way, the preceding discussion was based mostly on the situation of U.S. interexchange carriers, including figures from AT&T, which is certainly a prototypical U.S. interexchange carrier. What about other carriers? To get some feeling for the cost components seen by different types of carriers, let's zero in on annual capital-related spending as a measure of the proportion of costs related to network hardware (as opposed to other items such as sales).

Continuing to rely on financial statements from annual reports, some interesting figures are shown in Table 12.2.

Regarding Table 12.2, note first of all that we have now switched to percent of revenue, as opposed to percent of operating cost, since revenue appears to be reported on a more uniform basis across the spectrum of companies listed here. Second, while most of the U.S. companies plus Deutsche Telekom publish a figure for depreciation and amortization, others offer different indexes of capital-related spending, as described in the table notes. Finally, the authors are aware that accounting standards differ around the world, but we are very definitely not experts on that subject.

With all of this information, it seems possible to make some sense out of the percentages displayed in Table 12.2 and to relate them to the differing network businesses run by these companies. As expected, the AT&T of 1997, as an almost pure U.S. interexchange carrier, has the lowest ratio of capital cost to revenue, reflecting the relative dominance of other costs, such as sales and advertising, in that sector. The U.S. RBOCs (Bell Atlantic, SBC, US West) and European ex-monopoly national operators (BT, Deutsche Telekom, France Telecom) show a markedly higher ratio of capital spending to revenue, on the order of 20 percent. This higher rate reflects the fact that these networks own more hardware per

Table 12.2   Depreciation (or Other Measure of Capital Spending) as Percent of Revenue

COMPANY (YEAR)	PERCENT
AT&T (1997)	7.7
Bell Atlantic (1998)	18.6
BT (1998)	19.3[a]
Deutsche Telekom (1998)	25.3
France Telecom (1998)	18.9[b]
MCI WorldCom (1997)[c]	12.6
PSInet (1998)	24.4
SBC (1998)	18.0
Sprint (wireline, 1998)	22.7[d]
US West (1998)	22.4[e]

Source: Derived from company annual reports.

[a]Purchase of tangible fixed assets.
[b]Amortissements des immobilisations corporelles et incorporelles.
[c]Pro forma—as if MCI and WorldCom had already merged in 1997.
[d]Net cash used by investing activities.
[e]Cash used for investing activities.

customer endpoint, notably the local loop itself and the associated local (class 5) switch termination. To some degree, the figure may also reflect lower sales and advertising costs in these markets, which, while they are no longer legal monopolies, do not yet have the full-blown competitive dynamics of the U.S. interexchange carrier industry. Deutsche Telekom and US West come out at the high end, which may reflect continuing infrastructure building in eastern Germany in the former case and the rural sparseness of the mountain West in the latter. The MCI WorldCom figures, which by an accountant's magic make it appear that these two companies had already merged in 1997, represent an intermediate case, with the former MCI being a nearly pure interexchange carrier, while WorldCom included some significant *competitive local exchange carrier* (CLEC) assets. Sprint, a company with both a long-distance and a local side, winds up looking more like a local carrier on this scale.

PSInet is a very interesting case. This company is a large, facilities-based ISP. Since it is engaged in an intensive program of building and acquiring facilities, depreciation and amortization come out at the high end—at 24.4 percent of revenue, the figure is higher than for any of the telephone-type companies except Deutsche Telekom. PSInet's annual report notes that this figure is expected to go even higher as it reduces its dependence on leased facilities from other carriers and builds/acquires more of its own.

At first glance, it would appear that opportunities for savings through the application of new network technology would be even greater in the case of the RBOCs and ex–national monopolies than in the U.S. interexchange carrier case that we examined in some detail, simply because network hardware costs are relatively greater. However, keep in mind that the increased network costs are almost entirely on the access side; so, in actuality, there is relatively less opportunity to save by consolidating traffic from different types of customers on a converged core network—the core network is a small thing compared with all the last-mile hardware going out to homes and businesses. (This may stretch the point a bit in the European national carrier case, but not for the RBOCs, which, in spite of the Telecom Act of 1995, still have very small long distance businesses.)

For these access-intensive businesses, access consolidation, rather than central network consolidation, may present the largest opportunities. Transmission technology solutions, such as running high-speed fiber access to business locations and utilizing DSL solutions to replace multiple phone lines for consumers, will achieve the first-order savings in the access area. The integration of the Internet and telecommunications may play an enabling role in access consolidation, however, by providing a common format for the carriage of multiple media on these high-speed access technologies.

So, returning to the question at hand: Is the technology driving the integration of the Internet and telecommunications relevant to the public carrier industry? All public carriers of any size are themselves sorting through the issues we have discussed. Currently, most are sufficiently convinced of the technology's potential relevance to conduct experiments or trials, and to include it in their target architectures and migration plans. In addition, a small number of new carriers have placed much bigger bets by making Internet-based infrastructures their major market differentiator.

Enterprise Viewpoint

Turning from the carrier world to the world of the enterprise, a number of things are markedly different. To see why, let's try thinking about costs in terms of the categories used in the discussion of interexchange carriers.

Access and other interconnection.   This is a set of costs peculiar to the regulatory situation of IECs and does not apply to enterprise networks in this form at all.

Selling, general, and administrative.   In contrast to the huge sums spent by IECs on sales and marketing, most managers of enterprise networks should presumably be able to get away with modest internal information campaigns to make users aware of the network and its capabilities.

Network and other communication services.   Remember that this is where the operations costs are. These will certainly be a big factor in any decision to adopt a strategy for integrating the Internet and telecommunications in the enterprise, just as they are for the IECs. For enterprises, another recurring expense associated with the network is the cost of services purchased from carriers—let's think of these costs as residing in this category.

Depreciation and amortization.   Depending on the amount of network equipment they own outright, enterprises may have substantial hardware-related costs in this category. In many cases, they will own things like PBXs, routers, LAN switches, inside wiring, and telephones.

So, to summarize, in terms of the cost categories, compared with carriers, enterprises will typically see a much higher percentage of their costs in the categories actually related to building and operating the network, as opposed to persuading users to use it or dealing with regulatory arcana such as carrier-to-carrier access charges.

These cost differences begin to hint at the really fundamental advantage that enterprises have over carriers in seeking to integrate the Internet and telecommunications and the reason why, in many instances, they will be earlier to adopt. The fact is that enterprises overall will typically have more detailed knowledge of and better control over demand, usage patterns, traffic levels, QoS requirements, and network utilization. Okay, we hear the rueful laughter from network managers convinced that they are at the mercy of an arbitrary and capricious user population. Just consider, by contrast, the world of the large public carriers. First, they must run elaborate television advertising campaigns and mount costly promotions to attract consumers to their services, and at the same time, they must support sophisticated marketing efforts to woo business customers. Then they must live in terror that some falloff in quality or lapse in network reliability will cause mass desertion to the equally heavily advertised services and promotions of one or more rivals. Finally, to engineer their networks with the proper amount of equipment to carry the traffic load at the expected high quality of service, they must rely entirely on statistical estimation methods—and face the consequences when the tried-and-true ones are thrown off by something like the sudden popularity of hour-long Web browsing sessions.

So, if you as an enterprise network manager do have, relatively speaking, a solid and detailed knowledge of your firm's network demand, usage patterns, traffic levels, QoS requirements, and network utilization, you can apply this to understand in which portions of the network the integration of the Internet and telecommunications may have immediate, quantifiable payoffs. If the transcontinental links in the IP intranet are underutilized, fill them up with VoIP. If the firm is opening a new office in Orlando, study the possible life cycle cost advantages of an IP PBX and a single wire to the desktop for voice and data. Think twice about routing the chairperson's phone calls through a voice-on-packet compression box, but think hard about applying the same technology to routine international phone traffic.

Quite possibly, you will find that the conclusion stated in this chapter's title, "The Technology Is Relevant," will apply right now to at least some part of the enterprise network for which you are responsible.

Private Networks and Carrier Services

So far, we have been discussing the economics of carriers and enterprise networks as if they were independent. They are not, of course. In fact, anyone who has been managing enterprise networks for some time is well aware that tariffs and services that are available from public carriers can have a dramatic impact on the optimum architecture choices for private networks. The rapid evolution of private voice and data network architectures through the 1970s and 1980s affords some good examples.

At the beginning of this period, it was typical for a company's private voice network to be constructed of PBXs interconnected by private analog tie lines leased from carriers, and for the data network to be based on an entirely separate collection of analog leased lines that interconnected things like front-end processors and terminal cluster controllers. The next step in the evolution occurred with the availability of tariffed T1 services from the carriers. These stimulated the development of multiplexers, which could place both voice and data traffic on the same T1 line. With the ready availability of leased T1 lines and multiplexers, it became common to design enterprise networks that integrated voice and data transport on the leased lines.

The next moves were made by the carriers. They applied the new technology of the Intelligent Network to create virtual private voice network services within the public network infrastructure, and also began to raise the prices of private lines, including T1s, to a level that better reflected the operations costs of these special services. Ultimately, the economics of the virtual private network carrier services became so compelling in comparison with private lines that many companies migrated to these services for their voice needs. Initially, most of the data traffic remained on private lines, but then a new generation of carrier data services emerged, notably ones based on frame relay technology, and significant migration of enterprise data traffic to these carrier services occurred.

It will be quite interesting to see what carrier service options for enterprise networks emerge in the era of Internet-telecommunications integration. Since we have seen that the application of packet technology to the integration of voice and data provides at least some modest opportunities for cost savings to carriers, it would be logical for carriers to develop attractively priced IP-based virtual private integrated voice-data services and to offer them to enterprise customers, effectively passing on the savings. Of course, some enterprises may be in a position to realize even greater savings with a go-it-alone approach, but for others, as in the past, carrier services may provide an attractive option.

Regulation and Its Impact

Let's turn to another topic that has generated a vast amount of literature in the academic and trade press—government regulation and its impact on the feasibility and attractiveness of network convergence.

Most writers assume that in the long run there will be relatively little regulation of services such as Internet telephony. This assumption is certainly consistent with the trend of the last two decades toward greatly reduced regulation of telecommunications in general, and, barring some unpredictable political sea change, it will almost certainly be the case. In the nearer term, however, regulation is definitely having an impact, especially on the carrier side. Some regulation benefits the integration of the Internet and telecommunications and some makes it more difficult; some regulatory effects are deliberate and others are inadvertent, caused by the collision of new technology with regulations designed with older technology in mind. Some of the strangest regulatory effects are seen in the field of international communications, where they are driven by the different rates at which deregulation is proceeding in different countries.

At one extreme end of the spectrum, quite a few countries have actually made Internet telephony illegal. This is particularly true for so-called class 1 (phone-to-phone) and class 2 (computer-to-phone) Internet telephony, which competes directly with embedded telephony providers. In some countries, the embedded telephony provider is still a government owned and operated entity that has a legal monopoly on telephone service. It is inherently difficult for a government to enforce a prohibition against class 3 (computer-to-computer) Internet telephony, because unless you look inside the packet payloads, it looks like a data application. Making it illegal to operate gateways to support class 1 or class 2 service is a little easier. Singapore, whose embedded operator will have a legal monopoly through the year 2000, takes the pragmatic approach of stating that a user who wants to engage in Internet telephony from a standard telephone set may do so only by using a gateway that is located at that user's premises.

In the United States and Europe, regulators have appeared reluctant to write too many new regulations that deal explicitly with Internet telephony. The European Commission has studied the matter and has decided that, for the time being, no action is needed because Internet telephony service is not comparable with the ubiquitous, high-quality voice service that is available over the public telephone networks of Europe.

The U.S. Federal Communications Commission (FCC) has also devoted extensive study to Internet telephony but has balked at several opportunities to impose regulation, giving the overall impression that it wishes to encourage this new form of telecommunications for its possible competitive benefits. This has left most providers of Internet telephony in the United States in the beneficial status of being information service providers that do not need to pay carrier access charges to the LECs or contribute to universal service funds. Furthermore, their rates are not regulated by the federal or state governments. So, overall, this situation is quite favorable to the Internet telephony providers, and it is not expected to change at least until, through improvements in the quality of service and ownership of their own transmission facilities, they might begin to resemble existing telephony providers so much that legal logic would require them to be subject to the same rules.

One more aspect of the U.S. regulatory environment that benefits Internet service providers in general is worth mentioning, because it may also help their entry into the field of Internet telephony. This is the predominance in the United States of flat-rate local calling. In most areas of the United States, it is possible for consumers to get a local calling tariff at a flat rate per month, independent of the actual minutes of use. This practice started long ago, when primitive electromechanical switching systems without central control units were not able to do much in the way of usage recording. When electronic switching systems were introduced starting in the 1960s, the telephone companies attempted to move to a local measured-service system, but met great resistance from consumers and public utility commissions, and largely backed off.

The flat-rate system has obvious benefits for consumers who want to dial up to an Internet service provider and then engage in Web browsing. It also helps

Internet telephony by, first, creating a larger market base of ISP subscribers and, second, limiting the amount of telephone network charges incurred to enter the Internet. Flat-rate local calling is less available outside of the United States, and this has somewhat hampered the growth of consumer Internet access in other parts of the world.

One can view the availability of the flat-rate system to ISPs and their customers as somewhat unfair, since Internet users typically exceed by a large amount the average monthly usage on which the tariff is based, and thus have the cost of their long-holding-time calls subsidized by other users. When Internet usage by consumers first took off, some telephone companies used this argument along with the switch and network congestion caused by unexpectedly long holding times in petitioning to regulators that something must be done about the way ISP services are regulated. However, the telephone companies are increasingly using technology to identify calls to ISPs and route them off to data networking equipment, which is less sensitive to call holding time.

It is probably in international communications that Internet telephony has benefited most from the existing regulatory regime—one that came into being long before this technology existed. The subject of how international telephony prices are determined based on bilateral negotiation of accounting rates is a fascinating and rather complex one. The bottom line is that there are many pairs of countries for which the price of a telephone call as charged to the user appears to be far above the marginal cost of providing the call.

The international accounting rate system would appear to be unsustainable in the long run, given the probable future of competitive, privatized international networks. In the meantime, the system has been under attack from multiple directions. On the regulatory front, the U.S. FCC has initiated various unilateral actions designed to bring prices more into line with costs. In the business realm, the artificial prices create opportunities for arbitrage. One way of exploiting this, for example, is to find situations where there are very high calling rates between country A and country B, but much more reasonable rates between both A and C and B and C. A business can then be created of routing calls from A to B via C. There are also many situations where it costs much more to call from A to B than to call in the opposite direction (B to A). These cost differences have given rise to the well-known call-back industry.

A different approach to getting around (or exploiting) the accounting rate system is technological—finding some way of routing international phone calls without using the international public network. This is where Internet telephony comes into the picture. If a call can be sent over the Internet from a computer in country A to a computer in country B, or, by using gateways, from the domestic phone network in A, then over the Internet, then to the domestic network in B, the international phone network and its potentially high prices can be avoided entirely.

While this Internet bypass of the international phone network appears to be a golden opportunity for Internet telephony, at least until the international accounting rate system finally collapses, there are several things to keep in mind. Perhaps the most important is that there are other, simpler technological end runs that can be made around the international public network. The most straightforward is to lease an international private line and use it to route calls that bypass the international switched network. The line can connect private networks within the two countries, and thus be used by a business for its internal calls; or the line can be connected to the domestic network on one or both sides and used to provide a cut-rate international calling service to subscribers. This is called *international resale*, and its use predates Internet telephony.

International resale of private lines actually has a number of advantages over Internet telephony. It can be accomplished with tried-and-true voice equipment, without the need for packet-circuit gateways. Voice quality can readily be made equivalent to that of the international public telephone network. On the other hand, there are a few advantages on the Internet telephony side. As discussed earlier, voice compression, while possible in circuit-switched networks, may be more readily available with packet voice, and, given the inherent high costs of international calling, more users may be willing to make a trade-off for lower cost, even if it involves some degradation of quality. Also, it is probably true that it is harder to regulate the use of the Internet for bypass of the international public network. This point is significant because the resale of international private lines for voice is actually only legal among a relatively small number of technologically advanced countries with progressive regulatory regimes.

So, we have seen that in the short run, regulation cuts both ways—sometimes favoring the integration of the Internet and telecommunications and sometimes making this integration more difficult to achieve without running afoul of the law. In the long run, the consensus is that all types of networks will compete on their technical and economic merits, and that regulators will gracefully claim victory for the benefits that this competition will bring to users.

Multimedia: Voice as One Application among Many

In the preceding sections, we have posited that there are at least some sets of circumstances in which the technology used to integrate the Internet and telecommunications is relevant in its simplest form—that of Internet telephony, in which the Internet plus appropriate hardware and software mimics the functions of public or private circuit-switched networks in carrying point-to-point voice calls.

A much more powerful case for the relevance of the technology can be made for multimedia applications. With multimedia, voice is just one form of communication among several that must be handled at once. Consider, for example, the case of multimedia conferencing, described in detail in Chapter 9. When one service must deal not only with voice, but also with video, text, graphics, and still pictures, a flexible, common transport medium is advantageous. As we also mentioned, the control of complex communications scenarios such as multimedia conferences is also greatly aided by the application of Internet technology, such as the Web and browser interfaces.

Also, we have been speaking about voice as a single application with, implicitly, one set of requirements. This is a habit carried over from traditional telephony, which defined voice as a 4-kHz signal and then built a massive worldwide network optimized for the transport of that signal. However, with the flexibility afforded by packet-based voice transport, different kinds of voice and audio applications can be accommodated by changing bit rates, coders, and quality options. Examples would be high-quality voice for conference or lecture applications and CD-quality audio for music. Another assumption of traditional telephony that need not hold in the multimedia environment is that voice (or audio) must be transported as a real-time signal. With packet voice/audio, files could be sent using low bandwidth at less-than-real-time rates for later listening, or large stored voice files could be sent between voice-mail systems using high bandwidth at greater-than-real-time rates.

In considering these kinds of scenarios, for perspective, one must keep in mind that there is a kind of inverse relation between the size and complexity of the type of multimedia communications and how often it occurs. For example, in today's telephone networks, by far the greatest number of minutes of use are generated by telephone calls between exactly two people; three-way calls generate considerably fewer minutes; calls involving many endpoints and the exchange of fax and images in addition to voice generate still fewer total minutes; and so on. By making multimedia communication more convenient and more cost effective, the integration of the Internet and telecommunications has the potential to increase its use, but an inverse relationship of this kind will, most likely, still apply.

A case that is less complex than a full-blown multimedia, multipoint conference, but that may be very important because of its frequency of occurrence, is the kind of communication that often takes place today from the business desktop, in which a phone conversation is augmented by reference to simultaneously viewed Web pages, graphics files, or documents. This scenario is amenable to improvement by applying the integration of the Internet and telecommunications in any of its several forms: either by carrying all of the communication over an IP network or, in the fashion of click-to-dial and Web-based conference calling, by using the Internet and a browser interface to control the voice portion of the communication, which may still be carried over the circuit-switched telecommunications network.

Specialized Applications and Their Requirements

This section is similar to the preceding one in that it examines the relevance of the integration of the Internet and telecommunications from an application point of view. However, in a sense, it looks at the opposite case: Rather than considering multimedia applications in which multiple media are active at the same time and there may be distinct advantages at the application level from the carriage of all media types over one network, here we consider specialized applications—monomedia ones, if you will.

Of course, this is a setup. If you want to really annoy the advocate of an integrating technology (let's pick as an example ATM, which is somewhat neutral because it is not directly the subject of this book), all you need to do is describe a particular application in detail (pick one—voice telephony will do, or high-definition television, and so on) and go on to show how much more economically and with what greater quality of service it can be handled by a specialized network, perhaps one that is already in existence. The advocate of the integrating technology will reply, quite correctly, that if only *all* of the applications could be carried on the new, integrated network, then abundant benefits of economies of scale and operational cost consolidation would result. How do you get to that state, though, if each application viewed by itself would not experience compelling benefits from rolling over to the integrating technology?

This is a quite fundamental dilemma in the field of communications network architecture, and it is not easily solved. For the particular case of integration of the Internet and telecommunications, there are several things you could say in answer to it. As we discussed in the earlier sections on economics, it may be that the spectacular growth of IP-based applications, if it continues for some time, will make the jump to an operationally less costly integrated network easier. This would be so because, with IP traffic dominant, most of the investment that carriers would be making in an integrated, IP-based network would be needed anyway simply to keep up with the demand for IP-based services.

Also, recall that the integration of the Internet and telecommunications as we have defined it includes scenarios in which, for instance, voice can continue to ride on a circuit-switched network while integration is achieved at the control level. That may be a helpful case to cater to the needs of specialized voice (or other) applications that require the characteristics of a real circuit-switched network.

However, in the absence of some government mandate that all applications shall ride on one national information infrastructure, there is simply nothing to stop entrepreneurs from offering specialized networks designed to optimally support the needs of specific applications, whether these are based on an old technology like circuit switching or on some technology that has not yet been invented. The degree to which this happens will depend on the potential market size for such applications, the willingness of users to pay for optimized performance, and the ingenuity of inventors.

Summary and Conclusions

Here, the authors would first like to acknowledge that this chapter was written at the strict insistence of our editors, who, though strong advocates for the Internet themselves, also understand its technical underpinnings in an extremely detailed way, and so have a strong aversion to the kind of ill-informed hype that often passes for expert prophecy in the literature of network convergence. So we were put to the task of justifying, in a concluding chapter, the *relevance* of technologies used to integrate the Internet and telecommunications—about which we are admitted enthusiasts. We hope that we have succeeded in a balanced and restrained way in convincing you that the technology is relevant to at least a subset of the problems faced by those who have to build and operate networks on behalf of end users.

A summary of the main points would be as follows:

- The biggest long-term payoff of the integration of the Internet and telecommunications for carriers is likely to be operations savings from network consolidation. In the nearer term, most operators will feel their way along with experiments and trials, while some start-ups will deploy converged networks from day one as a market differentiator.

- Enterprises are generally in a better position to assess and realize near-term benefits from the integration of the Internet and telecommunications in selected portions of their operations due to their different cost structure and generally more controlled environment.

- The existing regulatory environment cuts both ways—sometimes it makes the integration of the Internet and telecommunications attractive where it otherwise would not be, and sometimes it makes this integration harder to achieve. In the long term, regulation will be much less of a factor.

- Some applications—multimedia, for example—are a natural fit for the integration of the Internet and telecommunications. There will always be specialized applications that may be better served by specialized networks.

A few final words: The business environment of the communications industry is changing with a rapidity that has never been experienced before. The technical landscape is also characterized by change, much of it coming about as the technical experts on telecommunications and data networking encounter each other with increasing frequency and as each community comes to better appreciate, learn about, and draw upon the vast fund of know-how accumulated by the other over decades of largely separate development. It's a pretty wild ride for those of us whose job it is to navigate the resulting crosscurrents; and it's a time of new opportunities for everyone who uses telecommunications and the Internet. Let's all make the most of it!

Bibliography

Books

Bellamy, J. 2000. *Digital Telephony*, 3d ed. New York: John Wiley & Sons.

Black, U. 1997. *Residential Broadband Networks—xDSL, HFC, and Fixed Wireless Access.* Upper Saddle River, NJ: Prentice Hall.

Chen, W. 1998. *DSL: Simulation Techniques and Standards Development for Digital Subscriber Line Systems.* New York: Macmillan.

Cheswick, W. R., and S. M. Bellovin. 1998. *Firewalls and Internet Security: Repelling the Wily Hacker.* New York: Addison-Wesley.

Davis, R. H. 1999. *ATM for Public Networks,* New York: McGraw-Hill.

Faynberg, I., L. R. Gabuzda, M. P. Kaplan, and N. J. Shah. 1997. *The Intelligent Network Standards: Their Application to Services.* New York: McGraw-Hill.

Ferguson, P., and G. Huston. 1998. *Quality of Service: Delivering QoS on the Internet and in Corporate Networks.* New York: John Wiley & Sons.

Ferguson, P., and G. Huston. 2000. *Quality of Service,* 2d ed. New York: John Wiley & Sons.

Grinberg, A. 1995. *Computer Telecom Integration: The SCAI Solution.* New York: McGraw-Hill.

Held, G. 2000. *Next-Generation Modems.* New York: John Wiley & Sons.

Huitema, C. 1995. *Routing in the Internet.* Upper Saddle River, NJ: Prentice Hall.

Huston, G. 1999. *ISP Survival Guide: Strategies for Running a Competitive ISP.* New York: John Wiley & Sons.

ITU. 1999. *Yearbook of Statistics 1999, Chronological Time Series 1988–1997.* International Telecommunications Union. Telecommunication Indicators Series.

Geneva: Telecommunication Development Bureau. www.itu.int/ti/publications.

Kaufman, E., and A. Newman. 1999. *Implementing IPsec: Making Security Work on VPNs, Intranets, and Extranets.* New York: John Wiley & Sons.

Kleijn, W., and K. Palisal (eds.). 1995. *Speech Coding and Synthesis.* New York: Elsevier Science.

Kosiur, D. 1998. *Building and Managing Virtual Private Networks.* New York: John Wiley & Sons.

Minoli, D., and E. Minoli. 1998a. *Delivering Voice over Frame Relay and ATM.* New York: John Wiley & Sons.

Minoli, D., and E. Minoli. 1998b. *Delivering Voice over IP Networks.* New York: John Wiley & Sons.

Robertson, J. H. 1947. *The Story of the Telephone.* London: Pitman.

Rose, M. T., and K. McCloghrie. 1994. *How to Manage Your Network Using SNMP.* Englewood Cliffs, NJ: Prentice Hall.

Stallings, W. 1989. *ISDN and Broadband ISDN.* New York: Macmillan.

Standage, T. 1998. *The Victorian Internet.* New York: Walker & Company.

Starr, T., J. Cioffi, and P. Silverman. 1999. *Understanding Digital Subscriber Line Technology.* Upper Saddle River, NJ: Prentice Hall.

Stevens, W. Richard. 1994. *TCP/IP Illustrated*, vol. 1: *The Protocols.* New York: Addison-Wesley.

Tanenbaum, Andrew S. 1996. *Computer Networks*, 3d ed. Upper Saddle River, NJ: Prentice Hall.

Papers and Articles

Armitage, G. 2000. "MPLS—The Magic Behind the Myths." *IEEE Communications Magazine* 38(1)(January):124–131.

Atai, A., and J. Gordon. 1997. "Architectural Solutions to Internet Congestion Based on SS7 and Intelligent Network Capabilities." *Bellcore* (now Telcordia) *White Paper.*

Ayanoglu, E., N. Dagdeviren, G. Golden, and M. Maxo. 1998. "An Equalizer Design Technique for the PCM Modem: A New Modem for the Digital Public Switched Telephone Network." *IEEE Transactions on Communications* 46(6):763–774.

Bieszad, A., P. K. Biswas, W. Buga, M. Malek, and H. Tan. 1999. "Management of Heterogeneous Networks with Intelligent Agents." *Bell Labs Technical Journal* 4(4)(October–December):109–135.

Bradner, S. 1999. "IP Phone or Internet Phone?" *Network World* (October 4).

Calvert, K. L., S. Bhattacharjee, E. W. Segura, and J. Sterbenz. 1998. "Directions in Active Networks." *IEEE Communications Magazine* 36(10)(October):72–78.

Clark, D., S. Shenker, and L. Zhang. 1992. "Supporting Real-Time Applications in an Integrated Services Packet Network: Architecture and Mechanisms." *Proceedings of SIGCOMM '92* (August):14–26.

Codding, G. A. 1952. "The International Telecommunications Union, An Experiment in International Cooperation." Leiden: E.J. Brill.

Cox, R., and P. Kroon. 1996. "Low Bit-Rate Speech Coders for Multimedia Communication." *IEEE Communications Magazine* (December).

Demers, A., S. Keshav, and S. Shenker. 1990. "Analysis and Simulation of a Fair Queuing Algorithm." *Journal of Internetworking: Research and Experience* 1(September):3–26.

Economides, N. 1996. "The Economics of Networks." *International Journal of Industrial Organization* 14(6)(October):673–699.

Hubaux, J., C. Gbaguidi, S. Koppenhoefer, and J. Y. Le Boudec. 1998. "The Impact of the Internet on Telecommunication Architectures." *Technical Report SSC/1998/001*. Swiss Federal Institute of Technology (EPFL) (January).

Huitema, C., J. Cameron, P. Mouchtaris, and D. Smyk. 1999. "An Architecture for Residential Internet Telephony Service." *IEEE Internet Computing* 3(3)(May/June):50–56.

International Telegraph Union. 1881. *Journal Telegraphique* V(11)(November 25):225–231.

Kozik, J., W. A. Montgomery, and J. J. Stanaway. 1998. "Voice Services in Next-Generation Networks: The Evolution of the Intelligent Network and Its Role in Generating New Revenue Opportunities." *Bell Labs Technical Journal* 3(4)(October–December):124–143.

Kumar, V. P., T. V. Lakshman, and D. Stiliadis. 1998. "Beyond Best-Effort: Router Architectures for Differentiated Services of Tomorrow's Internet." *IEEE Communications Magazine* 36(5)(May):162–164.

Lakshmi-Ratan, R. A. 1999. "The Lucent Technologies Softswitch—Realizing the Promise of Convergence." *Bell Labs Technical Journal* 4(2):174–195.

Low, C. 1997. "Integrating Communication Services." *IEEE Communications Magazine* 35(6)(June):164–169.

Low, C., D. Skov, and N. Raguideau. 1996. "An Architecture for Fast Deployment of IN-based Personal Services." *Proceedings of the IEEE Intelligent Network Workshop IN'96*, Melbourne, Australia (April).

Marcus, W. S., I. Hadzic, A. J. McAuley, and J. M. Smith. 1998. "Protocol Boosters: Applying Programmability to Network Infrastructures." *IEEE Communications Magazine* 36(10)(October):79–83.

Nagle, J. 1987. "On Packet Switches with Infinite Storage." *IEEE Transactions on Communications* COM-35(April):435–438.

Pekarich, S. 1978. "UNIX Time-Sharing System: No. 4 ESS Diagnostic Environment." *The Bell System Technical Journal* 57(6)(July–August):2265–2274.

Prywes, N. 2000. "Active Networks—Components, Networks, and Intelligent Communications Applications." *Tutorial 1B Delivered to 6th International Conference on Intelligence in Networks*, Bordeaux, France (January).

Raz, D., and Y. Shavitt. 1999. "An Active Network Approach to Efficient Network Management." *Technical Report 99-25, DIMACS* (May).

Schulzrinne, H., and J. Rosenberg. 1998. "A Comparison of SIP and H.323 for Internet Telephony." *Proceedings of the 1998 Workshop on Network and Operating System Support for Digital Audio and Video (NOSSDAV '98)*, Cambridge, England (July).

Schulzrinne, H., and J. Rosenberg. 1999. "The IETF Internet Telephony Architecture and Protocols." *IEEE Network Magazine* 13(3)(May/June):18–23.

Tebbs, R. 1999. "Real-Time IP Facsimile: Protocol and Gateway Requirements." *Bell Labs Technical Journal* 4(2):128–145.

Weiss, Walter. 1998. "QoS with Differentiated Services." *Bell Labs Technical Journal* 3(4)(October–December):48–62.

Werbach, K. 1997. "Digital Tornado: The Internet and Telecommunications Policy." *FCC OPP Working Paper Series*, no. 29.

Zhang, L. 1991. "Virtual Clock: A New Traffic Control Algorithm for Packet Switching Networks." *ACM Transactions on Computer Systems* 9(2)(May): 101–124.

ITU-T Recommendations

Recommendation E.164	ITU-T. 1997. "The International Public Telecommunication Numbering Plan." *Recommendation E.164*. Geneva: International Telecommunication Union. www.itu.int/itudoc/itu-t/rec.
Recommendation F.700	ITU-T. 1996. "Framework Recommendation for Audiovisual/Multimedia Services." *Recommendation F.700*. Geneva: International Telecommunications Union. www.itu.int/itudoc/itu-t/rec.
Recommendation F.702	ITU-T. 1996. "Multimedia Conference Services." *Recommendation F.702*. Geneva: International Telecommunications Union. www.itu.int/itudoc/itu-t/rec.
Recommendation G.711	ITU-T. 1988. "Pulse Code Modulation (PCM) of Voice Frequencies." *Recommendation G.711*. Geneva: International Telecommunications Union. www.itu.int/itudoc/itu-t/rec.

Recommendation G.723.1 ITU-T. 1996. "Dual Rate Speech Coder For Multi-media Communications Transmitting at 5.3 and 6.3 kbit/s." *Recommendation G.723.1.* Geneva: International Telecommunications Union. www.itu.int/itudoc/itu-t/rec.

Recommendation G.726 ITU-T. 1990. "40, 32, 24, 16 kbit/s Adaptive Differential Pulse Code Modulation (ADPCM)." *Recommendation G.726.* Geneva: International Telecommunications Union. www.itu.int/itudoc/itu-t/rec.

Recommendation G.729 ITU-T. 1996. "Coding of Speech at 8 kbit/s Using Conjugate-Structure Algebraic-Code-Excited Linear-Prediction (CS-ACELP)." *Recommendation G.729.* Geneva: International Telecommunications Union. www.itu.int/itudoc/itu-t/rec.

Recommendation G.729A ITU-T. 1996. "Reduced Complexity 8 kbit/s CS-ACELP Speech Codec." *Recommendation G.729 Annex A.* Geneva: International Telecommunications Union. www.itu.int/itudoc/itu-t/rec.

Recommendation G.729B ITU-T. 1996. "A Silence Compression Scheme for G.729 Optimized for Terminals Conforming to Recommendation V.70." *Recommendation G.729 Annex B.* Geneva: International Telecommunications Union. www.itu.int/itudoc/itu-t/rec.

Recommendation H.225.0 ITU-T. 1998. "Call Signaling Protocols and Media Stream Packetization for Packet-Based Multimedia Communication Systems." *Recommendation H.225.0.* Geneva: International Telecommunications Union. www.itu.int/itudoc/itu-t/rec.

Recommendation H.245 ITU-T. 1998. "Control Protocol for Multimedia Communication." *Recommendation H.245.* Geneva: International Telecommunications Union. www.itu.int/itudoc/itu-t/rec.

Recommendation H.320 ITU-T. 1999. "Narrow-Band Visual Telephone Systems and Terminal Equipment." *Recommendation H.320.* Geneva: International Telecommunications Union. www.itu.int/itudoc/itu-t/rec.

Recommendation H.323 ITU-T. 1998. "Packet-Based Multimedia Communications Systems." *Recommendation H.323.* Geneva: International Telecommunications Union. www.itu.int/itudoc/itu-t/rec.

Recommendation H.324   ITU-T. 1998. "Terminal for Low Bit-Rate Multimedia Communication." *Recommendation H.324.* Geneva: International Telecommunications Union. www.itu.int/itudoc/itu-t/rec.

Recommendation I.356   ITU-T. 1996. "B-ISDN ATM Layer Cell Transfer Performance." *Recommendation I.356.* Geneva: International Telecommunications Union. www.itu.int/itudoc/itu-t/rec.

Recommendation I.610   ITU-T. 1999. "B-ISDN Operation and Maintenance Principles and Functions." *Recommendation I.610.* Geneva: International Telecommunications Union. www.itu.int/itudoc/itu-t/rec.

Recommendation Q.700   ITU-T. 1993. "Introduction to CCITT Signalling System No. 7." *Recommendation Q.700.* Geneva: International Telecommunications Union. www.itu.int/itudoc/itu-t/rec.

Recommendation Q.701   ITU-T. 1993. "Functional Description of the Message Transfer Part (MTP) of Signalling System No. 7." *Recommendation Q.701.* Geneva: International Telecommunications Union. www.itu.int/itudoc/itu-t/rec.

Recommendation Q.711   ITU-T. 1996. "Functional Description of the Signalling Connection Control Part." *Recommendation Q.711.* Geneva: International Telecommunications Union. www.itu.int/itudoc/itu-t/rec.

Recommendation Q.721   ITU-T. 1988. "Functional Description of the Signalling System No. 7 Telephone User Part (TUP)." *Recommendation Q.721.* Geneva: International Telecommunications Union. www.itu.int/itudoc/itu-t/rec.

Recommendation Q.730   ITU-T. 1997. "ISDN User Part Supplementary Services." *Recommendation Q.730.* Geneva: International Telecommunications Union. www.itu.int/itudoc/itu-t/rec.

Recommendation Q.771   ITU-T. 1997. "Functional Description of Transaction Capabilities." *Recommendation Q.771.* Geneva: International Telecommunications Union. www.itu.int/itudoc/itu-t/rec.

Recommendation Q.931   ITU-T. 1998. "ISDN User-Network Interface Layer 3 Specification for Basic Call Control." *ITU-T Recommendation Q.931.* Geneva: International Telecommunications Union. www.itu.int/itudoc/itu-t/rec.

Recommendation Q.1201 ITU-T. 1992. "Principles of Intelligent Network Architecture." *Recommendation Q.1201.* Geneva: International Telecommunications Union. www.itu.int/itudoc/itu-t/rec.

Recommendation Q.1202 ITU-T. 1997. "Intelligent Network—Service Plane Architecture." *Recommendation Q.1202.* Geneva: International Telecommunications Union. www.itu.int/itudoc/itu-t/rec.

Recommendation Q.1203 ITU-T. 1997. "Intelligent Network—Global Functional Plane Architecture." *Recommendation Q.1203.* Geneva: International Telecommunications Union. www.itu.int/itudoc/itu-t/rec.

Recommendation Q.1204 ITU-T. 1993. "Intelligent Network Distributed Functional Plane Architecture." *Recommendation Q.1204.* Geneva: International Telecommunications Union. www.itu.int/itudoc/itu-t/rec.

Recommendation Q.1205 ITU-T. 1993. "Intelligent Network Physical Plane Architecture." *Recommendation Q.1205.* Geneva: International Telecommunications Union. www.itu.int/itudoc/itu-t/rec.

Recommendation Q.1208 ITU-T. 1997. "General Aspects of the Intelligent Network Application Protocol." *Recommendation Q.1208.* Geneva: International Telecommunications Union. www.itu.int/itudoc/itu-t/rec.

Recommendation Q.1211 ITU-T. 1993. "Introduction to Intelligent Network Capability Set 1." *Recommendation Q.1211.* Geneva: International Telecommunications Union. www.itu.int/itudoc/itu-t/rec.

Recommendation Q.1213 ITU-T. 1995. "Global Functional Plane for Intelligent Network CS-1." *Recommendation Q.1213.* Geneva: International Telecommunications Union. www.itu.int/itudoc/itu-t/rec.

Recommendation Q.1214 ITU-T. 1995. "Distributed Functional Plane for Intelligent Network CS-1." *Recommendation Q.1214.* Geneva: International Telecommunications Union. www.itu.int/itudoc/itu-t/rec.

Recommendation Q.1215 ITU-T. 1995. "Physical Plane for Intelligent Network CS-1." *Recommendation Q.1215.* Geneva: International Telecommunications Union. www.itu.int/itudoc/itu-t/rec.

Recommendation Q.1218 ITU-T. 1995. "Interface Recommendation for Intelligent Network CS-1." *Recommendation*

	Q.1218. Geneva: International Telecommunications Union. www.itu.int/itudoc/itu-t/rec.
Recommendation Q.1221	ITU-T. 1997. "Introduction to Intelligent Network Capability Set 2." *Recommendation Q.1221.* Geneva: International Telecommunications Union. www.itu.int/itudoc/itu-t/rec.
Recommendation Q.1223	ITU-T. 1997. "Global Functional Plane for Intelligent Network Capability Set 2." *Recommendation Q.1223.* Geneva: International Telecommunications Union. www.itu.int/itudoc/itu-t/rec.
Recommendation Q.1224	ITU-T. 1997. "Distributed Functional Plane for Intelligent Network Capability Set 2." *Recommendation Q.1224.* Geneva: International Telecommunications Union. www.itu.int/itudoc/itu-t/rec.
Recommendation Q.1225	ITU-T. 1997. "Physical Plane for Intelligent Network Capability Set 2." *Recommendation Q.1225.* Geneva: International Telecommunications Union. www.itu.int/itudoc/itu-t/rec.
Recommendation Q.1228	ITU-T. 1997. "Interface Recommendation for Intelligent Network Capability Set 2." *Recommendation Q.1228.* Geneva: International Telecommunications Union. www.itu.int/itudoc/itu-t/rec.
Recommendation T.38	ITU-T. 1998. "Procedures for Real-Time Group 3 Facsimile Communication over IP Networks." *ITU-T Recommendation T.38.* Geneva: International Telecommunications Union. www.itu.int/itudoc/itu-t/rec.
Recommendation T.120	ITU-T. 1996. "Data Protocols For Multimedia Conferencing." *Recommendation T.120.* Geneva: International Telecommunications Union. www.itu.int/itudoc/itu-t/rec.
Recommendation T.121	ITU-T. 1996. "Generic Application Template." *Recommendation T.121.* Geneva: International Telecommunications Union. www.itu.int/itudoc/itu-t/rec.
Recommendation T.122	ITU-T. 1998. "Multipoint Communication Service—Service Definition." *Recommendation T.122.* Geneva: International Telecommunications Union. www.itu.int/itudoc/itu-t/rec.
Recommendation T.123	ITU-T. 1999. "Network Specific Data Protocol Stacks for Multimedia Conferencing." *Recommendation T.123.* Geneva: International Telecommunications Union. www.itu.int/itudoc/itu-t/rec.
Recommendation T.124	ITU-T. 1998. "Generic Conference Control." *Recom-

	mendation T.124. Geneva: International Telecommunications Union. www.itu.int/itudoc/itu-t/rec.
Recommendation T.125	ITU-T. 1998. "Multipoint Communication Service Protocol Specification." *Recommendation T.125.* Geneva: International Telecommunications Union. www.itu.int/itudoc/itu-t/rec.
Recommendation T.126	ITU-T. 1997. "Multipoint Still Image and Annotation Protocol." *Recommendation T.126.* Geneva: International Telecommunications Union. www.itu.int/itudoc/itu-t/rec.
Recommendation T.127	ITU-T. 1995. "Multipoint Binary File Transfer Protocol." *Recommendation T.127.* Geneva: International Telecommunications Union. www.itu.int/itudoc/itu-t/rec.
Recommendation T.128	ITU-T. 1998. "Multipoint Application Sharing." *Recommendation T.128.* Geneva: International Telecommunications Union. www.itu.int/itudoc/itu-t/rec.
Recommendation V.70	ITU-T. 1996. "Procedures for the Simultaneous Transmission of Data and Digitally Encoded Voice Signals over the GSTN, or over A 2-Wire Leased Point-to-Point Telephone Type Circuits." *Recommendation V.70.* Geneva: International Telecommunications Union. www.itu.int/itudoc/itu-t/rec.
Recommendation X.25	ITU-T. 1996. "Interface between Data Terminal Equipment (DTE) and Data Circuit-Terminating Equipment (DCE) for Terminals Operating in the Packet Mode and Connected to Public Data Networks by Dedicated Circuit." *Recommendation X.25.* Geneva: International Telecommunications Union. www.itu.int/itudoc/itu-t/rec.
Recommendation X.219	ITU-T. 1988. "Remote Operations: Model, Notation and Service Definition." *Recommendation X.219.* Geneva: International Telecommunications Union. www.itu.int/itudoc/itu-t/rec.
Recommendation X.224	ITU-T. 1995. "Information Technology—Open Systems Interconnection—Protocol for Providing the Connection-Mode Transport Service." *Recommendation X.224.* Geneva: International Telecommunications Union. www.itu.int/itudoc/itu-t/rec.
Recommendation X.500	ITU-T. 1997. "Information Technology—Open Systems Interconnection—The Directory: Overview of Concepts, Models and Services."

Recommendation X.500. ISO/IEC 9594-1:1997. Geneva: International Telecommunications Union. www.itu.int/itudoc/itu-t/rec.

Recommendation X.519   ITU-T. 1997. "Information Technology—Open Systems Interconnection—The Directory: Protocol Specifications." *Recommendation X.519.* ISO/IEC 9594-5:1995. Geneva: International Telecommunications Union. www.itu.int/itudoc/itu-t/rec.

Recommendation X.680   ITU-T. 1997. "Information Technology—Abstract Syntax Notation One (ASN.1): Specification of Basic Notation." *Recommendation X.680.* ISO/IEC 8824-1:1997. Geneva: International Telecommunications Union. www.itu.int/itudoc/itu-t/rec.

Recommendation X.690   ITU-T. 1997. "Specification of ASN.1 Encoding Rules: Basic, Canonical, and Distinguished Encoding Rules." *Recommendation X.690.* Geneva: International Telecommunications Union. www.itu.int/itudoc/itu-t/rec.

Requests for Comments (RFCs)

RFC 821   Postel, J. 1982. "Simple Mail Transfer Protocol." *RFC 821* (August). Standards Track: Internet Standard 0010.

RFC 822   Crocker, D. 1982. "Standard for the Format of ARPA Internet Text Messages." *RFC 822* (August). Standards Track: Internet Standard 0011.

RFC 1006   Rose, M., and D. Cass. 1987. "ISO Transport Service on Top of the TCP: Version 3." *RFC 1006* (May). Standards Track: Internet Standard 0035.

RFC 1035   Mockapetris, P. V. 1987. "Domain Names: Implementation and Specification." *RFC 1035* (November). Standards Track: Internet Standard 0013.

RFC 1055   Romkey, J. 1988. "A Nonstandard for Transmission of IP Datagrams over Serial Lines: SLIP." *RFC 1055* (June). Standards Track: Internet Standard 0047.

RFC 1109   Cerf, V. 1989. "Report of the Second Ad Hoc Network Management Review Group." *RFC 1109* (August).

RFC 1144   Jacobson, V. 1990. "Compressing TCP/IP Headers for Low-Speed Serial Links." *RFC 1144* (February). Standards Track: Proposed Standard.

RFC 1155   Rose, M. T., and K. McCloghrie. 1990. "Structure and Identification of Management Information for TCP/IP-Based Internets." *RFC 1155* (May). Standards Track: Internet Standard 0016.

RFC 1157   Case, J., M. Fedor, M. Schoffstall, and J. Davin. 1990. "A Simple Network Management Protocol (SNMP)." *RFC 1157* (May). Standards Track: Internet Standard 0015.

RFC 1212   Rose, M. T., and K. McCloghrie. 1991. "Concise MIB Definitions." *RFC 1212* (March). Standards Track: Internet Standard 0016.

RFC 1321   Rivest, R. 1992. "The MD5 Message-Digest Algorithm." *RFC 1321* (April). Informational.

RFC 1332   McGregor, G. 1992. "The PPP Internet Protocol Control Protocol (IPCP)." *RFC 1332* (May). Standards Track: Proposed Standard.

RFC 1418   Rose, M. 1993. "SNMP over OSI." *RFC 1418* (March). Standards Track: Proposed Standard.

RFC 1570   Simpson, W. 1994. "PPP LCP Extensions." *RFC 1570* (January). Standards Track: Proposed Standard.

RFC 1618   Simpson, W. 1994. "PPP over ISDN." *RFC 1618* (May). Standards Track: Proposed Standard.

RFC 1633   Braden, R., D. Clark, and S. Shenker. 1994. "Integrated Services in the Internet Architecture: An Overview." *RFC 1633* (June). Informational.

RFC 1661   Simpson, W. (ed.). 1994. "The Point-to-Point Protocol (PPP)." *RFC 1661* (July). Standards Track: Internet Standard 0051.

RFC 1771   Rekhter, Y., and T. Li. 1995. "A Border Gateway Protocol 4 (BGP-4)." *RFC 1771* (March). Standards Track: Draft Standard.

RFC 1772   Rekhter, Y., and P. Gross. 1995. "Application of the Border Gateway Protocol in the Internet." *RFC 1772* (March). Standards Track: Draft Standard.

RFC 1773   Traina, P. 1995. "Experience with the BGP-4 Protocol." *RFC 1773* (March). Informational.

RFC 1774   Traina, P. (ed.). 1995. "BGP-4 Protocol Analysis." *RFC 1774* (March). Informational.

RFC 1830   Vaudreuil, G. 1995. "SMTP Service Extensions for Transmission of Large and Binary MIME Messages." *RFC 1830* (August). Experimental.

RFC 1869   Klensin, J., N. Freed, M. Rose, E. Stefferud, and D. Crocker. 1995. "SMTP Service Extensions." *RFC 1869* (November). Standards Track: Internet Standard 0010.

RFC 1870   Klensin, J., N. Freed, and K. Moore. 1995. "SMTP Service Extension for Message Size Declaration" *RFC 1870* (November). Standards Track: Internet Standard 0010.

RFC 1889   Schulzrinne, H., S. Casner, R. Frederick, and V. Jacobson. 1996. "RTP: A Transport Protocol for Real-Time Applications." *RFC 1889* (January). Standards Track: Proposed Standard.

RFC 1890   Audio-Video Transport Working Group, and H. Schulzrinne. 1996. "RTP Profile for Audio and Video Conferences with Minimal Control." *RFC 1890* (January). Standards Track: Proposed Standard.

RFC 1891   Moore, K. 1996. "SMTP Service Extension for Delivery Status Notifications." *RFC 1891* (January). Standards Track: Proposed Standard.

RFC 1894   Moore, K., and G. Vaudreuil. 1996. "An Extensible Message Format for Delivery Status Notifications." *RFC 1894* (January). Standards Track: Proposed Standard.

RFC 1902   Case, J., K. McCloghrie, M. Rose, and S. Waldbusser. 1996. "Structure of Management Information for Version 2 of the Simple Network Management Protocol (SNMPv2)." *RFC 1902* (April). Standards Track: Draft Standard.

RFC 1905   Case, J., K. McCloghrie, M. Rose, and S. Waldbusser. 1996. "Protocol Operations for Version 2 of the Simple Network Management Protocol (SNMPv2)." *RFC 1905* (January). Standards Track: Draft Standard.

RFC 1906   Case, J., K. McCloghrie, M. Rose, and S. Waldbusser. 1996. "Transport Mappings for Version 2 of the Simple Network Management Protocol (SNMPv2)." *RFC 1906* (January). Standards Track: Draft Standard.

RFC 1907   Case, J., K. McCloghrie, M. Rose, and S. Waldbusser. 1996. "Management Information Base for Version 2 of the Simple Network Management Protocol (SNMPv2)." *RFC 1907* (January). Standards Track: Draft Standard.

RFC 1939   Myers, J., and M. Rose. 1996. "Post Office Protocol—Version 3." *RFC 1939* (May). Standards Track: Internet Standard 0053.

RFC 1994   Simpson, W. 1996. "PPP Challenge Handshake Authentication Protocol (CHAP)." *RFC 1994* (August). Standards Track: Draft Standard.

RFC 1998   Chen, E., and T. Bates. 1996. "An Application of the BGP Community Attribute in Multi-home Routing." *RFC 1998* (August). Informational.

RFC 2003   C. Perkins. 1996. "IP Encapsulation within IP." *RFC 2003* (October). Standards Track: Proposed Standard.

RFC 2026   Bradner, S. 1996. "The Internet Standards Process—Revision 3." *RFC 2026* (October). Best Current Practice.

RFC 2045   Freed, N., and N. Borenstein. 1996. "Multipurpose Internet Mail Extensions (MIME) Part One: Format of Internet Message Bodies." *RFC 2045* (November). Standards Track: Draft Standard.

RFC 2046   Freed, N., and N. Borenstein. 1996. "Multipurpose Internet Mail Extensions (MIME) Part Two: Media Types." *RFC 2046* (November). Standards Track: Draft Standard.

RFC 2047   Moore, K. 1996. "Multipurpose Internet Mail Extensions (MIME) Part Three: Message Header Extensions for Non-ASCII Text." *RFC 2047* (November). Standards Track: Draft Standard.

RFC 2048   Freed, N., J. Klensin, and J. Postel. 1996. "Multipurpose Internet Mail Extensions (MIME) Part Four: Registration Procedures." *RFC 2048* (November). Best Current Practice.

RFC 2049   Freed, N., and N. Borenstein. 1996. "Multipurpose Internet Mail Extensions (MIME) Part Five: Conformance Criteria and Examples." *RFC 2049* (November). Standards Track: Draft Standard.

RFC 2060   M. Crispin. 1996. "Internet Message Access Protocol—Version 4rev1." *RFC 2060* (December). Standards Track: Proposed Standard.

RFC 2138   Rigney, C., A. Rubens, W. Simpson, and S. Willens. 1997. "Remote Authentication Dial In User Service (RADIUS)." *RFC 2138* (April). Standards Track: Proposed Standard.

RFC 2139   Rigney, C. 1997. "RADIUS Accounting." *RFC 2139* (April). Informational.

RFC 2165   Veizades, J., E. Guttman, C. Perkins, and S. Kaplan. 1997. "Service Location Protocol." *RFC 2165* (June). Standards Track: Proposed Standard.

RFC 2197   Freed, N. 1997. "SMTP Service Extension for Command Pipelining." *RFC 2197* (September). Standards Track: Draft Standard.

RFC 2205   Braden, R. (ed.), L. S. Berson, S. Herzog, and S. Jamin. 1997. "Resource ReSerVation Protocol (RSVP)—Version 1 Functional Specification." *RFC 2205* (September). Standards Track: Proposed Standard.

RFC 2206   Baker, F., J. Krawczyk, and A. Sastry. 1997. "RSVP Management Information Base Using SMIv2." *RFC 2206* (September). Standards Track: Proposed Standard.

RFC 2207   Berger, L., and T. O'Malley. 1997. "RSVP Extensions for IPSEC Data Flows." *RFC 2207* (September). Standards Track: Proposed Standard.

RFC 2208   Mankin, A. (ed.), F. Baker, B. Braden, S. Bradner, M. O'Dell, A. Romanow, A. Weinrib, and L. Zhang. 1997. "Resource ReSerVation Protocol (RSVP)—Version 1 Applicability Statement Some Guidelines on Deployment." *RFC 2208* (September). Informational.

RFC 2209   Braden, R., and L. Zhang. 1997. "Resource ReSerVation Protocol (RSVP)—Version 1 Message Processing Rules." *RFC 2209* (September). Informational.

RFC 2211   Wroclawski, J. 1997. "Specification of the Controlled-Load Network Element Service." *RFC 2211* (September). Standards Track: Proposed Standard.

RFC 2212   Shenker, S., C. Patridge, and R. Guerin. 1997. "Specification of Guaranteed Quality of Service." *RFC 2212* (September). Standards Track: Proposed Standard.

RFC 2215   Shenker, S., and J. Wroclawski. 1997. "General Characterization Parameters for Integrated Service Network Elements." *RFC 2215* (September). Standards Track: Proposed Standard.

RFC 2216   Shenker, S., and J. Wroclawski. 1997. "Network Element Service Specification Template." *RFC 2216* (September). Informational.

RFC 2231   Freed, N., and K. Moore. 1991. "MIME Parameter Value and Encoded Word Extensions: Character Sets, Languages, and Continuations." *RFC 2231* (November). Standards Track: Proposed Standard.

RFC 2251   Wahl, M., T. Howes, and S. Kille. 1997. "Lightweight Directory Access Protocol (Version 3)." *RFC 2251* (December). Standards Track: Proposed Standard.

RFC 2306   Parsons, G., and J. Rafferty. 1998. "Tag Image File Format: F Profile for Facsimile." *RFC 2306* (March). Informational.

RFC 2326   Schulzrinne, H., A. Rao, and R. Lanphier. 1998. "Real Time Streaming Protocol (RTSP)." *RFC 2326* (April). Standards Track: Proposed Standard.

RFC 2327   Handley, M., and V. Jacobson. 1998. "SDP: Session Description Protocol." *RFC 2327* (April). Standards Track: Proposed Standard.

RFC 2393   Shachan, A., R. Monsour, R. Pereira, and M. Thomas. 1998. "IP Payload Compression Protocol (IPComp)." *RFC 2393* (December). Standards Track: Proposed Standard.

RFC 2401   Kent, S., and R. Atkinson. 1998. "Security Architecture for the Internet Protocol." *RFC 2401* (November). Standards Track: Proposed Standard.

RFC 2402   Kent, S., and R. Atkinson. 1998. "IP Authentication Header." *RFC 2402* (November). Standards Track: Proposed Standard.

RFC 2403   Madson, C., and R. Glenn. 1998. "The Use of HMAC-MD5-96 within ESP and AH." *RFC 2403* (November). Standards Track: Proposed Standard.

RFC 2404   Madson, C., and R. Glenn. 1998. "The Use of HMAC-SHA-1-96 within ESP and AH." *RFC 2404* (November). Standards Track: Proposed Standard.

RFC 2405   Madson, C., and N. Doraswamy. 1998. "The ESP DES-CBC Cipher Algorithm with Explicit IV." *RFC 2405* (November). Standards Track: Proposed Standard.

RFC 2406   Kent, S., and R. Atkinson. 1998. "IP Encapsulating Security Payload (ESP)." *RFC 2406* (November). Standards Track: Proposed Standard.

RFC 2407   Piper, D. 1998. "The Internet IP Security Domain of Interpretation for ISAKMP." *RFC 2407* (November). Standards Track: Proposed Standard.

RFC 2408   Maughan, D., M. Schertler, M. Schneider, and J. Turner. 1998. "Internet Security Association and Key Management Protocol (ISAKMP)." *RFC 2408* (November). Standards Track: Proposed Standard.

RFC 2409   Harkins, D., and D. Carrel. 1998. "The Internet Key Exchange (IKE)." *RFC 2409* (November). Standards Track: Proposed Standard.

RFC 2411   Thayer, R., N. Doraswamy, and R. Glenn. 1998. "IP Security Document Roadmap." *RFC 2411* (November). Informational.

RFC 2421   Vaudreuil, G., and G. Parsons. 1998. "Voice Profile for Internet Mail—Version 2." *RFC 2421* (September). Standards Track: Proposed Standard.

RFC 2451   Periera, R., and R. Adams. 1998. "The ESP CBC-Mode Cipher Algorithms." *RFC 2451* (November). Standards Track: Proposed Standard.

RFC 2458   Lu, H., M. Krishnaswamy, L. Conroy, S. Bellovin, F. Burg, A. DeSimone, K. Tewani, P. Davidson, H. Schulzrinne, and K. Vishwanathan. 1998. "Toward the PSTN/Internet Internetworking—Pre-PINT Implementations." *RFC 2458* (November). Informational.

RFC 2474   Nichols, K., S. Blake, F. Baker, and D. Black. 1998. "Definition of the Differentiated Services Field (DS Field) in the IPv4 and IPv6 Headers." *RFC 2474* (December). Standards Track: Proposed Standard.

RFC 2475   Blake, S., D. Black, M. Carlson, E. Davies, Z. Wang, and W. Weiss. 1998. "An Architecture for Differentiated Services." *RFC 2475* (December). Informational.

RFC 2543   Handley, H., H. Schulzrinne, E. Schooler, and J. Rosenberg. 1999. "SIP: Session Initiation Protocol." *RFC 2543* (March). Standards Track: Proposed Standard.

RFC 2570   Case, J., R. Mundy, D. Partain, and B. Stewart. 1999. "Introduction to Version 3 of the Internet-standard Network Management Framework." *RFC 2570* (April). Informational.

RFC 2571   Wijnen, B., D. Harrington, and R. Presuhn. 1999. "An Architecture for Describing SNMP Management Frameworks." *RFC 2571* (April). Standards Track: Draft Standard.

RFC 2572   Case, J., D. Harrington, R. Presuhn, and B. Wijnen. 1999. "Message Processing and Dispatching for the Simple Network Management Protocol (SNMP)." *RFC 2572* (April). Standards Track: Draft Standard.

RFC 2574   Blumenthal, U., and B. Wijnen. 1999. "User-based Security Model (USM) for Version 3 of the Simple Network Management Protocol (SNMPv3)." *RFC 2574* (April). Standards Track: Draft Standard.

RFC 2575   Wijnen, B., R. Presuhn, and K. McCloghrie. 1999. "View-based Access Control Model (VACM) for the Simple Network Management Protocol (SNMP)." *RFC 2575* (April). Standards Track: Draft Standard.

RFC 2578   McCloghrie, K., D. Perkins, and J. Schoenwaelder. 1999. "Structure of Management Information Version 2 (SMIv2)." *RFC 2578* (April). Standards Track: Internet Standard 0058.

RFC 2579   McCloghrie, K., D. Perkins, and J. Schoenwaelder (eds.). 1999. "Textual Conventions for SMIv2." *RFC 2579* (April). Standards Track: Internet Standard 0058.

RFC 2580   McCloghrie, K., D. Perkins, and J. Schoenwaelder. 1999. "Conformance Statements for SMIv2." *RFC 2580* (April). Standards Track: Internet Standard 0058.

RFC 2589   Yaacovi, Y., M. Wahl, and T. Genovese. 1999. "Lightweight Directory Access Protocol (v3): Extensions for Dynamic Directory Services." *RFC 2589* (May). Standards Track: Proposed Standard.

RFC 2597   Heinanen, J., F. Baker, W. Weiss, and J. Wroclawski. 1999. "Assured Forwarding PHB Group." *RFC 2597* (June). Standards Track: Proposed Standard.

RFC 2598   Jacobson, V., K. Nichols, and K. Poduri. 1999. "An Expedited Forwarding PHB." *RFC 2598* (June). Standards Track: Proposed Standard.

RFC 2608   Guttman, E., C. Perkins, J. Veizades, and M. Day. 1999. "Service Location Protocol, Version 2." *RFC 2608* (June). Standards Track: Proposed Standard.

RFC 2609   Guttman, E., C. Perkins, and J. Kempf. 1999. "Service Templates and Service: Schemes." *RFC 2609* (June). Standards Track: Proposed Standard.

RFC 2616   Fielding, R., J. Gettys, J. Mogul, H. Frystyk, L. Masinter, P. Leach, and T. Berners-Lee. 1999. "Hypertext Transfer Protocol—HTTP/1.1." *RFC 2616* (June). Standards Track: Draft Standard.

RFC 2661   Townsley, W., A. Valencia, A. Rubens, G. Pall, G. Zorn, and B. Palter. 1999. "Layer Two Tunneling Protocol (L2TP)." *RFC 2661* (August). Standards Track: Proposed Standard.

Additional Standards Efforts

ANSI X3.4-1986 (R1997)   ANSI. 1986. "Information Systems—Coded Character Sets—7-Bit American National Standard Code for Information Interchange (7-Bit ASCII)." *ANSI X3.4-1986 (R1997).* American National Standards Institute. www.ansi.org.

IETF MPLS WG   Rosen, E. C., A. Viswanathan, and R. Callon. 1999. "Multiprotocol Label Switching Architecture." IETF MPLS Working Group. Work in Progress (August).

IETF MPLS WG   Andersson, L., B. Jamoussi, M. K. Girish, and T. Worster. 1999. "MPLS Capability Set." IETF MPLS Working Group. Work in Progress (August).

Acronym List

AAA	Authentication, Authorization, and Accounting
ACD	Automatic Call Distribution
ACH	Attempts per Circuit per Hour
ACL	Agent Communication Language
ACM	Address Complete Message
AD	Adjunct
ADPCM	Adaptive Differential Pulse-Code Modulation
ADSL	Asymmetric Digital Subscriber Line
AF	Assured Forwarding
AH	Authentication Header
AIN	Advanced Intelligent Network
ANI	Automatic Number Identification
ANSI	American National Standards Institute
API	Application Programmer's Interface
AS	Autonomous System
ASN	Abstract Syntax Notation
ASR	Automatic Speech Recognition
ATM	Asynchronous Transfer Mode
AWGN	Additive White Gaussian Noise

BA	Behavior Aggregate
BCP	Best Current Practice
BCSM	Basic Call State Model
BER	Basic Encoding Rules
BGP	Border Gateway Protocol
B-ISDN	Broadband ISDN
BRI	Basic Rate Interface
CCAF	Call Control Agent Function
CCF	Call Control Function
CCH	Connections per Circuit per Hour
CCIS	Common Channel Interoffice Signaling
CCITT	Consultative Committee for International Telephony and Telegraphy
CCS	Common Channel Signaling
CD	Compact Disk
CDR	Call Detail Record
CHAP	Challenge Handshake Authentication Protocol
CLEC	Competitive Local Exchange Carrier
CLI	Calling Line Identification
CMIP	Common Management Identification Protocol
CO	Central Office
CODEC	Coder/Decoder (combined in one device)
CoS	Class of Service
CPA	Calling Party Address
CPE	Customer Premises Equipment
CPU	Central Processing Unit
CR	Carriage Return (an ASCII character)
CS	Capability Set
CS-ACELP	Conjugate-Structure Algebraic-Code-Excited Linear Prediction
CSL	Component Sublayer
CSLIP	Compressed Serial Line Internet Protocol
CSTA	Computer-Supported Telephony Applications
CT	Computer Telephony
CTI	Computer-Telephony Integration
DIT	Directory Information Tree
DLC	Digital Loop Carrier
DNIS	Dialed Number Identification Service

DNS	Domain Name System
DOI	Domain Of Interpretation
DP	Detection Point
DPC	Destination Point Code
DPCM	Differential Pulse-Code Modulation
DS	Differentiated Services
DSL	Digital Subscriber Line
DSP	Digital Signal Processor
DSS1	Digital Subscriber Signaling Number One
DTMF	Dual-Tone-Multi-Frequency
ECMA	European Computer Manufacturers' Association
EDI	Electronic Data Interchange
EDP	Event Detection Point
EISA	Enhanced Industry System Architecture
ESMTP	Extended Simple Mail Transfer Protocol
ESP	Encapsulating Security Payload
ETSI	European Telecommunications Standards Institute
FCC	Federal Communications Commission
FE	Functional Entity
FEC	Forwarding Equivalence Class
FIPA	Foundation for Intelligent Physical Agents
GCC	Generic Conference Control
GSTN	Global Switched Telephone Network
HDSL	High-bit-rate Digital Subscriber Line
HDSL2	High-bit-rate Digital Subscriber Line 2
HLR	Home Location Register
HTML	Hypertext Markup Language
HTTP	Hypertext Transfer Protocol
IAM	Initial Address Message
IANA	Internet Assigned Number Authority
ICP	Intelligent Call Processor
ICW	Internet Call-Waiting
IDR	Interdomain Routing
IEEE	Institute of Electrical and Electronics Engineers
IETF	Internet Engineering Task Force
IF	Information Flow
IKE	Internet Key Exchange
ILEC	Incumbent Local Exchange Carrier

IMAP	Internet Message Access Protocol
IN	Intelligent Network
INAP	Intelligent Network Application Part
INR	ISUP Information Request
IP	Intelligent Peripheral; Internet Protocol
IPCP	IP NCP
IPIP	IP encapsulation within IP
IPsec	Internet Protocol Security
ISDN	Integrated Services Digital Network
ISO	International Organization for Standardization
ISOC	Internet Society
ISP	Internet Service Provider
ISUP	ISDN User Part
ITU-T	International Telecommunications Union—Telecommunications Standardization Sector
IXC	IntereXchange Carrier
JTAPI	Java Telephony Application Programmer's Interface
LAC	L2TP Access Concentrator
LAN	Local Area Network
LATA	Local Access and Transport Area
LCP	Link Control Protocol
LDAP	Lightweight Directory Access Protocol
LD-CELP	Low-Delay Code-Excited Linear Prediction
LDP	Label Distribution Protocol
LEC	Local Exchange Carrier
LF	Line Feed (an ASCII character)
LNP	Local Number Portability
LNS	L2TP Network Server
LSH	Label-Switched Hop
LSP	Label-Switched Path
LSR	Label-Switching Router
L2TP	Layer Two Tunneling Protocol
MASIF	Mobile Agent System Interoperability Facilities
MBFT	Multipoint Binary File Transfer
MCS	Multipoint Communication Service
MCU	Multipoint Control Unit
MD	Message Digest [algorithm]
MEGACO	Media Gateway Control

MF	Multifrequency
MG	Media Gateway
MGC	Media Gateway Control
MIB	Management Information Base
MIME	Multipurpose Internet Mail Extensions
MOS	Mean Opinion Score
MPLS	Multiprotocol Label Switching
MSC	Mobile Switching Center
MSIA	Multipoint Still Image and Annotation
MSO	Multisystem Operator
MTP	Message Transfer Part
NAS	Network Access Server
NAT	Network Address Translators
NCP	Network Control Point; Network Control Protocol
NHR	Nonhierarchical Routing
NT	Network Terminator
NTM	Network Traffic Management
OA&M	Operations, Administration, and Management
ODP	Open Distributed Processing
OMAP	Operation, Maintenance, and Administration Part
OPC	Originating Point Code
OSI	Open Systems Interconnection
OSS	Operations Support System
PBX	Private Branch eXchange
PC	Personal Computer
PCM	Pulse Code Modulation
PDA	Personal Digital Assistant
PDN	Public Data Network
PE	Physical Entity
PHB	Per-Hop Behavior
PIC	Point in Call
PIN	Personal Identification Number
POP	Point of Presence; Post Office Protocol
POTS	Plain Old Telephone Service
PPA	Packet Phone Adapter
PPP	Point-to-Point Protocol
PRI	Primary Rate Interface
PSDN	Packet Switched Data Network

PSTN	Public Switched Telephone Network
PTT	Post, Telegraph, and Telephone
QoS	Quality of Service
RAD	Remote Access and Diagnostics
RADIUS	Remote Authentication Dial-In User Service
RAID	Redundant Array of Inexpensive Disks
RAM	Random Access Memory
RAS	Remote Access Server
RBOC	Regional Bell Operating Company
RDN	Relative Distinguished Name
RFC	Request for Comments
RFI	Request for Information
RFP	Request for Proposal
Rspec	Reservation Specification
RSVP	Resource reSerVation setup Protocol
RTCP	Real-Time Control Transport Protocol
RTP	Real-Time Transport Protocol
RTSP	Real-Time Streaming Protocol
SA	Security Association
SCCP	Signaling Connection Control Part
SCE	Service Creation Environment
SCEAF	Service Creation Environment Agent Function
SCEF	Service Creation Environment Function
SCF	Service Control Function
SCP	Service Control Point
SDF	Service Data Function
SDL	Specification and Description Language
SDP	Service Data Point
SDSL	Single-Pair Digital Subscriber Line; Symmetric Digital Subscriber Line
SG	Signaling Gateway; Study Group
SG&A	Selling, General, and Administrative
SI	Still Image
SIB	Service-Independent Building Block
SIP	Session Initiation Protocol
SLA	Service Level Agreement
SLC	Signaling Link Code
SLIP	Serial Line Internet Protocol

SLP	Service Location Protocol
SLS	Signaling Link Selection
SMAF	Service Management Agent Function
SMF	Service Management Function
SMS	Service Management System
SMTP	Simple Mail Transfer Protocol
SN	Service Node
SNMP	Simple Network Management Protocol
SOHO	Small Office/Home Office
SPI	Security Parameter Index
SRF	Specialized Resource Function
SSF	Service Switching Function
SS No. 7 (or SS7)	Signalling System No. 7
SSP	Service Switching Point
STP	Signaling Transfer Point
TAPI	Telephony Application Programmer Interface
TASI	Time Assignment Speech Interpolation
TC (or TCAP)	Transaction Capabilities
TCA	Traffic Conditioning Agreement
TCP	Transmission Control Protocol
TDD	Telecommunications Device for the Deaf
TDM	Time Division Multiplexing
TDP	Trigger Detection Point
TIA	Telecommunications Industry Association
TIPHON	Telecommunications and Internet Protocol Harmonization Over Network
TMN	Telecommunications Management Network
T1	ANSI-accredited standards committee for telecommunications; line operating at first level of North American digital hierarchy
TRIP	Telephony Routing Information Protocol
TSL	Transaction Sublayer
Tspec	Token Bucket Specification
TTS	Text-To-Speech
TUP	Telephone User Part
UDP	User Datagram Protocol
URI	Uniform Resource Identifier
URL	Uniform Resource Locator

VAD	Voice Activity Detection
VC	Virtual Circuit
VCR	Video Cassette Recorder
VDSL	Very-high-rate Digital Subscriber Line
VLL	Virtual Leased Line
VoIP	Voice over Internet Protocol
VP	Virtual Path
VPIM	Voice Profile for Internet Mail
VPN	Virtual Private Network

Index